# Ungrateful Daughters

*Also by Maureen Waller*

1700: Scenes from London Life

*Maureen Waller*

# Ungrateful Daughters

*The Stuart Princesses Who Stole
Their Father's Crown*

ST. MARTIN'S GRIFFIN ❧ NEW YORK

www.stmartins.com

Library of Congress Cataloging-in-Publication Data

Waller, Maureen
    Ungrateful daughters : the Stuart princesses who stole their father's crown / Maureen Waller.
        p.  cm.
    Originally published: London : Hodder & Stoughton, 2002.
    Includes bibliographical references and index.
    ISBN 0-312-30711-X (hc)
    ISBN 0-312-30712-8 (pbk)
    1. Mary II, Queen of England, 1662–1694. 2. James II, King of England, 1633–1701—Family. 3. Great Britain—History—William and Mary, 1689–1702. 4. Great Britain—Anne, 1702–1714. 7. Queens—Great Britain—Biography. I. Title.

DA462.A3 W27 2003
947.06'.8—dc21                                                    2002031879

First published in Great Britain by Hodder and Stoughton, a division of Hodder Headline

First St. Martin's Griffin Edition: February 2004

10  9  8  7  6  5  4  3  2  1

For Brian, with love

# Contents

# List of Illustrations

**Endpapers**

Letters of Princess Anne and Princess Mary to Frances Apsley. Reproduced by kind permission of the Right Hon. the Earl Bathurst from the Bathurst Papers on loan to the British Library

**Section One**

Mary Beatrice of Modena, Duchess of York by Simon Verelst (Yale Centre for British Art, Paul Mellon Fund/photograph Bridgemann Art Library, London)

The Three Eldest Children of Charles I by Anthony Van Dyck
(The Royal Collection © 2002, Her Majesty Queen Elizabeth II)

Charles I and James, Duke of York during the civil war. Studio of Sir Peter Lely
(Courtesy Sotheby's Picture Library, London)

James, Duke of York and Anne Hyde, Duchess of York in the 1660s by Sir Peter Lely (National Portrait Gallery, London)

Princess Anne by Sir Peter Lely
(The Royal Collection © 2002, Her Majesty Queen Elizabeth II)

Princess Mary dressed as Diana by Sir Peter Lely
(The Royal Collection © 2002, Her Majesty Queen Elizabeth II)

Mary Beatrice, Duchess of York in riding costume by Simon Verelst
(The Royal Collection © 2002, Her Majesty Queen Elizabeth II)

## List of Illustrations

Sarah Churchill, Duchess of Marlborough, and Barbara Berkeley, Lady Fitzharding, playing cards by Godfrey Kneller
(Reproduced by kind permission of His Grace the Duke of Marlborough)

King William III in old age with a candle by Godfried Schalcken
(Rijksmuseum, Amsterdam)

Queen Anne in coronation dress c. 1702. Studio of John Closterman
(National Portrait Gallery, London)

Prince James Francis Edward c. 1712. Studio of Alexis Simon Belle
(National Portrait Gallery, London)

# Acknowledgements

I wish to thank Her Majesty Queen Elizabeth II for kind permission to make use of material in the Royal Library and the Royal Archives at Windsor and to reproduce paintings in the Royal Collection.

Special thanks go to my agent, Jonathan Lloyd at Curtis Brown, and to my editor, Roland Philipps, for their kindness, encouragement and support. I should also like to thank Sheila Crowley, Karen Geary, Briar Silich, Diane Banks and Lizzie Dipple at Hodder & Stoughton for their unstinting efforts on my behalf. Thanks also to Juliet Brightmore for her expertise and enthusiasm in gathering the illustrations.

I am extremely grateful to my husband, Brian MacArthur, and to Barry Turner for kindly giving their valuable time to read and comment on the script. I should like to thank the following friends for offering encouragement and support along the way: Elizabeth Buchan, Lucy Ferguson, Sue Fletcher (she knows what for), Peter Lavery, Diana Mackay and Bob Tyrer.

Finally, I am most grateful to the staff of the London Library, who offered me a lifeline sending me a steady stream of books when I was unable to come in to the library, and to the staff at the British Library for their wonderfully efficient service.

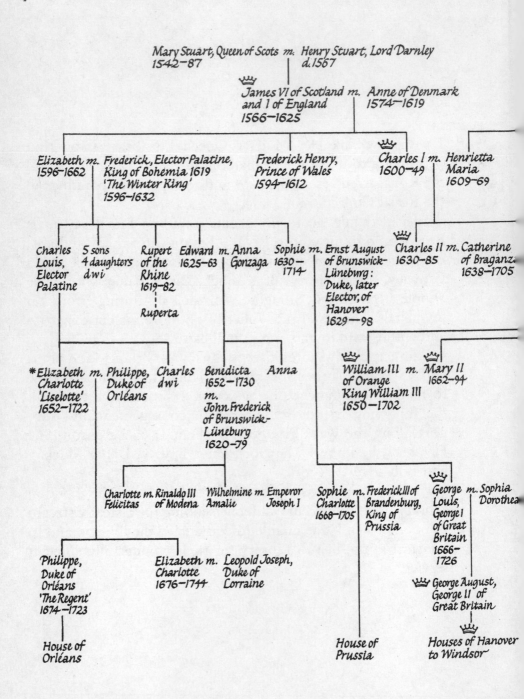

Mary Stuart, Queen of Scots *m.* Henry Stuart, Lord Darnley
1542–87           d. 1567

James VI of Scotland *m.* Anne of Denmark
and I of England    1574–1619
1566–1625

Elizabeth *m.* Frederick, Elector Palatine,    Frederick Henry,      Charles I *m.* Henrietta
1596–1662   King of Bohemia 1619    Prince of Wales     1600–49    Maria
            'The Winter King'      1594–1612                        1609–69
            1596–1632

Charles   5 sons    Rupert    Edward *m.* Anna    Sophie *m.* Ernst August    Charles II *m.* Catherine
Louis,    4 daughters   of the    1625–63   Gonzaga    1630–    of Brunswick-    1630–85    of Braganza
Elector    d w i      Rhine                     1714    Lüneburg:               1638–1705
Palatine          1619–82                            Duke, later
                  Ruperta                         Elector, of
                                              Hanover
                                              1629—98

*Elizabeth *m.* Philippe,   Charles    Benidicta      Anna           William III *m.* Mary II
Charlotte    Duke of    d w i     1652–1730                  of Orange     1662–94
'Liselotte'    Orléans              m.                         King William III
1652–1722                    John Frederick         1650–1702
                             of Brunswick-
                             Lüneburg
                             1620–79

Charlotte *m.* Rinaldo III    Wilhelmine *m.* Emperor     Sophie *m.* Frederick III of    George *m.* Sophia
Felicitas    of Modena      Amalie       Joseph I      Charlotte    Brandenburg,   Louis,    Dorothea
                                           1668–1705   King of     George I
                                                   Prussia     of Great
                                                           Britain
                                                                  1666–
                                                                  1726

Philippe,         Elizabeth *m.* Leopold Joseph,                      George August,
Duke of         Charlotte    Duke of                          George II of
Orléans         1676–1744   Lorraine                         Great Britain
'The Regent'
1674–1723

House of                                      House of       Houses of Hanover
Orléans                                       Prussia       to Windsor

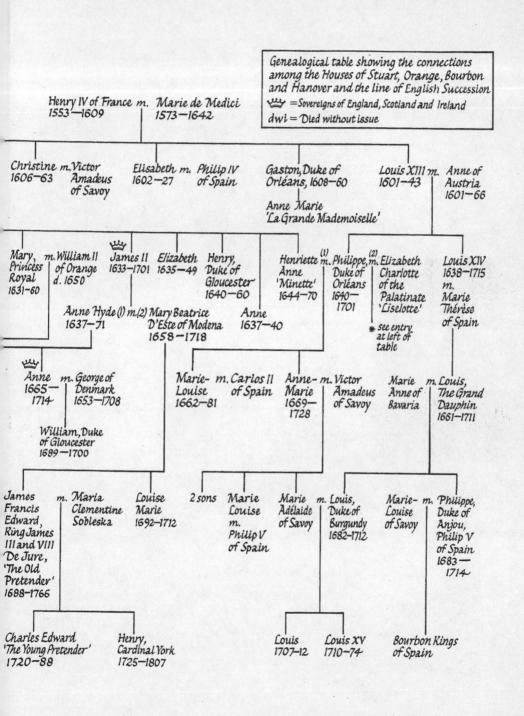

Genealogical table showing the connections among the Houses of Stuart, Orange, Bourbon and Hanover and the line of English Succession

👑 = Sovereigns of England, Scotland and Ireland

dwi = Died without issue

Henry IV of France m. Marie de Medici
1553—1609          1573—1642

Christine m. Victor          Elisabeth m. Philip IV          Gaston, Duke of          Louis XIII m. Anne of
1606–63   Amadeus           1602–27      of Spain           Orléans, 1608–60         1601–43    Austria
          of Savoy                                                                              1601–66

                                                            Anne Marie
                                                     'La Grande Mademoiselle'

Mary,     m. William II   👑                                    (1)          (2)
Princess     of Orange   James II  Elizabeth  Henry,        Henriette m. Philippe, m. Elizabeth    Louis XIV
Royal        d. 1650     1633–1701 1635–49    Duke of       Anne      Duke of    Charlotte   1638–1715
1631–60                                       Gloucester    'Minette'  Orléans    of the      m.
                                              1640–60       1644–70    1640–      Palatinate  Marie
          Anne Hyde (1) m.(2) Mary Beatrice        Anne                1701      'Liselotte'  Thérèse
          1637–71        D'Este of Modena          1637–40                                   of Spain
                         1658–1718                                           * see entry
                                                                              at left of
                                                                              table

👑
Anne     m. George of                                      Anne– m. Victor    Marie   m. Louis,
1665–       Denmark          Marie– m. Carlos II           Marie    Amadeus   Anne of    The Grand
1714        1653–1708        Louise     of Spain           1669–    of Savoy  Bavaria    Dauphin
                             1662–81                        1728                          1661–1711

          William, Duke
          of Gloucester
          1689–1700

James     m. Maria       Louise    2 sons   Marie     Marie    m. Louis,    Marie–  m. Philippe,
Francis      Clementine  Marie              Louise    Adélaide    Duke of    Louise     Duke of
Edward,      Sobieska    1692–1712          m.        of Savoy    Burgundy   of Savoy   Anjou,
King James                                  Philip V             1682–1712              Philip V
III and VIII                                of Spain                                    of Spain
De Jure,                                                                                1683–
'The Old                                                                                1714
Pretender'
1688–1766

Charles Edward          Henry,                          Louis    Louis XV    Bourbon Kings
'The Young Pretender'   Cardinal York                   1707–12  1710–74     of Spain
1720–88                 1725–1807

# Cast of Characters in the Royal Family

*Charles II*
The eldest son of King Charles I, he was restored to the throne in May 1660, although he counted his reign from the day after the execution of his father on 30 January 1649.

*Queen Catherine of Braganza*
The devoutly Catholic, Portuguese wife of Charles II. She had no children.

*The Dowager Queen Henrietta Maria*
The Catholic daughter of Henri IV of France and Marie de Medici, she was the widow of Charles I and mother of Charles II; James II; Henry, Duke of Gloucester; Mary, the Princess Royal; Henriette Anne, Duchess of Orléans; and Elizabeth and Anne, who died during their childhood. Never popular in England, she died in France in 1669.

*James II*
The second son of Charles I. He was Duke of York and Albany before succeeding his brother Charles II to the throne in 1685.

*Anne Hyde, Duchess of York*
The daughter of the Chancellor, Sir Edward Hyde, later Earl of Clarendon, and maid of honour to Charles I's daughter, the Princess of Orange, she was the first wife of James, Duke of York and mother of the Princesses Mary and Anne. She converted to Catholicism shortly before her death in 1671.

*Queen Mary Beatrice*
The Catholic Princess from the Italian duchy of Modena,

second wife of James, Duke of York and later his Queen Consort. She bore James several children, of whom only James Francis Edward and a daughter, Louise Marie, survived.

### Princess Mary of Orange, later Queen Mary II

The elder daughter of James, Duke of York and his first wife, the commoner Anne Hyde. As a child, she was known as the Lady Mary of York. She married her cousin, Prince William of Orange, in 1677. She became Queen Mary II in 1689 and died childless six years later.

### Princess Anne of Denmark, later Queen Anne

The younger daughter of James, Duke of York and his first wife, the commoner Anne Hyde. She married Prince George of Denmark in 1683. She had seventeen pregnancies but none of her offspring survived her. She succeeded William III to the throne in 1702 and died in 1714.

### William Henry, Duke of Gloucester

The only surviving son of Princess Anne and Prince George of Denmark was born in July 1689 and regarded as the Protestant heir to the throne after his mother. He died shortly after his eleventh birthday in 1700.

### Mary, the Princess Royal, Princess of Orange

The eldest daughter of Charles I and Henrietta Maria, she married Prince William II of Orange in 1642. She died of smallpox during a visit to London at Christmas 1660.

### Prince William of Orange, later King William III of England

The only son of Mary, the Princess Royal and Prince William II of Orange was born a week after his father's death in 1650. He became Stadholder of the Dutch Republic in 1672 and five years later married his cousin, Princess Mary of York. He was offered the crown jointly with his wife in 1689 and died childless in 1702.

### James Francis Edward, Prince of Wales

The only surviving son of James II and his second wife, Mary Beatrice of Modena, he was born in June 1688. When he was less than six months old, his mother fled with him to safety in France. He never recovered his father's crown and became known in English Protestant circles as 'the Old Pretender'. He died in Rome in 1765.

### Louise Marie

The daughter of James II and Mary Beatrice, she was born at St Germain-en-Laye in 1692. James called her La Consolatrice, the daughter sent to comfort them in their exile. She died of smallpox in 1712.

### Henriette Anne, Duchess of Orléans

The youngest daughter of Charles I and Henrietta Maria, she was brought up in exile and comparative poverty in France. She was Charles II's favourite sister, known affectionately as Minette. On the restoration of her brother, Charles II, to the English throne, she married her cousin, Philippe, Duke of Orléans, the homosexual brother of Louis XIV of France. They had two children, Marie-Louise and Anne-Marie. Henriette Anne died after a visit to England in 1670.

### Louis XIV

The Catholic King of France, first cousin of Charles II and James II, who wished to imitate his royal absolutism. His territorial aggression won him the life-long enmity of the Protestant Prince William of Orange, who organised a series of European alliances against him.

### Elizabeth of Bohemia

The only surviving daughter of James I and sister of Charles I of England, she married the Protestant German prince, Frederick, Elector Palatine, to whom the Czechs offered the crown of Bohemia in 1618, triggering off the Thirty Years'

War. She reigned in Prague as Queen of Bohemia for one winter, hence her title 'the Winter Queen', before fleeing the Habsburg Emperor's advancing Catholic forces. The mother of thirteen children and godmother to James, Duke of York, she spent the rest of her life in penury in The Hague, before dying in London in 1662.

### Prince Rupert of the Rhine

The third son of the Queen of Bohemia, he fought for his uncle, Charles I, in the English civil war. He settled in London after his cousin Charles II's restoration to the throne. He lived with the actress Peg Hughes, by whom he had a daughter, Ruperta. Prince Rupert stood godfather to Princess Mary at her christening in April 1662. He was the advocate of a marriage between Princess Anne and his nephew George of Hanover in 1680, but his hopes were disappointed.

### Sophie of the Palatinate, Duchess, later Electress, of Hanover

The twelfth child of the Queen of Bohemia, she was briefly considered as a possible bride for her cousin, the exiled Charles II of England. She married Ernst August, Bishop of Osnabruck, Duke and later Elector of Hanover, and became the mother of seven children. Nominated in the 1701 Act of Settlement to succeed Queen Anne to the English throne, she died in June 1714 at the age of eighty-four, just two months before Anne.

### Elizabeth Charlotte (Liselotte) of the Palatinate, Duchess of Orléans

The granddaughter of Elizabeth of Bohemia, the child of her eldest surviving son, Charles, Elector Palatine, she was known affectionately in the family as Liselotte. She was a childhood playmate of William of Orange and once considered as a prospective bride for him, before her father married her to Philippe, Duke of Orléans, the widowed husband of Henriette

Anne of England. She kept up a life-long correspondence with her beloved aunt, Sophie of Hanover.

*George Ludwig of Brunswick-Lüneburg, Elector of Hanover*
The eldest son of Sophie of Hanover. Once a suitor of Princess Anne, he inherited the throne from her as George I in 1714.

*George August, Electoral Prince of Hanover*
The son and heir of George Ludwig, he became George II of England in 1727.

*James Scott, formerly Crofts, Duke of Monmouth*
The eldest bastard of Charles II and his mistress Lucy Walters, his father doted on him and married him to the wealthy heiress, Anne Scott of Buccleuch. During the exclusion crisis when the Earl of Shaftesbury and the Whigs wanted to exclude the Catholic James, Duke of York from the throne, they espoused the cause of Monmouth, the Protestant Duke, whom they claimed was legitimate. Monmouth led a rebellion against James II, was defeated at Sedgemoor, captured and executed in 1685.

*James Fitzjames, Duke of Berwick*
The bastard son of James II and his mistress Arabella Churchill, sister of John Churchill. Berwick remained loyal to his father and his brother James Francis Edward and, like his Churchill uncle, was one of the great military commanders of the age.

# Author's Note

## The calendar

During the period covered in this book the English calendar was ten days behind the rest of Europe in the seventeenth century and eleven days behind Europe in the eighteenth century. Contemporaries corresponding between England and continental Europe would usually give both dates, such as 2/12 August 1680. For the purposes of this book, all dates for events taking place in both England and Europe are given in the Old Style, that is, as they pertained in England at the time.

Officially, the New Year in England began on 25 March, so that for the period 1 January to 24 March, contemporaries often used the style 6 February 1664–5. This is apparent in the diaries of Evelyn and Pepys, for instance. I have adhered to the modern New Year date of 1 January, so that I refer to the above – Princess Anne's birthday – as 6 February 1665.

## Spelling

I have quoted the letters written by Princesses Mary and Anne before marriage just as they appear in the original in the Bathurst Papers on loan to the British Library, not least because they have so much charm. Their handwriting was rather good and their standard of spelling and punctuation no worse, and very often better, than that of other women – and men – of their time. Otherwise, almost all quotations are given in modern usage to make them easier to read.

## Money

A £ was equivalent to approximately £75 in today's money, so that when King William expressed surprise to Lord Godolphin that Princess Anne could spend as much as £30,000 a year – £2.25 million in today's money – we can sympathise with him. Similarly, when Princess Anne's friends in Parliament were demanding an allowance of £70,000 a year for her in 1689, it meant £5.25 million in today's terms.

# Ungrateful Daughters

# Prologue

---

## The Arms of England Inn, Faversham, Kent
## December 1688

The seamen peered through the gloom at the tall, gaunt figure sitting motionless by the fire. Swathed in a broad-brimmed black hat and long dark cloak, he bore an uncanny resemblance to the late King Charles I as he faced his judges, just before they signed his death certificate. This king had the same look. He was distant and removed, somehow above it all. Some detected an aura of majesty about him, others cold arrogance. The long white face with its thin curling lip was etched with misery.

They had boarded the customs boat in the night, and, as they suspected, found it full of escaping papists. The tall man with the black hat and cloak was the first to catch their eye. Here was a priest, perhaps the notorious Father Petre, the Jesuit who had sat on the King's Council and tried to drag England back to Rome. The heavy gold cross he carried seemed to confirm their suspicions, and he was most reluctant to part with it. A stash of diamonds and the coronation ring lay hidden in his breeches, but it was the cross he cared about. When a Westminster chorister had seen its glimmer and reached into the broken tomb of St Edward the Confessor to retrieve it three years ago, it had seemed like a gift from this most holy of ancestors, this sanctified king, direct to James in the year of his accession.

It was only when they had hauled him back to the inn that someone who had served in the navy when James was Lord High Admiral recognised King James II. Even down here in

I

Kent they knew the King had fled the capital just as his son-in-law, the Dutchman William of Orange, was poised to take it. Now, by all accounts, London was given over to the mob, who were burning and looting Catholic houses and places of worship. The old seaman had thrown himself at the King's feet and asked his blessing. James's late brother King Charles II would have turned this into a triumph. The most charming and accessible of kings, he would have allowed them all to kiss his hand, he would have called for a round of drinks and told them stories, and asked about their lives and women. Before long they would have been carrying him back to Whitehall and throwing out the Dutch invader. But James lacked his brother's common touch. He had brusquely pushed the seaman aside, drawn himself apart and started issuing orders. Calling for a quill, paper and ink, he had sat down to write a series of letters, each one betraying his frenzied state of mind, before tearing most of them up and consigning them to the fire.

Tankards in hand and puffing on their pipes, the seamen now stared at their prisoner. He looked straight ahead, unseeing. Perhaps he was remembering the first time he had escaped his enemies. He had been fourteen years old. His father, King Charles I, had known he was going to die and he had urged James to flee, so that Cromwell and the Parliament men would not be able to set him up as a puppet king. The King was ordained by God, not man, the crown was hereditary and passed strictly from father to eldest surviving son and only after that to any daughters. Charles I had impressed on all his younger children that none of them should be crowned while their eldest brother Charles was alive and in exile. James had staged an elaborate game of hide-and-seek with his younger siblings, Elizabeth and Henry. They were still looking for him long after he had escaped through the garden at St James's and been smuggled away down the river dressed as a girl.

And now James's daughters, Mary and Anne, seemed to be doing exactly what his long dead father had warned against.

They were taking the crown while their brother, the infant Prince of Wales, was still alive – upsetting the natural order of succession, making the monarchy elective. James had been outraged when William of Orange's manifesto had questioned the authenticity of James's precious son, the Prince of Wales. How could anyone seriously believe that such a fond father as James would oust his beloved daughters from the succession just to put a changeling on the throne? The whole business of casting aspersions on the Prince of Wales's birth, pretending that someone else's child had been smuggled into Queen Mary Beatrice's bed in a warming-pan for the royal couple to pass off as their own, was just a convenient fabrication of the Protestants. It was the pretext William needed for his unlawful invasion of his father-in-law's kingdom.

William had been planning the invasion for months, ever since the announcement of the Queen's pregnancy at Christmas 1687 had thrown the Protestants into a panic. He had been conspiring with those discontented Protestant nobles and squires who had been too busy skulking in their country houses to come forward to support their lawful sovereign in his hour of need. The Dutchman had landed in the West Country on 5 November with a massive foreign army and not one of James's subjects had put up any resistance. The royal army, once James's pride and joy, had been no better. While James had been suffering from an interminable nosebleed at the camp at Salisbury, his most senior officers – men such as John Churchill, whom James had raised from nothing – had gone over to the enemy without a fight. James had despaired, not so much because of their disloyalty, but because God had evidently withdrawn His favour from him. He had returned to London a dispirited and broken man, already resolved to flee for his life. And now William was at Syon on the edge of London, poised to take over the kingdom.

Pray God, the Queen and his son were now safe in France. James had feared for their lives. Just as his mother, the Catholic Queen Henrietta Maria, had been threatened with impeachment by Parliament in the 1640s, so Parliament was now threatening to impeach Queen Mary Beatrice. Before that could happen, there was always the chance she might fall victim to the fury of the mob. Even when she had arrived in England as James's second wife, a fifteen-year-old Catholic princess from the Italian duchy of Modena, the London rabble had been threatening to tear her to pieces, spurred on by a silly rumour that she was the daughter of the Pope.

James was convinced that his son, born to Mary Beatrice and himself after fifteen years of marriage, was a gift from God. James Francis Edward had been conceived after James had bathed in the holy well of St Winifrede. His birth was a miracle, a sign that God wanted James to have a Catholic son and heir to carry on his good work of bringing England back to the true faith. Nothing was more terrible for James to contemplate than that William would hunt down the child and kill him, or bring him up a Protestant, which was why he had ignored the advice of the loyal Lord Dartmouth and spirited the child and his mother off to France.

James's thoughts turned to his other children, his Protestant daughters by his first wife, the commoner Anne Hyde. A knife seemed to stab his heart when he remembered his younger daughter Anne's defection to his enemies. He had returned to Whitehall from his fast depleting army at Salisbury to find she had fled in the night, no doubt prompted by her fool of a husband who had so disloyally deserted the army and her lady of the bedchamber, that minx Sarah Churchill. Anne's desertion cut him to the very depths of his being. He had loved her, cherished her and lavished a generous allowance on her, rushed to comfort her and sit by her bedside every time she had lost a child. The shock of her desertion had pushed James in his anguished mental state over the edge, even though he was happily ignorant of the malicious letters she had been writing to her sister Mary all these months, throwing doubts on the Queen's pregnancy and the authenticity of their brother.

He wondered about his elder daughter, Mary. He still could

not believe that she understood what her husband William was about in invading his father-in-law's kingdom. She was too good. But then James knew only too well how much his beloved daughter was dominated by her husband. She was a malleable young woman who would do anything to win the love and approval of the emotionally cold man she had married. Mary was the rightful heiress to the crown only after her brother, the Prince of Wales. But if she and her sister denied their brother's birthright and stole the crown now, James knew that Mary was such a loyal and dutiful wife she would give it to William. For all William might protest that he came only to safeguard English liberties and restore the rule of law, James knew that he was after the crown and he would prevail on Mary to give it to him.

James had never trusted his nephew and son-in-law, William. His sister Mary's boy was a cold fish, he had none of his mother's sense of family and he did not seem to like England at all. James thought it perverse that William should identify himself so totally with those insolent Dutch Republicans that he should have spent his life defending their miserable country when they would not even make him their king. Most of all, James loathed William's stern Calvinism. He had hated giving his precious daughter Mary to him in marriage. He had wanted her to marry the Dauphin, to be Queen of France. But Charles had insisted that she marry her cousin William to appease the Protestants, to assure them that the crown would eventually pass into safe Protestant hands. James revered the monarchy too much to go against the King's wishes. He always obeyed his brother.

James had loved Mary best of all his children. He thought of her as a little girl, brought to St James's from her nursery at Twickenham. He had adored her. She was a real Stuart, with the long almond-shaped dark eyes and luminous white complexion of her tragic great-great-grandmother, Mary, Queen of Scots. She had been tall for her age, lithe and graceful, dancing and skipping round his feet and holding her arms up for him to lift her. He had loved playing with her. Once he had taken her into a meeting with Mr Pepys and had hardly been able to tear his attention away to look at the naval accounts. He had been so proud of Mary's beauty and precocity, carrying her about the palace, showing her off to all the courtiers.

There was a shout outside, someone pushing his way through the press of onlookers at the doorway. The prisoner was to be taken to the mayor's house for his own safety, then perhaps back to London. James thought with dread of his father's trial and execution. The adolescent boy had never recovered from his father's death. His father had been weak, he had tried to compromise with his enemies, and they had killed him anyway. James thought a king should be strong; he looked with approbation at his cousin, the absolute Catholic monarch Louis XIV across the Channel. James had none of the subtlety of his brother Charles II, who knew how to bend with the wind. James had been open and frank to the point of idiocy in declaring himself a Catholic, and thought it only reasonable that he take his subjects with him, back to the true Church. He never had any time for opposition. Either you were with the monarchy or against it. Anyone who opposed his wishes was no better than Cromwell and those factious republicans.

On the first leg of his escape across the Thames to Lambeth, James had thrown the Great Seal into the river to confound his enemies, to cause confusion in government, and to prevent a Parliament being called. Then the gold cross of the Confessor, his talisman, had been snatched from him. James had been at his most Lear-like and distraught when he had discovered that both his daughters had ranged with his enemies against him, but he was also disturbed by the loss of his cross. Now, he seemed to have suffered a nervous collapse, crying and muttering to himself. James had often dwelled on the fate of fallen kings and he must surely have contemplated his own end now, as a prisoner of the ruthless William. James knew that William wanted the crown, even if those who had invited him here were fooling themselves that he did not, but how was

6

he to get it while James was alive? James's wild imaginings, fuelled by his father's terrible end and the events of the 1640s, told him that he would have to die. To be executed as a public spectacle as his father Charles I had been, or to be put away like Edward II and Richard II and done to death in some dark corner – which would be his fate?

It remained to be seen whether this palace revolution, this *coup*, would claim its victim, or if it would be bloodless.

# Part One

*The Family*

# I

# Queen Mary Beatrice

'It is strange to see how the Queen's great belly is everywhere ridiculed, as if scarce any body believed it to be true'

– Henry Hyde, Earl of Clarendon

In the balmy late summer of 1687 Bath received a royal visit. Every morning, to the strains of an Italian orchestra, the pale Queen Mary Beatrice and her attendants, wearing voluminous yellow canvas gowns to disguise the female shape, entered the sulphurous warmth of the Cross Bath for treatment. In the balconies above, men in cumbersome periwigs and women sporting black patches, *mouchoirs* held to noses to ward off the noxious fumes of the bath, leaned forward to watch the royal consort submerging herself in the waters believed to be so conducive to fertility. In the afternoons the Queen amused herself riding in her coach around the pleasant countryside bordering the River Avon, accompanied by her red-coated guards and a military tune. At her early evening drawing rooms, the gentry flocked to see the tall, willowy Italian Queen, who received them very graciously and allowed them to kiss her hand.

This pleasant interlude was interrupted in the first week of September by the arrival of King James II. He had been on a progress through the western counties, pausing with his Catholic priests to touch for the King's Evil, running his fingers over the swollen necks of those subjects suffering from scrofula – bovine tuberculosis – who flocked to the churches for the royal cure. As God's representative on earth, the monarch was believed to have the healing touch first manifested by his forbear, the Saxon King, St Edward the Confessor. The power of suggestion was obviously efficacious, because many believed they were cured by the royal touch. James, too, needed divine intervention. He had made a detour to St Winifrede's Well at Holywell in Flintshire to pray for a son.

Conception must have taken place almost immediately after the reunion. By the time the Queen returned to London in late October, she knew that the miracle had indeed occurred, and that she was expecting a child in either June or July 1688; the physicians thought the latter. News of the pregnancy began to leak out before Christmas. The Tuscan ambassador, Terriesi, heard the rumours. 'There is a strong hope that the reported pregnancy of the Queen will soon be confirmed,' he wrote, adding ominously: 'it would be impossible to describe the passion of those who do not desire it, nor the schemes and reflections of both parties, in case it should be true.'

The King and Queen, as devout Catholics, were convinced that the pregnancy was a miracle, and as such it was sure to bring the longed-for son and heir. The Roman Catholics could not conceal their glee, encouraged that the King's efforts to bring them into the political establishment and allow them freedom of worship would be perpetuated by a Catholic dynasty. The Protestants were seriously depressed for the same reason. They felt that the Catholics seemed a little too confident that the child would be a boy and survive. This attitude raised suspicions in some Protestant minds that the pregnancy was a hoax, a Catholic plot to foist a changeling on the nation and deny the true Protestant heirs the throne. Even if they did not believe such an absurd fabrication, it was convenient to pretend to do so.

The Protestant heirs were the King's two daughters by his previous marriage to Anne Hyde, the Princess Mary of Orange and her younger sister, the Princess Anne of Denmark, as well as his nephew and son-in-law, Prince William of Orange. William's claim as third in line was bolstered by his marriage to Princess Mary, but some argued that as the son of the eldest daughter of Charles I he had a better claim than James's daughters, whose mother was only a commoner. None of them was pleased at the news of the impending birth. As Terriesi told his master the Grand Duke of Tuscany: 'the Orangists, therefore, refuse to believe it . . . or impudently declare it to be a fiction.'

Of all those who stood to lose by the birth of a Catholic heir, no one was more visibly affronted than the King's younger daughter, the Princess Anne, who was afraid for her beloved Anglican Church, and eaten up with jealousy and dislike for her stepmother. Terriesi noted during the Christmas festivities: 'No words can express the rage of the Princess of Denmark at the Queen's condition, she can dissimulate it to no one; and seeing that the Catholic religion has a prospect of advancement, she affects more than ever, both in public and in private to show herself hostile to it, and [to be] the most zealous of Protestants, with whom she is gaining the greatest power and credit at this conjunction.'

Rumours spread and pamphlets spilled out of presses – many of them in the Dutch Republic – questioning the reality or legitimacy of the royal baby. The die-hard core of opposition to James and his Catholic religion had used the same technique during the Queen's previous pregnancy in 1682, although their efforts were wasted on that occasion. The baby had been a daughter, so had not posed any threat to her sisters' place in the succession, and she had died within a few weeks of her birth. Now, in the winter of 1687, Mary Beatrice was understandably 'afflicted at hearing of the satires (which are already being published) against her; and indeed,' concluded the admiring Tuscan ambassador, 'most innocent in all her actions, she has never given cause to any one save to worship her.'

At Christmas 1687 the Queen's pregnancy was officially announced and a proclamation in the New Year appointed two days of public prayer for her: Sunday, 15 January in London and 29 January in the rest of the kingdom. That fervent

Anglican and loyal supporter of the Crown, Henry Hyde, Earl of Clarendon, uncle to the Princesses Mary and Anne, attended church at St James's Piccadilly, and was shocked at the behaviour of the congregation. Hardly anyone had bothered to bring the service sheet issued by the government with the order of prayers to be said for the Queen. Even worse, as Clarendon confided in his diary: 'it is strange to see how the Queen's great belly is everywhere ridiculed, as if scarce any body believed it to be true. Good God, help us!'

It was ridiculous for the Queen's detractors to infer that she was past her childbearing years. She was only twenty-nine years old. At the same time, it is hard to see how anyone could be sanguine about the outcome of the royal pregnancy. By 1688 Mary Beatrice had been married nearly fifteen years and had no surviving children to show for it. James had despaired many times that none of his sons would live. Those Protestants who chose to believe the rumours of a hoax did so out of a combination of fear and political expediency. Suspicion of Catholic intentions was so fierce by the third year of James's reign that some might genuinely have thought that the Catholics would stop at nothing to advance their religion. But no one who knew the Queen – least of all her stepdaughters, to whom she had always been kind – could seriously believe that she would perpetrate a lie.

James had still been Duke of York and a widower for two years when he married Princess Maria Beatrice Eleonora D'Este of Modena in the autumn of 1673. When Parliament got wind of the Catholic match, they angrily demanded that it be annulled. No good had ever come of a member of the royal family marrying a Catholic, they argued; such a marriage disturbed the minds of the King's Protestant subjects, encouraged alliances abroad detrimental to the Protestant religion, and increased the numbers of Catholics in the kingdom. This

Princess was especially worrying, because her family was reported to be so close to the papal court.

As head of state and head of the family, Charles II refused to compromise his honour by reneging on his brother's marriage. It was too late. The marriage had taken place by proxy in Modena and the bride was on her way. Charles would not ask her to return to Modena. In truth, there were probably few eligible royal princesses in Europe who were not Catholic. And as a secret convert himself, it was understandable, although politically suicidal, that James wished to marry a fellow Catholic.

On a lighter note, James had also stipulated that his new bride must be beautiful. During his first marriage to Anne Hyde, James had been flagrantly unfaithful and, as his sworn enemy Gilbert Burnet observed, he was not always 'very nice in his choice'. The King maintained that his brother's mistresses were so ugly that his priests must have given them to him as penance. Charles was a cynic and found it hilarious that James wanted his wife to be beautiful. What did a wife's face matter when you saw it so often you ceased to notice it?

Henry Mordaunt, Earl of Peterborough, was despatched to scour the courts of Europe, encumbered by a cache of jewellery worth £20,000, the Duke's wedding present to his bride. When Peterborough saw the portrait of the young Princess Maria Beatrice D'Este at the Paris home of her late aunt the Princess de Conti, he knew he had found his future Queen. As he recalled in his memoirs:

The Princess Mary of Este appear'd to be at this time about fourteen years of age; she was tall, and admirably shaped, her complexion was of the last fairness, her hair black as jet, so were her eyebrows and her eyes; but the latter so full of light and sweetness so they did dazzle and charm too. There seemed given unto them from nature, sovereign power; power to kill and power to save; and in the whole turn of her face, which was of the most graceful oval could be framed, there was all the features, all the beauty, and all that could be great and charming in any humane creature.

At the ducal court of Modena, Peterborough met with an unexpected rebuff. The prospective bride told him that she had never heard of England, nor of the Duke of York, and that she had no wish to marry. As soon as age permitted, she intended to take her vows as a nun in the convent next door. It was now that Pope Clement X intervened, the first time a papal brief had been addressed to one so young. He wrote in Latin, which the Princess understood well:

Ever since it reached Our ears that it was the intention of the Duke of York to make an alliance with your Nobility, We have been giving thanks to the Father of Mercies, Who . . . is preparing for Us, in the Kingdom of England, an ample harvest of joy . . . You will therefore understand, dear daughter in Christ, the anxiety which filled Us when We were informed of your repugnance for marriage. For although We appreciated that this was due to your desire, most laudable in itself, to embrace religious discipline; in the present circumstances it hinders the progress of religion, and We were sincerely grieved . . . We therefore earnestly exhort you . . . to reflect upon the great advantage which would accrue to the Catholic faith in the aforementioned Kingdom through your marriage, and trust that, inflamed with zeal for the good which may result, you will open to yourself a field of merit wider than that of the virginal cloister.

The reluctant Princess bowed her head in resignation. Peterborough stood in for the Duke of York when the proxy marriage took place at the ducal palace on 30 September 1673 before a vast crowd of nobility, followed by a sumptuous reception.

Peterborough immediately dashed off a letter assuring Charles II that he would find his new sister-in-law worthy of the honour he had done her. 'Sire, you will find this young princess to have beauty in her person and in her minde, to be faire tall, well-shap'd and very healthfull.' He also noted that the Italian Princess had beautiful white teeth, a rarity among the English. He warned the King that the widowed Duchess of Modena – Cardinal Mazarin's niece, the former Laura Martinozzi, whom Charles had known as a young man in exile in Paris – would be accompanying her daughter to England. She promised her stay would be short, however, and certainly planned to leave before the Parliament *'infuriato'* – so hostile to the marriage – reconvened after Christmas.

According to Rachel, Lady Russell, James was in the drawing room at Whitehall with a group of courtiers when the French ambassador, Colbert de Croissy, brought in the letters announcing that the proxy marriage had taken place. James turned to his companions saying, 'Then I am a married man.' He immediately sent off a message to his elder daughter the Lady Mary that 'he had provided a playfellow for her.' Mary at eleven was barely four years younger than her new stepmother. From the mullioned windows of St James's Palace the Duke's daughters, Mary and Anne, might have seen the angry bonfires lit to protest at the marriage of their father to a Catholic.

The new Duchess of York began her journey to England on her fifteenth birthday, 5 October 1673. In France Louis XIV, who had done much to promote the marriage, gave her a splendid reception and took her on a tour of his new palace at Versailles. One of the reasons that the marriage was so unpopular with the English Parliament was that it was deemed to be part of the hated French alliance, and, indeed, Louis XIV was providing a proportion of the dowry. While Parliament was raging against the marriage in England, the bride was delayed in France owing to a bout of dysentery.

Eventually, on 21 November, she sailed to Dover on the yacht *Catherine*. James, with a small party of attendants, stood on the shore to meet her. As the young Duchess, tired and shaken by the rough crossing, stepped out of the boat, James came forward to greet her. She promptly burst into tears. To the fifteen-year-old girl, her forty-year-old bridegroom must have looked impossibly old. James was tall and fair like his grandmother Anne of Denmark, but his once handsome face betrayed years of debauchery and there was a sneer, a cruel curl to his lip. If she was disappointed, he was delighted with her. At a private house in the town, the Bishop of Oxford hastily read aloud the marriage contract, the Duke placed a ruby ring on her finger, and, as he so succinctly put it in his little red morocco-bound notebook with the engraved silver clasp, the bride was bedded that same night.

During the early days of her marriage, the new Duchess had a disconcerting habit of bursting into tears whenever she looked at her bridegroom, but she immediately liked her brother-in-law the King, who came in the royal barge to meet her at Greenwich. Charles II had the black eyes, the swarthy skin and saturnine features of his Medici ancestors and Mary Beatrice must have derived some comfort from this Italian affinity. Charles was always charming and gracious to women and he was full of admiration for his new sister-in-law's youth and beauty and good manners. He decided she was worth all the trouble she had caused him with his fractious Parliament.

As they progressed up the river, Mary Beatrice's uncle, Prince Rinaldo D'Este, was impressed by the number of ships acknowledging their passing, and Charles proudly showed the bride the magnificent city that had taken shape after the Great Fire of 1666. When they arrived at Whitehall Palace, he took her by the hand and led her inside, where Queen Catherine waited to greet her at the top of the stairs. The two women should have been friends if only because of their shared religion, but Catherine was less than welcoming to her new sister-in-law, seeing her as a young and beautiful woman who would probably bear an heir to the throne where she herself had failed.

After the sunlit ducal palace at Modena, Mary Beatrice

would have found Whitehall dark, damp and depressing. Later she described it as the largest and most uncomfortable house in the world. The palace complex consisted of a rambling warren of buildings housing the royal and state apartments, private quarters and government offices, which stretched for half a mile along the River Thames. The only architectural splendour it could boast was Inigo Jones's Banqueting House with its Rubens ceiling depicting the divine status of the Stuart monarchy. The Banqueting House was a cruel reminder to the royal family of the fate of Charles I, for he had stepped from its balcony on to a public stage erected for his execution.

At the Restoration some of the royal portraits and other treasures had been returned to Whitehall. There were exquisite Indian cabinets, looking-glasses from France, and a bevy of clocks whose chiming kept the King's attendants awake through the night. For all its grandeur, when the court was in residence the palace was dirty and stinking. Anyone who was at all fastidious found the smell of the King's favourite spaniels, which were allowed to produce their pups and give suck wherever they pleased, noisome and repellent. Dressed in their lace-edged finery and expensive silks and velvets, courtiers would urinate and defecate in any convenient corner. The layout of the palace, the dark rooms and secret nooks and crannies, the easy access to the often fog-bound river steps and small private gardens, made it perfect for the sort of lascivious intrigue that was so typical of Charles's court.

The palace offered the royal family little or no privacy. There was open access to the court, although in the *Ordinances for the Government of the Household* the porters were ordered 'not to permit any stragling and masterless men, any suspitious person, or uncivill, uncleanly, and rude people, or beggars to come within our Court'. Charles was the most accessible of kings. Unlike his remote and majestic father, the long years of poverty and exile during the Interregnum had made Charles a little too casual and familiar with his subjects. His tall figure would be seen advancing through the press of people in the picture galleries. He and his family would dine in state, worship in the royal chapel where the public came to stare at them and listen to the music, receive visitors in their bedchambers, invite a favoured few into their closets – the little rooms where they kept their personal valuables and correspondence. The King might snatch some occasional moments of peace and solitude carrying out experiments in his laboratory or fishing in all weathers, but more often than not he spent his days amidst the throng. He was always there to receive petitions, to give an ear to his subjects, and he had revived the custom of touching for the King's Evil, the afflicted being admitted to the Banqueting House for the royal cure, a timely reminder of his divinely ordained status.

The new Duchess of York never forgot that she had come to England on a mission to help her fellow Catholics, suffering from religious persecution and discrimination. She decided that the best way she could advance the Catholic cause would be by example. She would be a perfect wife, a model of propriety, holding her place at the centre of court life. She would not hide herself away in prayer like the sour and childless Queen Catherine at her dower palace of Somerset House along the river. Catherine had long since resigned herself to her husband's infidelity. Consequently, the most splendid apartments at Whitehall – they had been redecorated several times before she declared them adequate – belonged to the King's mistress, Louise de Kéroualle, Duchess of Portsmouth.

On her last visit to England in 1670, the King's sister, Henriette Anne, Duchess of Orléans – his beloved Minette – had offered him a jewel as a parting gift, but Charles had replied that the only jewel he wanted was her Breton maid of honour, Louise de Kéroualle. The girl was sent to Charles shortly after the death of Minette that same year and quickly found her way into the royal bed. Of course, the Duchess of Portsmouth was a French spy, a Catholic, and steeped in political intrigue. The rabble hated 'Carwell', as they called her, and once attacked a carriage thought to be hers. The

King's Cockney mistress, Nell Gwynne, stuck her head out, shouting, 'Good people, be civil! I am the *Protestant* whore.'

Strictly speaking, the Duchess of York was not obliged to meet the King's mistress. However, when Mary Beatrice's ravishing cousin, Hortense Mancini, Duchess Mazarin, deserted her husband and arrived in London dressed as a man and accompanied by a black page – inciting the admiration of Charles II who promptly seduced her and gave her a pension – she felt it was her duty to visit her. The Duchess of Portsmouth complained that she had been slighted. So James had to take his wife to visit her too. The Queen took offence at this and publicly snubbed the young Mary Beatrice by turning her back on her at a court ball.

As Duke of York and heir to the throne, James had some of the best apartments at Whitehall, next to the King's and with a view of the river. On his first marriage, Charles had also given his brother the old red-brick Tudor palace of St James as his official residence, and he tended to stay there mostly during the summer months when they were not at Windsor. Within the precincts of St James's Palace was an exquisite little Catholic chapel designed by Inigo Jones, but Mary Beatrice was disappointed to find that this was reserved for the Queen's use, and that she would have only a makeshift arrangement next to her bedchamber. The palace had been extensively refurbished during the Duke's marriage to Anne Hyde, for whom the balcony had been made overlooking St James's Park. There was a fine view of the canal that the King had cut through the park, which was used for skating in winter. And early in the morning one might catch a glimpse of the King striding along, accompanied by a bevy of fawning courtiers, grasping place-seekers and ordinary petitioners for justice running to keep up with him.

There were plenty of beggars at court, though not of the kind proscribed by the *Ordinances*. The courtiers who vied with each other for royal favour and the perquisites of office were vain, shallow, immoral, venal and corrupt. The court was a massive gambling den, where fortunes were carelessly hazarded at card games. The young Duchess of York hated to play and to lose money, but she was told that it would cause offence if she did not do so. She walked a perilous path among the cynical and sophisticated courtiers. The English duchesses took umbrage when she offered her mother a chair when she dined publicly with her, while etiquette dictated that they had to stand. Her mother protested that, unlike them, she was a reigning duchess, moreover one who did not need to call a Parliament to raise taxes. Always sensitive about points of etiquette, Mary Beatrice decided that for the rest of her mother's visit she would dine privately with her, rather than cause offence to the English ladies.

Young and innocent, Mary Beatrice was happiest in the company of her two stepdaughters, with whom she played games of hide-and-seek and blind man's buff. Her Italian lady of the bedchamber, Countess Lucrezia Pretonari Vezzani, noted that she liked to divert herself 'with the Princesses, whose conversation is much to her taste and satisfaction'. Since their mother's death in 1671, Mary and Anne had been removed from their father's care, in case he should contaminate them with his Catholicism, and had their own household at Richmond Palace. With the arrival of their young stepmother, the two Princesses were invited to St James's more frequently.

Mary Beatrice became particularly fond of the Lady Mary, who was closer to her in age. Mary was charming, affectionate and intelligent, and the two became friends. Tall and graceful like herself, Mary loved to dance. Mary Beatrice might have found it harder to warm to the younger girl, who was less open and more suspicious than her sister. Lady Anne had a slight cast in her eye, so that she appeared to be looking at a person askance, which was rather disconcerting.

Subjected to her mother's strict discipline, Mary Beatrice had received a far superior education to that given these Stuart Princesses. Besides Italian, she was fluent in French and Latin and soon spoke and wrote the English language better than they did. Women's education was not high on the agenda in Restoration England and no one minded about Mary and Anne's lack of it. As long as they observed the strict tenets of the Anglican faith, they were allowed to while away the rest of the time playing cards. Both girls had a good ear, however, and were able to share their stepmother's love of music. She invited Italian musicians to England and the first Italian opera was performed in London the year after her marriage.

In the New Year of 1674, Mary Beatrice was observed by the Venetian ambassador to be so inconsolable at the departure of her mother that a court ballet she was to have attended that evening had to be postponed. In December her uncle, Prince Rinaldo, had written to her younger brother, the reigning Duke Francesco of Modena: 'The Duchess of York succeeds marvellously. She is loved tenderly by her husband, admired by the court, and respected by that wretched party, the Parliamentarians, despite the fact that they hate the marriage . . . I think we shall shortly leave here, because I see that Parliament is infuriated and determined to reassemble in January . . . It would not do for us to be found here.'

On leaving her daughter, the Duchess of Modena drew some consolation from the fact that the Duke was a good man who was obviously very fond of his young wife.

While English girls of good family were reported to be tearing each other's eyes out for a place in the Duchess of York's household, Mary Beatrice had the comfort of retaining at least a few of the Italians she had brought with her. Her old childhood friend, the Countess Lucrezia Pretonari Vezzani, remained as lady-in-waiting and the devoted Pellegrina Turini as woman of the bedchamber. She was allowed to keep Dr James Ronchi as her chaplain and almoner, and Father Antonio Guidici as her confessor, as long as they kept a low profile. More menial Italian servants included two cooks, so perhaps the Duchess was able to avoid the worst excesses of the English diet, which consisted of vast helpings of meat, a few vegetables swimming in butter, milky puddings and chalky bread. Lord Peterborough's wife was rewarded with the prize post of groom of the stole, worth £400 a year; she needed it as their silver plate was in pawn. A young Protestant widow, Susan, Lady Bellasys, whose father-in-law Lord Bellasys was a prominent, but moderate, Catholic, became lady of the bedchamber.

Among her four maids of honour was a bright girl with beautiful flaxen hair, Sarah Jennings, whose elder sister Frances had aroused James's interest when she waited on his first wife. Mrs Margaret Dawson, who had attended Anne Hyde in all her confinements, was one of the six women of the bedchamber. Mary Beatrice's secretary was a Catholic convert, Edward Coleman, who would soon be engaged in treasonable correspondence with France. Other members of the Duchess's household included a starcher, a seamstress, a laundress, a lace mender, two gentleman ushers, four gentleman waiters, four pages of the backstairs, a master cook, a necessary woman, eighteen watermen for her barge, a master of the horse, two esquires, eight footmen, four coachmen, postillions and helpers and grooms, and two chairmen to carry her in her sedan.

Fortunately, the Duke of York was by this time a rich man and, unlike the more profligate King's servants, members of the well-ordered York household were always paid promptly. The Duchess herself received £5,000 a year pin money, a vast sum for 'her personal service, dress, pocket money, play, etc.'.

———

Once Mary Beatrice was left alone with her husband, something curious happened. She started to fall in love with him. 'After her [mother's] departure,' she recalled many years later, 'I became very fond of my husband, and my affection for him increased with every year that we lived together. It was sinful for any one to love an earthly creature as I loved him.' She recognised that he was 'a very good man, and wishes me well and would do anything to prove it to me'. She drew consolation from the fact that he was a good Catholic, 'so firm and steady in our holy religion'. She was not to be consoled for long. Mary Beatrice had been in England for four months when she was incensed to discover that she was not the only object of the Duke's affections.

She learned that James had a mistress, Arabella Churchill, and that she had just given birth to their fourth child. Installed in a house in the newly built, fashionable St James's Square, Arabella led a quiet and discreet life. She was unlikely to cause Mary Beatrice embarrassment by flaunting herself at court, but a young bride with a passionate Italian temperament was understandably jealous of the very existence of her husband's mistress and their children.

It was through Arabella's influence that her handsome younger brother, John Churchill, had been taken into the Duke's household as a page. John had improved his fortunes by becoming the lover of his cousin, the King's voracious mistress Barbara Villiers, Duchess of Cleveland, who had preceded the Duchess of Portsmouth as *maîtresse en titre*. By 1675, thanks to the encouragement of his patron the Duke of York, Churchill was a colonel in the army and embarking on a turbulent courtship with the Duchess's maid of honour, the fifteen-year-old Sarah Jennings, ten years his junior but far more challenging than Barbara Villiers had ever been.

Royal brides were glorified breeding machines. James still had no male heir and it was Mary Beatrice's duty to give him one. She became pregnant soon after the marriage, but suffered an early miscarriage. Then, in January 1675, her first child was born. On the previous night, she had sat up until midnight playing ombre with the young Duchess of Monmouth – wife of the King's eldest bastard, James – she had had a good supper and slept well. In the morning she heard two masses, dined with her stepdaughters, and that evening gave birth to a princess. It was common practice for witnesses to attend a birth, to encourage the woman in labour and to swear there had been no foul play if the child died. At the birth of a potential heir to the throne witnesses were essential and on this occasion the Queen and many ladies of quality were present. Men, too, attended a royal birth, if only to hover in the background. The King was present this time and on leaving he embraced his brother with great affection. If James was disappointed that the child was a girl, he must have been relieved that his young wife seemed to be able to bear children with no trouble.

Within the privacy of her closed bed curtains, the Duchess quickly had her child baptised in the Catholic faith by her chaplain. When the King discovered this, he took absolutely no notice of her pleas. He explained that, like the Duke's elder daughters Mary and Anne, her daughter was a child of state and must be brought up a Protestant. She was given a public baptism in the Anglican Church and named Katherine Laura after the Queen and the Duchess of Modena. Her sisters, Mary and Anne, and the Duke of Monmouth were godparents. In October, she died of convulsions. 'You were a witness of the joy of my marriage,' a stricken Mary Beatrice wrote to Prince Rinaldo, 'and you can judge of my sorrow at the loss of its first-fruit by the death of my daughter, the Princess Katherine Laura, which happened last Sunday.'

In August 1676 the Duchess gave birth to another daughter, Isabella. Again, her labour was fast, so much so that the King and Queen did not arrive in time. Under pressure to produce a son, Mary Beatrice was disappointed at the sex of the child. James was at pains to reassure her that he did not mind in the least and presented her with a fine silver filigree bowl and dishes. After this birth, Mary Beatrice's health went into decline, not helped by the constant bleedings she was subjected to by the English physicians. The Lady Isabella was a child of almost ethereal blonde beauty, but so delicate she was not expected to live long.

In the autumn of 1677 Mary Beatrice casually mentioned to her brother that 'the Prince of Orange arrived two days ago to treat of some affair with the King. I have not yet seen him, as he went direct to His Majesty, who is at Newmarket.' She could have had little idea that this man, her husband's nephew, would become their implacable enemy and encourage the basest slanders on her reputation. The reason for the Prince's visit was soon clear. He was to marry his cousin and Mary Beatrice's stepdaughter, Mary, and they were to leave for Holland within days. 'I am much grieved to lose her,' Mary Beatrice told her brother, 'because I hold her in much affection, and she is really a princess of great merit.'

Mary Beatrice was again heavily pregnant and at the wedding in Mary's bedchamber a few nights later, the King jovially urged the officiating Henry Compton, Bishop of London, to 'make haste, lest his sister the Duchess of York should be deliver'd of a son, and so the marriage be disappointed'. There was a sting in his remark. The marriage had been arranged to placate the Protestants, who were incensed at James's increasingly blatant Catholicism. At Easter 1676 he had thrown aside all pretence as to his religion and ceased to attend Anglican services, much to his wife's satisfaction. Even moderate Protestants were disturbed, John Evelyn commenting that the Duke's non-appearance at the royal chapel was 'to the infinite griefe and threatened ruin of this poor nation'. For the Whigs, James's public stand was a gift, enabling them to rouse anti-Catholic hysteria to a new fury. The marriage of his daughter to the Calvinist Prince of Orange was the price James had to pay for his religious convictions, offering the nation hope of an eventual Protestant succession.

A few days later, the longed-for son and heir made his appearance. He was named Charles and created Duke of Cambridge, the ill-omened title held by three of James's sons by his first wife, all of whom died in their infancy. The Prince of Orange must have been seething with suppressed fury as he took his place with the King and the little Lady Isabella as sponsors at the baptism of the boy who had displaced Princess Mary in the succession. He was not the only one who was angry at the turn of events. The French ambassador, Paul Barillon d'Amoncourt, Marquis de Branges, reported to Louis XIV: 'The people of London show no pleasure at the birth of the Duke of York's son, and it has damped the joy that they had at the marriage of the Prince of Orange.'

There was a virulent strain of smallpox endemic in London and it now cut a swathe through the court. Lady Anne, who was observed to be sickening for some days, succumbed. As did the royal governess, Lady Frances Villiers, who had carried the infant Duke of Cambridge to the font. She died. Mary Beatrice did not endear herself to the Protestant courtiers when she revealed that Lady Frances had appeared to her in a dream, telling her that she burned in Hell. The Princess of Orange, who clung weeping to her stepmother, departed without being allowed to visit her sister in the sickroom to say goodbye.

Lady Anne's attack was mild, and on leaving her bed, the convalescent's first visit was to her stepmother in her lying-in chamber. Bending over the cradle, Anne gave her infant brother a kiss – and, in all innocence, sealed his fate. Apparently recovered yet still infectious, Anne could well have been responsible for passing on the smallpox to her brother. Within a few days the baby sickened, the nurses Mrs Chambers and Mrs Manning were blamed for concealing an eruption that had broken out at his navel and under his arm 'instead of using a coal leafe to draw it out', and he followed his half-brothers to the grave. His nineteen-year-old mother was prostrate with grief, telling her brother that 'great as was my joy when he was born, so much the greater is my anguish at his loss, but we must have patience, God knows what he does.' The Duke, according to the Princesses' chaplain Dr Lake, 'was never known to grieve so much at the death of any of his children'.

The ageing court poet Edmund Waller, whom Mary Beatrice had invited to pen a verse in her copy of Tasso soon after her arrival in England, put the loss of the boy down to the mother's youth and wrote to offer her hope:

*The failing blossoms which a young plant bears*
*Engage our hopes for the succeeding years;*
*Heaven, as a first-fruit, claimed that lovely boy*
*The next shall live to be the Nation's joy.*

At the same time Barillon was writing gloomily to Louis XIV: 'Many people believe that the Duke of York will never have children that will live. This death can only be advantageous to the Prince of Orange, strongly raising hopes for the future, and strengthening his party in England at the present conjuncture.'

Whatever was happening on the political horizon, there was no lessening of the Duchess of York's affection for her stepdaughter, Princess Mary, whom she dubbed her dear Lemon in complement to her husband's title of Orange. In the first week of October 1678 Mary Beatrice announced in a letter to her brother her intention of paying her a visit at The Hague:

The King has prorogued Parliament again until the end of this month, wishing to go to Newmarket on Tuesday next for three weeks, my lord Duke will go too, as he never leaves the King's side. I also am going a journey to Holland to see the Princess of Orange who is with child and has been ill, she is better now and very anxious to see me and her sister; we have as great wish to see her, for certainly I love her as if she were my own daughter, and also I have a wish to see that country. My lord Duke is pleased that I should visit his daughter and divert myself, and the King has given me permission.

Mary Beatrice's party, consisting of Lady Anne, the Duchesses of Monmouth and Buckingham, the Countesses of Richmond and Peterborough and Lady Henrietta Hyde, travelled to The Hague incognito. The visit was a great success and she returned happily reassured about Mary's welfare. James immediately wrote a rare effusive letter of thanks to his son-in-law. The Duchess, he wrote, was 'so satisfied with her journey and with you, as I never saw anybody; and I must give you a thousand thanks from her and from myself, for her kind usage by you: I should say more on this subject, but I am very ill at compliments, and you care not for them.'

––––––

In the winter of 1678 Mary Beatrice returned from her journey of pleasure into a political maelstrom. The carefree early years of her marriage when she had to some extent been protected from the full fury of the parliamentary opposition and anti-Catholic hysteria were over. Now, she and James were embarking on a period of exile, when it sometimes looked as if he might be excluded from the succession altogether.

The wild accusations of the disreputable, defrocked minister Titus Oates, who had infiltrated Catholic seminaries on the Continent, fell on fertile ground. He claimed that the Jesuits were plotting to incite rebellion in the three kingdoms of England, Scotland and Ireland. There was a plot to kill the King, which with time grew ever more fantastical, implicating the Queen and then his brother. Rousing old suspicions, he said that there was a plot to set fire to London; popular belief already held the Catholics responsible for the Great Fire of 1666, as the inscription on the Monument attested. With the capital and all the shipping on the Thames in flames, a few thousand Catholics were to slaughter a far greater number of Protestants. Anti-Catholic hysteria was such that any plot, no matter how far-fetched or illogical, was credited. Oates provided just enough circumstantial evidence for the King's minister, Thomas Osborne, Earl of Danby, to feel the plot warranted investigation.

Oates gained further credibility when Sir Edmund Berry Godfrey – the magistrate to whom he had first disclosed details of the plot – was murdered. His body was found in a ditch on Primrose Hill, but it was maintained that he had been killed at the Queen's residence, Somerset House. The Queen's physician, Sir George Wakeman, was arrested, as were several innocent Catholic peers and priests, many of whom in due course suffered a traitor's death on the basis of Oates's tenuous and contradictory evidence. As John Evelyn later reflected, the testimony of a man like Oates should not have been used against the life of a dog.

Letters written on his own initiative to France by the Duchess of York's secretary Edward Coleman, a fanatical Catholic convert, seemed to contain evidence of some Catholic design on England, and he too was arrested. Among the papers he had so carelessly left to be seized at his house were copies of letters from Mary Beatrice to the Pope, but she was unconcerned, knowing that the letters were merely complimentary and perfectly innocent.

Mary Beatrice's concern was for her husband, as she explained to her brother on 24 November 1678:

Affairs here are getting rather worse than better, every day they invent new stories and new plots, which are too long and confused to write, also all the couriers are stopped, and all letters opened, so that one can write nothing. You can imagine how afflicted I am, principally for the danger in which I see my lord Duke, for he has many enemies who do him all the harm they can with his brother. I hope however that the number of his friends may prove the greater, and that the affection his brother bears him will prevent him from believing the evil which is said of him.

Charles's tactic was to try to defuse the situation by ordering a full investigation of the plot to dispel any impression that the court was implicated or favourable to popery and by enforcing the penal laws against the Catholics. This prompted Mary Beatrice to write to her brother: 'I am much afflicted also for the misery of the poor Catholics, which is really extreme; they are all banished from London, and may not come within ten miles of it, and many poor people are dying of hunger and privation.' By December she was deploring the fact that some of the Catholics, 'constrained by necessity, are abandoning our holy faith ... To my great sorrow, I have been forced to dismiss all my English Catholic servants, as Parliament has forbidden them to appear at court.'

Coleman was hanged, drawn and quartered. Emboldened by his success, Titus Oates had the temerity to point the finger of accusation at the King's Catholic wife: 'I, Titus Oates, accuse Catherine, Queen of England, of high treason', implicating her in the plot to murder Charles. The King refused to believe such nonsense. He had always been sceptical about the veracity of the plot and felt vindicated when Oates was found to be completely ignorant of the layout of Somerset House, where he claimed to have overheard the plotters.

Anthony Ashley Cooper, Earl of Shaftesbury, and the Whigs, who some felt were no better than republicans, ruthlessly exploited the anti-Catholic hysteria, their main object being to prevent a Catholic successor coming to the throne. Even the French ambassador, Barillon, had to admit: 'The aversion the English nation has to a Roman Catholic King appears impossible to surmount.' Charles prorogued Parliament before Christmas 1678, then dissolved it in January. If Whig extremism was beginning to make more moderate opinion feel uneasy, reminding them of the 1640s, the new Parliament promised to be no less factious, however. The Tory leader, Danby, advised the King to order James out of the country, at least until tempers cooled. Charles made a futile attempt to persuade his brother to return to the Anglican Church, if only to avert a crisis, but James remained adamant. The Yorks were to go to Brussels in the Spanish Netherlands under the dominion of the King of Spain. They were not permitted to take their daughters, Anne and Isabella.

The English resident, Sir Richard Bulstrode, noted their arrival on 27 March 1679:

Their Royal Highnesses arrived here with three of the Prince of Orange's yachts. I had notice the night before of their coming, and had 20 coaches ready to receive them, wherein they were conducted incognito to their lodgings at the Prince de Lignes'.

Her Highness was much indisposed with her coming by sea, and is not yet recovered of it. Immediately after their arrival here they were visited and welcomed in his Excellency's name [the Governor of the Spanish Netherlands] and by several persons of the greatest quality . . . Her Highness being still something indisposed received the visits in her bed, the better to avoid all exceptions as to matters of ceremony, which is much stood upon in this court, especially among the grandees of Spain, who pretend a privilege much greater than others, but by this means all disputes will be avoided.

The one advantage of being in Brussels for Mary Beatrice was that it gave her easy access to her dear Lemon, the Princess Mary, at The Hague. In mid-April she wrote to her brother: 'Tomorrow I leave for Holland to see the Princess who is ill with fever and pains, but with no further hope of a child . . . which is very displeasing to us all. I shall stay with her several days, until she recovers, she having as great a desire to see me as I have to see her, and then we shall return here until it pleases the King and Parliament to let us go home again. You can imagine how passionately I desire our return.'

She was destined to be disappointed. The King made their chief enemy, the Whig leader Lord Shaftesbury, President of the Council, perhaps in an attempt to rein him in. In May the Whigs brought in the Bill for the exclusion of the Duke of York from the English throne, adding that if he ever returned from foreign parts he was to stand accused of high treason. On 1 June the Bill passed the Commons by 207 votes to 128 and Charles moved swiftly to prorogue Parliament. To add insult to injury, James received a letter from the Pope, warning him against excess of zeal. It could only do the Catholic cause harm, he warned. It was clear to James that his exile was to be prolonged and he sent to England for his coaches and his hounds, there being every opportunity to enjoy his favourite pastime of hunting in the countryside around Brussels.

The Yorks' residence in a Catholic country gave the Duchess

of Modena an opportunity to visit her daughter, whereas her presence was never welcome in London. The two had not seen each other for five years and she found Mary Beatrice grown into a beautiful woman. 'She is very tall,' she told Prince Rinaldo, 'but rather thin, full of goodness and grace. The Duke adores her, and thanked me again for having bestowed her upon him.' James and Mary Beatrice had been separated from their daughters for five months and in August petitioned successfully to have them with them during the parliamentary recess. The Duchess of Modena was able to see her granddaughter, Isabella, who was now three years old. Soon after the arrival of the Princesses, James was called to England urgently. The King had fallen gravely ill at Windsor. He arrived to find Charles recovering from a chill. Charles was pleased to see him, but it was judged too soon for his exile to be revoked. The blow was softened when the place of exile was changed from Brussels to Edinburgh. At least it would give James a foothold in the kingdom if the King should die suddenly and he had to seize the throne by force. The Yorks were to travel there directly by sea.

James lost no time in shepherding his family to Holland, from where they were to set sail. They stopped briefly at The Hague to dine with the Prince and Princess of Orange, who then accompanied them as far as Maesland Sluys. None of them realised it, but James and Mary Beatrice were never to see William and Mary again. The crossing was so rough that Mary Beatrice was vomiting blood. A request to put in at the Downs and continue the journey to Scotland by land was granted. The King was truly concerned for his sister-in-law, pressing her to stay in London with the children. She refused.

In his memoirs, James pays tribute to her loyalty, to the fact that although she was not more than twenty years of age she chose 'even with the hazard of her life, to be a constant companion of the Duke her husband's misfortunes and hardships. But it was a sensible trouble to His Royal Highness to see the Duchess thus obliged to undergo a sort of martyrdom for her affection to him, and he ... to be thus sent a sort of vagabond about the world.' For Mary Beatrice, the greatest tribulation was to be separated from her small daughter again, especially as her health was giving cause for concern. The Yorks made the best of their stay in Edinburgh and the Scottish nobility was delighted to have a court at Holyrood again.

In December 1680 the Exclusion Bill was carried in the Commons again, but Charles had plenty of allies in the Lords keen to uphold hereditary right, who threw it out. Far from buckling under popular pressure as the Whigs had expected, Charles had proved immutable on the question of his brother's succession. The succession was sacrosanct, he would in no way agree to its being altered either by his own action or that of Parliament. To play for time, or to defuse the opposition, he indicated he was prepared to discuss limitations on the powers of a Catholic successor. Early in December 1680 Mary Beatrice summarised the situation for her brother, perhaps echoing her husband's views:

O Dio! How things have changed! The House of Commons passed that Exclusion Bill against the Duke, but the House of Lords rejected it, so it means nothing; it is true that now they are trying to do worse, even in the Lords; to make laws limiting the Duke's authority, if ever he becomes King, and in a word to make of him a king of cards, which would be worse than the exclusion. God knows what effect these proposals will have. It is always in the King's power to save his brother, if he will; others speak of banishing him; as yet we know not what will be resolved upon, we are only certain that it will be nothing good for us.

It seemed particularly cruel that the four-year-old Lady Isabella should be prevented from living with her parents in exile, especially as her health was deteriorating and she died in February 1681 at St James's Palace. A grieving Mary Beatrice wrote to a nun at Modena that God had taken from her 'one of the dearest things I had in the world, and which I hoped

He would have left me in His goodness to be a comfort in my afflictions'. The following month she gave birth to another child, who also died. Sick and bereft, she wrote to the convent at Modena: 'But I console myself with the thought that I have more angels to pray for me, and I ought to esteem myself honoured that, while other women give their children to the world, I have given all mine to God, in whose mercy I still hope that He may some day comfort me by giving me a male child who shall live, and yet in the end gain Heaven.'

In England the situation had calmed down sufficiently for the King to give permission for Lady Anne, now sixteen, to travel to Edinburgh to spend some time with her parents. At Holyrood Mary Beatrice introduced the novelty of drinking tea – a rare and expensive commodity – at her receptions and the ladies of the court indulged in country dancing and card parties. The countryside round Edinburgh was unsuitable for hunting, but Lady Anne rode out in the hills with her stepmother. Mary Beatrice loved to ride, and she looked especially dashing in the fashionable feathered hat and long male riding coat worn over the trailing skirt that the ladies of the court had adopted. She had a serious accident in Scotland when her horse threw her, her long skirt became entangled, and she was dragged for some distance. She lost consciousness and was badly bruised. The accident was all the more serious since she was pregnant again, as she confided to Lady Bellasys in the spring of 1682.

By May 1682 the Duke and Duchess of York's exile was over. The plot had burned itself out and Parliament had been dissolved in March 1681, never to meet again in this reign. Fearful of the horrors of civil war being revisited on the nation, the Tories' natural inclination was to support the monarchy. They upheld the principles of divine right and hereditary succession and were firm supporters of the established Anglican Church. Moderate opinion everywhere preferred to take their chances with the lawful successor to the throne, albeit a Catholic, than encourage the dubious ambitions of the Whigs.

There was a backlash against violent extremists. The Whigs seemed to be finished. Their leader, the Earl of Shaftesbury, slunk off to Holland, where he died in January 1683. The discovery of a real plot to assassinate the King and the Duke of York on their return from Newmarket in June 1683 revived their popularity. Whether through shrewdness or good fortune, Charles had managed the situation well, although it had taken a terrible toll on his health. The royal prerogative had not been impaired, his brother's succession was assured and there were to be no limitations on his power.

Mary Beatrice's misfortunes were not over with her exile, however. On 15 August 1682 she gave birth to a daughter, 'all passing so quickly that not only the King and the Duke, but even the nurse did not arrive in time'. Significantly, the Whigs had been putting it about that the pregnancy was a hoax, until the sex of the child was known. The Duke's enemies, according to Barillon, were rejoicing that he had not got a son, while the Duchess of Portsmouth told him that the King was very disappointed because he felt a son would have helped 'to dissipate the factions of the malcontents'. Three weeks later the Lady Charlotte Mary died of convulsions and James was once again despairing that none of the children of his second marriage would live.

––––––––––

Mary Beatrice was grief-stricken at the sudden death of King Charles II on 6 February 1685, confessing to the nuns at Chaillot many years later that she had loved him from the start, long before she had come to love her husband. His death and the surprisingly smooth succession of James to the throne meant that England had one of the most beautiful queens in its history. There was some concern that Mary Beatrice's health was too frail for her to undergo the rigorous coronation ceremony, but in the event she carried the day very well.

Three crowns had been made especially for her. On her way to the abbey she wore a circlet of gold enriched with diamonds. An imperial crown adorned with precious stones surrounded with *fleurs-de-lys* and surmounted by a cross was placed on her head at the moment of her coronation. On leaving the abbey, she wore a crown of gold encrusted with pearls and diamonds. Every seam of her dress was covered with diamonds and cordons of pearls held her train to the dress. It was observed that during the Anglican ceremony she showed every sign of devotion. She was seen to depart from etiquette after the ceremony by joining Princess Anne and her husband in their box, chatting amiably with them before joining the King for the banquet in Westminster Hall. The new Queen endeared herself to the people by taking upon herself the liability of all the small debtors in the kingdom imprisoned for sums under £5, releasing many hundreds from prison.

One of her first acts as Queen was to write to William of Orange, telling him: 'Pray follow my example and write to me without any ceremony for it is not to be minded between such friends as we are.' Mary Beatrice had been universally loved as Duchess of York, but as Queen some felt she became too grand. She still hated to lose money at cards, as Evelyn noted when she lost £80 one evening at basset and looked extremely concerned, adding, 'her outward affability much changed to stateliness since she has been exalted'.

Gilbert Burnet, who was William's creature, chose to imply that Mary Beatrice had been concealing her true character all along. While praising her grace and beauty, he said that she behaved in so obliging a manner, and seemed so innocent and good, that everyone was fooled. 'So artificially did this young Italian behave herself, that she deceived even the oldest and most jealous persons, both in the court and country,' he wrote in his *History*, which put a Williamite gloss on the Revolution. 'She avoided the appearances of a zealot, or a meddler in business, and gave herself up to innocent cheerfulness; and was universally esteemed and beloved, as long as she was Duchess.'

Mary Beatrice's chief critic was her stepdaughter Anne, who wrote to her sister Mary:

The Queen, you must know, is of a very proud, haughty humour; and though she pretends to hate all form and ceremony, yet one sees that those that make their court this way, are very well thought of. She declares always that she loves sincerity and hates flattery, but when the grossest flattery in the world is said to her face, she seems extremely well pleased with it. It really is enough to turn one's stomach to hear what things are said to her of this kind, and to see how mightily she is satisfied with it.

All kings and queens were subject to flattery, it was the nature of court life, and Princess Anne's criticism of her stepmother might be put down to jealousy. She might also have been angry because the Queen had succumbed to Sunderland's insinuating charm. Robert Spencer, Earl of Sunderland was the most devious, self-serving politician of the age. He had supported the Exclusion Bill, yet somehow managed to worm his way into James II's favour. Princess Anne hated both him and Lady Sunderland, perhaps because he was prepared to abandon the Anglican religion and become a Catholic. Being rather naïve, Mary Beatrice considered him a friend, so much so that she sent his son Lord Spencer as an envoy to her brother. Unfortunately, Lord Spencer had a drink problem and was a grave diplomatic embarrassment. Time would prove that Sunderland was no friend.

James and Mary Beatrice's court was undoubtedly thin. As early as October 1686 John Evelyn noticed that a court ball held in honour of the King's birthday was not well attended. There might have been some truth in Princess Anne's assertion that 'All ladies of quality say that she is proud that they don't care to come oftener than they must needs, just out of mere duty.' The whole tone of court life had changed. Where it had been given over to pleasure, riotous and dissolute, now it was formal, stately and moral. It was forbidden to appear drunk before the Queen or to fight at court. Many courtiers probably stayed away not so much because of the Queen's manner, but because they found the overt Catholicism obnoxious.

Without the restraining influence of Charles II, who had insisted his brother and his wife worship in private, James and Mary Beatrice now practised the Catholic religion flagrantly. They went publicly to mass, leaving the door open. John Evelyn went along to view the splendour of the new Catholic chapel at Whitehall and to enjoy the singing of the Italian tenor, Cifaccio. He was scandalised by the sight of a Catholic bishop and the Jesuit priests in their rich vestments, the elaborate ceremony and gilded ornaments, the swinging censer and the waft of incense. 'I could not have believed I should ever have seen such things in the King of England's palace,' he wrote, 'after it had pleased God to enlighten this nation.' Even when James reviewed his troops on Hounslow Heath he took a portable altar, where he and the Queen heard mass in public. They surrounded themselves by priests and for the first time since the sixteenth century a papal nuncio was received at court. It was all too blatant and caused offence to Anglican sensibilities.

Mary Beatrice continued in delicate health. The Tuscan ambassador watched her avidly, since if she died he intended to recommend his master's daughter, the Princess of Tuscany, as James's next wife. One of the reasons for Mary Beatrice's wan appearance was the fact that her husband was planning to introduce his two sons by Arabella Churchill, James and Henry Fitzjames, created Dukes of Berwick and Albemarle respectively, to court in September 1685. They had been educated by the Jesuit Father Petre and brought up as Catholics and were to continue their education in France. Worse than this was her husband's continuing affair with Catherine Sedley, who had already borne him a daughter.

Catherine, the only daughter and heiress of the rakish poet Sir Charles Sedley, had replaced Sarah Jennings as one of her maids of honour. The affair with James had begun in about 1678 and continued intermittently whenever he was in England. Ironically, Sir Winston and Lady Churchill had hoped to secure Catherine as the bride of their son John, who had no money of his own and needed her inheritance. But he had been irresistibly drawn to Sarah Jennings, and Mary Beatrice when Duchess of York had somehow contrived to make this match financially viable. The Churchills' marriage, which at first remained secret, might even have taken place in her apartments. John Evelyn described Catherine as 'none of the most virtuous, but a wit'. This, of course, was her attraction for James, who had always been more drawn by a woman's wit than her looks. As Catherine herself quipped, 'It cannot be my beauty because I haven't any, and it cannot be my wit because he hasn't enough of it himself to know that I have any.'

There were some, namely the King's former brothers-in-law, Henry Hyde, second Earl of Clarendon, and Laurence Hyde, Earl of Rochester, who thought that a Protestant mistress would be good for him, perhaps divert him from some of his more extreme religious measures. At first, James was so moved by his new dignity as king that he tried to pension Catherine off. When their eight-month-old son, James Darnley, died the day before the coronation, however, James might have visited Catherine to commiserate. Whatever his good intentions, she soon regained her ascendancy over him. In January 1686 James gave her a title. Mary Beatrice was reported to be moping. John Evelyn confided in his diary: 'Passed the Privie Seale, amongst others, the creation of Mrs Sedley . . . Countess of Dorchester, which the Queen took very grievously, so that for two dinners, standing neare her, I observed she hardly eate one morsal, nor spoke one word to the King, or to any about her, tho' at other times she us'd to be extreamly pleasant, full of discourse and good humour.'

Where other royal wives had endured their husband's infidelity, Mary Beatrice was not prepared to tolerate it. Barillon was following the unfolding scandal avidly and reported to Louis XIV: 'She loves her husband in all sincerity; she is Italian and very proud. Her grief manifested itself very plainly. I believe it is strengthened and encouraged underhand. She has openly declared she will not suffer the public scandal it is intended to establish, that she will not see the new Countess, and that if the King does not separate from her, she will retire to a convent, in any country that may be.'

The force of Mary Beatrice's resistance surprised James, and she left him in no doubt of his choice. Either he gave up Catherine Sedley, or she would carry out her threat to enter a convent. She summoned James to her bedchamber, where Father Petre and other priests confronted him. They pointed out to James the harm it would do the reputation of a Catholic king to be seen disporting himself with a heretic mistress. He conceded and Catherine was ordered to leave the country. She prevaricated and resisted, retorting that she was a freeborn Englishwoman. Eventually, she departed for Ireland – temporarily, for it was soon reported that a house was being prepared for her in St James's Square and a pew reserved at St Ann's Church – and Mary Beatrice regained her serenity. The affair with James might be over, but the court had not seen the last of Catherine Sedley.

The Queen never meddled in politics, but she undoubtedly exercised a strong influence over James and she was blamed for his excesses. Princess Anne certainly held her responsible, as she told her sister: 'One thing I must say of the Queen, which is that she is the most hated woman in the world of all sorts of people; for everybody believes that she pressed the King to be more violent than he would be of himself; which is not unlikely, for she is a very great bigot in her way, and one may see by her that she hates all Protestants.' This was not quite fair. Mary Beatrice's outlook was European and Catholic. She was naturally devout. As a foreigner in England, insulated from the mainstream of English life and probably ignorant of its history, she absorbed her politics from her husband. Unfortunately, James's take on English affairs was somewhat skewed and his cause had

42

never been helped by the simple fact of his having taken a Catholic wife.

As a convert, James was zealous, whereas the Queen, brought up in the Catholic faith, was moderate. Like James, she wanted their Catholic subjects to be free to practise their religion and to have the penal laws repealed. But she differed with James as to the means. Like all the more moderate Catholics, the Queen understood that these reforms must be carried out legally and tactfully. She neither liked nor trusted the Jesuit Father Petre, who had gained such a hold over James and eventually found his way on to the Privy Council, because his methods and ambitions were so extreme. The Pope, with whom Mary Beatrice regularly communicated, was no friend of the Jesuits and he discouraged any rash action that would do the Catholic cause more harm than good.

The Queen was touched when William of Orange sent over his cousin, William Frederick of Nassau, Count Zuylestein, to offer condolences on the death of her mother in August 1687. The Duchess of Modena had left her daughter one of the finest pearl necklaces in Europe, her Monti estates and a considerable sum in cash. Mary Beatrice was distraught by her mother's death and the court was plunged into deep mourning. The event provided a convenient cover for the real purpose of Zuylestein's visit. He was to have covert talks with the English nobility, to sound out their opinions on James's regime, perhaps even to test their loyalties for the future. William liked to keep his finger on the pulse of English affairs. When the Queen left for Bath at the end of that month, she noticed that the court was very depleted and she suspected that the courtiers might not return. As James made his progress in the western counties, he must surely have wondered why so many of the nobility and gentry appeared to be absent from their estates. The news of the Queen's pregnancy towards the end of the year meant that William would almost certainly decide to intervene in English affairs.

William knew the value of propaganda. The Queen and

her pregnancy must be discredited. Scurrilous broadsheets appeared on the streets, some of them claiming that Father Petre or the papal nuncio, Count D'Adda, was the father of her child. *On the Queen's Conception* read:

> *And the spirit of Love*
> *Shall descend from above,*
> *Though not as before, in the shape of a dove,*
> *Yet down he shall come, in some shape or other,*
> *Perhaps like Count Dada, and make her a mother.*

Rumours were also put about that the Queen had suffered a miscarriage early in the pregnancy and that she was wearing a cushion. Cartoons depicted her pinning one on. One of Burnet's scurrilous suggestions after the event was that in the spring the Countess of Clarendon had entered the Queen's bedchamber to find her moaning and repeating the words, 'Undone, undone.' One of her women was taking something out of the bed, which she believed was 'linen taken from the Queen'. At that moment Lady Powis entered the room and hustled Lady Clarendon out. All this sounds like snippets of gossip sewn together to make an allegation.

Certainly Mary Beatrice had some scares of miscarriage. On one occasion a careless or malicious bedchamber woman, Mrs Elizabeth Bromley, burst in with the news that the Duke of Modena was dead. Tradesmen were at the door, she told her mistress, demanding what the arrangements were to be for mourning. Mary Beatrice took the letter, read the first lines about the seriousness of her brother's illness, and fainted. In fact, the rest of the letter described his amazing recovery. Afterwards, she wrote to Princess Mary on 15 May: 'I was soundly frightened . . . I am now within six weeks.' Here, as elsewhere, she was relying on the physicians' reckoning. Her own theory, which proved correct, was that she had conceived as soon as she and James had met at Bath in the first week of September, so that she was due in the second week of June.

All this time the Queen was ignorant of the nature of

the correspondence between her two stepdaughters. Burnet claims that 'all things about her person were managed with a mysterious secrecy, into which none were admitted but a few papists. She was not dressed or undressed, with the usual ceremony.' In his memoirs, James maintains that, on the contrary, his daughter Anne regularly attended the Queen's toilette and handed her her shift, so that she must have seen the pregnancy was real. Burnet says that the Princess 'went so far in desiring to be satisfied by feeling the motion, after she said she was quick, as she could without breaking with her'. By her own later admission, Anne had never been invited to feel the baby kick in any of Mary Beatrice's previous pregnancies, so that there was nothing abnormal about her not being asked to do so on this occasion. Anne, however, was only too eager to plant in her sister's mind the idea of the Queen's 'false belly':

For, methinks, if it were not, there having been so many stories and jests made about it, she should, to convince the world, make either me or some of my friends feel her belly; but quite contrary, whenever one talks of her being with child, she looks as if she were afraid one should touch her. And whenever I happen to be in the room as she has been undressing, she has always gone into the next room to put on her smock. These things give me so much just cause for suspicion that I believe when she is brought to bed, nobody will be convinced it is her child, except it prove a daughter. For my part, I declare I shall not, except I see the child and she parted.

It is possible that Mary Beatrice sensed her stepdaughter's venom and so recoiled from letting her touch her and a natural modesty took over when she was undressing under such a hostile stare. It seems that Anne was so inquisitive that the Queen once struck her in the face with a glove in exasperation. Mary Beatrice was aware of the scurrilous allegations, but she disdained to stoop so low as to react to them. Her pride was her downfall. It would have been far better if she had paraded naked in front of the English

Protestant ladies in her bedchamber and let them feel the child kicking in order to counter the rumours. But, of course, she expected to be confined in public. Someone as virtuous as Mary Beatrice could never have anticipated that her enemies would also throw doubt on what happened in a birth chamber full of witnesses.

# 2

## *Princess Anne of Denmark*

*'I can't help thinking Mansell's wife's great belly is a little suspicious . . . there may be foul play intended. I will do all I can to find it out, if it be so: and if I should make any discovery, you shall be sure to have an account of it'*

– Princess Anne of Denmark to her sister the Princess of Orange

When Princess Anne was still a very small child, it seemed that all the maternal figures in her life were destined to leave her. At only three years old, she was taken away from her parents, the Duke and Duchess of York, and brought to France to live with her grandmother, the Queen Dowager Henrietta Maria, at her château at Colombes outside Paris. The purpose of the visit was to find a treatment for Anne's sore eyes, which could not stand bright light and would not stop watering. Perhaps the French physicians would succeed where the English had failed. It was here in France that the Stuart Princess had her portrait painted. Serious grey eyes showing no sign of her malady looked out of a stubborn little face under a halo of light auburn curls. She clutched a small spaniel in a pose that could have lasted only a minute. There was already a hint of the self-protective survivor she was to become in the set of the vulnerable shoulders.

Her grandmother had been suffering from consumption, but, even so, everyone was taken by surprise at her death in August 1669. The four-year-old was transferred to the household of her aunt, the charming Henriette Anne, Duchess of Orléans, at the palace of St Cloud. She placed the chubby little girl in the nursery with her own two daughters, Marie-Louise who was two years her senior, and the baby, Anne-Marie. The English

47

Princess must have been happy there, because years later she fondly remembered Anne-Marie in her will as her closest living relative. The security and comfort of the nursery world was abruptly shattered the following year by the sudden death of the young Duchess of Orléans, only two weeks after she had completed a successful diplomatic mission to her brother King Charles II in England. There were whispers of foul play. Some suspected that 'Madame' had been poisoned by 'Monsieur', her jealous and spiteful husband, or by some of his homosexual cronies. A post-mortem indicated a ruptured appendix.

A stickler for etiquette, Monsieur, who loved to wear female finery and cosmetics, immediately had the two older children rigged out in full court mourning and ordered the courtiers to make all three children official visits of condolence for their loss. La Grande Mademoiselle, daughter and sole heiress of the late Gaston, Duke of Orléans, protested to her cousin Louis XIV that the children looked absurd in the flowing violet veils and long velvet trains designed for adults. Small as they were, they made stumbling progress in the cumbersome clothes. As tactfully as possible, the English intervened to extract their princess from the Orléans household. They used the thin excuse that her eyes were now cured, which in reality would never be the case. Louis XIV gave the five-year-old Princess Anne a very handsome leaving present, 'two braceletts of pearle besett with diamante valued at 10,000 crowns'. He could not have anticipated that this small girl, who was so shy and taciturn and had to screw up her eyes to look at a person, would grow up to be his great adversary.

After two years' absence, the Lady Anne of York – as she was called in England as a child – returned to her parents at St James's Palace. She could barely have remembered her mother, Anne, Duchess of York, the large bejewelled lady who had made such a pet of her as an infant, inviting her to sip chocolate and feeding her titbits, so that she became as round as a ball. Her mother was no great beauty, but she was handsome and voluptuous. Clever and witty, she had ensnared

48

James, Duke of York into a clandestine marriage – they had exchanged vows before witnesses and then consummated the union, which amounted to a marriage in the eyes of the Church – at Breda a few months prior to the Restoration. For a royal duke and the heir to the throne to marry a commoner was a huge misalliance: if he had only waited a few months, after his brother's restoration to the throne he could have married any princess in Europe. When the secret began to leak out and Anne's first pregnancy became glaringly obvious in the autumn of 1660, it embarrassed the royal family and scandalised society.

Even the bride's father, Sir Edward Hyde, a Wiltshire lawyer who had turned to politics and become Charles II's Lord Chancellor, was appalled. He said that he would rather she was the Duke's whore than his wife and urged the King to punish her for her presumption by sending her to the Tower. The Stuarts' royal relatives in Europe were shocked and disgusted that James should make such a base marriage. His aunt and godmother, Elizabeth, Queen of Bohemia, was incredulous. She was living at The Hague when Anne Hyde was resident there as maid of honour to the Princess of Orange, so she was in a position to know that the girl had taken physick to try to induce an abortion. Surely she would not have done such a thing, she claimed in a letter to her son the Elector Palatine, if she had been legally married when she became pregnant? Her daughter and James's cousin, Sophie of Brunswick-Lüneburg, later Electress of Hanover, could never quite bring herself to regard the children of the marriage as her equals.

And now, on Lady Anne's return from France, her parents were again embarrassing the monarchy. In her absence, the Duke and Duchess of York had taken the drastic step of abandoning the Anglican faith of their youth and converting to Roman Catholicism. The King urged them to keep it secret. Nothing was more abhorrent to the English political nation and public opinion than Catholicism. The conversion of the

49

heir to the throne was to have enormous and far-reaching consequences both for him and for his children.

———————

Anne Stuart was born on one of the coldest days in living memory, 6 February 1665, the year of the plague. Her mother's labour was so fast that it is doubtful that the King and Queen and many of the witnesses deemed necessary at a royal birth arrived at St James's on time. She was the fourth child and second daughter of the Duke and Duchess of York. The first child, Charles, Duke of Cambridge, whose birth had been so clouded by the murky circumstances of his parents' marriage, had died of convulsions when he was seven months old. Even his parents were somewhat relieved at his death, since there would always have been doubt about his right to succeed to the throne. He was conceived well before his parents underwent a second marriage ceremony in London in September 1660. There could be no doubt of the legality of this marriage and of the legitimacy of the children who followed. In April 1662 the Lady Mary was born. She was ousted from her place in the succession by the arrival of a brother, James, Duke of Cambridge, in July 1663.

On the birth of a second daughter to the Duchess of York, Charles II wrote to his sister the Duchess of Orléans in France, showing how undervalued a princess was:

I am very glad to hear that your indisposition of health is turned into a great belly. I hope you will have better luck with it than the Duchess here had, who was brought to bed Monday last of a girl. One part I shall wish you to have, which is that you may have as easy a labour, for she despatched her business in little more than an hour. I am afraid your shape is not so advantageously made for that convenience as hers is; however, a boy will recompense two grunts more.

Lady Anne was named in honour of her mother. Her christening in the Chapel Royal at St James's presented an interesting contrast in youth and old age. The godparents included her three-year-old sister Lady Mary, held up at the font by her governess, Lady Frances Villiers; the fourteen-year-old Duchess of Monmouth, the Buccleuch heiress who had been married to the King's eldest bastard; and the septuagenarian Gilbert Sheldon, Archbishop of Canterbury. The Chancellor, created Earl of Clarendon in the wake of his daughter's marriage, seemed particularly pleased with this new granddaughter, perhaps because she resembled the Hydes and had such a placid temperament. She might already have been exhibiting his stubborn expression. But she was delicate and would need to survive the perils of infancy, the attentions of the royal physicians, and the plague which raged in London and then in the provinces through the first two years of her life.

Years later when Anne looked at a portrait of her mother, she admitted to her friend Sarah Churchill that she could not remember what she looked like. The Duke and Duchess spent the summer of 1665 in York with their children and in the autumn the family took up residence in the Oxford colleges with the rest of the court avoiding the plague-ridden capital. It is likely that when the court returned to London in the spring of 1666, the York children were sent off to the healthier environment of Richmond Palace further up the Thames, the traditional nursery of the royal children. A new baby, Charles, Duke of Kendal, soon joined them. Here they had their own 'family' or household. The world Lady Anne was most familiar with consisted of her siblings, her wet nurse Mrs Martha Farthing, her governess Lady Frances Villiers, the under-governess Mrs Mary Kilbert, and other servants including nurses, rockers, a dresser, a seamstress, a necessary woman, a laundress and a page of the backstairs. Lady Anne seems to have been very loyal to her 'family'; she was always to show her ladies and her more menial servants kindness and consideration and many of them served her devotedly to the end of their lives.

Throughout their childhood, the York children spent little time with their parents. Though she made a pet of her daughter

Anne, the Duchess was not a particularly maternal woman. She had demands elsewhere. She was the second lady in the kingdom. The Duchess was rather a stately figure and commanded respect, but she was also good company, generous and friendly. She had the knack of attracting people of merit and her court at St James's was far more brilliant than that of Queen Catherine at Whitehall. Anne was a stronger character than her husband, and observers of the marriage noted that while she was not able to control the Duke's rampant womanising, she dominated him in every other respect. The Duchess was no passive figure taking a back seat in political and social affairs: she was intelligent and involved in all matters that concerned the Duke and his interests.

Much of her attention must have been concentrated in a vain effort to keep her errant husband in check. James was an incorrigible womaniser. There were the obvious affairs with ladies of the court that were common knowledge and caused the Duchess intense jealousy and humiliation. And there were the more sordid illicit couplings. The Duke's pimps were said to bring women to his closet at Whitehall, so that, according to one of the gossip-loving Pepys's sources, 'he hath come out of his wife's bed, and gone to others laid in bed for him.'

The Duchess alleviated her unhappiness at her husband's infidelity by overeating. This, together with the annual pregnancies that were the lot of upper-class women who did not breast-feed their infants, destroyed what pretensions she ever had to a good figure. She became grossly overweight. She also spent her husband's money furiously, amassing jewels for herself. She was in the advantageous position of having borne heirs to the throne, but she must have worried that they were delicate and sickly.

Gilbert Burnet, who it must be remembered was hostile to the Duke, repeated some scurrilous story that Lord Southesk had purposely contracted a venereal disease which he passed on to his wife, believing that the Duke was involved with her. Burnet maintained that James passed the disease on to the Duchess and that their offspring suffered as a result: 'his children were born with ulcers, or they broke out upon them soon after; and all his sons died young, and unhealthy.' That 'Willis, the great physician, being called to consult for one of his sons, gave his opinion in those words, *male stamina vitae*, which gave such offence, that he was never called for afterwards.' James's children, Burnet concluded viciously, were nothing but 'the dregs of a tainted original'.

James would have been fortunate indeed to escape some sort of venereal infection as a result of his promiscuity. But whether it was of a nature to affect his children is a moot point. The bedchamber woman, Mrs Dawson, who served both James's wives, noticed that every one of their children was born with red spots round the eyes, which soon disappeared. Both Mary and Anne suffered from 'sore eyes' throughout their lives. Neither of their parents had such a defect. In Anne's case, it was more extreme, taking the form of a 'defluxion'. This made her squint, which, according to contemporaries, lent her face a sour, petulant look. The disability added to her natural shyness. As she grew up, she preferred the closet to the drawing room, and would rather move in a small circle of known acquaintances than large gatherings where she would be unable to see people. Using poor eyesight as an excuse, she would rarely pick up a book, although she was able to manage an expansive correspondence.

It may be that, as girls, Mary and Anne escaped some of the more zealous attentions the royal physicians visited on the boys, who were considered more important. Royal children seem to have been as much in peril from the so-called cure as the disease. In the late spring of 1667 Lady Anne's four-year-old brother, James, Duke of Cambridge, was very ill and covered with spots – whether from smallpox or measles is unknown. Smallpox, of course, could be deadly, but measles or some other childhood illness could have been overcome with good nursing, had it not been for the intervention of the physicians with their ignorant and misguided practices. Even the toughest infant might have been defeated by the bleedings, emetics, vomits and weird and dangerous concoctions the physicians prescribed. Both the Duke's sons were at St James's when Pepys reported the poignant news that they were gravely ill. Apparently, their mother divided her attentions anxiously between them, not knowing which of them would die first, the elder of 'some general disease' or the younger of convulsions, of which he had had four in one morning.

Obviously everyone was very concerned, because after James these boys were the sole male heirs to the throne. When their brothers died within a month of each other, the Ladies Mary and Anne were briefly second and third in line to the throne. But their mother was already pregnant with her sixth child. On 14 September 1667 Pepys reported: 'The King and Queen and the Duke of York and the whole court is mighty joyful at the Duchess of York's being brought to bed this day, or yesterday, of a son; which will settle minds mightily.' The child was given the ancient Saxon royal name, Edgar, and he was the third and by no means the last of Lady Anne's brothers to hold the luckless title, Duke of Cambridge.

The Duchess admitted she was never well again after the birth of Edgar. This was the year in which her mother died, leaving the Chancellor bereft, and that of his fall from office. A scapegoat had to be found for the Dutch war. It had started so promisingly in the year of Lady Anne's birth when her father as Lord High Admiral had won a naval victory off Lowestoft, becoming a popular hero for a rare moment. But it had ended disastrously, with the Dutch sailing up the Medway and towing away the *Royal Charles*. Among other grievances, Clarendon was held responsible for marrying the King to a barren woman, supposedly so that his own grandchildren would inherit the crown. In fact, Queen Catherine had three miscarriages, so that she was not exactly barren. Gout-ridden and grieving for his wife and grandsons, Edward Hyde went into exile at

Rouen, never to see the Duke and Duchess or his remaining grandchildren again.

On the night of Clarendon's fall, Lady Anne's parents dined alone in melancholy mood. They had good reason to be. George Villiers, second Duke of Buckingham, who now gained ascendancy among a loose assortment of government ministers known as the Cabal from the first initial of each name or title – Clifford, Arlington, Buckingham, Ashley Cooper and Lauderdale – was no friend to James. He sought to destroy him by launching an enquiry into his conduct of naval affairs. He prompted the King to take an interest in the Roos divorce case. It was something of a *cause célèbre* because divorce, with permission to remarry, was still so rare. In the case of aristocrats, such as the Roos couple, where a marriage had to be dissolved because a legitimate heir was needed for a great estate, the case was heard in the House of Lords. Charles duly attended the proceedings and declared they were as good as a play. This was probably part of Buckingham's plan for Charles to divorce the Queen and remarry, so dislodging James and his children from the succession. And he encouraged the pretensions of the King's eldest bastard, James, Duke of Monmouth, to the throne. These were all ideas shared by a fellow member of the Cabal, Anthony Ashley Cooper, Earl of Shaftesbury, and his Whig followers, who were to become such vociferous opponents of the Duke of York.

While Buckingham was in favour, James entered a period of isolation. It was now, at the beginning of the year 1669, that he took the most momentous and politically damaging decision of his life. He abandoned the High Anglicanism of his youth and embraced Roman Catholicism. He was encouraged to some extent by Charles's private revelation to James and two trusted Catholic members of the Cabal, Thomas, Lord Clifford and Henry Bennet, Lord Arlington, that he was a Catholic in his heart, and wanted to further the cause of Catholicism in his realm. Charles probably only meant to suspend the penal laws against Catholics and give them a measure of religious toleration. He was far too shrewd to alienate his subjects by making public profession of a faith most of them feared and hated, still less by attempting to impose it on them.

While Lady Anne was sharing her children's nursery at St Cloud, Henriette Anne, Duchess of Orléans, came to Dover in June 1670 for talks with her brother. The Duke and Duchess of York followed Charles down to the coast to greet her, although James did not play a key role in the discussions, spending two weekends in London quelling riots in the wake of the new Conventicle Act, which forbade meetings of Protestant Dissenters. Minette had come to forge a treaty of alliance between England and France. This contained a secret clause promising that Louis XIV would subsidise Charles while he dispensed with Parliament to facilitate the imposition of royal absolutism and the conversion of England to Catholicism. The immediate consequence of the treaty, however, was not England's conversion, but another war with the Dutch, which James bitterly opposed.

Frank to the point of foolishness and entirely lacking his brother's political sense, James resented the need to keep his conversion a secret. The Duchess had followed suit in embracing the Catholic faith. Some thought she did so in a bid to retain her hold over her husband, but that does not do her justice. An extremely intelligent woman, well schooled in religious doctrine, she wrote an impressive paper explaining the reasons for her conversion. A staunch Anglican, her father was horrified by her decision and wrote to warn her of the inevitable consequence: 'That she would bring all possible ruin upon her children, of whose company and conversation she must expect to be deprived; for, God forbid, that, after such an apostasy, she should have any power in the education of her children.'

The question did not arise, because the Duchess was already entering upon her final illness. James's Catholic leanings had always been suspected, which is one of the reasons he was generally unpopular, but fears of the Duchess's conversion arose when she ceased to attend Anglican services. She had always been a regular churchgoer, taking communion about once a month. She used her illness as an excuse not to attend church, but it was observed that her chaplains were not invited to pray with her either. By the time Lady Anne returned from France in July 1670, her mother was already a very sick woman. The previous year, she had borne another daughter, Lady Henrietta, who did not survive. Another pregnancy followed and on 9 February 1671 she gave birth to Lady Katherine, despite the fact that she was in the advanced stages of cancer.

On 30 March 1671, just weeks after she had given birth to her eighth child, the thirty-three-year-old Duchess returned to St James's after a hearty dinner with her brother's in-laws, the Burlingtons, at their house in Piccadilly and promptly collapsed. Her sister-in-law, Queen Catherine, who had always been fond of her, rushed from Whitehall to be with her. Her brother, Henry Hyde, Lord Cornbury, described by James as 'a violent Church of England man', refused to come near her because he suspected that she had become a Catholic. As Anne lay dying, James was anxious not to have her disturbed by the intercession of well-meaning Anglican clergy. He took the Reverend Mr Blandford aside and divulged the truth of her conversion to him. Blandford was kind enough to restrict himself to generalities. He approached the dying woman and asked her merely if she 'continued in the truth'? 'Truth, truth,' Anne replied through mists of pain and delirium, 'what is truth?' The Duke asked her if she knew him and she replied, 'Aye.' A few moments later she stirred and muttered, 'Duke, Duke! Death is terrible – death is very terrible', and died.

The Duchess's diseased and grossly corpulent body was in such an advanced state of decomposition that she could not lie in state, receiving the public honours normally accorded royalty. Her young maid of honour, Margaret Blagge, was appalled by the whole business:

The Duchess dead, a princess honoured in power, had much witt, much mony, much esteeme: she was full of unspeakable tortur, and died (poor creature) in doubt of her religion, without the sacrament, or divine by her, like a poore wretch; none remembered her after one week, none sorry for her; she was tost and flung about, and every one did what they would with that stately carcase. What is this world, what is greatness, what to be esteemed, or thought a wit?

As for Lady Anne of York, who had just passed her sixth birthday, she had lost three crucial maternal figures – her grandmother, her aunt and her mother – all within two years of her short life. Inured to loss at so young an age, perhaps she had already started to develop a self-protective shell to hide her vulnerability. Naturally reserved, she would always be cautious in whom she placed her trust. But when she did find someone she felt she could trust, she gave her affection wholeheartedly.

At the time of her mother's death, Lady Anne was considered so delicate she was not given long to live, but she confounded the predictions. It was Edgar and Katherine who followed their mother to the grave within a few months of her death. Mary and Anne were the sole survivors of the eight children born to the Duke of York and his English commoner wife. He was now free to make a suitable marriage with any princess of his choice. As for his daughters, Charles II did not trust his Catholic brother with their upbringing. Second and third in line to the throne, they were declared children of state, to be brought up as good little Protestants to appease the nation. Perhaps because they were close in age and thrown so totally on each other's company, already imperceptibly alienated from their father because of his religion, the sisters were devoted to each other and grew up good friends.

———

In spite of the tragedies in her young life, Lady Anne seems to have been a happy child. Although she did not have her sister Mary's striking beauty and tall, graceful figure, she was bonny with rich auburn curls and soon became rosy-cheeked in the healthy surroundings of Richmond Palace. The Ladies Mary and Anne were brought up with the daughters of Sir Edward and Lady Frances Villiers, their governess, together with other young girls who were selected as company for the Duke's daughters. Sarah Jennings, later Churchill, with whom Anne was to have such a passionate friendship, certainly became well acquainted with the household after she became a maid of honour at court. There may be some truth in Sarah's claim that 'we had used to play together when she was a child, and she even then expressed a particular fondness for me.' But Sarah was five years older, and the two did not become close until much later.

The Restoration was a low point in the education of women. In a court notorious for its immorality, women were encouraged to be ornaments or playthings rather than scholars. Unlike the Tudor princesses of the sixteenth century and their own great-great-grandmother, Mary Stuart, Queen of Scots, Mary and Anne were not to enjoy a Renaissance education. In spite of their proximity to the crown, they learned nothing of history, geography, constitution or law. Their knowledge of English spelling and grammar was rudimentary. They had no Latin or Greek, but they did learn French, and could both speak and write it competently. It was their only foreign language. Like her father, Lady Anne was musical and she had tutors for the harpsichord and the guitar, at which she excelled. Both girls learned to dance under a French dancing master who had instructed their grandmother, Henrietta Maria. Her poor eyesight seems to have prevented Anne from taking an interest in art, or perhaps even sharing her sister's lessons with the dwarf art master, Mr Gibson. Emphasis was placed on domestic accomplishments such as needlework. In a court very taken up with dogs and horses, learning came low in the list of priorities for royal princesses.

The only criterion for Mary and Anne's education was that they receive a good grounding in the Protestant religion. Charles chose as their religious tutor Henry Compton, Bishop of London, a younger son of the Earl of Northampton. He had pursued a military career until taking holy orders. A fierce Anglican, he was a vigorous opponent of Catholicism. James loathed him and had the satisfaction of blocking him from the see of Canterbury when it became vacant in 1677. Compton instilled in the Duke's daughters an unshakeable conviction that the Church of England was the one, true Church, and that the Church of Rome was in grave error, scarred by centuries of abuse and deviation from the pure truth. Writing long after she had quarrelled with Anne, Sarah Churchill wrote that Anne was 'ignorant of everything but what the parsons had taught her when a child'.

Anne proved an apt pupil in matters of religion. If she was not bright enough to read the subject deeply or engage in theological debate, she could at least repeat Compton's lessons pat. 'I must tell you that I abhor the principles of the Church of Rome as much as it is possible for any to do, and I as much value the doctrine of the Church of England,' she assured her sister a few years later. 'And certainly there is the greatest reason in the world to do so, for the doctrine of the Church of Rome is wicked and dangerous, and directly contrary to the Scriptures, and their ceremonies – most of them – plain, downright idolatory.'

Showing that she had absorbed all Compton's teaching to the letter, she continued: 'But God be thanked we were not bred up in that communion, but are of the Church that is pious and sincere, and conformable in all its principles to the Scriptures. Our Church teaches no doctrine but what is just, holy and good,' she concluded with a note of satisfaction, 'or what is profitable to salvation; and the Church of England is, without all doubt, the only true Church.' Just as the Church of

Rome appealed to James's authoritarian nature, so the Church of England provided Anne with a much needed rock of stability from her insecure youth.

James remained a distant figure for his children, but he and his younger daughter did share one very characteristic trait: their obstinacy. Sarah Churchill recalls an incident that illustrates this:

When they [Mary and Anne] were children, walking in the park together, a dispute was started between them, whether something they saw at a great distance were a man or a tree; her sister being of the former opinion, and she of the latter. When they came so near that their eyesight could convince them it was a man, the Lady Mary said, Now sister, are you satisfied that it is a man? But Lady Anne, after she saw what it was, turn'd a way, and persisting still in her own side of the question, cried out, No, sister, it is a tree.

The atmosphere at Richmond Palace seems to have been rather like a girls' boarding school, with best friends, jealousies, fallings-out and mischief behind the back of the governess. Lady Mary had a schoolgirl passion for an older girl, Frances Apsley, whom she called Aurelia. Although Lady Anne was so much younger than Frances, she succeeded in becoming her friend too, and her sister suffered pangs of jealousy when Frances gave Anne a cornelian ring. Later, Anne copied her sister in writing letters full of devotion to Frances, addressing her as her 'Deare Semandra'. The name was taken from Lee's *Mithridates*, in which the girls had taken part in a court performance. Anne had played the role of Semandra, but in her correspondence she allotted the female role of 'Wife' to Frances, playing the role of the 'Husband', Ziphares, herself. Whereas her sister Mary would always be the submissive wife, it is interesting that Anne chose to play the male lead in her friendship with Frances. Avoiding some of the excessive protestations of love that filled Mary's letters to Frances, Anne at fourteen was to display a sincere yet more restrained love for her friend:

Deare Semandra, none deserves more love from everybody then you nor none hass a greater share in my heart then your self exsepting whom you know I must love better. I am not one of those who can express a great deale & therfore it may be thought I do not love so well but whoever thinks so is much mistaken for tho I have not may be so good a way of expressing my self as some people have yet I asure you I love you as well as those that do & perhaps more then some.

When the sisters appeared 'all covered with jewels' in John Crowne's masque *Calisto, or the Chaste Nymphe* at court in December 1674, rehearsals had proved such a disaster that professional actors were brought in to bolster the performance. One of them was the famous actress Mrs Barry. Charles II noticed that his niece Anne had a particularly mellifluous speaking voice – it was described as 'a sort of charm' – and retained Mrs Barry to train her voice. Anne's timidity and bashfulness prevented her from speaking in public, but when she could not avoid it, such as when she addressed her Parliament, the listeners were mesmerised.

There was one matter upon which the Duke of York and his daughters' Anglican chaplains, Dr Lake and Dr Doughty, agreed. Every year without fail the anniversary of King Charles I's execution on 30 January was held as a day of mourning, prayer and fasting. The Duke of York's daughters observed the occasion with the strictest solemnity and clad in black. It was a timely reminder that their grandfather had died a martyr for the Anglican faith, even if their father the Duke of York appeared to have forgotten this, and of what happened to kings when they crossed the will of the people.

––––––––––

The Duke of York seems to have been lost without a wife. His apartment at Whitehall, shared with a large rampaging dog called Mumper, apparently became very run down in the two-year period between the death of his first duchess and the arrival of the second. His remarriage in the autumn of 1673 might have been expected to make a profound change in the lives of his daughters, but in all essentials this was not so. Their routine continued. Lady Anne was probably so settled in her own little world at Richmond Palace that a stepmother made little difference to her. The girls spent more time in London and their fifteen-year-old stepmother was undoubtedly kind and gracious. But, perhaps because in age Mary Beatrice was more like an older sister, she never seems to have fulfilled the role of a mother to them.

At this early stage there is no evidence of the hostility that later became so marked in Anne's relationship with her stepmother. Nor, on the other hand, do the letters of either party reveal any evidence of real affection between them. Anne's attitude to Mary Beatrice seems to have been one of indifference. As with her father, relations were harmonious, if superficial. The Italian Mary Beatrice probably found Mary's character more sympathetic. Mary possessed a Latin temperament, derived from her French and Italian ancestors. She had a sort of feverish charm, was highly emotional and loved to chatter. The phlegmatic Anne, so much more like her mother's English family, must have watched in amazement as her new stepmother wept copious tears every time she looked at her father. To brighter, quicker minds, Anne was slow and plodding. Reserved and cautious, secretive even, she was watchful and kept her own counsel.

Already firm Protestants at eleven and eight, the Duke's daughters must have been aware of the crucial religious divide between themselves and their new stepmother. Their father had already lost his office as Lord High Admiral because of the new Test Act, requiring all office-holders to deny the doctrine of transubstantiation, a fundamental Catholic belief. The Act was designed to smoke out secret Catholics in government, and, indeed, no good Catholic could swear the oath. Court and servants' gossip and their own observation of the angry bonfires lit in protest at the Duke's marriage to a Roman

Catholic princess can have left the girls in no doubt as to the unpopularity of their father's second marriage.

James's stubborn refusal to renounce the Catholic faith he had so eagerly embraced meant that he had little say in his daughters' education, nor in Lady Mary's case, in the choice of her marriage partner. For Lady Anne, her sister's marriage to their Dutch cousin, Prince William of Orange, meant separation from her sister, who was to leave immediately for the United Provinces. This probably represented a far greater upheaval in Anne's world than her father's remarriage had done four years previously. Anne was not well enough to attend the marriage ceremony, a hurried and joyless occasion at St James's. Her chaplain, Dr Lake, recalled in his diary entry that it had been rather a momentous week: 'This week hath produced four memorable things. The Lady Mary and the Prince of Orange were married on the Sunday; the Duchesse was brought to bed of the Duke of Cambridge on the Wednesday; the Archbishop of Canterbury [Sheldon, Anne's godfather] dyed on the Friday; and on the same day Lady Anne appear'd to have the small pox.'

Smallpox was highly contagious and very often fatal. Dr Lake was concerned that he was not allowed to go into Anne's chamber to read prayers, for fear of spreading the infection. He admitted that he was troubled because Anne's nurse 'was a very busy, zealous Roman Catholick, and would probably discompose her if she had the opportunity'. He obtained permission from Compton to attend the Lady Anne exclusively. Lake's diary reveals some rather touching fatherly concern on the part of the Duke, who did not want to upset Anne with news of her sister's departure. 'The Duke visited her every day of her sicknesse,' he wrote, 'and commanded that her sister's departure should be conceal'd from her; wherefore there was a feigned message sent every morning from the Princess to Her Highness to know how she did.'

Smallpox was apt to disfigure the victim for life but, like

her father, Lady Anne was fortunate to emerge with her skin only lightly scarred. The Duke had to admit that her sister had already left, news which the stolid Anne 'appear'd to bear very patiently'. An immediate bonus was that she inherited her sister's far superior apartment at St James's; another was that she would no longer fall under the shadow of the more vivacious Mary, who could be very imperious with her younger sibling. The world of Richmond Palace that the sisters had shared ended with Mary's marriage, but now Anne suffered a further wrench when their governess, Lady Frances Villiers, died of smallpox. Unfortunately for Anne, Lady Henrietta Hyde, the wife of her younger uncle, Laurence, replaced her kindly governess. Anne disliked her intensely.

Freed from the sickroom, Anne rushed to visit her step-mother and greet her new baby brother. At this stage, the fact that their stepmother was likely to bear the Duke other children, potential heirs to the crown, does not seem to have concerned Mary and Anne. They were both fond of their little sister, Lady Isabella, born in September 1676, and genuinely grieved when each of their half-siblings died. Charles, Duke of Cambridge, quickly followed the others to the grave.

———

When James and Mary Beatrice went into exile in March 1679, they were compelled to leave their surviving children behind. It was not until that summer that the Ladies Anne and Isabella were allowed to travel to Brussels, accompanied by Lady Bellasys, for a brief visit to their parents. Shortly after their arrival James was urgently recalled to England when the King fell ill. He arrived in London secretly and made for Sir Allen Apsley's house in St James's Square, where he spent the night before proceeding to Windsor.

Anne was obviously hoping that the event marked the end of her father's exile. As she wrote to Lady Apsley: 'I find you weare mightely surprised to see the Duke, indeed we weare all

mightely surprisde at it heare at first & did not know what
to think but now I hope in god it will be for the best & that
I shall be so happy to bring the Dutchess over with me but I
know not whethere I have any ground for these hopes, I hope
I have for I have a good heart thank God or els it would have
bin down long ago.'

The fourteen-year-old girl went on to describe to Lady Apsley
her delight in the celebrations marking the marriage of her
cousin, Marie-Louise of Orléans, to King Carlos II of Spain:

I was to see a ball at the court incognito which I likde very well it
was in very good order & some danced well enough indeed there
was Prince Vodemont that danced extreamly well as well if not
better then ethere the Duke of Monmouth or Sr E. Villiers which
I think very exstrodinary last night againe I was to see fyer works
and bon fyers which was to celebrate the King of Spaines weding
& they weare very well worth seeing indeed.

The letter goes on to reveal a lively interest in her surroundings
and betrays a need for security that she seemed to derive
from them. It is apparent that she had a close, affectionate
relationship with her little sister and companion:

All the people heare are very sivil & exsept you be othere ways to
them they will be so to you, as for the town it is a gret & fine town
methinks tho the streets are not so cleane as they are in holland yet
they are not so dirty as ours they are very well paved & very easy
they only have od kind of smells, my sisster Issabellas lodgings &
mine are much better then I expected & so is all this place, for our
lodgings they weare all one great room & now are devided with
boards into severall, my sister Issabella has a good bedchamber with
a chimny, & in it there is a little hole to putt by things between her
room & mine there is a indeferent room without a chimney then
mine is a good one with a chimney which was made a purpose for
me. I have a closet and a place for my trunks & thers a little place
wheare our women dine & over that such anothere.

To her old friend Frances Apsley, she revealed a schoolgirl's appreciation of all the treats she had enjoyed at the ball, such as 'Limonade cinemont water & chocolate sweet meats all very good'. She was already showing signs of a rigid anti-Catholicism in her next remark: 'All the fine churches & monasterys you know I must not see, so can give you no good account of them, but those things which I must needs see as theire images, which are in every shope & corner of the street the more I see of those foolerys & the more I heare of that religion the more I dislike it.'

When the Yorks returned to England and embarked on a second period of exile in Scotland, Anne travelled with her parents as far as Hatfield. Here she probably witnessed the scorn and contempt with which some of the nobility were beginning to treat her father. When the travel-weary party reached Hatfield, it was to find the Earl of Salisbury absent. Very mean fare and kindling had been left for the royal guests and the Duke insisted that so poor a lord must not be out of pocket for them, pressing on the steward eight shillings, which was accepted. With their parents exiled in Edinburgh, Anne was alone but for their attendants when four-year-old Isabella died at St James's in February 1681. The loss of so many siblings was not unusual in the seventeenth century, but it did not make the grief any less intense.

By the time the Duke and Duchess of York returned from exile in May 1682, Lady Anne was seventeen, already well past the age when a princess might expect to be married. In the autumn of 1680 there had been some talk of Anne marrying her second cousin, George Ludwig of Hanover, the eldest son of that Sophie who so deplored the marriage of her cousin the Duke of York to a commoner. Rachel, Lady Russell, who was usually quite well informed, wrote that Henry Sidney had told her that the 'Duke of Hanover is coming over to take our Lady Anne away', adding: 'They say this young Hanover is one of the handsomest and best bred men of the age.' In fact, he was short, blond with bulging blue eyes, and rather dull.

The main advocate of the marriage seems to have been the

King's cousin and Sophie's brother, Prince Rupert of the Rhine, who had long been resident in London. Roger Coke's *Detection* maintains that George came on purpose to see the Lady Anne, but that 'not liking her person, he left the kingdom, without making any motion to the King or the Duke of York, for their consent to marry her'. It continues: 'many affirmed, that the Lady, to her dying day, had an aversion to him, in particular for the suppos'd slight put upon her.'

The meeting between Lady Anne and George of Hanover seems to have been a stilted affair, since they were both so shy and taciturn. Conversation was presumably conducted in French, since George did not speak English either then, or later, when he became king. The Prince stayed in London from December to the following March. The fact that the marriage rumours came to nothing was much more likely to have been owing to reasons of state rather than any personal aversion. Lady Anne would surely not have taken umbrage when she understood that George's subsequent marriage to his paternal cousin, Sophie Dorothea of Celle, arranged by his father at the time of George's visit to London, made perfect sense in Hanoverian dynastic terms. The claim that she had always hated her Hanoverian successors because of George's supposed rejection of her as a young woman was one put about by her enemies thirty years later. It is probably true that Anne never forgot a slight, but it is a moot point that she felt slighted in this instance. Her own subsequent marriage was so happy that it is unlikely that she would harbour any regrets for one that might have been.

Although her conversation was rather limited, George could have found nothing wrong with Lady Anne's looks. She had not yet put on the excessive weight that came with years of childbearing and other health problems. With her rich dark brown auburn-tinted curls, the lovely arms and hands that contemporaries considered such an asset to a woman's beauty, and a generous, sensual mouth, she soon attracted an unwanted suitor. John Sheffield, Lord Mulgrave, was one of

Charles II's favourite courtiers, a thirty-five-year-old bachelor with an eye for the ladies. The innocent and inexperienced young Princess was no doubt flattered to receive the attentions of such a sophisticated admirer. Mulgrave maintained that his crime was 'only ogling', but it was enough to warrant his being despatched to Tangiers in a leaky boat. Gossip, of course, had it that he had seduced the Princess. Princess Mary in Holland strongly disapproved of the whole business, believing that her sister must take some of the blame for being implicated in such a scandal. She spilled out her feelings in a letter to Frances Apsley:

*Hage Nov. ye 27th (1682)*

If I coud love you better then I did before your last letter woud make me do so, to see the consern you are in for my pore sister. I am sure all who are truelly her friends must be so, for my part I never knew what it was to be so vext & trobled as I am at it, not but that I believe my sister very innocent however I am so nice upon the point of reputation that it makes me mad she should be exposed to such reports, & now what will not this insolent man say being provokt, oh my dear Aurelia tis not to be imagined in what conserne I am that I should ever live to see the ondly sister I have in the world, the sister I love like my own life thus abussed & wronged. I could writ thus till tomorrow morning & not express half I have in my heart, but keep it to yourself, for tho tis a thing so publicke grown yet I have not the heart to spake of it but to my best friends adieu then dear Aurelia I deserve some pittie as well as my pore sister for all her afflictions I recon as my own.

Probably not as chastened as her sister would have liked, Anne retained a fondness for her admirer. When she became Queen, she created him Duke of Buckingham and gave him a piece of St James's Park, where he built Buckingham House – 'the house that Jack built' – eventually to become the royal residence in London. Meanwhile, the upshot of the Mulgrave scandal was a determined drive on the part of the King and the Duke to find an acceptable husband for Lady Anne. Their choice fell on the eminently suitable Prince George, brother to King Christian V of Denmark.

The fact that George was a Protestant – albeit Lutheran – pleased both Anne and the nation. He was twelve years older and they were distant cousins, since Anne's great-grandmother, the wife of James I, had been a Danish princess. John Evelyn noted that 'he had the Danish countenance, blond; a young gentleman of few words, spake French but ill, seemed somewhat heavy; but reported valiant.' Prince George had been trained for a military career and had shown courage in the field against the King of Sweden. He was neither clever nor witty, as Charles soon discovered: 'I have tried him drunk and I have tried him sober and there is nothing in him.' But he was kind and considerate to Anne, prepared to take second place in their household, and she was delighted with him.

Anne's wedding took place at ten o'clock at night on 28 July 1683 in the Chapel Royal at St James's Palace. It was a joyous occasion. Bishop Compton presided and afterwards the couple sat at the head of the table at a small family supper, before the bedding ceremony. James had provided a dowry of £40,000 and the couple were to receive an annual allowance from the King of £20,000, to be supplemented by income from Prince George's Danish estates. Although she was now to be known as the Princess of Denmark, Anne was fortunate in that she was to reside in England. The King gave her as an outright gift the Cockpit at Whitehall as her official London residence.

Prince George turned out to be that rare creature in Charles II's court, a faithful husband. The couple shared a bedchamber all their married life. George's only problem was his inertia. He drank far too much, in common with nearly everyone else in London and at court at that time, and he ate too much. When he confided to the King a worry about his weight, Charles advised him: 'Walk with me, hunt with my brother, and do justice to my niece, and you will not be fat.' As for the drinking, Charles could not help comparing the kindly but dull young man to 'a great jarr, or vessel, standing still and receiving unmoved and undisturbed so much liquor, every time it came to its turn'.

James had had the satisfaction of snubbing his other son-in-law, Prince William of Orange, by not informing him of the proposed marriage until negotiations had been concluded. It greatly concerned William that his sister-in-law and cousin make a marriage compatible with his interests. The Hanoverian alliance would have pleased him, since he was in constant touch with that family and, by and large, could rely on their support. He was less pleased with a Danish alliance, since Denmark came within the French sphere of influence. James had dashed off one of his increasingly snide letters to William: 'I must now inform you of a proposal which has been made to his Ma. and approved of by him: it is a marriage between Lady Anne and Prince George of Denmark: it was this day approved of, of which I would not fail to give you notice. It is now very late and I am to go a hunting tomorrow morning so that I have not time to say more but that you shall still find me as kind to you as you desire.'

It irritated William that Prince George outranked him. The son of a monarch and brother of a reigning sovereign was obviously the superior of an elected Stadholder, so that Prince George would take precedence over William in England. Princess Mary, however, was pleased that her sister seemed so well settled, as she confided to Frances Apsley: 'You may believe twas no small joy to me to heer she liked him & I hope she will do so every day more & more for els I am sure she cant love him & without that tis impossible to be hapy wch I wish her with all my heart as you may easely imagin knowing how much I love her.'

Just prior to her marriage, Anne had the added joy of persuading her father to allow her friend Sarah, Lady Churchill, to transfer from the Duchess of York's household to her own. There was resistance to the proposal at first, possibly because there were some – Anne's uncle, Laurence Hyde, Earl of Rochester, for one – who felt that Sarah would not be a good influence on Anne. But James liked to think of himself as an indulgent father and acceded to her wishes. Anne wrote off excitedly to Sarah: 'The Duke of York came in just as you were gone, and made no difficulties, but has promised me that I shall have you, which I assure you is a great joy to me. I should say a great deal for your kindness in offering it, but I am not good at compliments. I will only say that I do take it extreme kindly, and shall be ready to do you all the service in my power.'

In her *Conduct*, Sarah says that the Princess encouraged her always to speak frankly to her and never flatter or dissemble. According to Sarah, it was in the Princess's best interests to hear the truth. Nor did the Princess stand on her rank and suggested that during Sarah's absences from court they correspond as Mrs Morley and Mrs Freeman. 'My frank, open temper naturally led me to pitch upon Freeman,' Sarah recalls, 'and so the Princess took the other, and from this time Mrs Morley and Mrs Freeman began to converse as equals, made so by affection and friendship.' The two women were now at the height of their friendship. Sarah had already borne several children and Anne was about to embark on childbearing, so the older woman was able to advise the younger and they shared common interests in pregnancy and small children for a while. Sarah seems to have been genuinely fond of her young mistress at this time, although she must have found Anne's clinging dependence on her increasingly irksome as the needs of her own growing family became paramount to her.

John, Lord Churchill was still a member of the Duke of York's household, but his wife's friendship with Princess Anne drew him inexorably into the Cockpit circle, where the Churchills were soon dominant. Prince George was a great admirer of John Churchill, who had escorted him to England for the marriage. He had also known John's brother George as a page at the Danish court – he was now a captain in the navy – while the other brother, Charles, was a colonel in the army. The Cockpit circle also included the Duke of Grafton – Charles II's bastard by Barbara

Castlemaine – and Lord Ossory, the grandson of the Duke of Ormonde.

The Stuart sisters' childhood friend Frances Apsley had married, rather later than usual, Sir Benjamin Bathurst, some years her senior. He had been director of the East India Company. Now she asked Anne for a place in her household for her husband, who duly became comptroller, or treasurer. The Princess's other Richmond playmate, Barbara Villiers – a kinswoman of Charles II's erstwhile mistress – was now married to Colonel Berkeley, in command of Anne's dragoons. In due course, Barbara would take charge of the royal nursery, as her mother Frances had done before her. Anne's cousin Lord Cornbury, the son of Henry Hyde, Earl of Clarendon, was Prince George's master of the horse. When her aunt Lady Clarendon – who 'looked like a madwoman, and talked like a scholar' – left with her husband to take up office in Ireland, Anne breathed a sigh of relief and replaced her as first lady of the bedchamber with Sarah Churchill. The vibrant Sarah provided all the passion and excitement that Anne lacked in her relationship with her cosy nonentity of a husband.

The Denmarks spent their time in the idle pursuits of the aristocracy. Any activity at all seems to have been an effort for Prince George. 'We talk here of going to tea, of going to Winchester, and everything else except sitting still all summer which was the height of my ambition,' he complained. 'God send me a quiet life somewhere for I shall not be long able to bear this perpetual motion.' Gambling for high stakes meant that their income was never sufficient to cover their needs and Anne's father frequently stepped in to pay her gambling debts. Apart from cards, Anne enjoyed all the usual country pursuits. She joined the King and the Duke at Newmarket – Charles's love of horses and racing prompted him to launch the races there, while Anne would later be responsible for Royal Ascot – where she attended cock fights. Like her father, she loved to hunt and she and her stepmother hunted for hares with small beagles. Anne was not particularly keen on the theatre, unlike her uncle and her father who were patrons of it, nor was she a reader, so that her conversation, Sarah commented tartly, centred on 'trifling fashions, rules of precedence, and observations upon the weather'.

As a royal princess third in line to the throne, Anne's duty was to provide heirs for the House of Stuart. Three months after her marriage, she embarked on the first of the seventeen pregnancies that were to break her heart and wreck her health. In May 1684 she gave birth to a stillborn daughter. 'I believe you will be sorry to hear of my daughter, the Pcs. of Denmark, being delivered of a dead child,' James informed William, 'they say it had been dead some days before, so that it is a great mercy it come as it did, and that she is so well after it.' The following month she accompanied her stepmother to Tunbridge Wells, where the Duchess was to take the waters and Anne was to convalesce. By the end of the year, Anne was pregnant again. The fact that she was pregnant might have accounted for the fact that she does not seem to have been present when her uncle, King Charles II, died on 6 February 1685, making a deathbed conversion to the Catholic faith. It was Anne's twentieth birthday and she gave some credence to the ridiculous rumour that the Jesuits had poisoned her uncle to make way for her Roman Catholic father.

---

The surprisingly smooth accession of King James II, the first Roman Catholic king in over a century, triggered the gradual awakening of Anne's political conscience. Suddenly she was the sole member of the royal family participating in Anglican services in the Chapel Royal at Whitehall. An assiduous church-goer, she became ostentatious in her support of Protestantism. Bishop Compton, dismissed from the Privy Council because of his opposition to James's wish to repeal the Test Act, remained her religious adviser and mentor. As James's Catholic policies increasingly seemed to offer a threat to the Anglican Church, she also attended sermons given by some of the more vociferous anti-Catholic preachers. Publicly the King accorded his daughter all the honours due to her rank, ordering the courtiers who served her at table to do so kneeling. But he knew that she was a magnet to the silent opposition and he kept a close watch on her household, placing spies about her person.

Anne's antipathy to her stepmother seems to have coincided with Mary Beatrice becoming Queen. Perhaps Anne was jealous of the Queen's exalted rank and her hold over her father. Certainly she harboured some unexplained resentment. Possibly she blamed her for the fact that her allowance, which now stood at £30,000 a year, had not been increased as she wished. 'Ye Queen sent me . . . a watch with her picture on it set with diamonds,' she wrote sarcastically to Sarah a few months after the coronation, 'for wch present I must return her most thankful acknowledgments but among friends I think one may say without being vain that ye goddess might have showered down her favours on her poor vassals with more liberality.'

Anne did not trouble to hide her dislike of the Queen, or refrain from criticism of her, within the confines of her own household. She might have been influenced by Sarah, or been aiming to impress Sarah by her disdain for her father's wife. Anne was determined to think the worst of her stepmother, writing to her sister two years later: 'She pretends to have a great deal of kindness to me, but I doubt it is not real, for I never see proofs of it, but rather the contrary.' As usual, she pretended a cool indifference to her. 'It is not for me to complain, and as long as she does not make the King unkind to me, I don't care what she is.' One wonders if Mary Beatrice realised how two-faced her stepdaughter was, as Anne's next remark reveals: 'I am resolved always to pay her a great deal of respect, and make my court very much to her, that she may not have any just cause against me.'

Whatever their personal feelings for each other, they could not be divorced from the religious question. While Anne was increasingly seen as the representative of Anglicanism, Mary Beatrice was regarded by many as the leader of the opposing

Catholic party. Anne felt that the Queen influenced the King to be more bigoted than he would otherwise have been, although she also blamed Lord Sunderland and the priests for her father's extreme policies. Her greatest fear was that her father would try to enforce her conversion. The King undoubtedly wished both his daughters to convert, if only, as he believed, to save their immortal souls. 'Nobody has yet said anything to me about religion,' she wrote to her sister in April 1686. The King had given her the devotional papers of Charles II and her mother, explaining the reasons for their belief that the Church of Rome was the true Church. Later that summer, she was writing to Mary: 'I am of your opinion that it is more likely he will use fair means rather than force; and I am in as great expectation of being tormented if he had not some hopes that in time he may gain either you or me.'

Anne assured her sister that she did everything she could not to acquiesce in the overt Catholicism of her father's court:

You must know there was never grace said at the King's table by a priest till after I went to Tunbridge this year; when I came back and found it so whenever I dined with Their Majesties, I always contrived when grace was saying to be either talking to somebody or looking another way, which the King observing, one day he came to me and asked whether I did it on purpose or by chance, and bid me be ingenuous, which I was, and told him I did do it on purpose. Upon that, he said it was looking upon them as Turks, and looked disrespectfully to him; and he said he found by this that I had very ill impressions made on me about his religion.

Princess Mary obviously wrote frequently to urge her sister to stay firm to her religion, advising her also not to employ Catholics in her household. Anne assured her that she would 'rather beg my bread than ever change'. She did, however, after much prevarication, have to greet the papal nuncio, Count D'Adda, in July 1686.

The birth of her child, Lady Mary, on 1 June 1685 at Whitehall increased Anne's political importance. William and

Mary's marriage had produced no children, so the future of the dynasty seemed to rest with Anne. Anne might never, so far, have been ambitious of the crown for herself, but the arrival of children undoubtedly gave her a stake in it. Lady Mary, named for her aunt, was a poor scrap of a child who seemed to have inherited her mother's eye problems. A second daughter, Lady Anne Sophia, was born prematurely on 12 May 1686. The King visited his daughter in her lying-in chamber at Windsor, bringing a Catholic priest with him. Anne promptly burst into tears at the sight of the priest and her father sent him away. She spent another summer convalescing at Tunbridge Wells and by the end of the year she was pregnant for the fourth time in her four-year marriage.

Early in the New Year of 1687, Anne wrote a letter to her sister that, as things turned out, was unbelievably poignant:

I have always forgot to thank you for the plaything you sent my girl. It is the prettiest thing I ever saw, and too good for her yet, so I keep it locked up and only let her look on it when she comes to see me. She is the most delighted with it in the world and in her language gives you abundance of thanks. It might look ridiculous in me to tell you how much court she makes to your picture without being bid, and may sound like a lie, and therefore I won't say anything more of her, but that I will make it my endeavour always to make her a very dutiful niece.

A few days later, Anne suffered a miscarriage, brought on, she suspected, by a new dance called the riggadoon, which had involved a great deal of jumping. She was still recovering when Prince George and their two infant daughters succumbed to smallpox. Anne nursed her family devotedly, but first Lady Anne Sophia and then Lady Mary died within days of each other in the first week of February. The autopsy showed that the elder girl was 'all consumed, but the younger quite healthy, and every appearance for long life'. A few days later the bereaved couple withdrew to Richmond to mourn their children. 'The good Princess has taken her chastisement very heavily,' Rachel, Lady Russell wrote, observing of the grieving parents: 'Sometimes they wept, sometimes they mourned in words; then sat silent, hand in hand; he sick in bed, and she the carefullest nurse to him that can be imagined.'

Childless again, Princess Anne applied to her father in March 1687 to allow Prince George to visit his family in Denmark, while she went to her sister the Princess of Orange in Holland. At first James agreed, then a few days later he changed his mind and permission was refused. 'So that it is plain he has spoke of it to somebody that persuaded him against it,' Anne told her sister, 'and it is certain that that body was Lord Sunderland, for the King trusts him with everything.' Anne's intentions in visiting her sister might have been innocent. On the other hand, did the King really want the two Protestant heirs to the throne colluding? Anne believed that Sunderland was 'afraid that you should be told a true character of him, and this I really believe is the reason why I was refused coming to you; though maybe he and the priests together give other reasons to the King.' Anne went on to tell her sister exactly what she thought of Sunderland:

Everybody knows how often this man turned backwards and forward in the late King's time; and now, to complete all his virtues, he is working with all his might to bring in popery. He is perpetually with the priests and stirs up the King to do things further than I believe he would of himself. Things are come to that pass now, that, if they go on much longer, I believe in a little while no Protestant will be able to live here.

It is interesting that hitherto Anne never blamed the King directly for his policies, always attributing the blame to someone else: the Queen, Sunderland, Catholic priests. The refusal to grant her permission to travel infuriated Anne, who was so used to having her own way, and caused her estrangement from her father, pushing her into the opposite camp. In the same letter, she announced her intention of communicating with Everard van Weede van Dijkvelt, the agent whom William had sent to England to sound out the nobility about future plans. Anne admits that she has never ventured to speak to Dijkvelt 'because I am not used to speak to people about business' and also because she knew she was being watched. She decided to have Lord Churchill speak to Dijkvelt on her behalf.

Presumably he did so, and two months later Churchill wrote to William himself to assure him that the Princess was prepared 'to suffer all extremities, even to death itself, rather than be brought to change her religion'. Whether or not he realised that William and Mary suspected the Churchills were opportunists who might change their religion if it suited their ambitions, Churchill also added his reassurances that 'all my places and the King's favour I set at naught, in comparison of being true to my religion.' By that time, Anne told her sister that she had been talking to Dijkvelt herself and it was clear from her letter that she had been taken into her sister and brother-in-law's confidence: after all, her support was important to the Prince of Orange's scheme.

Anne knew that she had made an irrevocable step in joining the opposition to her father. 'Pray don't let anybody see this,' she urged in her letter of 13 March to Mary, 'nor speak of it: pray let me desire you not to take notice of what I have said to anybody except the Prince of Orange, for it is all treason that I have spoke.' She warned 'one dares not write anything by the post' and, henceforth, the sisters used trusted messengers to carry their letters. When Dijkvelt returned to Holland in June 1687, he brought a secret code for the sisters to use. Anne had always, even to her sister, referred to her father as 'the Duke' or 'the King', implying a formal, distant relationship. Now he became 'Mansell' in their increasingly disrespectful and dangerous correspondence.

From the discovery of her fifth pregnancy in the spring of 1687, Anne absented herself from court as much as she decently could, dividing her time between Richmond and Hampton Court. At the King's insistence, she returned to the Cockpit in early October, just as her father and stepmother returned from their visit to Bath and the West Country. On 22 October, two months before her time, Anne gave birth to a stillborn son, who had apparently lain dead inside her for a month. It was shortly after this latest disappointment in her childbearing efforts that she would have heard the disquieting rumours that her stepmother was pregnant. Worried for her religion, still grieving for the loss of her own children, her body and emotions in turmoil from repeated pregnancies that came to nothing, Anne now turned all her furious jealousy and pent-up anger on the hated stepmother, whose child – if a boy – would continue the Catholic tyranny.

Far from there being a Catholic plot to perpetrate a false pregnancy and smuggle someone else's child into the Queen's bed, it seems much more likely that there was a Protestant plot to discredit the pregnancy and throw doubt on the child's legitimacy from the first. The chief perpetrator was Princess Anne, whose support lent the malicious rumours credibility. Princess Mary's side of the correspondence no longer exists, but it seems that it was Anne who first implied that the pregnancy was a hoax and persuaded her sister to believe it. On 14 March 1688 she picked up her crow's quill pen and wrote a highly seditious and damaging letter to Mary:

I have now very little to say, however would not miss writing by this bearer by whom you told me I might say anything; and therefore knowing nothing else of any consequence I must tell you I can't help thinking Mansell's wife's great belly is a little suspicious. It is true indeed she is very big, but she looks better than she ever did, which is not usual: for people when they are so far gone, for the most part look very ill. Besides, it is very odd that the Bath, that all the best doctors thought would do her a great deal of harm, should have had so very good effect so soon, as that she should prove with child from the first minute she and Mansell met, after her coming from thence. Her being so positive it will be a son, and the principles of that religion being such that they will stick at nothing, be it never so wicked, if it will promote their interest, give some cause to fear

80

there may be foul play intended. I will do all I can to find it out, if it be so: and if I should make any discovery, you shall be sure to have an account of it.

The following month Princess Anne was reported to be so ill she was in danger of death. In the early hours of the morning of 16 April she apparently suffered another miscarriage. Her uncle, Lord Clarendon, went to visit her and found the King at her bedside. In his diary entry, Clarendon made an interesting comment, namely that 'the rumour among the women was, that she had only had a false conception.' It is possible that Anne was so overwrought by events and so desperate to bear a child after the failure of so many pregnancies, that she had been experiencing a false pregnancy. Given that she was so busy implying that the Queen's pregnancy was false, it would be ironic if it were true.

She needed to convalesce. The advice of the royal physicians was sought as to whether or not it was a good idea for her to attend a spa. They gave different opinions, perhaps prompted by conflicting interests, Anne's Sir John Lower thinking it was a good idea, the Queen's Sir Charles Scarborough being against it for the time being. In his *History*, Gilbert Burnet claimed that Anne's friends urged her to stay in London. According to his account, it was James who 'pressed her to go to the Bath, since that had so good an effect on the Queen', the implication being that there was some conspiracy to get Anne out of the way just when the Queen's confinement was due.

The conflicting dates of the Queen's expected confinement were an honest mistake, and one made frequently at this time when there was so much ignorance about pregnancy. Although Mary Beatrice believed that conception had taken place when the King met her at Bath in early September, she had bowed to the professional opinion of the physicians in accepting the later date. All her letters to Princess Mary gave the July date and arrangements were being made for the lying-in accordingly. The confusion over the dates, however, gave the King's enemies a chance to imply that as soon as Princess Anne was out of town, the Queen hurriedly revised her dates so as to be confined away from the prying eyes of her stepdaughter.

Far from wanting his daughter away from court at this time, James had everything to gain from her attendance at the birth. But he was concerned for her health and wanted to do what was best for her. Even Burnet, one of his severest critics, had to admit that he was a kind and indulgent father. It is most unlikely that James ever succeeded in making his obstinate daughter do anything she did not want to do, so that it was probably *he* who acceded to *her* wishes to leave London for a period of recuperation. He might well have hoped that she would return in time for the birth, but, of course, in going to Bath instead of her usual Tunbridge Wells she had placed herself that much further from London.

William's plans to intervene in English affairs were well advanced and Anne had some knowledge of them. It would serve his interests splendidly if the veracity of the royal birth were thrown into doubt. Anne's presence at the birth would be crucial in proving its authenticity. She had no intention of being a witness or offering her word as proof of it. She had nothing whatsoever to gain from the perpetuation of a Catholic dynasty and possibly something to gain from its overthrow. It must have been with a great deal of satisfaction that she took her leave of the heavily pregnant Queen in the third week of May, offering as her parting shot the meaningful words, 'Madam, I think you will be brought to bed before I return.'

# 3
## Princess Mary of Orange

_'And though I know you are a good wife, and ought to be so, yet for the same reason I must believe you will still be as good a daughter to a father that has always loved you so tenderly'_

— James II to Princess Mary

In the old palace of Richmond, a dwarf was frequently to be seen emerging from a panelled closet and hurrying along dark galleries whose mullioned windows looked towards the shining Thames. He wore the serious expression of someone on an important mission and clutched a parchment letter in his hand. Mr Gibson, the dwarf drawing master, was one of the few entrusted to carry the precious, secret correspondence between the Lady Mary of York and a young lady of the court nine years her senior. The Princess's letters were the romantic outpourings of a girl starved of love, whose passionate nature craved its fulfilment. Hers was a world of the imagination, which so far held at bay harsher realities.

It may be significant that Lady Mary's attachment to Frances Apsley began about the time of her mother's death in 1671, when Mary was almost nine years old. It is impossible to gauge what effect the loss of her mother had on the child. The Duchess of York was a formidable woman and there is no reason to believe that her relationship with her eldest daughter was at all close. The Duke and Duchess were distant beings, who seldom saw their children. The birth of Mary, on 30 April 1662, was greeted with disappointment because she was a girl. Few of the nobility bothered to visit the Duchess in her lying-in chamber to offer their compliments, which they surely would have done had they known that the new occupant of the royal cradle would one day be Queen.

Born at her parents' official residence at St James's Palace, the baby Princess was baptised according to the rites of the Church of England in the Chapel Royal there a few days later. Her godparents were the valiant old Cavalier, Prince Rupert of the Rhine, her father's friend and cousin, and the Duchesses of Buckingham and Ormonde. Lady Mary was named after her great-great-grandmother, Mary, Queen of Scots, quite a coincidence since she came to resemble her so closely in looks. She inherited the dark, almond-shaped slanting eyes, the alabaster skin and the rich brown locks so typical of the Stuart women, as well as the tallness of the Scottish Queen, which made both women stand out among their contemporaries.

When Lady Mary was just over two years old, Samuel Pepys was charmed by the sight of the Duke playing with her 'just like an ordinary private father of a child'. The Duke liked to think of himself as a fond father, but in reality he was more taken up with his work as Lord High Admiral, the court, his hunting and his women than his children. If he made a fuss of his elder daughter on the few occasions she was brought to St James's from her nursery at Richmond or her maternal grandparents' house at Twickenham, where she spent some of her early childhood, such an event was rare.

A sensitive child, Lady Mary must gradually have become aware of the tensions between her parents because of the Duke's womanising. She was three years old in the year of the plague, when the Yorks went on progress to the north, removing their three children – Mary, James and Anne – from the pestiferous capital. It was here at York that Lady Mary's mother took her revenge for all the jealousy and humiliation she had suffered because of her husband's infidelities. She was particularly galled at his latest fling with the pasty-faced Arabella Churchill, who had made such an exhibition of herself on the journey north by falling off her horse and lying with her long legs on display. The Duchess embarked on a flirtation with the good-looking Henry Sidney, a son of the Earl of Leicester who had been appointed groom of the bedchamber to the Duke and master of the horse to the Duchess.

As Sir John Reresby recalled: 'This Duchess was a very handsom woman, had a great deal of wit; therefore it was not without reason that Mr Sidney, the handsomest youth of his time, then of the Duke's bedchamber, was so much in love with her, as appeared to us all, and the Duchess not unkind to him, but very innocently.'

The affair was almost certainly innocent. When James left York in late September 1665 to rejoin the court, which had by now set up camp in the Oxford colleges, the Duchess followed more slowly with the children, and Sidney accompanied them. Like all men who set one standard for themselves and another for their wives, James was furious at the interest that Sidney was showing in his wife. Lady Mary's parents were not speaking to each other by the end of the year, when the Duke suddenly banished Sidney from the court. The double standard continued, for a few months later Pepys was complaining that the Duke had 'gone over to his pleasures again, and leaves off care of business, what with his woman, my Lady Denham, and his hunting three times a week'.

With the return of the court to London, Lady Mary and her siblings took up residence at their nursery at Richmond Palace, under the care of their kindly governess, Lady Frances Villiers, and Lady Mary's nurse – 'my mam' – the gossiping Mrs Frances Langford. Not very well educated himself, James was not the sort of man to have a high opinion of the female mind, and probably thought that a good education would be wasted on his daughters. He does not seem to have drawn up a programme of studies for them, as he later did for the Prince of Wales, which was a pity as his elder daughter was highly intelligent. Lady Mary's command of English spelling, grammar and punctuation remained execrable, although her standard was slightly higher than that of many other women of her time. She made good progress in French under Peter de Laine, who found her a diligent pupil.

Mary seems to have inherited something of her grandfather Charles I's love of the visual arts. She proved a talented pupil of Mr Gibson, her drawing master, who was a fine miniaturist and taught her to paint on ivory. Above all, she had a good ear for music and learned to dance under the direction of the elderly Frenchman, Mr Gorey, who had taught all the royal family and earned a generous £400 a year. Just short of Mary's seventh birthday, Pepys noticed her at Whitehall: 'I did see the young Duchess, a little child in hanging sleeves, dance most finely, so as almost to ravish me, her ears were so good.'

As she grew older, Lady Mary must have found her mother an increasingly revolting sight. The Duchess had always been a big eater. A courtier joked that it was an edifying sight to see her at table, where she indulged her gargantuan appetite. The Duke, in contrast, was abstemious. Vigorous hunting, the gratification of his sexual appetites, and perhaps some of the consequences of his dissipation meant that he was lean and seemed to be wasting away. The memory of her mother's grossly swollen and corpulent figure probably accounted for Lady Mary's later terror of becoming fat. Her mother was constantly pregnant, bearing one child after another in her crowded lying-in chamber, ruining her health in the process. Her efforts were largely wasted. Her children were weak and sickly, most of them dying in their infancy. And the Duchess herself was rumoured to have spent long periods of time towards the end of her life so covered in sores, whether from a venereal disease or some other cause, that she had to hide from view.

The deaths of so many of her siblings – five of them during her own childhood – must have left an indelible impression on Mary, perhaps sowing the seeds of the morbidity that would be so fundamental to her adult personality. As a child in the nursery she must have been aware of the anxious whispers and panic of the nurses and rockers every time one of her siblings fell sick, perhaps frightened by the presence of the black-clad physicians with their doomed expressions and desperate remedies. Then there were the suddenly empty cradles, the little waxen corpses laid out in dark candlelit chambers swathed in black, and the burials with all the pomp of royal mourning.

Even as her mother gave birth to her eighth child, she was dying of cancer. Lady Mary must have known that her mother was desperately ill, her suffocating bedchamber given over to the bleeding and purging, the violent effects of 'physick' and 'vomits', the odour of sickness and burning of herbs, the shrieks of pain for which there was no remedy or relief. There is no evidence that Lady Mary was brought to say a final goodbye to her mother on her deathbed, perhaps because of the hushed-up scandal over the Duchess's change of faith. When she died at the end of March 1671, neither the Duke nor the remaining children attended her interment at Westminster Abbey. The court soon forgot the Duchess and resumed its frivolous, fleeting pleasures, and Lady Mary seems to have retained only the vaguest memory of her.

---

In her letters to Frances Apsley, Lady Mary, the rather neglected child, assumes an air of world-weary sophistication. 'If I had any nuse to tel you I wold,' she tells her older friend, 'but hear there is none worth a chip.' And, 'Tho St Jeames is so dul as to aford no news dear husban now windsor may shake hands with it for I have drained it so dry in my last letter.' Living mostly apart from her uncle's dissolute court but surrounded by chattering servants, Lady Mary picked up snippets of barely understood gossip. Of her chaplain, Dr Doughty, she reported: 'Dr D. Mrs is come to dine with him may be she is his W.'

Mary's glamorous cousin James, Duke of Monmouth, the King's eldest bastard who had been married to the wealthy heiress Anne Scott of Buccleuch, was obviously having an affair with another lady of the court, Eleanor Needham. Apparently, Mary wrote: 'It is very trew that Mrs Needham did wright a letter to the Duches but what it was I can not tel for nobody did see it but herself but this I can tel the duches said that if it ware trew that was in the letter she wold be found very inosent but she wold not belive it to be trew.'

Steeped in the romances of Madame de Scudéry and the works of Dryden, Beaumont and Fletcher and other poets and playwrights, twelve-year-old Lady Mary made her court debut at Christmas 1674 when she appeared in the title role of John Crowne's masque *Calisto, or the Chaste Nymph*. As the young ladies waited in the wings drinking in the sights of the court and surreptitiously casting an eye at young gallants such as the Duke of Monmouth, the young Margaret Blagge, future wife of Sidney, Lord Godolphin, fumed at the frivolity of it all. She had no wish to join in the excited chatter of the Ladies Mary and Anne and Sarah Jennings, nor did she wish to join in the supper and dancing after the performance. As Margaret's elderly friend John Evelyn noted, the performers appeared all covered in jewels, and Margaret had the mortification of losing a diamond lent by the Countess of Suffolk. After the servants combed the stage and wings and failed to find it, the Duke of York made good the loss.

It was after this exciting glimpse of the grown-up world that Lady Mary's letters to Frances Apsley became more passionate. She started to address her friend as Aurelia, the part she had played in the masque. Otherwise, she was her dear husband, Mary playing the role of wife and signing off as Mary Clorine. Although she used quires of paper dashing off letters written with a 'new croe quil pen' to her beloved Frances, they were invariably full of excuses for her tardiness in writing:

Why dear cruel loved blest husban do you think I do neglect my wrighting you your self know I could not Monday senat [sennight, in other words, seven nights or a week ago] was the King's beirth day so tusday I slept till eleven a cloke thursday morning I was so busie trying on mantos and a gown that I did not see Mr Gipson nor had I time to wright Saturday you know I could not wright Tusday last I took fisike [physick] so pray judg yourself when I could wright I confese dear Aurelia I am in fault if my dear dear dear husban think so.

The arrival of her father's second wife, the fifteen-year-old Mary Beatrice D'Este of Modena, in the autumn of 1673 brought Mary a new friend, very different from her own mother. The Italian and English Princesses had more in common than might have been supposed. They were both very religious, albeit devotees of opposing faiths. Bishop Compton and her chaplains had taught Lady Mary that Roman Catholicism was one of the worst evils in the world – and indeed, she had at first been very upset to hear her father was marrying a Roman Catholic – but the young Duchess of York worshipped privately and did not enter into religious discussion with her stepdaughters.

The new Duchess was beautiful and kind, prepared to spend time talking to her stepdaughters, and not too grown-up to join in their games. Just as she admired the older and very pretty Frances Apsley, Lady Mary must have admired her stepmother. And the love-starved girl must have basked in the attention she gave her. Four months into the marriage, Mary Beatrice joined the Duke's daughters at Richmond when she discovered James was carrying on his affair with Arabella Churchill. Far from looking disdainfully on her stepmother's tears like her stoical sister Anne, the emotional Lady Mary would have sympathised with her distress at her husband's betrayal. Her feelings eventually found expression in a letter to Frances: 'Who can imagin that my dear husband can be so love sike for fear I do not love her but I have more reson to think that she is sike of being wery of me for in tow or three years men are alwais wery [weary] of their wifes and looke for Mrs. [mistress] as sone as thay can gett them.'

Soon Lady Mary herself had reason to be jealous of a rival. Her irritating younger sister Anne was emulating her in writing copious letters to Frances and winning her affection. 'I have still the marks that you loved me once,' Mary wrote sadly, '& now I do not dout but my hapy sister has the cornelian ring unhapy I should have had she wil wright to you now unkind Aurelia.' She that has it 'wil have your haert tow & your letters tow oh thrice hapy she is hapyer then ever I was for she has tryoumpht over a rival that wonce was hapy in your love til she with her aluring charmes removed unhapy Clorine from your haert.' Frances and Anne had sat whispering and laughing together 'whilst pore unhapy I sate reading of a play my haert redy to breake.' Mary refused to give her rival the satisfaction of seeing her cry.

Frances evidently assured Mary that she came first, and soon Mary was writing:

What can I say more to perswade you that I love you with more zeal then any lover can I love you with a love that ner was known by man I have for you excese of friandship more of love then any woman can for woman and more love then ever the constanest love had for his Mrs. you are loved more then can be exprest by your ever obedient wife vere afectionate friand humbel sarvent to kis the ground where on you go to be your dog in a string your fish in a net your bird in a cage your humbel trout.

Some time in 1676 Frances moved with her parents, Sir Allen and Lady Apsley, out of their apartment at St James's Palace into their newly built house at 20 St James's Square, where Lady Mary's father had installed his mistress Arabella Churchill and their brood at Number 21. Much given to over-dramatising, Lady Mary saw her friend's removal even so short a distance from the palace as a disaster:

If I shoud dy I coud not take my leav of you dear husband for then I shoud think you were going where I should never see you more and indeed I think it is almost as bad for now I shal very seldom or never see you but in a grave vissit with your mother . . . for if I see Mrs Apsley [Frances] as I don't dout but I shal very often at chapel or in my one chamber some time yett I shal never think you my husband if I don't talk with you as we used to do for I love Mrs Apsley better then any woman can love a woman but I love my dear Aurelia as a wife should doe a husband nay more then is able to be exprest my dear will excuse me if my letter be not as it shoud be for I am in great haest to be drest for Mr Liley [Lely, the painter, to do her portrait] wil be here at ten of the cloke so I though unwilling must take my leave of me dearest dearest dear and am your obedient and loving wife.

Lady Mary knew full well that her governess Lady Frances Villiers would not approve of the nature of her correspondence with Frances Apsley, any more than the Duke and Duchess would have done. The following letter to Frances reveals how furtive Mary was being about her letter-writing in general, and also, incidentally, how much Sarah Jennings had insinuated herself into the royal sisters' confidence:

*Sunday too a cloke*

Becaus my dearest Aurelia comes to me but onely Sundays and holy days I thought it convenient to lett her know how I took her name in vain for fear that in seven days and nights I might forgett it yester day my sister and myself both ritt to Mrs barkly [Barbara, one of Lady Frances's daughters, with whom they had been raised at Richmond] in my closet in ye after noon. while I danced with Mr Gory my sister ritt she went to dance in hast and left her letter for me to seal so I put it in my poket while I ritt my own letter thinking to seal um both together Mrs Jenings came in ye mean time to feach ye letters so for haste I called her in to seal my sisters while I sealed my own letter all this while my closet dore was open Lady [Lady Frances Villiers] came in and was almost at ye dore before I hard her so I started up run to ye dore and mett her, I had a new manto [manteau, the fashionable new dress with the skirt open at the front to reveal a different coloured petticoat] on so I asked how she liked the make and blushed as red as fire, but thank god my bake [back] was to her that she coud not see me. She ansard me that question and asked me what I was doing in my closett I told I had carryed Mrs Jenings in to se ye Duchises picture and that she showed me a new way of sealing a letter that I had ritt to Mrs Apsly she said she was very ingenous and so went away for if she shoud know I ritt to Mrs Barkly she woud be more angry than she is with her if it be possible.

After Lady Mary's fourteenth birthday, her preceptor Bishop Compton suggested to the Duke of York that it was time she was confirmed according to the rites of the Anglican Church. Still smarting from the fact that his daughters had been made children of state and removed from his care, James did everything he could to resist Compton's request. He replied that just as he had no control over Lady Mary's religious upbringing, so he could not give his consent. He added that 'it was much against his will that his daughters went to church and were bred Protestants; and that the reason he had not endeavour'd to have them instructed in his own religion, was because he knew if he should have attempted it, they would have immediately been quite taken from him.' Compton simply went over his head and gained the King's permission to proceed. In his fury, James retaliated by refusing even to put in a token appearance at Anglican services from Easter 1676.

Endearingly innocent for her age, Lady Mary was still protesting her undying love for Frances, even though they now only saw each other regularly at church. The romantic girl who had only known life in palaces and worn the richest silks and finest lawns next to her skin swore that she would live with Frances and 'be content with a cotage in the contre [country] & cow a stufe peticot & wastcot in sumer & cloth in winter a litel garden to live upon the fruit & herbs it yeelds or if I could not have you so to myself I would go a beging be pore but content what greater hapynes is there in the world then to have the company of them on loves to make your hapynes compleat.'

Her idyll was about to be rudely shattered by the arrival on the scene of a real husband.

———

Towards the end of October 1677, Lady Mary and her sister were at St James's when they heard of the sudden return of the court from Newmarket several days earlier than expected. An informal meeting had been arranged between Lady Mary and her cousin, Prince William of Orange, who had joined his uncles at the races and accompanied them back to London. It is not certain whether Mary had encountered William on a previous visit when she was still only a child, but the impression she would have formed now, through the romantic eyes of a girl of fifteen, is unlikely to have been favourable.

The Dutch Prince was old – nearly twenty-seven – and seemed older still because his slight frame was hunched and stooped. At five feet six and a half inches, he was of average height for a man of his time, but small compared with his Stuart uncles, who were just over six feet tall, and he would have had to look up at Mary, who was five feet eleven. In the damp, fog-thickened London air and the dark candlelit rooms of St James's, he wheezed as if unable to breathe. There was no court repartee in the few words he did utter in a thick Dutch accent. Unlike the fashion-conscious fops of the court with their periwigs and gaudy clothes, this Prince wore his own dark hair loose and a black suit, so plain as to look like one of the despised Dissenters. His features were aquiline, with a nose 'curved like the beak of an eagle'. Only his dark eyes made an impression, lighting up with a brilliant lustre when he saw something he admired. And he admired the beauty, the gentle disposition, the charm and the good manners of the tall girl standing before him. So much so, that he instantly went to his uncle the King and asked for her hand in marriage.

Rumours of a marriage between William and Mary had occurred intermittently, but until now he had not been in a position to think of it. He had been too busy fighting for his country's survival in the face of French aggression. He had considered the matter very seriously, however, confiding to Sir William Temple, the English Ambassador at The Hague, that he had to be sure of his wife's character. For William, this was more important than other considerations, for 'if he should meet with one to give him trouble at home, 'twas what he should not be able to bear, who was like to have trouble enough abroad in the course of his life.' He had already taken the precaution of asking Lady Temple to make enquiries about the Lady Mary's character from her governess, but he also wanted to assure himself that she was the right choice. When he had opened negotiations with his uncles at Newmarket, he had shocked them by saying that he must meet the young lady before any proposal could be made.

James was outraged. Naturally, he considered Mary a great prize in the marriage stakes. Not only was she the first daughter of the Crown, the heir-presumptive to the throne, but she was a beauty. For some time, James had been strung along by the French ambassador, Barillon, who on instructions from Louis XIV had led him to believe that a marriage between Mary and the Dauphin was in the offing. Such a marriage would have the additional advantage, in James's eyes, of necessitating her conversion to Catholicism. James had no wish to see Mary wed to this stern Dutch Calvinist, who was merely an elected Stadholder of the Dutch Republic. He neither liked nor trusted his nephew and his insistence on inspecting Mary before deciding whether or not to marry her gave him no high opinion of his manners.

The King was ruled by other considerations. Perhaps if he

married his niece to her Protestant cousin some of the heat would be taken off him, whose nefarious dealings with Catholic France had long been suspected. The marriage was the culmination of Thomas Osborne, Earl of Danby's efforts towards a pro-Dutch alliance. James's blatant Catholicism had caused Charles endless trouble with his Parliament and he recognised that some concession had to be made to Protestant sentiments. Charles had promised his brother that he would not dispose of Mary's hand without first obtaining his consent. Of course, he being Charles, this promise was ignored. ''Od's fish,' he declared when reminded of it, 'I know I promised, but he *must* give his consent.' Ever obedient to the King's wishes, James gave in, but with an ill grace.

Something of James's disapproval must have communicated itself to his highly strung daughter when, after dinner at Whitehall on 21 October, he came to St James's and led her into her closet to break the news of her impending marriage. Mary promptly burst into tears. Her chaplain, Dr Lake, noted that 'she wept all that afternoon and all the following day.' James made the best of it when it was announced in council that evening, declaring with the usual undertone of sarcasm that perhaps now they would believe that he always had the good of the country in mind. When Louis XIV heard the news, he protested to James that he had given his daughter to his mortal enemy. While commenting publicly that William and Mary were nothing but a couple of beggars who were well matched, in private he knew that their marriage was the equivalent to him of the loss of an army.

While the various male egos considered what the impending marriage meant to them and haggled over terms for a European peace treaty, the weeping girl reached for quill and paper and wrote a frantic letter to her Aurelia: 'If you do not come to me some time today dear husband that I may have my bellyful of discours with you I shal take it very ile. if you can before you goe to diner when you come from Mr Lily [Lely] for I have a great deal to say to you concerning I do not know how to tel in the letter. if you com you wil mightyly oblige your faithful wife, Mary Clorine.'

The country was ecstatic about the marriage of two Protestant heirs to the throne. Church bells pealed and bonfires were lit to celebrate. In the succeeding days the members of the Privy Council, the Lord Mayor and aldermen and the judges trooped to St James's to congratulate the couple. On Lord Mayor's Day, all the royal family attended the show in the City, followed by a lavish banquet. The City noted with approval William's serious dress and demeanour, one City wife commenting, 'What a nice young man he looked, not like those popinjays at the court!'

The marriage ceremony at which Bishop Compton officiated took place on William's twenty-seventh birthday, Sunday, 4 November 1677, between eight and nine o'clock at night. It was a small private family affair held in the bride's apartments at St James's. A slightly inebriated Charles gave his tearful niece away and his quips were the only mark of joviality in the otherwise subdued atmosphere. When William laid the coins symbolic of his worldly goods on the prayer book, Charles urged his niece to 'Gather it up, gather it up and put it in your pocket, for 'tis all clear gain.' The solemn couple must have looked a strange sight before the clergyman, the red-eyed, statuesque Mary being so much taller than her wheezing bridegroom. A heavily pregnant Duchess of York looked on, no doubt moved to pity for her young stepdaughter, whom she knew she would miss dreadfully. The bride's sister, Lady Anne, was absent, as she was unwell.

After supper, Queen Catherine and the Duchess of York undressed the bride for the bedding ceremony. It was eleven o'clock, one hour later than the groom's usual bedtime. At the French court, the couple's irrepressible second cousin Liselotte – who had once been considered as a possible bride for William – was soon spreading the word that William had gone to bed in his woollen drawers. When King Charles suggested they were inappropriate, William replied that as he and his wife were to live together a long time, she better get used to his habits. The couple sat up in bed to drink the customary hot posset, then as everyone left the room, the King pulled the bed curtains closed with a flourish and words that must have made the couple wince: 'Now, nephew, to your work. Hey! St George for England!'

The day after the wedding, William's closest friend, Hans Willem Bentinck, came to present Princess Mary with William's magnificent wedding present to her: £40,000 worth of jewels, including the huge pearls she wore in all her subsequent portraits and the ruby ring 'she came to value above her kingdom'. The value of the jewellery was equivalent to Mary's dowry, which was paid late by her chronically insolvent uncle, in tiny grudging instalments, or not at all. After the ceremony, Mary's tears continued and she proved obdurate when William urged her to move out of St James's, where Lady Anne and others now lay sick of the smallpox, to join him in the riverside apartment he had been lent at Whitehall. Mary was adamant that she would not leave her home until the last minute. Observers noticed that 'he was a very fond husband, but she was a very coy bride, at least before folks.'

They could not leave London until after Queen Catherine's birthday ball on 15 November, where Princess Mary appeared wearing all her new jewels. By this time, William had completely run out of patience with his sulky adolescent bride and was anxious to leave his uncle's dissolute court and return to business in Europe. It was not that he did not care for Mary, just that there was no sense to be made of the situation while they lingered in London. His coolness towards Mary at the ball, where he danced with her only once, was noticed with indignation. This was the moment that William acquired the names 'Caliban' and the 'Dutch Abortion', names that Lady Anne came to use so freely in her letters to Sarah Churchill about her detested brother-in-law. It was also the moment the belief took root that William treated his wife badly.

After the ball, Princess Mary changed into her travelling

clothes, but to William's intense annoyance their departure was delayed because the wind had changed, preventing their sailing for Holland. Four days later, the couple said their good-byes to the royal family. Queen Catherine tried to comfort the weeping Mary by telling her that she, too, had left her country to come to a strange land to marry. Mary replied ingenuously, 'Yes, Madam, but you were coming *into* England, I am going *out* of England.' Mary's tears increased as she clung to her stepmother, who was still in her lying-in chamber after the recent birth of a son. Unlike William, Mary does not seem to have been at all put out by the arrival of a brother ousting her from the succession. She had always shown fondness for her stepmother's babies, referring sadly to 'the pore dear distresed bab' when the first of them, Katherine Laura, hovered between life and death, and later confiding in her aunt, the Countess of Clarendon, her great love for the little Lady Isabella.

Mary had never had smallpox, so that she was not allowed to visit her sister Anne in her sickroom to say goodbye. She left her two letters and urged the Duchess of Monmouth to accompany her to church when she was better, since she would now be the only Protestant in a family of Catholics. Lady Frances Villiers, who had cared for Mary all her life, lay sick of smallpox and close to death, and many of the party who were to accompany her to Holland were too ill to leave. Nevertheless, among the forty attendants she was permitted by her marriage contract – a nuisance and an unnecessary expense in William's opinion – were her old nurse Mrs Langford and three of the Villiers sisters, Anne, Elizabeth and Katherine, with whom she had passed her childhood at Richmond. The courtier Henry Saville had noted the competition among the 'beggarly bitches' to win a place at the Princess of Orange's court and when John Churchill had asked William what it would cost to join the Princess's household, William had replied scornfully that offices were not for sale at *his* court.

The King and the Duke accompanied the couple down the Thames as far as Erith, where they dined. As they boarded the yachts that were to take them to Holland, it was clear that the wind was again veering in the wrong direction. Nothing would induce William to return to London, at the King's invitation, for another bout of emotional parting. Instead, the couple and their attendants made towards Canterbury to await a change in the weather. Prince William did not have enough cash for an extended stay and had to send to the town's mayor for a loan, which was refused. It was the dean of the cathedral, Dr Tillotson, who came to their rescue, a kindness William and Mary never forgot. In due course, they appointed him Archbishop of Canterbury.

The crossing a few days later was rough and, as the couple travelled in separate yachts, William had to watch his wife's being tossed in the water. She was the only person on board who was not seasick. Their arrival found the Dutch port of Rotterdam iced up. They embarked on sloops that took them to a fishing village further along the coast and William apparently carried his exhausted wife up the beach. There were no coaches to meet them and the party walked three miles along the icy lanes before being picked up and driven to the palace of Honselaersdijck. Here Mary's mother, Anne Hyde, maid of honour to the previous Princess of Orange, had played games of ninepins with young English gallants in the gallery. Now it was one of several splendid homes of which William's fifteen-year-old wife would be mistress.

---

To Mary's surprise and delight, she liked her new country, and the Dutch people immediately took her to their hearts. When William had sought the permission of the States-General for his proposed marriage to Mary, as he was bound to do if his allowance were to be continued, they gave it cautiously. The memory of the last Stuart princess who had married into the House of Orange – William's mother Mary, the Princess Royal, the eldest daughter of Charles I – was not such as to endear them to the idea of another.

But this Mary Stuart was completely different. When she made her entry into The Hague on 14 December in a golden coach drawn by six piebald horses, the impression she gave was one of beauty. While her regal bearing was evident, she clearly had none of the previous Mary's proud aloofness or haughty contempt for the Dutch. She gave the impression of being pleased and of wanting to please. This Mary, William's wife, had heard nothing but jokes and sneers about the hated Dutch republicans all her life at the English court, but she was curious and intelligent enough to make up her own mind about her new people. And she liked what she saw.

At The Hague, Mary was taken to the second of her new homes, the Binnenhof, the old, dark palace that housed both the Orange private quarters where William spent much of his early childhood and some of the offices of the States-General, to watch a spectacular firework display. William had coached Mary carefully as to how she was to receive the ladies presented to her. According to English court custom, she was to kiss the wives of nobles on the cheek, but give the oligarchs' wives her hand to kiss. Despite their proud republicanism, the regents protested to William at this distinction, to which he merely replied, 'Are you noble?' When they answered in the negative, but claimed their office gave them equal rank, William retorted, 'No office ennobles its possessors.' It was the only cool note in Mary's welcome, and not a fault that could be attributed to her. She won the Dutch over with her easy charm, her gaiety and conversation, while the good house-wife in her admired their order, neatness and cleanliness, the antithesis of what she had been used to in London.

As Princess of Orange, Mary had particular hours when she was at home to receive visitors, either at the Binnenhof or at Honselaersdijck. If she wanted more privacy, she could retreat to the House in the Wood outside The Hague, a charming house which had belonged to William's grandmother, or to Soestdijck, where she enjoyed long country walks. She also accompanied William to Dieren, a hunting lodge in the wild

wooded country where he loved to pursue the sport. She travelled around her new country by barge and the Dutch people
were treated to the sight of the Princess and her ladies passing along the canals embroidering while her chaplain read
to them. Mary made every effort to learn Dutch and soon
spoke it well enough to make friends among the ladies of her
new court.

The palace at Honselaersdijck, built in the Dutch Renaissance style and similar to the Palais du Luxembourg in Paris,
was one of the most beautiful private houses in the Republic.
As it was only seven miles from The Hague, a trip there was
a popular excursion for the inhabitants. Here they could see
the Prince and Princess of Orange on the occasions they dined
in public in the great dining room with its painted ceiling
of shepherds and shepherdesses disporting themselves. Visitors could admire the family portraits in the great gallery –
William and Mary were to assemble the best of them here at
Honselaersdijck – and the two Rembrandts, *The Burial* and
the *Resurrection of Christ*, acquired by William's grandfather,
Prince Frederik Hendrik. They might even meet the Prince in
his audience chamber with the new sash windows that were
so far unknown in England.

At Honselaersdijck, William could indulge his passions for
art and gardening, which Mary came to share. They had both
inherited their grandfather Charles I's appreciation of fine
painting and William had gone to some trouble to add to his
collection prior to the marriage. The garden with its statuary
and fountains was one of the glories of the palace and William
and Mary were not only interested in its design and planning,
but also in the introduction of new plants from more exotic
climes. Once she settled in her new home, she might frequently
be seen strolling in the garden with her ladies or in discussion
with the gardeners. Later, William would buy Het Loo in
Gelderland and the couple would spend many hours poring
over their plans for its transformation into a palace, designing
its furnishings to accommodate Mary's growing collection of

blue and white porcelain. In its gardens Mary, who loved birds, would have an aviary.

On her marriage, Mary was given the whole left wing of Honselaersdijck for her own use and William had made sure that it was decorated and furnished with care. In her study with its yellow and violet satin, embroidered with gold and silver, William had placed a copy of Van Dyck's *Madonna and Child*. A painting of William's grandmother, Amalia von Solms, as Diana by Honthorst adorned her audience chamber with its walls of pale blue flowered damask. Virtue, Labour and Vigilance looked down from the painted ceiling of Mary's bedchamber, which was hung with green damask trimmed with gilt cord and had matching curtains. The furniture was of English lacquer. The walls of the dressing room were covered with fashionable gilded leather with flowers and cherubs painted by Duval. The palace also boasted marble bathrooms with running hot water, an unheard-of luxury after the squalor of the English palaces. Having gone to so much trouble to prepare a fitting home for his bride, William was less than pleased when Mary's Anglican chaplain, Dr Hooper, persuaded her to transform her private dining room into a chapel, leaving her to eat in a poky dark parlour. Coming to inspect the new arrangements, William kicked the altar step, asking disdainfully what it was for, as such fripperies were not needed in his own Calvinist religion.

The couple spent the first weeks of their marriage quietly ensconced at Honselaersdijck getting to know each other. Soon the impressionable young girl, so hungry for affection, had fallen in love with her solemn husband. Mary had the sense to understand that, hitherto, William had led a typical bachelor life in exclusively male company. With his male friends, loyal, long-term companions of the hunting field and his military campaigns, William relaxed and was at his most jovial, sharing animated conversation over a few bottles. The intensely feminine Mary had no intention of intruding into this male world and showed no jealousy of William's preference for their company. Fortunately, she was on the best of terms with William's closest friend, Bentinck, who would shortly make a love match with one of her ladies, Anne Villiers. After the stresses of his public life, the gentle Mary would offer William peace and tranquillity. When he came to join her in her rooms, they spoke in English together, and she would entertain him with light chatter, a delightful distraction from the cares of state.

Life at William's court was far more sedate than at Whitehall, but it obviously agreed with Mary. Its sobriety calmed down her over-excitable temperament. There would be the occasional ball when she would indulge her love of dancing, sometimes until dawn, but otherwise social life consisted of private dinner parties with friends such as the Bentincks, tea parties in which the expensive new drink was imbibed, and endless games of cards. While regretting that the Princess of Orange had taken up card playing on Sundays, something she never did in England, her former chaplain Dr Lake heard that 'the princess was grown somewhat fat, and very beautiful withal'. Apparently her silver chocolate-pot was in constant use. At the same time, Lake expressed concern that she had attended an English nonconformist service at The Hague. He need not have worried. Mary's Anglican chaplain, Dr Hooper, soon had her reading Eusebio's *Church History* and Hooker's *Ecclesiastic Polity*, much to William's disgust when he found her struggling through them.

On Mary's marriage, Frances Apsley, who was not to marry until 1682, had been in a quandary as to how to proceed with their relationship. A rough draft survives of her letter to Mary broaching the subject:

Synce it was my hard fate to loose the greateste blessing I ever had in this worlde, which was the deare presenc of my most beloved wife, I have some comfort thatt shee is taken from mee by so worthy and so great a prince for so hee is in the oppinnion of all goode men. Yr Highness has putt a harde taske uppon me to treate you with the same familiarity as becomes a fond husband to a beloved wife hee doates uppon, whom I ought to reverence and adoare as the greatest princes now alive, when I flatter myselfe with the blessing god and yr selfe have given mee in so deare a wife I thynck what the scripture ses thatt man and wife are butt ony body and then your hart is myne, and I am sure myne is yours. Butt if I behave myselfe to you as I am bound in duty to yr Hyghness I mustt aske yr pardon for my presumption, yett synce my life dependes uppon itt for I can live no longer then your favour shynes uppon mee, itt wil be a great charritye in yr Hyness to continnue your love and bounty to a husbande that admyres you and doates upoon you and an obediient servantt thatt will always serve and adoare you.

In her busy new life, Mary rose before dawn to reply to Frances. But she could not conceal the fact that she had 'played the whore' a little, and that she was very much in love with her new husband. When the time came in February 1678 for William to return to the army, Mary accompanied him as far as Rotterdam, where her uncle, Laurence Hyde, Earl of Rochester, was pleased to note 'a very tender parting on both sides'. In consternation, Mary wrote to Frances expressing a sorrow she had never known:

I supose you know the prince is gone to the Army but I am sure you can geuse at the troble I am in I am sure I coud never have thought it half so much I thought coming out of my own contry parting with my friands and relations the greatest that ever coud as long as thay lived happen to me but I am to be mistaken that now I find till this time I never knew sorow for what can be more cruall in the world then parting but parting so as may be never to meet again to be perpetually in fear for god knows when I may see him or wethere he is nott now at this instant in a batell I recon him now never in safety ever in danger oh miserable live that I lead now.

Mary confided in Frances that she put on a cheerful appearance in company, but alone in her closet 'I give my self up to my griefe and mallancholly thoughts'. The partings were to be the pattern of William and Mary's married life, the anxiety she never ceased to feel for him undermining her health. Deep introspection and sadness were an increasingly prevalent aspect of Mary's mentality, not helped, as she became absorbed in religious devotion, by her own belief in her unworthiness before an exacting God.

Mary was already pregnant, but nevertheless she set off in a bone-jolting coach in the harsh conditions of a northern winter to join William first at Antwerp then at his castle at Breda. The result was disaster. Mary had a miscarriage. If she had been at home at The Hague, it is likely that she would have been able to call on the services of Dr Drelincourt, the brilliant gynaecologist and embryologist, or Cornelis Solingen, a renowned surgeon and obstetrician. Neither was available at Breda, and it is possible, in view of Mary's subsequent gynaecological history, that an infection set in with this first miscarriage that rendered her sterile. Neither Mary nor her family understood this. Indeed, Mary would never cease to hope for children, although her nurse, Mrs Langford, was heard to mutter that William never really gave her cause to expect them. Meanwhile, it was clearly not advisable for a young woman in a delicate condition to be gadding about after her soldier husband. Her father wrote anxiously from London, expressing his sorrow at the miscarriage and urging 'pray let her be carefuller of herself another time'.

Mary's health remained poor following her miscarriage, but then in the late summer of 1678 she found it impossible to contain the joyful news that she seemed to be pregnant again. She wrote to Frances, confiding a secret that 'I would hardly give me self leave to think on it nor no body leave to spake of it nott so much as to my self and that I have not yett ritt the Duchess word who has always chargd me to do it in all her letters ... If you love me don't tell it because I woud nott have it known yett for all the world since it cannott be above 6 or 7 weeks att most.'

When she did hear of Mary's pregnancy, her stepmother Mary Beatrice was very concerned about her 'dear Lemon'. She decided to bring her sister, Lady Anne, and a small party including the Duchess of Monmouth to The Hague to cheer her up, while the rest of the English court was at Newmarket. 'I love her as if she were my own daughter,' Mary Beatrice told her brother, as she set out in the autumn of 1678. James waited anxiously for every Dutch post to hear how Mary did and wrote to his son-in-law: 'I was very glad to see by the last letters that my daughter continued so well, and hope now she will go out her full time. I have written to her to be very careful of herself, and she would do well not to stand too much, for that is very ill for a breeding woman.' Mary Beatrice found Mary in good health and spirits and her pregnancy seemed to be progressing well. Nothing could have been further from the truth.

In March 1679 the Duke and Duchess of York went into exile in Brussels, from where Mary Beatrice was able to pay her stepdaughter another quick visit. By this time, it was clear that something was wrong. As time progressed and Mary's expected delivery date came and went, it became apparent that she was not pregnant at all. The sickness and malaise and lack of periods which had been taken for pregnancy, the intermittent fevers she had been experiencing which had been taken for the ague, or malaria, common in the Low Countries, were possibly symptoms of an ongoing gynaecological infection.

Mary Beatrice was disconcerted to find that William had grown impatient with the whole business. He was tired of his young wife's emotional demands and chronic ill health. Mary Beatrice told her brother the sad news that Mary had 'no further hope of a child', adding indignantly that 'she had passed the nine months since her pregnancy in great loneliness which strongly displeases us.' The impression of William's cruelty towards Mary was one she took away with her and coloured James's view of him in the future.

After the devastating revelation that she was not, after all, with child, the fevers continued, accompanied by an agonising pain in her hip. But in May 1679 James was writing optimistically to William: 'I am exceedingly glad to hear my daughter has missed her ague, I hope she will have no more now the warm weather is come.' Perhaps fearing that she had outworn William's patience, Mary agreed to go to Aix-la-Chapelle in August to take the waters. After a month, she felt much better. Henry Sidney, her mother's one-time admirer who was now the English envoy at The Hague, noted that William and Mary had a happy reunion in September. A month later, Mary had her last meeting with her father and stepmother when she took her leave of them as they left the Low Countries for their new place of exile, Edinburgh. In spite of the change in James's fortunes, he still liked to think that they were all 'family', with mutual interests. It was inevitable, however, that Mary's father and husband would end up on opposite sides of the political and religious divide. When it came to it, there was no question which side Mary, the loyal and malleable wife, would choose.

---

James gradually alienated Mary's affections, partly through his querulous attitude to William, partly through his interference in her marriage, and partly through the threat he posed to the Anglican Church and his clumsy attempts to convert her to Catholicism.

It was easy to offend James, who saw everything in simple terms – loyalty or betrayal – venting his wrath on anyone who went against him. He was incensed when William received James, Duke of Monmouth at The Hague. The Protestant Monmouth had been a thorn in James's side ever since the Earl of Shaftesbury and the Exclusionists had proposed him as an ideal alternative successor to the crown. Monmouth's pretensions had already earned him banishment from court, but his involvement in the Rye House Plot in 1683, which planned to assassinate the King and the Duke of York as they returned from Newmarket, had alienated the King from this beloved son. Whether he would eventually forgive Monmouth, as he always had his past misdemeanours, remained to be seen. Monmouth went into exile.

Charles might have indicated to William that he would take it kindly if Monmouth were to be received at The Hague, but James was furious at what he saw as William's betrayal and sent one of his angry letters to the hapless Mary: 'And let the Prince flatter himself as he pleases, the Duke of Monmouth will do his part to have a push with him for the crown, if he, the Duke of Monmouth, outlive the King and me . . . it will become you very well to speak to him [William] of it.'

Even William found Monmouth's charm irresistible and Mary had always been very fond of her handsome cousin. Soon the trouble-making French ambassador, Jean Antoine de Mesmes, Count D'Avaux, was reporting with relish that The Hague was given over to balls and parties at which the Duke of Monmouth always led the Princess of Orange out to dance first. Every day Monmouth visited the Princess and dined with the Prince and accompanied the Princess on public walks in the Mall. 'Nobody could understand,' he wrote, 'how the Prince of Orange, who is the most jealous man alive, permitted all the airs of gallantry which were observed by everyone between the Princess of Orange and M. de Monmouth.' Soon the ambassador was scandalised by the sight of Monmouth and the Princess learning to skate together. 'It was a most extraordinary thing to see the Princess of Orange with very short skirts partly tucked up, and iron skates on her feet, learning to slide now on one foot and now on the other.'

The fun came to an abrupt halt when the news of the death of King Charles II and the accession of Mary's father as James II reached The Hague in February 1685. Monmouth's continuing presence at The Hague was an embarrassment, which William made plain, underlying the theory that he had only entertained him to please the late King. William gave him a large sum of money and advised him to go to Vienna to join the Habsburg Emperor's army fighting the Turks. It was good advice. Both William and Mary extracted promises from Monmouth that he would not make an attempt on the English throne. But the promises were worthless. For all his charm, Monmouth was the weak puppet of more ruthless men. Within months, Monmouth's rebellion had ended in ignominious failure and Mary's father had sent her charming cousin to be butchered on the block by the notorious public executioner, Jack Ketch.

With her father's accession to the throne Mary, as the elder of his two surviving children, became heiress-apparent to the three kingdoms, and she was served at table on bended knee. This was a privilege that came automatically. Where it was in his power to do more, as he should have done, James did nothing. He awarded Mary no allowance and sent her no jewels or presents in recognition of her new dignity. Indeed, Mary's dowry had never been fully paid and she had a mere £4,000 a year for her own spending money. Out of this, she would ask Frances to buy her the latest fashions in London, although as the recognised leader of fashion in The Hague she was careful not to 'bring up such a fashion heer which the pursses could not bear'. She gave generously to charity. Unlike her younger sister Anne in London, who enjoyed a large income from the late King and now her father, Mary had no gambling debts for an indulgent father to pay. Anne, of course, lived in a society that wasted its wealth on costly apparel and lost fortunes at the gaming tables. When he was eventually taxed with his failure to make Mary an allowance, James retorted that he could not be sure that the money would not be used against him. Mary was not a greedy or acquisitive person, but her father's meanness, neglecting to give her some token recognition of her new status, must have saddened her.

William had always resented Mary's English household, whose gossiping and intrigues reminded him of Whitehall. He must have been aware that they blamed him for his perceived coldness to Mary. If Mary herself felt that William was cold to her, she was too proud, discreet and loyal to complain of it to anyone. Now some of her servants conspired to cause further trouble and they might even have been encouraged in their intrigues by James himself, who had never approved of his daughter's marriage and who might, as King, have hoped to break it. He was only too eager to believe the worst of William and the idea that he treated Mary badly, bolstered by the evidence of Mary Beatrice's second visit in 1679, was one his enemies loved to put about. Mary's servants saw their opportunity to cause trouble in William's liaison with Elizabeth Villiers.

Elizabeth was one of the daughters of Mary's governess, Lady Frances, with whom she passed her childhood in Richmond. She had accompanied the Princess to Holland in 1677. Elizabeth was no beauty – she was known as Squinting Betty because of a cast in her eye – but she had a scintillating wit that held even Jonathan Swift enthralled. Elizabeth was some years older and a good deal more sophisticated than William's adolescent bride and she attracted him in a way an innocent young girl could not. William does not seem to have been very interested in sex, but it is probable that his relationship with Elizabeth was at least partly sexual, if only because her brother-in-law, Bentinck, thought her behaviour disgraceful. There was almost certainly an extra, more important dimension, however. Witty and intelligent, Elizabeth captivated William by her conversation, and it was these qualities that put her in great demand on the diplomatic social circuit at The Hague. It is possible that she acted as an agent for William, and their late-night trysts were more likely to have been debriefing sessions than sexual encounters.

Whatever the exact nature of their relationship, discontented members of Mary's household determined to make mischief out of it. Mary probably learned of her husband's affair in the spring of 1680, when emotional disturbance typically made her so ill that it was thought she would die. She recovered, managing to put her knowledge of the relationship between William and Elizabeth at the back of her mind. Although it never ceased to trouble her and she might have mentioned it in her last letter to William many years later, Mary and William continued to live in happiness and harmony together, at least to all outward appearances.

In the autumn of 1685, however, Mary's gossiping 'mam' Mrs Langford, her old friend Anne Trelawney, her recently appointed Anglican chaplain Dr Covell and his assistant decided to bring William's continuing affair with Elizabeth to her attention. They had kept the new English envoy, Bevil Skelton – an unwise choice of James's whom William loathed – informed of their intrigues and he had sent his reports back to James in London in the diplomatic bag. James's evident interest in the affair spurred them on. They persuaded Mary that William's late nights, which he excused by pointing to his voluminous correspondence, were being passed in Elizabeth's bedchamber. If she did not believe them, they suggested she should stand at the bottom of the stairs one night and see for herself.

When William emerged from Elizabeth's room at two o'clock one morning to find his wife standing outside, his fury knew no bounds. He managed to convince Mary that it was not what it looked like. Only too anxious to believe him, the weeping Mary threw her arms round her husband and begged his forgiveness. Having appeased his devoted and trusting wife, William set a trap for her intriguing servants and confiscated their incriminating correspondence. Dr Covell had written to Skelton: 'Your Honour may be astonished at the news, but it is too true the Princess's heart is like to break . . . we dare no more speak to her. The Prince hath infallibly made her his absolute slave, and there is an end of it.'

William lost no time in sending all four of them packing

and James was prevailed on to recall Skelton to London. Mary was sorry to lose Mrs Langford, who had been with her all her life, but as she told Frances, 'when what is past cant be recaled the lesse one thinks of it the better.' Mary sent Elizabeth to England on some pretext, but news of her disgrace had already reached Whitehall and her father begged William and Mary to take her back. When she returned to The Hague she took up residence with her sister Katherine, but her strange liaison with William continued.

In the year of the accession of the Catholic King James in England, Louis XIV revoked the Edict of Nantes, which had allowed French Protestants freedom to practise their religion. Thousands fleeing persecution poured into the Dutch Republic, where they found religious toleration. Mary was shocked at the tales of Catholic atrocities the refugees brought with them. She set up a charitable institution for Huguenot girls at The Hague and donated generously to funds to help the refugees. She was also incensed that Louis, who had taken possession of William's principality of Orange in the south of France, now sent his dragoons to kill and torture the Protestants who had sought refuge there.

She who had never interfered in politics now turned to her father for help. His protests to the French were half-hearted and he excused himself to Mary by saying it was not a matter worth going to war over. 'The only thing I ever asked the King, my father, to do was to use his influence with the King of France to prevent the seizure of the Principality of Orange,' she recalled sadly. 'But my father preferred to join with the King of France against my husband.'

As heiress-apparent to her father's crown, Mary was beginning to take an interest in politics. Above all, she was concerned for the Anglican Church in the face of her father's evident determination to undermine it. She protested to James when Henry Compton, Bishop of London, the man who had confirmed and married her, was brought before the hated Ecclesiastical Commission and suspended when he refused to dismiss Dr Sharp for preaching an anti-Catholic sermon. James rebuked her for meddling in such matters. William and Mary were in favour of religious toleration, the suspension of the penal laws against Catholics and Dissenters. But they could never agree to the abolition of the Test Act, as James wished, because they felt that it guaranteed the supremacy of the Anglican Church. When seven bishops refused to read James's second Declaration of Indulgence, which was a repetition of the first, from the pulpit and he had them arrested for seditious libel, Mary asked her chaplain to write on her and her husband's behalf to Archbishop Sancroft. She wished him 'to express their real concern for your grace and all your brethren, and for the good cause in which your grace is engaged; And your refusing to comply with the King is by no means looked upon by them as tending to disparage the monarchy, for they reckon the monarchy to be really undervalued by illegal actions.'

James hoped to convert one or both of his daughters to the Catholic faith. Those who did not know her thought that Princess Anne was the more likely to convert and there was a disturbing rumour that James intended to ignore the claim of the Princess of Orange and make Anne his successor. Rumour also had it that he might declare his marriage to Anne Hyde null and void, so disinheriting both Mary and Anne. Mary's letters to Anne do not survive, but from Anne's replies, there is no doubt that the elder sister sought constant reassurance that Anne would stay firm in her religion.

Mary herself entered into correspondence with James, asking him to explain the reasons for his conversion to Catholicism. He did so at some length and he was impressed by the cogent argument she wrote in reply. James then sent her the devotional papers of Charles II and of her mother, Anne Hyde, but she remained unimpressed. 'I found her reasons as strange as they were surprising for a woman of whom I had always heard it said that she possessed great intelligence,' she wrote of her mother.

Finally, she read the book James had sent her, *Reflections on Differences in Religion*, and again rebutted its arguments. 'I have found nothing in all this reading but an effort to seduce feeble spirits,' she wrote, 'no solid reasoning, and nothing that could disturb me the least in the world, so much that the more I hear of this religion the more pleased I am with my own, and more and more thanks have I to render to my God for His mercy in preserving me in His true faith.'

Gilbert Burnet, a Scottish clergyman who had taken refuge at William and Mary's court when James came to the throne, read Mary's responses to her father. 'It gave me an astonishing joy to see so young a person all of the sudden, without consulting any one person, to be able to write so solid and learned a letter, in which she mixed with the respect that she paid a father so great a firmness, that by it she cut off all further treaty,' he wrote. 'And her repulsing the attack, that the King made upon her, with so much resolution and force, did let the popish party see, that she understood her religion as well as she loved it.'

Mary was no longer the naïve, innocent young girl who had left England in 1677. She had matured and used her time wisely, making up for the shortfalls in her education. When she was not suffering from the old complaint of sore eyes, she read books on history and divinity. She read over and over again Drelincourt's *A Christian Defence against the Fears of Death*, a tome that only encouraged her inherent morbidity. If anything, Mary had become too wrapped up in religion, spending many hours in solitary contemplation. She had always been very influenced by her Anglican chaplains, but now she saw the hand of God in everything, and Mary's God was wrathful. Her personal confidences in her journal are larded with references to Him, making her sound more like a Puritan of the 1640s than a daughter of Charles II's court. A natural melancholy in Mary's character, accentuated by sorrow that she was childless, seems to have been exacerbated by her awareness of God as judge of all

her actions and her constant fear that he would find her
wanting.

The Prince of Orange had always encouraged his wife to
play a subservient, frivolous role. He did not invite her to discuss weighty affairs with him, perhaps taking her gay chatter
at face value. Gilbert Burnet was the first to recognise that
Mary possessed a formidable intelligence and he could not
praise her too highly. 'She had great knowledge, with a true
understanding, and a noble expression,' he wrote. 'There was
a sweetness in her deportment that charmed, and an exactness
in piety and virtue that made her a pattern to all that saw her.'
Burnet imparted his knowledge of English politics to her. 'She
knew little of our affairs, till I was admitted to wait on her,' he
boasted. 'And I began to lay before her the state of our court,
and the intrigues in it, ever since the Restoration; which she
received with great satisfaction, and showed true judgement,
and a good mind, in all the reflections that she made.'

Burnet also claims to have raised a matter with Mary that
William had never been able to bring himself to discuss with
her in all the years of their marriage. Whether he had the
audacity to do this of his own volition, was prompted to do
so by William whose ambitions it served, or just invented the
scene when writing his *History* after the Revolution to put
himself in a good light, is a moot point. He asked Mary
what her intentions towards her husband were when she
became Queen. Mary did not understand. Burnet explained
that as Queen Regnant she would have the superior role,
while William would merely be her consort. Since he knew
their marriage had been 'a little embroiled' of late, he had
the temerity to advise that she should have the real authority
vested in her husband, while she should be content to play the
lesser role.

It is hard to believe that Mary was so ignorant of English
royal custom, but, according to Burnet, the next day she asked
him to bring William to her. She stated that 'she did not know
that the laws of England were so contrary to the laws of God,

as I had informed her: she did not think that the husband was ever to be obedient to the wife: she promised him he should always bear rule; and she asked only, that he would obey the command of "husbands love your wives," as she should do that, "wives be obedient to your husbands in all things." ' True or not, the incident perfectly describes the role Mary embraced in the dual monarchy with William.

Any thoughts of Mary inheriting her father's crown were thrown into jeopardy by the announcement of the Queen's pregnancy, which seems to have taken everyone by surprise. Although Mary Beatrice suspected she was pregnant in October 1687, she waited another month to tell Mary the news, and even then she seems to have given the impression that she was not quite sure. Mary said that she wrote 'always in very dubious terms'. However, she received the news with pleasure. She always rejoiced at other people's good fortune in having children, although her own hopes had been disappointed.

A tiny prickle of doubt might have started in Mary's mind when James followed up Mary Beatrice's tentative disclosure with a letter dated 29 November definitely confirming the pregnancy. He spoke of it 'in a manner so assured and that in a time when no woman could know anything for certain that there was certainly cause enough to raise a small suspicion', Mary wrote in her journal, perhaps with the benefit of hindsight, since she wrote it up properly from notes at the end of every year. Of course James, who had prayed for a son at St Winifrede's Well, believed in miracles. As a Protestant, Mary might not have fully appreciated this. By the time he wrote to Mary, his wife was over two months pregnant. From the first, however, Mary seems to have been under the impression that conception had taken place later than it had and that the baby was not due until July – the date mistakenly given by the royal physicians. It was an unfortunate misunderstanding that, in due course, would help convince Mary that there had been some 'trickery'.

There is no evidence to suppose that Mary was annoyed

because a brother would oust her from the succession. 'I rendered thanks to God that this news did not trouble me in any fashion,' she wrote in her journal, 'God having given me a contented spirit and no ambition but to serve my Creator and conserve my honour without stain.' Mary had no wish to leave her adopted country, where she was loved and happy. She knew that she had a far better life as Princess of Orange than she would as Queen of England. 'This it has pleased the Lord to make of me contents me and, in the state where I am, I am better able to serve Him than I should have been in a post more eminent.' She confided in her journal that all the King's family should rejoice in the fact that he might have a son, except that 'one cannot do so without being necessarily alarmed by the thought of a papist successor.'

If Mary did not want the crown for herself, she recognised that she should feel obliged to want it to please the Prince and to protect her beloved Church of England. 'Besides the interest of the Church,' she wrote, 'the love that I have for the Prince made me wish him all that he merits, and though I regret not to have more than three crowns to bring him, it is not my love that blinds me; no, I can see his faults, but I say this because I know also his merits.'

Mary decided to place her trust in God, 'so that even if I see a son born I shall not discourage myself, though I fear the consequences of this birth on feeble spirits'. From the evidence of her journal, Mary at first had no thoughts of discrediting the Queen's pregnancy or of doubting its veracity. In March 1688 all that changed when she received the first of her sister's letters implying that foul play could be intended. Presumably this was the source Mary was referring to when she wrote in her journal: 'In this time I received such a relation of the pregnancy of the Queen which gave me just reason to suspect there had been some deception.' At the same time, Anne was at pains to warn her sister and brother-in-law not to think of visiting England, implying that she feared some attempt on their lives. Possibly Anne feared that the Princess of Orange would be able to witness for herself the state of the Queen's pregnancy.

There is no evidence at all to suggest that Mary and Anne were colluding to perpetrate the idea that the Queen's pregnancy was a hoax, a plot to foist someone else's child on the nation. Indeed, the older sister was dependent on the younger for her information and formed her impressions largely from what she told her. Mary had decided to place her trust in God and wait upon events. After all, she might have reasoned, her sister would be there to witness the birth. It probably never occurred to Mary that Anne would be silly or malicious enough to leave town just when the Queen might be expected to go into labour. Her sister's unexpected absence from the birth would throw Mary into a quandary. The truth was important to Mary: what was she supposed to believe?

# 4
## King James II

*'He was bred with high notions of the kingly authority, and laid it down for a maxim, that all who opposed the king were rebels in their hearts'*

– Bishop Burnet

In May 1641 the idyllic childhood of the seven-year-old James, Duke of York and Albany, second son of King Charles I of England, Ireland and Scotland, came to an abrupt end. The London rabble surrounded Whitehall Palace shouting for the head of the King's chief minister, Thomas Wentworth, Earl of Strafford. Fearful for the safety of his family and hoping to buy time, Charles I gave them what they wanted. Strafford was duly executed on Tower Hill. The bloody sacrifice of a loyal servant was not enough, however. Still the enemies of the King were not satisfied. They wanted more and more concessions. The young James, often at his father's side during these years of turmoil, saw that concessions bought the King nothing. Clearly, it did not do for a king to be weak. A king must be strong and meet opposition with force.

Charles applied force, but so ineptly that it made matters worse. With civil war looming in 1642, Charles sent his second son ahead of him into the garrison at Hull, whose munitions he wished to retrieve for the royalist cause. The governor, Sir John Hotham, welcomed the boy and his escort, then promptly slammed the gates in the King's face. James was indignant at the King's humiliation and his own first experience of imprisonment left him bitter. Never one to forget a slight or forgive those he perceived to be his enemies, James was later to gloat when he heard that Hotham and his son had fallen foul of the Parliament and were to be executed, even though they were losing their lives in the royalist cause. In August 1642 James was with his father when he raised his standard in a field at Nottingham, declaring war on his subjects, although he always maintained they were the aggressors. On a frosty day shortly after his ninth birthday, James had his first taste of battle when he and his brother, Charles, Prince of Wales, the elder by three years, watched the opening engagement of the civil war, the slaughter at Edgehill. It was a war from which James drew all the wrong lessons, forming rigid political opinions that he failed to modify with age and experience.

James's second imprisonment came after Parliament's forces took the royalist stronghold of Oxford, where he had spent three years barely applying himself to his books and listening avidly to tales of military campaigns. The King had surrendered himself to the Scots, who sold him to the English, and he was now a prisoner of the army. James was forcibly separated from his servants, even his dwarf whom he wished to retain, and taken into the Earl of Northumberland's custody. He joined his younger siblings, Elizabeth and Henry, at St James's Palace. It was now that the King, imprisoned at Hampton Court, was permitted to have several meetings with his children, which took the form of deathbed admonitions. He impressed on them always to be loyal to their brother Charles and never to allow the hereditary line of succession to be altered. He urged James, who was likely to be set up as a puppet king by Parliament, to flee.

James had already been planning his escape. Incriminating letters were discovered by Parliament. He refused to reveal the key to the ciphers, until threatened with the Tower. He promised to make no further escape attempts. In fact, a new plan was soon hatched with help from outside. James started playing hide-and-seek with his siblings in the evenings. He hid so well that it took them at least half an hour to find him. On the evening of his escape, he locked up Elizabeth's little dog and hid until the children had given up the search. Then he slipped down the stairs and through the garden, using a key that had been smuggled in to him to pass into the park. Colonel Bampfield hurried him off to a safe house, where he changed into female clothes. He was then hustled into a barge at Billingsgate. The barge-master grew suspicious when he saw his young passenger hitching up his stocking in a most unladylike manner, but he accepted a bribe to slip past the lookout post at Gravesend under cover of darkness. James took ship for Holland, and arrived at his sister Mary, the Princess of Orange's court a penniless exile.

The fifteen-year-old James had just reached Paris when he heard the news of his father's public execution at Whitehall on 30 January 1649. The judicial murder of their king by the English shocked all Europe, even the republican Dutch. James never spoke of it directly, but it is evident that he never recovered from the brutal death of a father he loved deeply. Years later, during the exclusion crisis, he was to remind his brother Charles of the fate of those predecessors who had fallen into the hands of their enemies: 'Remember Edward II and Richard II, and the King our father.' Scarred by the experiences of his youth, James's outlook on life became fixed, immutable. Forty years later and beyond, James clung to the beliefs of the Cavalier Party of 1642, expecting a repetition of the terrible events of that year every time the monarchy encountered the least sign of opposition.

The immediate consequence of his father's death was that James came under the care of his mother, the Queen Dowager Henrietta Maria, who seems to have disliked him intensely. She was certainly very unkind to him, making loud, unfavourable comparisons between him and Charles, exploiting the mutual jealousy between the brothers who, nevertheless, loved each other. Consciously or otherwise, both her older sons held her responsible for their father's downfall, and they resented her relationship with Lord Jermyn, whom she was later rumoured to have married. She was no doubt frustrated by James's implacable obstinacy. Ironically, she placed difficulties in the way of his exercise of the Protestant religion, although she made no overt attempt to convert him to Catholicism.

James loved France, where he was among his mother's people, and his cousin Louis XIV, five years his junior, was said to be very fond of him. To escape dependence on his mother, James had the sense to see that he had to make himself acceptable to the French court, which might offer him a future. Tall and fair with fine features and blue eyes, James was considered far more handsome than his brother Charles, who had not made a good impression. Unlike his brother, James had a facility for languages, although his speech was often impeded by a nervous stutter. His cousin La Grande Mademoiselle, daughter of Gaston, Duke of Orléans, was impressed: 'I have found staying with the Queen of England her second son, the Duke of York. He is extremely good-looking and well made, and of fair complexion; he speaks French well and this gives him an advantage over the King his brother, for nothing in my opinion goes more against a man than lack of words.'

Shortly after James's eighteenth birthday, he embarked on the happiest years of his life when he joined the French royal army under Marshal Turenne, the greatest commander of the age. A military career had been mapped out for James since his father had made him Lord High Admiral at the age of three. Lacking his elder brother's quick mind and cunning, the rather plodding James was never going to be a politician, nor, from his choice of companions in exile, was he a good judge of men. The army's firm structure, the clear lines of command and duty, appealed to his authoritarian nature. His royal rank brought him no special privileges in the French army. He quickly gained promotion on his own merits, winning a reputation as a dashing, courageous cavalry leader, and became a lieutenant-general after two years. James's heroics on the battlefield threatened to overshadow his brother's more feckless existence.

He might well have ended up a marshal of France, but a treaty between Cromwell and Cardinal Mazarin dashed his hopes. The Stuart brothers were expelled from France and, ever obedient to his brother's wishes, James reluctantly took up arms against his former comrades in the service of Spain. At the Battle of the Dunes in June 1658, James fought heroically against the combined French and English forces, and there is a story that after the battle the victorious French looked for him among the prisoners, hoping to release their popular former comrade. The fortunes of the Stuarts in exile were at their lowest ebb when James accepted the offer of paid employment as Lord High Admiral of Spain at the beginning of 1660.

In the backbiting, peripatetic, debt-ridden Cavalier court in exile, in which the royal brothers were reduced to their last worn suit of clothes and could never be sure where their next meal was coming from, there were some compensations. Charles and James were young. Liberated from the restrictions of their father's austere chastity, the brothers indulged in sexual promiscuity. A young Charles had been disconcerted when his mistress, Lucy Walters, casually took up with another man while he was away on campaign in Scotland and England, trying to recover the crown. She died of the pox, leaving a son, James Crofts, whom Charles owned as his. More experienced in the ways of the world, Charles became cynical and never expected loyalty from anyone. James's sexual appetite was even more voracious than his brother's and he was less discriminating in his choice of women. Now, in the last, hopeless days of a long exile, he found himself trapped into marriage.

He had met Anne Hyde, the daughter of his brother's Lord Chancellor, Sir Edward Hyde, when she had come to Paris in the spring of 1656 as one of his sister the Princess of Orange's maids of honour. Anne's attraction lay in the strength of her personality, her wit and her lively intelligence. For a man who was already a bit of a bore despite his good looks and dashing reputation as a soldier, it is curious that James found wit so seductive in a woman. He admitted in his memoirs that he fell in love with Anne principally because of her witty conversation.

When the Princess of Orange returned to The Hague a year later, James continued to pursue Anne Hyde. Whatever appeal she had, Anne knew how to exploit it. And she was far cleverer than James. She refused to yield to his advances. 'She indeed shew'd both her wit and her vertue in managing the affaire so dexterously,' James recalled ungallantly in his memoirs, 'that the Duke overmaster'd by his passion, at last gave her a promise of marriage some time before the Restoration.' Perhaps James thought the promise, which took the form of a contract, could later be rescinded. For the moment, it did the trick. Anne gave him everything he desired.

To marry without the King's consent to assuage his sexual appetite was a foolish error of judgement on James's part. He was probably taken by surprise at his brother's sudden restoration to the throne in May 1660. Now James would be a grandee who could have the hand of any princess in Europe, a princess who would represent a useful alliance with a foreign power and bring a dowry to Charles's empty treasury. With the added prospect of so many new beauties ripe for seduction at the English court, James might well have been regretting his impetuosity. But he was no longer a free man. Anne was already pregnant and brandishing that incriminating piece of paper.

---

In May 1660 the Stuart monarchy was restored amidst universal acclamation, but James could never rid himself of the idea that there were republicans lurking round every corner intent on its destruction. When James later boasted to his confidant, the French ambassador Paul Barillon, that he knew the English and they only understood force, he revealed that he did not know the English at all. More at home with the absolutist monarchy of France, James had no concept of the subtleties of English government. There were no checks on the power of the monarchy before the calling of the Long Parliament in 1640, at the restoration of the monarchy in 1660, on James's accession in 1685, or at the time of William's invasion in 1688. The King was expected to use his prerogative within the spirit of the constitution, not to override it. There was a delicate balance between King and Parliament, with each respecting the other's prerogatives and privileges. Government should be part of an ongoing dialogue between the two. When Charles and later James resorted to proroguing and dissolving successive Parliaments, the monarchy was showing not strength but weakness.

Far from wanting to attack the monarchy, the landed aristocrats and squires who sat in the two Houses of Parliament, operated as JPs in the counties, and were closely associated with the Anglican clergy, were relieved at its return. They were determined that such a bunch of radicals as had been thrown up during the late civil wars and Commonwealth would never get into power again. They would do anything, almost, to avoid another civil war and republic. Charles's government was weak not because it lacked backing, but because it was chronically poor and inept. But Charles was flexible. He was motivated by a determination never to go on his travels again. Unlike his late father, he was not a man of high principle. He was a realist and a cynic. Above all, he knew how to bide his time to get the better of his opponents.

Unlike Charles, who was clever but lazy, James was diligent but not very bright and had little imagination. George Villiers, second Duke of Buckingham, who had joined the brothers in the royal nursery after the assassination of his father, knew them well. He put it succinctly when he told Burnet that 'the King could see things if he would, and the Duke would see things if he could.' To be fair, James's education had been sadly neglected since the outbreak of the civil war, but, unlike his brother, he seemed to have learned nothing from the school of life. James was obstinate and opinionated. He had no patience with opposition. He would not countenance even a reasonable argument in contradiction of his wishes. He saw criticism as disloyal, something that must be firmly crushed.

As the King's brother, James resumed his office as Lord High Admiral and was invited to sit in all his councils. He was given wealth, power and patronage. Knowing that he could always rely on his brother's loyalty, Charles kept James as his close confidant through most of the twenty-five years of his reign in England, excepting the brief periods when James was in exile. No other king in English history has enjoyed such a long apprenticeship at the heart of government. Yet James almost immediately diminished his reputation by the revelation of his secret marriage to Anne Hyde, and by his attempts to extricate himself from it.

Shortly after the Restoration, James confessed to Charles that he and Anne were contracted and that she was pregnant, begging Charles's permission to marry her publicly. Charles's first instinct was to refuse. It was scandalous for a royal duke to marry someone so far below him in rank. Not only the royal family, but also James's 'family', his servants, took exception to him marrying a commoner. The bride's own father was opposed to it, no matter the disgrace of having a pregnant daughter on his hands.

Then Charles capitulated. Anne's father was loyal and industrious, a useful servant of the Crown, and Charles had no wish to shame the man by rejecting his daughter. Besides, he had experts look into the marriage contract, and it was found to be valid in the eyes of the Church. James went through a second marriage ceremony with Anne on 3 September 1660 at her father's rented mansion, Worcester House in the Strand, where, unknown to her father, James had taken to visiting her bed at nights. This ceremony was secret, too, but there could be no doubt of its legality. James's Anglican chaplain, Dr Crowther, officiated and the young Lord Ossory, son of the Duke of Ormonde, and Anne's maid Ellen Stroud acted as witnesses. They later gave depositions to the Privy Council. But before they did, James began to have second thoughts.

Faced with the determined onslaught of his mother, Henrietta Maria, and his sister, Mary, Princess of Orange, James was beginning to waver. His mother was coming hotfoot from France 'to prevent, with her authority, so great a stain and dishonour to the crown'. His snobbish sister was furious that her former maid of honour would take precedence over her when she visited her brother's court. They encouraged James's boon companions, the disreputable rakes with whom he had made friends in exile – the Earl of Arran, Harry Jermyn (Lord Jermyn's nephew), Sir Richard Talbot ('lying Dick Talbot') and Tom Killegrew – to claim they had enjoyed Anne's sexual favours, in orders to besmirch her reputation and cast doubt on the legitimacy of her child.

Their allegations were so crude they must have made James wince. However, he craved his mother's pardon 'for having placed his affection so unequally, of which he was sure there was now an end; that he was not married, and had now such evidence of her unworthiness, that he should no more think of her'. On 22 October 1660 Anne was left to give birth to her first child without James's presence or support. Throughout her labour she had to endure the indignity of being interrogated by a clergyman – her old tutor, Dr Morley – as was usual when the marital status of the mother or the paternity of the father was in dispute. After the birth of a son, James neither visited her, nor sent his good wishes.

At Christmas 1660 everything changed. The smallpox epidemic that had killed the King's promising youngest brother, Henry, Duke of Gloucester, in September, now claimed his sister, the Princess of Orange. Before her death, she expressed her regret that she had sought to disparage James's marriage by lies. Anne's courage had won her the sympathy of the courtiers, who were disgusted at the behaviour of James and his cronies. It was unworthy of a prince. Seeing the game was up, James's friends confessed that they had lied only to protect him. Charles had long lost patience with his brother's shilly-shallying and told him 'he must drink as he had brewed, and live with her whom he had made his wife.' The courtiers dutifully made a dash to pay Anne their respects – a respect that soon became very sincere, because of her cleverness, her lively wit and friendliness, and the ease with which she assumed her new, exalted rank.

This whole affair had shown how easily James could be dominated by strong women and led by those he regarded as friends – friends to whom, having once placed his trust, he was ever loyal. Having made an honest woman of Anne, he lost no time in being unfaithful. 'He was perpetually in one amour or another,' Burnet noted with ill-disguised disdain. Courtiers removed their wives to the country to escape James's attentions. When Lord Chesterfield removed his to Derbyshire, the phrase 'to do a peak' caught on. Maids of honour took bets as to which of them the Duke would 'ogle' next. His duchess might fume with impotent jealousy, complain to the King and her father, the newly elevated Earl of Clarendon, but she made sure that she dominated the Duke in every other aspect of their life together. As Pepys remarked: 'The Duke of York is in all things but his codpiece, led by the nose by his wife.'

Quickly bored by the inactivity and comfort of court life, James sought an outlet for his energies in ferocious hunting. Whether at St James's or Windsor, he went out several times a week. His servants were paid danger money to keep up with his desperate pace, as he chased the stag and the fox (he was one of the first 'gentlemen' to indulge in fox-hunting) through swirling rivers and dense woodland and over vast distances. Sometimes he came back with cuts on his face, an eye almost lost, a collarbone broken. No wonder he was so impatient for a second Dutch war. In 1664 he had been awarded a large tract of land in North America taken from the Dutch and New Amsterdam had been renamed New York in his honour. It was only a matter of time before war would be declared against England's rival for overseas trade, the hated Dutch Republic.

At the outbreak of hostilities in 1665, James joined the fleet as Lord High Admiral. With his usual disregard for his personal safety, he fought in the Battle of Lowestoft on the deck of the *Royal Charles* in the thick of the fighting. When the battle was won and he retired to his cabin for a few hours' sleep, Henry Brouncker, one of his 'family', countermanded his orders to pursue the Dutch fleet. The sail was shortened and the Dutch were able to outrun their pursuers to the mouth of the Texel. If the English had kept pace with them, they would have been able to deal the final blow to the enemy fleet.

This whole affair is so mysterious that there is no certain proof whether Brouncker was acting purely for his own self-preservation in avoiding engagement with the Dutch, or had some other motivation. He was the sort of courtier who should not have been at sea in the first place. Typically, James could never bring himself to trust the more experienced officers and seamen who had served under Admiral Blake and the Commonwealth, because he suspected their republican sentiments. He found it more congenial to bring his own kind into the navy, and so 'began a method of sending pages of honour, and other young persons of quality, to be bred to the sea'. Popular opinion believed that the domineering Duchess of York had instructed her household that the Duke's life was to be preserved at all costs and that Brouncker interpreted this in his own way. Whatever her involvement, the outcome was one the Duchess would have wished. A grateful Parliament voted the Duke a large sum of money and begged him, as the heir to the throne, not to risk his life again.

The money was sorely needed, because the ducal household was in debt. James had large revenues from the confiscated lands of the regicides, the revenues of the post office and excise duties and licences on wine, and a proportion of the prize money from captured ships and their cargoes. He was a shareholder in the East India Company and the Royal Africa Company. All these sources of income were to yield larger amounts in the course of time. But in the 1660s the household was spending in excess of £60,000 a year, while its income was just over £40,000 a year. Although she liked to preside over meetings of the Duke's finance committee and strike out wages, the Duchess's personal extravagance did not help the situation. However, James was a good administrator and eventually gained a reputation for being careful with money. He shuddered at his brother's feckless spending, which, as James saw it, always made him dependent on Parliament.

The Duke and Duchess were badly shaken by the fall from power of Anne's father, Lord Chancellor Clarendon, at the end of the Dutch war in 1667. Clarendon and his sons, Henry and Laurence, exhibited the sort of steadfast loyalty to the Crown and the Anglican Church with which James, equally conservative, must have felt totally at ease. Accumulated grievances were laid at Clarendon's door: the disastrous Dutch war he had never wanted in the first place, the sale of Dunkirk to the French, the costly defence of Tangier, even the failure of Charles II's Queen, Catherine, to bear children. An angry crowd gathered outside his ostentatious new mansion in Piccadilly, nicknamed 'Dunkirk House', in the belief that Clarendon had personally benefited from the sale of the garrison that had proved too expensive to maintain. They cut down the newly planted trees and broke the windows. A gibbet was set up at the gate with a placard inscribed: 'Three sights to be seen, Dunkirk, Tangier and a barren queen.'

Like his father before him with Strafford, Charles was prepared to sacrifice a minister who had served him faithfully from the darkest years of his exile. He gave James the unpalatable task of persuading Clarendon to resign before Parliament could impeach him on charges of high treason. Clarendon was indignant that he should be asked to hand over the Great Seal, when nothing could be proved against him. James succumbed to a timely but mild attack of smallpox, saving him further embarrassment. Charles would have to do his own dirty work. He received Clarendon in the garden at Whitehall and dismissed him. As he left, the old man was jeered at by Lady Castlemaine, the voracious lady of pleasure whose extravagance he had tried to curb, standing at her window *en déshabille*. 'You, too, will grow old, my lady,' he told her. Factious courtiers had used Parliament to hound a loyal minister of the Crown from office and Charles had let it happen. For the rest of his reign, no minister would be able to serve the King without fear of impeachment from Parliament, which understood its new strength.

———

Temporarily out of favour with his brother, James now embarked upon a course of action that would seriously jeopardise the monarchy. He reveals in his memoirs that he was 'more sensibly touched in his conscience, and began to think seriously of his salvation'. As we have seen, he became a Catholic. The only surprise is that he did not do so sooner. At the French court he had come under a degree of pressure from his fiercely Catholic mother, but he had declined to embrace her religion, even when she had tried to convince him that he and his brother could rely only on Catholic support to restore the monarchy. He had attended mass, but solely to hear the music, which he loved. In truth, James had been an indifferent Anglican all along and there is no reason to doubt him when he says that it was only in 1669 that he decided to convert.

James embraced his new religion with a convert's fervour. He did not have the intellectual capacity to engage in theological debate. He always saw everything in simplistic terms: black or white, right or wrong. Once he had convinced himself that the Church of Rome was the one true Church, nothing would persuade him otherwise. Knowing what a furore his conversion would cause, James tried to persuade a Jesuit, Father Simon, to admit him into the Catholic Church while still allowing him to attend Anglican services for form's sake. When he refused, James turned to the Pope, who was equally adamant. Meanwhile, Charles was appalled by James's decision, and begged him to keep it secret. James was misled by Charles's confession to him and other trusted advisers that he was a Catholic at heart and wished to convert. He indicated that he wished to offer his Catholic subjects freedom of worship and relief from the penal laws. James was completely mesmerised by the prospect of Charles's 'Grand Design' to bring his realm back to the true faith. It was an idea, once sown, that James was never able to let go of, even although it was completely impracticable and his brother was largely motivated by the French subsidies that would accrue from his vague promises.

While Charles found it easy to lie and dissimulate to serve his ends, James was frank, open, convinced of his own rightness, eager to persuade others to do the same. James always displayed a tendency to impose his will on others, rather than take account of their views and inclinations. He was impatient of Charles's delay in declaring himself a Catholic and he longed to practise his new religion openly. He should have realised that news of his conversion, once it began to leak out, would incite a fresh wave of rabid anti-Catholicism – just the sort of public mood his co-religionists habitually took care to avert by keeping a low profile.

The Elizabethan government had done its work well in almost eradicating the old religion. A century later, only 5 per cent of a population that fell short of five million were believed to be Catholic. Most of them were nobility or country squires – people who could afford to pay the recusancy fines – rather than the lower class. Anti-Catholicism had become inherent in the English psyche. In the eyes of xenophobic Englishmen, Catholicism was something alien and equated with a foreign power – the Pope – and potentially subversive. Primed by Foxe's *Book of Martyrs* in every literate home, the English were prepared to believe that the Catholics would do anything, no matter how heinous, to impose their beliefs on others. Had they not been responsible for the Gunpowder Plot, an attempt to blow up the present King's grandfather, James I, and his Parliament? Any national disaster was laid at the Catholic door. Did a Catholic not start the Great Fire of London? The inscription on the Monument confidently blamed the fire on 'the treachery and malice of the Popish Faction . . . in order to the carrying on their horrid plot for extirpating the Protestant religion and old English liberty and introducing Popery and slavery'. Catholic foreigners might expect to be attacked in the street as 'papist dogs'.

The court with its French tastes – everything from periwigs to the use of the fork – had long been suspected of being pro-Catholic. The Queen was a Catholic, the King's new *maîtresse en titre*, Louise de Kéroualle, Duchess of Portsmouth, was a Catholic, some of the leading councillors and courtiers were Catholic. And now the King's brother, the heir to the throne, was making no secret of his inclinations. Soon there were whispers about an infamous secret clause in the Treaty of Dover, agreed in 1670 between the King and his sister Minette, the French King's sister-in-law. The King was being subsidised by that absolutist Catholic monarch, Louis XIV of France. Popery had always been associated with arbitrary government, but did these subsidies mean that the King could dispense with Parliament? Were the two kings planning to join forces to impose Catholicism on England? James might have been foolish enough to let slip something about the secret clause to the Duke of Buckingham. Before he died in the autumn of 1673 Lord Clifford, one of the three ministers in whom the King had confided his intended pro-Catholic policy, revealed it to fellow Cabal member the Earl of Shaftesbury, who instantly went into opposition.

These revelations came at just the time when the English were beginning to fear Louis XIV's aggression in the Low Countries. King Charles's pro-French foreign policy was clearly not in the best interests of the country. Did it not make more sense to join forces with the Protestant Dutch? His new minister, Thomas Osborne, shortly created Earl of Danby, was the leader of the emerging Tory Party – Tory being a derisive name associated with Catholic bandits in Ireland – which was a fervent supporter of the Crown and the Anglican Church. Danby wanted to steer the King towards an alliance with the Dutch Republic, but such an alliance went against all Charles's natural inclinations.

In such a climate of wild speculation and suspicion and after the scandal arising from Anne Hyde's conversion as revealed on her deathbed, it was extremely injudicious of James to take as his second wife a Roman Catholic. The whole affair could have turned out differently. Impulsive as ever, James had first proposed to the young Protestant widow, Susan, Lady Bellasys. She even had a paper to prove it, which she waved about for the entertainment of the court. Charles was totally exasperated when he heard of his brother's rash proposal and warned that he could not play the fool a second time. So, after an exhaustive search for the perfect royal beauty, James had settled for the Italian princess.

Maria Beatrice Eleanora D'Este of Modena was not just any Catholic princess, but one whose family had close ties with the papacy. Before long rumour had it that she was the daughter of the Pope himself. The fact that the duchy of Modena fell firmly within the French sphere of influence added to the unpopularity of James's choice. The English wasted no time in making their dissatisfaction at the proposed marriage known. Traditionally, they lit bonfires to celebrate their deliverance from popery, just as they lit them to protest when they felt threatened by it. A really good bonfire might burn the Pope in effigy with a cat sewn into the figure. Its screams added that extra touch of reality for the eager spectators. It was said that if Mary Beatrice had arrived in time for the frenzied Guy Fawkes' celebrations in 1673, she would have been torn to pieces. As it was, very few courtiers were intrepid enough to accompany James to Dover to meet her.

If James, the ageing roué of forty, thought his conversion to Catholicism and his marriage to a nubile fifteen-year-old were going to curb his lust, he was sadly mistaken. He tended to treat Mary Beatrice as a nice child he could dote on, while engaging his rampant sexuality with his Protestant mistresses, first Arabella Churchill, then her successor, the wickedly witty Catherine Sedley. When his Catholic wife resorted to sulking, then eventually turned on him with ferocity, he was shocked.

Mary Beatrice of Modena, second Duchess of York, was much admired
for her beauty and grace. Twenty-five years her senior, James introduced
his fifteen-year-old bride to his elder daughter with the words,
'I have brought you a new playfellow.'

Shortly after his invasion of England, William of Orange paused at Wilton to admire Van Dyck's portrait of the three eldest children of Charles I. It depicts William's uncles, the future Charles II and James II, and his mother, Mary, the Princess Royal. As he viewed the painting in 1688, William was about to hound James out of his kingdoms.

James, Duke of York, seen here with his father Charles I, drew all the wrong lessons from the civil wars. The experience left him convinced that any opposition to the monarchy was potentially subversive and republican and must be crushed.

No sooner had James made an honest woman of Anne Hyde than he embarked on a series of affairs. His wife was the stronger character, however, and dominated him in every other respect. 'The Duke of York is in all things but his codpiece, led by the nose by his wife,' Pepys remarked.

Separated from her mother as a small child, the Yorks' younger daughter, Lady Anne, would always seek her own security above all else.

Steeped in romances, drama and poetry, Lady Mary of York, seen here dressed as Diana, lived in a world of make-believe.

Mary Beatrice, Duchess of York, looked particularly striking dressed in the masculine riding habit the ladies of the court had made fashionable.

Princess Mary, the first daughter of the Crown, at the time of her
marriage to her cousin, Prince William of Orange, in 1677. She possessed
a sort of feverish charm, which was soon tempered at her husband's
more sober court.

The granddaughter of James I and the mother of George I, Sophie of the Palatinate, later Electress of Hanover, enjoyed a long friendship with her Stuart relatives, until a curt letter from Anne apparently hastened her death in June 1714. Had she lived two months longer she would have succeeded Anne as Queen.

Charles II had the dark saturnine looks of his Medici ancestors – one reason, perhaps, for the Italian Mary Beatrice to feel an immediate affinity with her charming, sardonic brother-in-law.

(*Left*) By the time Prince William of Orange married Princess Mary in 1677, he was already the Protestant champion of Europe, the saviour of his country and the veteran of many military campaigns.

(*Right*) Prince George of Denmark made a kindly but dull husband for Princess Anne. Charles II noted that he was completely vacuous: 'I have tried him drunk and I have tried him sober and there is nothing in him.'

Princess Anne, at the time of her marriage in 1683, displaying the charms that attracted such unwanted suitors as John Sheffield, Earl of Mulgrave. Her portraits give no indication of her eye problems, which apparently lent her a sour, petulant expression.

Dutch broadsheets which poured into England, casting aspersions on Queen Mary Beatrice's virtue and the authenticity of the Prince of Wales, were extremely cruel. Here we see Mary Beatrice sitting beside her son's cradle. The broadsheets routinely depict James Francis Edward holding a toy windmill, implying that he was in reality a miller's child, smuggled into the Queen's bed in a warming-pan. Father Petre has his arm round the Queen in a suggestive manner. Petre came from a family of English gentry, but in the broadsheets he is made to look foreign, xenophobia and anti-Catholicism being indistinguishable in the popular mind.

He tried to comply with the dictates of the priests. Full of self-disgust, he became more furtive about his womanising and his taste did not improve with age. 'My brother will lose his throne for his principles,' Charles despaired, 'and his soul for a bunch of ugly trollops.'

Parliament had done everything it could to persuade the King to stop James's unpopular Catholic marriage, but its appeals were futile. Charles and James maintained that a royal marriage was a private matter, and questions of marriage and the succession were no business of Parliament. They were displaying the sort of unwillingness to listen that eventually turned the Crown's most loyal adherents against it. James's Catholicism fuelled the parliamentary debates of the 1670s. As a direct result of his Catholicism, Parliament passed the Test Act, by which holders of office had to take an oath renouncing the doctrine of transubstantiation, central to Catholic belief. James had to resign as Lord High Admiral. A second Test Act meant that Catholic members could not sit in Parliament, although James's supporters managed to win an exemption for him. Apart from the restrictions forbidding them to worship either in public or in their own homes, Catholics were now deprived of civic rights. Far from rejoicing that the heir to the throne had declared himself a Catholic, fellow Catholics must have been wishing that the Duke had kept his religious beliefs to himself.

In deference to his brother's wishes, James participated in the Anglican Communion until 1672 – when he was officially admitted into the Roman Catholic Church – and continued to attend services until Easter 1676, when he took umbrage at Bishop Compton's confirmation of his daughter. After that, everyone drew the obvious conclusion about James's religion, although he worshipped in private. What were people supposed to think, therefore, when in August 1678 Titus Oates and Israel Tonge made allegations that there was a Jesuit plot to murder the King and replace him with James? If the heir to the throne had not turned Catholic, the conspiracy would not have had any credibility. As it was, it provided just the spark to set off a further, even more intense wave of anti-Catholic hysteria. One Protestant pamphleteer envisaged:

Your wives prostituted to the lust of every savage bog-trotter, your daughters ravished by goatish monks, your smaller children tossed upon spikes, or torn limb from limb, whilst you have your own bowels ripped up . . . and holy candles made of your grease (which was done within our memory in Ireland) your dearest friends flaming in Smithfield, foreigners rendering your poor babes that can escape everlasting slaves, never more to see a Bible, nor hear the joyful sounds of liberty and property. This, gentlemen, is popery.

The discovery of a cache of letters between the Duchess of York's secretary, Edward Coleman, and Louis XIV's confessor, Père La Chaise, which seemed to implicate James in a 'Grand Design' to impose Catholicism on England, brought James dangerously close to ruin.

Danby was pressing Charles to send his brother out of the country for his own safety. He was facing ruin himself. Louis XIV suspected him of trying to persuade Charles to defect to the Dutch interest and was determined to break him. At Louis's instigation, in the autumn of 1678 Ralph Montagu took revenge for his dismissal from the Paris embassy by revealing that Danby had been in correspondence with the French King about secret subsidies that, supposedly, would enable Charles to dispense with Parliament. Danby had done so only on the orders of Charles and almost certainly against his own inclinations. A furious Parliament decided to impeach Danby. He was dismissed and sent to the Tower. The upshot of this revelation was Tory disgust at the perceived hypocrisy of Danby and a massive Whig reaction.

The new Parliament, which met in March 1679, was almost totally hostile to the Crown and supported by the loud, angry, anti-papist London rabble. Kicking his heels in Brussels and sending for his hounds for the hunting with which he would now occupy his time, it probably did not occur to James that all this could have been avoided had he been prepared to keep his conversion strictly secret, or retire into private life. Ever convinced of his own rightness, James could congratulate himself that he was only obeying his conscience, leaving his brother to bear the strain.

The Earl of Shaftesbury and his followers, given the derisory appellation of Whigs after the rebellious Scottish Covenanters, now turned their attention to James and the succession. A Catholic could not succeed to the throne, they argued; he must be excluded. Desperate, they looked to James, Duke of Monmouth, that boy who had been known as James Crofts and brought to England in 1662 by Henrietta Maria and eagerly embraced by Charles as his beloved son. Even then there had been whispers that he might succeed his father the King before his uncle the Duke, because he was not really illegitimate. As early as October 1662 Pepys heard 'what great faction there is at court; and, above all, what is whispered, that young Crofts is lawful son to the King, the King being married to his mother. How true this is, God knows; but I believe the Duke of York will not be fooled in this of three crowns.' Now, attempts were made to find a mysterious black box, supposed to contain the marriage lines of his mother, Lucy Walters, with the then exiled King, Charles Stuart.

Charles had the Privy Council record not once but twice that he had never been contracted in marriage to anyone save Queen Catherine. His son, James, Duke of Monmouth, was a bastard. So strongly did Charles feel about this that he said that much as 'he lov'd the Duke of Monmouth, he had rather see him hang'd at Tyburn than own him as his legitimate son'. The opposition refused to listen. The fact that James always maintained that Monmouth was not Charles's son, but a by-blow of Robert Sidney – he even had a mole on his face like him and resembled that good-looking family far more than he did his reputed Stuart father – was considered sour grapes. The handsome, the charming, the weak, the pliable Protestant Duke was an ideal puppet for the Whigs, determined to exclude the Duke of York from the throne.

To James, the Whigs were dangerous republicans, the opposition he had always suspected had been waiting in the wings, determined to destroy the monarchy. If he had anything to do with it, the weakness of his father, the concessions he had made in the 1640s, would not be repeated. He bombarded his nephew and son-in-law, Prince William of Orange, with letters that reveal his increasingly dogmatic and reactionary state of mind. On 11 May 1679 he admitted to William: 'in my mind all things tend to a republick'. Three days later, when the first Exclusion Bill was passing through the House of Commons, he wrote:

You see how violently my enemies attack me, and that Wednesday last was the day both houses were to take into consideration my affair . . . I cannot now but look on the monarchy itself in great danger, as well as His Majesty's person, and that not from papists, but from the commonwealth party, and some of those who were lately brought into the council [Shaftesbury and the Whigs], that govern the Duke of Monmouth, and who make a property of him to ruin our family; and things go on so fast and so violently, and there are so very few left about His Majesty that have either will or courage to give good advice to him, that I tremble to think what will happen; for if His Majesty and the House of Lords stick to me, then one may expect great disorders, nay a rebellion; if His Majesty and they shall consent to what the Commons may do against me, I shall then look on His Majesty as less than a Duke of Venice, and the monarchy and our family absolutely ruined.

A few days later he was writing again in the same vein, and revealing his impatience at Charles's cautious tactics: 'so that except His Majesty begin to behave himself as a King ought to do, not only I, but himself and our whole family are gone.' In contrast to Charles, who simply dissolved Parliament to stop the passage of this first Exclusion Bill, James never made any secret of the fact that he was prepared to take up arms to defend his right to the succession. His letters to his brother and to William reveal his growing obsession with the Duke of Monmouth, who had been an irritation to his uncle even before the Whigs took up his cause. When James made his hurried, secret visit to the King's sickbed at Windsor in August 1679, he won the important concession that Monmouth, too, would be sent into exile.

In some ways, James's two periods of exile in Scotland, from the autumn of 1679 to the following February, and, after a brief interlude at the English court, from October 1680 to May 1682, strengthened his position. As Duke of York and Albany, the last title representing his long Scottish lineage, James found a ready welcome in Scotland. In contrast to his pleasure-driven, indolent brother, James was seen to be hardworking and decisive. His role as the King's representative came as a relief after the long tyranny of the Duke of Lauderdale. As a royal duke, James was able to rise above party to appeal to a broad section of Scottish society. There were some drawbacks to life at Holyrood, however, as he complained to William: 'I find you hunt almost every day, and that it is a place very proper for it; this country affords no such kind of hunting, for where the stags are there are such hills and bogs as 'tis impossible to follow any hounds, so that hare-hunting and shooting are the only sports one can have here; after June is once over there will be very good shooting at heath-pouts [grouse], of which and partridge there are great store here.' Apart from shooting when the weather was fair, he was 'abroad every day and playing at "goffe"' on the links at Leith, and in bad weather he practised the Scottish sport of curling.

Later, James's detractors would point to his cruelty towards the Scottish Covenanters and his attendance at torture sessions. It would be a mistake, however, to think that James ever agreed with religious persecution for its own sake. If he hounded the Covenanters, his reasons were political not religious. The Covenanters were rebels and James would have saved many of their lives, if only they had recognised King

Charles as their lawful sovereign. If the English did not want James as their king, there was every reason to believe that he would have been able to hold on to the kingdom of Scotland and even to use it as a platform from which to launch an attack on England.

By 1681, however, the situation in England was looking more favourable. The second Exclusion Bill was defeated in the Lords, mainly through the oratory of George Savile, Earl of Halifax. Although he was more inclined to the Whigs than the Tories, Halifax echoed Tory sentiments, indeed, the sentiments of all men with a vested interest in landed property, when he argued against exclusion. If the hereditary succession to the throne was tampered with, might not the same principles be applied to them and their estates? The Lords rejected the Bill. But Halifax was by no means oblivious to the dangers posed by James's religion and he introduced a scheme for limiting the prerogatives of a Catholic monarch. Ignoring the fact that Halifax had been largely responsible for saving his inheritance, James never forgave him for this 'betrayal'.

Tongue in cheek, Charles adopted a limitations scheme, which would have made William and Mary regents after his death, and offered it to the Whigs when Parliament met at Oxford in March 1681. The gamble worked. The Whigs were intransigent, replying that they would accept nothing less than James's exclusion. Charles dissolved Parliament and the Whigs, who had come into Oxford armed and belligerent, fled in every direction. Civil war, after all, was not an option.

The defeat of the Whigs did not make the idea of a Catholic successor any more palatable. James continued to resist all attempts to lure him back into the Anglican Church. 'Pray, once and for all, never say anything to me again of turning Protestant,' he had written to his friend George Legge, Earl Dartmouth from Brussels, 'do not expect it or flatter yourself that I shall ever be it, I never shall, and, if occasion were, I hope God would give me grace to suffer death for the true Catholic religion as well as banishment.' And more than two years later from Edinburgh: 'You are a man of conscience as well as honour, do but think what a base mean thing it would be in me, besides the sin of it, to dissemble and deny my religion; I hope by God's grace never to do so damnable a thing, and let my friends take their measures accordingly.'

Halifax told him frankly 'that except he became a Protestant his friends would be obliged to leave him, like a garrison that one could no longer defend.' James replied 'that then his case was more desperate than he understood it to be before, for that he could not alter his principles'. Worn out by his brother's recalcitrance, Charles left him to stew in Scotland.

James's release came from a most unexpected quarter. Charles's mistress, Louise, Duchess of Portsmouth, had supported exclusion, perhaps with the long-term view of getting her own bastard, Charles, Duke of Richmond, on the throne instead of Monmouth. Now she wanted to secure a loan, but she could only provide the necessary security if she could persuade James to exchange a proportion of his revenue from the post office for some of her income from a less reliable source. Knowing that his revenue could not be altered except by Act of Parliament – which was not sitting – James pretended to acquiesce, but on condition that he were allowed to come to London to oversee the transaction.

Once in London, James received a most extraordinarily warm welcome. Clearly, it was safe for him to return for good. He lost no time in returning to Edinburgh to wind up his affairs and to collect the Duchess and his daughter, Lady Anne. The ship in which he was travelling, the *Gloucester*, struck a sandbank off the Norfolk coast. No one could abandon ship before James gave the word and made the first move. Vital minutes in which lives might have been saved ticked by while he dithered, wondering if the ship could be saved. When he finally decided more time was lost and John, Lord Churchill held panicking men at bay at sword point, as James insisted that a large, heavy strongbox be lifted into the lifeboat with him. Lord Dartmouth asked pointedly if the box contained anything worth a man's life. To someone as self-obsessed as James, his memoirs were clearly more important. He does not seem to have insisted on his dogs accompanying him, as Burnet asserted, since Mumper was subsequently spotted floundering around in the water, along with hundreds of men who lost their lives, it being too late for them to save themselves after James's fatal delay.

James spent the last years of his brother's reign exacting vengeance on his enemies. He successfully sued a number of them, including Titus Oates, for malicious libel against great persons, winning vast sums in damages. He expressed satisfaction when the prominent Whig, Lord John Russell, and the republican, Algernon Sidney – brother of Henry, Anne Hyde's admirer, and of Robert, Monmouth's possible father – were brought to the scaffold for their alleged involvement in the Rye House Plot. Arrested and dragged before the King and the Duke, Monmouth admitted he knew of a plot, but was not implicated in the assassination aspect of it. Charles forgave him, but then thought better of it when Monmouth refused to sign a written statement. James had the satisfaction of once more seeing his troublesome nephew cast into exile.

So extreme was the Tory Anglican reaction against the defeated Whigs in the last years of Charles II's reign that James was able to resume his office as Lord High Admiral, albeit without the official title, in defiance of the Test Act. He regained a dominant position in his brother's councils, and was probably responsible for the move towards royal absolutism that now began to take effect. Arbitrary government suited his authoritarian nature and in due course he would use it as a means to further the Catholic cause rather than as an end in itself. In the last four years of the reign no Parliament was called, in defiance of the Triennial Act of 1664. Many new borough charters were issued allowing the Crown to nominate previously elected mayors, aldermen and burgesses, who would condone royal policies.

There was a massive swing of support in James's favour.

With their usual tendency to turn from the sinking to the rising sun, a far greater number of courtiers attended James's levées and couchées than were at the King's. 'The King walked about with a small train of the necessary attendants,' Burnet recalled, 'when the Duke had a vast following; which drew a lively reflection from [Edmund] Waller, the celebrated wit. He said the House of Commons had resolved that the Duke should not reign after the King's death; but the King in opposition to them was resolved he should reign even during his life.'

As Charles lay on his deathbed in the first week of February 1685, James bent down and asked in a whisper if he would like him to bring a priest. Charles eagerly agreed, admitting that he had delayed his reconciliation with Rome too long. James asked everyone to leave the room, except the Protestant Earls of Bath and Feversham, whose loyalty was assured. He then ushered in Father Huddlestone, disguised in a wig and cassock, that same priest who had saved Charles's life as he was being hunted down after Cromwell's victory at the Battle of Worcester and who had been excepted by Act of Parliament in all the laws enacted against the Catholics and the priests. Charles made his confession, took the sacrament, and received the last rites. Afterwards, he revived a little. At six the next morning he asked for the curtains to be opened, 'that I may once more see the day.' He died at noon and there was a stampede to greet the new King, who had retired to his apartment to weep and pray.

---

James saw kingship as a sacred trust. God had protected him through many dangers and misfortunes and brought him to this exalted position so that he could do His work. And God's work, as James saw it, was the advancement of Catholicism in England. It could only be a matter of time before he clashed with the vested interests, prejudices and fears of his subjects. James was able to come to the throne peacefully because the alternative, his exclusion and possible civil war, was too awful to contemplate. The political nation was holding its breath, prepared to give him a chance, hoping that it would not be too long before the Catholic King died and his Protestant successors, Mary and her husband William, came into their own.

With his usual shrewd foresight, Charles II had predicted that if ever his brother should reign, he would be so 'restless and violent, that he could not hold it four years to an end'. It was an uncannily accurate prediction. No sooner did he become King than James threw off all pretence about his religion. He abandoned the Anglican Chapel Royal at Whitehall to his daughter Anne and attended mass publicly at his own oratory, pending the completion at Christmas 1686 of a lavish new, Catholic, Chapel Royal in the palace. As was customary, courtiers accompanied the monarch to services, but now many of them stopped at the door.

Never one to be content to practise his own religion and let others practise theirs, James urged the Duke of Norfolk, carrying the sword of state before him, to proceed through the door into the Catholic oratory. Norfolk refused to budge. 'My lord, your father would have gone further,' the King told him. 'Your Majesty's father was a better man,' Norfolk replied, 'and he would not have gone so far.' When James tried to persuade his ministers to join him at Easter mass, his former brother-in-law, Laurence Hyde, Earl of Rochester, a fervent Anglican, made his excuses and left for the country. James held out the prospect of royal favour and high office to those who would agree to convert. Many resisted his attempts. Colonel Kirke, who had been in charge of the Tangier garrison, had the best excuse. He told James that he had already promised the King of Morocco that 'if ever he changed his religion, he would turn Mahometan'. Even those who did take the bait and convert did so with a degree of caution. The Earl of Peterborough, for example, kept his pew in his Anglican parish church, just in case.

When James said that he intended to 'establish' the Catholic religion in England, he meant that he wanted to give Catholics the same rights as Protestants, to allow them freedom of worship and to hold public offices. He was at pains to reassure the Anglican establishment that they would not lose out by granting Catholics equality. Neither the monastic lands they had inherited from Henry VIII's sequestration of Church property, nor the livings of the Anglican clergy would be threatened. In James's ideal world a repeal of the laws against Catholics would win many converts for Rome. His subjects would no longer hesitate to embrace the Catholic faith, he believed, once they were assured they could have access to the universities, to public office, a seat in Parliament, worship publicly without fear of arrest or incur the dreaded recusancy fines for non-attendance at the Church of England. There would be no need for force.

No one believed him. In the prejudiced eyes of the Anglican establishment, any relaxation in their vigilance against the Catholic threat would spell disaster. James might say he wanted only toleration for the Catholics, but he would not stop there. Surely this was the first move in a nefarious Catholic plot to force England back to Rome? Englishmen had only to look across the Channel at the persecution of the French Huguenots to see what the word of a Catholic king was worth. No Catholic monarch would tolerate heresy in his realm. Give the Catholics a bite and they would want the whole cake.

The Duke of Monmouth's landing at Lyme Regis in June 1685 and his call to the people to help him overturn the tyrant who, he claimed, had poisoned his father, the late King, and to recognise him as their lawful sovereign played right into James's hands. The rebellion gave him the excuse he needed to double the size of his army and introduce Catholic officers, who had hitherto served abroad, to deal with the emergency. The royal army was raw and untried, however, and James was anxious that it should not engage the rebels unless absolutely necessary. Monmouth was an experienced military commander but he had struck far too soon. James's rule was not yet sufficiently unpopular for the rebellion to have any hope of success. Crucially, the local gentry made no move to join him. Monmouth's morale was further undermined by the defeat of the Earl of Argyll's simultaneous rebellion in Scotland. Monmouth's ragged army made a surprise attack on the King's forces under the French-born, Catholic, Louis Duras, Earl of Feversham, at Sedgemoor during the night of 5 July and was crushed. The official, government-censored newspaper, the *London Gazette*, triumphantly reported that the Duke of Monmouth was found hiding in a ditch in shepherd's clothing a few days later.

He was brought to London, where he grovelled at James's feet, making excuses and pleading for his life. Always mindful of how a king ought to behave, James was disgusted at the abject behaviour of this bastard interloper. He had no intention of saving his life. There was little sympathy for Monmouth among the political nation, either. He was a rebel and must die a traitor's death. Judge Jeffreys, made irritable and vicious by an attack of the stone, and the violent Colonel Kirke were despatched to the West Country to make a terrible example of those who dared rebel against their lawful King. Hundreds were hanged and their bodies left to rot on gibbets, or they were transported, with favoured courtiers making profits from their sale into slavery in the colonies.

The emergency over, James had no intention of disbanding the army. Soldiers in peacetime were anathema to the English and an unnecessary expense in the opinion of Parliament. Parliament must already have been regretting its generosity in granting James all his brother's revenues – they were yielding far more than Parliament realised – for life and additional grants to refit the navy and deal with the Monmouth rebellion. Far from appreciating the trust Parliament was placing in him by making the Crown financially independent, James with his usual lack of magnanimity chose to warn the Commons: 'the best way to engage me to meet you often is always to use me well.' Now a Catholic monarch had in his hands a large standing army, albeit one with very little experience, with which he hoped to impress foreign powers and, if need be, impose the royal will and quell his subjects. What was there to stop these Catholic officers and soldiers terrorising the King's Protestant subjects as Louis XIV's dragoons were doing to the Huguenots in France? Already they were being billeted where they were not wanted and making a nuisance of themselves. James proudly held public reviews of his troops in Hyde Park and later had them camped at Hounslow, a menacing presence in striking distance of the capital.

The King's minister, Lord Halifax, warned him it was illegal to employ Catholics in the army, because they did not satisfy the requirements of the Test Act. James maintained that it was wrong for a king to be deprived of the services of any of his subjects. He used the royal prerogative to dispense Catholic officers from the penalties they incurred for not taking the oath stipulated in the Act. It was recognised that a king might use his dispensing power in certain, individual cases, but to apply such a power generally was against the spirit of the constitution. James decided to stage a test case. Sir Edward Hales, a Catholic officer, was prosecuted for holding office contrary to law, but pleaded the King's dispensation. James had taken the precaution of packing the bench with judges who shared his opinions – another misuse of the prerogative – so that when Lord Chief Justice Herbert found a pretext to call in all the judges, eleven out of the twelve found in the King's favour. 'The Kings of England,' the Lord Chief Justice confirmed, 'are absolute sovereigns; the laws of England are the King's laws; the King has power to dispense with any of his laws as he sees necessity for it; and the King is sole judge of that necessity.' The judgement made Parliament seem irrelevant and it was one to which James clung in the teeth of all opposition.

With no Catholic heir, James was impatient to effect the repeal of the penal laws and the Test Act, so that his Protestant successors would have no alternative but to recognise Catholic equality as a *fait accompli*. Unfortunately, he needed to win Parliament's support for these measures, and, given that the present Parliament was strongly Anglican, this was not going to be forthcoming. Before the second sitting of Parliament in the autumn of 1685, James had unwisely dismissed Halifax, who was far too clever for James's liking. James's tidy mind could not comprehend Halifax's 'trimming', the fact that he was neither a Whig nor a Tory. Besides, the man was an atheist. Halifax went straight into opposition, using his powerful oratorical skills against the abolition of the Test Act. In his accession speech, James had acknowledged the support the Anglican Church had always lent the monarchy, promising that in return he would take care to defend it, but now the interests of the Crown and the Church diverged. The Anglicans were hardly likely to agree to the repeal of an Act that guaranteed their monopoly of power. Only nine months after his accession, James prorogued Parliament in disgust.

James had taken the Anglicans for granted. Once they showed signs of resistance, he viciously turned against them. It was something of a contradiction for a Catholic monarch to be Supreme Governor of the Church of England, but James had no intention of surrendering the position. As the Anglican clergy became increasingly obstreperous, he established the Ecclesiastical Commission to act as a disciplinary body. His old foe, Bishop Compton of London, was the first to be called before it, to be castigated for allowing one of his clergymen to preach anti-papal sermons. James made himself even more obnoxious by breaking the Anglican monopoly at the Universities of Oxford and Cambridge. Most of the university colleges had been founded when England was still Catholic, James reasoned, so that his Catholic subjects should have the same right of access to them as the Anglicans. He was prepared to use his dispensing power to absolve Catholic dons or undergraduates from taking the oaths or attending prayers, so that they could remain at the universities. The continuing resistance of the fellows at Magdalen to James's order to appoint his nominees – the first totally unsuitable, the second still not to the college's liking – as president made James apoplectic with fury:

You have not dealt with me like gentlemen. You have done very uncivilly and undutifully . . . Is this your Church of England loyalty? . . . Go home and show yourselves good members of the Church of England. Get you gone, know I am your king. I will be obeyed and I command you to be gone. Go and admit the Bishop of Oxford head, principal, what do you call it of the college, I mean president of the college. Let them that refuse it look to it; they shall feel the weight of their sovereign's displeasure.

The vice-chancellor of Cambridge and the fellows of Magdalen College, Oxford, were deprived of their college livings for refusing to accept the King's instructions to suspend their statutes in favour of Catholics. Contrary to James's promise at his accession not to encroach on anyone's property, he was doing just that, since college fellowships were a form of freehold. The fact that the King was prepared to deprive his subjects of their properties in pursuit of his Catholic policies led to widespread alarm.

Ironically, James's dealings with the Vatican were no less tactless. He tried to bully Pope Innocent XI with the same arrogance he applied to his own subjects. He wrote repeatedly to demand a cardinal's hat for his adviser, Father Petre, and seemed unwilling to take no for an answer. Petre did not merit such a promotion and Pope Innocent had no intention of offering it to a Jesuit, anyway. James and Mary Beatrice demanded the same for her uncle, Prince Rinaldo D'Este, although he had never taken holy orders. They removed Cardinal Howard, of an ancient English Catholic family, as Protector of England in Rome and appointed Rinaldo in his place. Since he had no sense of humour, James failed to see that sending the inept Earl of Castlemaine, the cuckolded husband of his late brother's mistress, as his ambassador to the papal court made him a laughing stock. Mindful that James's zeal was doing the Catholic cause in England more harm than good, the Pope constantly urged James to modify his policies, but to no avail. When it came to the crunch, the Pope would not be in James's camp.

James alienated all the Crown's best ministers and natural supporters because he could not accept contradiction. Lord Rochester, a most loyal friend and supporter of the monarchy, could not bring himself to convert to Catholicism. He was driven out of office because James refused to employ a minister who did not hold the same views as his own. So much for his much vaunted notion of religious toleration. The King's other erstwhile brother-in-law, Henry Hyde, Earl of Clarendon, was dismissed from office in Ireland and replaced by the Catholic extremist Richard Talbot, Earl of Tyrconnel – 'lying Dick Talbot' in the Anne Hyde affair and married to Sarah Churchill's elder sister Frances – to effect radical changes in favour of the Catholics.

Robert Spencer, Earl of Sunderland, who had no principles other than satisfying his cravings for power and money to maintain his beloved Althorp, was able to slide into James's good graces, despite the fact that he had supported exclusion. He was prepared to do what more principled men such as Rochester would not: advance the cause of Catholicism. He even turned Catholic himself, rather late in the day in June 1688, after flirting with the idea for a long time. The danger of Sunderland was that he told James what he wanted to believe: that his crazy and impracticable ambitions for the Catholics were feasible. It is just possible that he was doing this intentionally, to bring down James's regime.

Under Sunderland's influence, James declined to listen to the more moderate Catholics at court – Lords Powis, Bellasys, Norfolk, Dover and Arundel – who opposed his 'unconstitutional' behaviour and any measure that would rebound on the Catholics. The Catholics were dangerously split. Sunderland allied himself with Father Petre, a man with nothing to lose and the leader of the Catholic extremists, and supported his appointment to the Privy Council. For a Jesuit to sit on the Privy Council was a shock to Anglican sensibilities. Just as it was a shock to see the King of England kneel to the papal nuncio, Count D'Adda, when he was received at Windsor in July 1687. The Duke of Somerset refused to present the nuncio, saying that it was against the law to recognise the Pope's representative. 'Do you not know I am above the law?' James retorted. 'You may be, sire,' the Duke replied, 'but I am not.'

Infuriated by the Anglicans' resistance to his policies, James lost patience with the natural adherents of the Stuart monarchy and turned to the Protestant Dissenters for support. This was a radical, perilous step, bound to alienate the Anglican establishment, whose monopoly of power was threatened. In a neat reversal, the Anglicans would become the state's minority, as religious toleration and equality of opportunity were extended to Catholics and Dissenters alike. It went against all James's long-held prejudices to embrace the Dissenters. These were the querulous Presbyterians who had opposed the Crown before and during the civil wars and the more extremist sects such as the Quakers and Anabaptists that had come into being during the great upheavals of the 1650s. These 'fanatics' were believed by the Anglican elite to pose a threat to Church and state and were identified with social revolution.

The Restoration had presented an opportunity to heal these religious divisions by extending toleration to all shades of Protestantism, as Charles II had intended in his Declaration of Breda of May 1660 when he promised 'liberty to tender consciences'. But the fiercely Anglican Cavalier Parliament that met in 1661 refused to pass up the chance for vengeance. They excluded all Protestant 'Dissenters' from the Established 'Anglican' Church, even the Presbyterians who had once been part of it, subjecting them to the severe disabilities prescribed in the Clarendon Code. Ejected ministers were not allowed to live within five miles of their former parishes. There were harsh penalties for those who attended any unofficial religious service involving more than five people, or for those who allowed their premises to be used for this purpose. Offices in the borough corporations were confined to those who participated in the Anglican Communion, encouraging the hypocrisy of 'occasional conformity'. As a result, the Quakers had been among the most persecuted of Charles II's subjects, hundreds of them dying in typhoid-infested gaols for their beliefs.

But now James was prepared to make common cause with these fellow outcasts to advance the Catholic religion. In a sense, he was precipitating revolution by himself being revolutionary: abandoning the traditional supporters of the Crown and embracing its former opponents. He alarmed a large part of the ruling class, the Tory Anglican landed aristocracy and gentry, by allying with an inferior social group, the largely Whig townspeople. Past attempts to enforce religious uniformity, he rightly if opportunistically asserted, had failed and divided the nation, 'as was sadly experienced by the horrid rebellion in the time of His Majesty's royal father'. Liberty of conscience would breed peace and harmony and, following the example of the Dutch Republic, encourage trade. 'Trade he had much at heart,' claimed the loyal Lord Ailesbury, 'and his topic was liberty of conscience and many hands at work in trade.'

Even James must have realised that he could not afford to ignore the political and economic strength of the City of London with its 100,000 Dissenters. Charles II had revoked the City's charter and purged the corporation of Dissenters. James now reinstated them in a bid for their support. James's Quaker friend William Penn helped draft a Declaration of Indulgence in 1687, offering religious toleration to all the King's subjects. James chose to ignore the fact that his brother had issued two such declarations in 1662 and 1672 and had been obliged to withdraw them when Parliament objected.

No matter how much he might stretch the royal prerogative

to get round the law, James needed Parliament to ratify his policies, if they were to be recognised by his Protestant successors. He needed to 'pack' Parliament to be sure of its support for his radical policies. The Anglican Tory office-holders Charles had nominated in the municipal boroughs were ousted and replaced by Catholics and Dissenters, some of them Whigs, whom James felt he could rely on to return MPs favourable to his policies. He resorted to a process of 'closeting', inviting MPs and office-holders for one-to-one interviews in his closet to sound them out. If they were elected to a new Parliament, would they support the repeal of the penal laws and the Test Act? Or would they vote for candidates pledged to do so? He applied enormous psychological pressure, not hesitating to threaten dismissal if they did not conform to his views.

It was a form of bullying and it was against the spirit of the constitution. A questionnaire was sent out to the lords lieutenant of the counties to discover who would vote for the repeal of the penal laws and the Test Act. Who was prepared to agree to religious toleration for their Catholic and Dissenter neighbours and live with them in harmony, as good Christians ought to do? Many declined to answer the questionnaire or to return the sort of answers the King wanted to hear.

James was so gratified by the loyal addresses of Catholics and Dissenters thanking him for his Declaration of Indulgence that he had them printed in the *London Gazette*. When the first batch of impulsive addresses dried up, pressure was applied to elicit more. But he could not fool himself that there was a rush of converts to Catholicism. Nor were there anything like enough Catholics capable of filling the number of offices he felt should be their share. Anglican clergy reported that their congregations did not become noticeably smaller. Nevertheless, the Anglicans' worst nightmare was an unholy alliance between Catholics and Dissenters, so that a move was now afoot to offer an olive branch to the Dissenters to divorce them from the Catholics. Halifax in his *Letter to a Dissenter* urged them to be suspicious of the Catholic *rapprochement*, warning them: 'you are therefore to be hugged now, only that you may be the better squeezed at another time.' Halifax had predicted that James's policies would fail of their own accord, because they were unrealistic, and it looked very much as if he were right.

Increasingly alarmed at the goings-on in England, fearful that James would alienate all support for the Crown and so jeopardise Mary's inheritance, William of Orange now intervened decisively to rein in the Dissenters. Rather than confronting his father-in-law directly, William instigated *Pensionary Fagel's Letter to James Stewart*, an open letter addressed to the King from the Grand Pensionary of Holland dated 4 November 1687. Thousands of copies were distributed in England. When Mary came to the throne, he promised all her subjects would enjoy 'full liberty of conscience'. They would no longer suffer under the penal laws. The letter implied that there was no need for the Dissenters to compromise themselves now by getting into bed with the Catholics to repeal the Test Act. At the same time, William and Mary reassured the Anglicans that they would never agree to the repeal of the Test Act, which they felt guaranteed the supremacy of the Church of England.

The question that dominated the spring of 1688, following the announcement of the Queen's pregnancy, was whether the prospect of a Catholic successor would make James's subjects more obedient, or drive them to outright rebellion? It can be argued that the prospect of a son made James even more fanatical. Was this not God's miracle, a sign that God approved his good work in the cause of the true religion? It meant that no one could afford to wait upon events any longer. Everything took on a new urgency. Decisions had to be made whether or not to interpose, to put a stop to James's crazed policies once and for all.

The reception to the news of the Queen's pregnancy increased James's suspicion of his own subjects and he demanded the return of the English and Scottish regiments serving in the

Dutch Republic to boost his army. His relations with William had been disintegrating for some time and they took a turn for the worse when William took refuge behind the States-General's refusal to release the regiments. Those officers who wished to do so could return to England, but the rest must remain. At the same time, James was demanding the forcible return of English exiles who had taken refuge in Holland, men such as Gilbert Burnet, who were busy preparing propaganda to be unleashed against him. Again, the Dutch refused to comply. In the face of William's defiance, James could only expostulate in impotent fury that he was head of the family and he would be obeyed.

Driven to ever more desperate measures, James turned to the recalcitrant Anglican Church and, perhaps inadvertently, declared outright war when, in April 1688, he ordered the clergy to read his second Declaration of Indulgence from the pulpit at Sunday services. In an age before the proliferation of newspapers, it was quite normal to use the pulpit to disseminate news, but in this instance it seemed as if the Anglican Church was being asked to preside over its own destruction. Sancroft, Archbishop of Canterbury, was one of seven leading churchmen to draw up a petition to the King. It protested against the order, questioning the validity of the dispensing power. Sancroft was not able to present the petition in person, because he was already under royal displeasure and forbidden the court. Compton, too, would have been a signatory if James had not already suspended him, but it is safe to assume that such a dogged opponent of James was offering advice somewhere in the background. Six of the seven signatories – Bishops Ken of Bath and Wells, White of Peterborough, Turner of Ely, Lake of Chichester, Lloyd of St Asaph and Trelawney of Bristol – were received in audience by the King and presented the petition.

Ever since the Restoration, the Anglican clergy had been so vociferous in their support of the royal prerogative and so wedded to the doctrine of passive obedience, that James was understandably taken aback when he read the petition. How dare the Anglican clergy defy him and question his dispensing power? James was incandescent with rage. 'This is a standard of rebellion,' he shouted. 'Is that what I have deserved who have supported the Church of England and will support it? I did not expect this from you . . . I will be obeyed in publishing my declaration . . . God hath given me the dispensing power and I will maintain it.' They were dismissed from his sight. A copy of the bishops' petition was published – it has never been ascertained who gave this secret document to the printer, but it is a fair guess that Compton had something to do with it – and they found themselves arraigned on a charge of seditious libel. All seven, the Archbishop of Canterbury among them, were sent to the Tower to await trial, their passage down the river being witnessed by thousands along the banks, some of them plunging into the water to beg their blessing.

When his longed-for son and Catholic heir the Prince of Wales was born on 10 June 1688, James might have effected a public relations coup by using his well-worn royal prerogative to extend a pardon to the bishops. It does not seem to have occurred to him to do so. Where was the spirit of reconciliation he never tired of preaching to others? An increasingly nervous Sunderland urged him to drop the case against the bishops. Even Lord Chancellor Jeffreys warned against the dangers of bringing the bishops to trial. But James was determined not to make his father's mistake. He would not yield, because he believed to do so was to show weakness before his enemies. He would crush the Anglican opposition once and for all.

The hearing went badly for the Crown. Lord Sunderland's appearance invited cries of 'Papist dog!' and people hissed as the case for the prosecution was made. Two of the judges were bold enough to condemn the dispensing power. 'If this be once allowed of, there will need no Parliament; all the legislature will be in the King,' Justice Powell warned. Given such a lead from the bench, the jury needed little encouragement to find the bishops not guilty, which they did on 30 June after deliberating about the verdict until the early hours of the morning. Lord Halifax, who was among a conspicuous presence of peers in the courtroom, led the cheering at the acquittal. It was echoed the next day by James's army encamped on Hounslow Heath. Even after the verdict, James determined to pursue and punish any of the clergy who had failed to read his declaration from the pulpit.

London went mad with joy and the news quickly spread to the provinces. After dark, in defiance of the Catholic King's ban on such anti-papist celebrations, bonfires were lit all over town. An effigy of the Pope was burned right outside St James's Palace. There had been a noticeable reluctance to light bonfires to celebrate the birth of the Prince of Wales, but now in a West Country still smarting from the savage reprisals following Monmouth's rebellion, they burned the child in effigy. Church bells rang and candles burned in every window of the capital.

That same night, seven men met at Lord Shrewsbury's house to draft a letter. There were three Whigs with grievances. William Cavendish, Earl of Devonshire, had been heavily fined for fighting at court. Edward Russell was the cousin of the famous Whig martyr who had been executed for participation in the Rye House Plot. Charles Talbot, Earl of Shrewsbury, had been denied office after converting to the Church of England from Catholicism in 1679. Of the Tories, Thomas Osborne, Earl of Danby, the brilliant minister who had arranged William and Mary's marriage as part of his pro-Dutch policy, had been living in semi-retirement since his release from the Tower. Richard Lumley, who likewise had converted from Catholicism in 1679, had become one of James's most outspoken critics. Only one churchman, James's old foe, Henry Compton, Bishop of London, subscribed to the letter.

The seventh subscriber, James's erstwhile *bête noire*, Henry Sidney, was the brother of the executed republican Algernon Sidney, and one of William's most ardent admirers. He was the driving force behind the scheme, the liaison between William and the conspirators. As he confided to William in a separate letter, these seven were perhaps not the most prominent men in the kingdom, but the best he could persuade to go so far. Lords Halifax and Nottingham had been party to the discussions, but hesitated to make the final commitment. The letter, after all, was treasonable, and the seven subscribers – later known as 'the immortal seven' – had taken the precaution of signing themselves by code-numbers only.

Next morning the sacked Admiral Arthur Herbert took ship for Holland, disguised as a common seaman. The letter was carefully concealed inside his clothes. One of the most important documents in English history, it did not offer William of Orange the crown. It merely invited him to come to restore English liberties and the rule of law.

# 5
## Prince William of Orange

*'You will all find the Prince of Orange a worse man than Cromwell'*
— James II

The birth chamber was entirely hung with black mourning, the only light coming from the guttering candles. As he was born a little prematurely, on 4 November 1650, he shared a birthday with his mother, Mary, the Princess Royal, who turned nineteen that day. The young woman was stunned with grief and shock. Only eight days previously, the husband she loved, Prince William II of Orange, had died of smallpox. Now she would be alone in a country she hated and among a people she despised. But the dead Prince's posthumous son, yet to be named, would be the hope of his house and of the Dutch people.

The naming of the young Prince of Orange was the occasion for one of many disagreements between his mother, the Princess Royal, and her mother-in-law, the Dowager Princess of Orange. The Princess Royal wanted to call her child Charles, after her ill-fated father, Charles I, who had been executed in January 1649. His grandmother wanted the boy to carry the Orange family names and he was duly christened William Henry. His spoilt Stuart mother, so used to getting her own way, refused to attend the ceremony, which took place at the Grote Kerk in The Hague on a freezing day towards the end of January 1651.

The House of Orange-Nassau was German by origin. William was brought up hearing of the heroism of his great-grandfather, William the Silent, who had led the Dutch Protestants in their revolt against Spanish rule in the sixteenth century. The independence of the Netherlands' seven northern provinces – Holland, Gelderland, Zeeland, Overijssel, Utrecht, Friesland and Groningen – which now made up the United Provinces or Dutch Republic, was finally recognised in the Treaty of Westphalia, which ended the disastrous Thirty Years' War of religion, only two years before William's birth.

William's family took its title from the tiny principality of Orange in the south of France, which had come to it through the marriage of William the Silent to Louise de Coligny, daughter of the Protestant French admiral. They also owned estates in the United Provinces, the Spanish Netherlands, Luxembourg, the German states and Franche-Comté. The House of Orange held a position of honour in the Dutch Republic. Traditionally, the Prince held the office of Stadholder, Chief Magistrate of the Republic, as well as the military offices of captain-general and admiral-general.

There was a great deal of jealousy, however, on the part of the wealthy oligarchs, particularly those of the richest and most powerful city of Amsterdam in the province of Holland, of these princely privileges. The House of Orange and the city of Amsterdam were more often than not in conflict over the Republic's policy, particularly regarding foreign affairs. Shortly before William's birth, his father had alienated the oligarchs still further when he arrested and briefly imprisoned Jacob de Witt and some of his faction. The Loevesteiners, as they came to be called, snatched their opportunity during William's minority to put an end to the House of Orange's power.

The fortunes of William's mother's family, the Stuarts, were at an exceedingly low ebb at the time of his birth. The marriage of Princess Mary, a stiff little girl with large dark eyes, and Prince William II of Orange had taken place in London in early 1642. Five years older than his bride, William had the good looks, personality, education and accomplishments to appeal to a princess brought up in the elegant court of Charles I. Indeed, he got on famously with his new brothers-in-law,

Charles and James. But her mother, Queen Henrietta Maria, was determined to fill her daughter's mind with her own prejudices. As a French Catholic Bourbon princess, the daughter of Henry IV and Marie de Medici, she despised the Dutch for their Calvinism, their republicanism and their preoccupation with trade and commerce. It must have come as a blow to her pride to leave the English crown jewels in pawn to the merchants of Amsterdam when she left her daughter with the Orange family a few months later. England was on the brink of civil war and the cash was desperately needed to buy arms for the royalist cause.

As Mary's mother had convinced her she was marrying beneath her, she did not hesitate to treat her new mother-in-law with contempt. Amalia von Solms-Braunfels was the daughter of a minor German prince, and Princess Mary was at pains to remind her, frequently, that she had once been a mere maid of honour to her aunt, Elizabeth, Queen of Bohemia. When Amalia's husband, Prince Frederick Henry, insisted that his son's eleven-year-old bride be treated, even by her parents-in-law, with all the honours due to a royal princess, Amalia must have been irritated beyond belief. So aware was Mary of her royal rank that when the regents came to congratulate her on the birth of her son and present her with a golden casket containing a letter of credit for 5,000 guilders, she would not even deign to touch it lest she contaminate herself. They had to put it down before withdrawing from her cold presence.

Even Mary's relatives, particularly Sophie, the second youngest of the Queen of Bohemia's thirteen children, found their cousin's proud haughtiness and insistence on always being addressed as Princess Royal a cause for amusement. Sophie derived some mischievous satisfaction, therefore, when she brought her brother's child, Liselotte – Elisabeth Charlotte of the Palatinate – for a visit to the Princess's court. The child had been warned to be on her best behaviour and was playing happily with Prince William, two years her senior, when she suddenly exclaimed, 'Who is the lady with the furious nose?' The adults froze. William laughingly told the little girl that the lady was his mother, the Princess Royal, who was suffering from a heavy cold. In disgrace, Liselotte was tactfully removed – by Anne Hyde, the Princess's maid of honour – and spent the rest of the afternoon rolling about with William on a Turkey carpet in the adjoining room.

In her lonely isolation after her husband's death, Mary found a sympathetic companion in her Aunt Elizabeth, known as the Winter Queen since her tenure as Queen in Bohemia had been that short. For many years the elder sister of Charles I had lived in penurious exile in The Hague. Never one to show much patience to any of her own large brood, Elizabeth was especially fond of her great-nephew, Prince William. He was a quiet, serious and solitary child. Elizabeth reported his attendance at an official event when he was only four years old: 'My little nephue was at the super and satt verie still all the time: those States that were there were verie much taken with him.'

The Princess Royal adored her brothers and was devoted to their interests. Although she was often absent, spending time with her mother in Paris and her brother Charles in his various refuges, it did not mean that she did not love her small son or neglected him. Charles, too, was fond of his nephew, so much so that Mary was jealous: 'You are so partially kind to him,' she wrote to her brother, 'that I fear at last my desiring your kindness to him will turn to jealousy and he may take some from me. I must assure you, that I shall obey all your commands except of loving him (though he is my only child) above all things in the world as long as you are in it.'

Mary saw Stuart and Orange fortunes as one. If her brother Charles were restored to the throne, she was sure the fortunes of the House of Orange would improve. In 1653, however, Johann de Witt, a staunch republican, had come to power as Grand Pensionary of Holland – the chief officer in the most dominant state of the Dutch Republic. He was strongly opposed to the House of Orange and, after the defeat of the Dutch in the first Anglo-Dutch war, agreed to Cromwell's demand that the Prince of Orange and his descendants would be for ever excluded from office. When the Act of Seclusion was passed by the States-General, there was rioting in the streets, as the people generally loved their Prince of Orange. Cheers of loyalty greeted the small boy every time he was lifted up at the window of the Binnenhof so that the crowd could see him.

The question of William's guardianship during his minority had been the occasion for another argument between Mary and her mother-in-law. Eventually it was decided that it would be shared between Mary, who had a half share, his grandmother Amalia and his uncle by marriage, the Elector of Brandenburg. His grandmother's secretary, Sir Constantyn Huygens, drew up a comprehensive plan for the education of a prince designed to be a patriot and a strong Calvinist. He was to learn history, geography, Latin, French, Dutch (in his mother's household only English was spoken), English and mathematics and take plenty of outdoor exercise to improve his weak constitution. His religious mentor, Pastor Trigland, instilled in the Prince an ardent belief in the Calvinist doctrine of predestination: he was to grow up convinced that he had some great destiny to fulfil. There is a story that one of William's tutors described the British Isles as 'a little world in themselves'. William was intrigued, saying, 'I wish I had a little world like this.' 'What would you do with it, Highness?' his tutor asked. 'Just give it to me,' William replied, 'and I will show you.'

When he was nine, William acquired a governor, Frederick van Nassau, Heer van Zuylestein, a bastard son of his grandfather Frederick Henry, and was sent to the university town of Leiden for further studies. In May 1660 he was brought back to The Hague to join the celebrations for his Uncle Charles's restoration. Having treated him as an embarrassment and a nuisance during his exile, the States-General could not now do enough for the new ruler of England. The young Prince William sat on his uncle, James, Duke of York's knee when the party of coaches made their triumphal entry into The Hague and at the dinner given by the States-General William sat beside his other uncle, Henry, Duke of Gloucester, whom he very much resembled. English visitors who had come to The Hague to collect their King took the opportunity to visit his young nephew, Pepys noting he was 'a very prettie boy', that his entourage was small 'for a prince, but yet handsome, and his tutor, a fine man'.

With the Stuart restoration, there were some hopes that William might, after all, regain the offices of his forebears. The Act of Seclusion was repealed, but Johann de Witt refused to make any promises about the Stadholdership. The boy was only nine, after all, and there was no knowing how he would turn out. For Mary, who had once told her brother that 'the greatest punishment of the world would be to live all my life here', the Restoration meant her longed-for return to her brother's court. William took his leave of her on 29 September 1660. Before she left, she had written anxiously to the States-General imploring them to have a care for her son, 'the being who is dearest to us in the world, and of his training in princely virtues and exercises'. Whether she meant to return or not, or had some premonition, is a moot point. That Christmas Eve, she died of smallpox, leaving ten-year-old William an orphan.

---

Emotional disturbance always affected William's delicate health and he was very ill following the news of his mother's death. By April 1661 he was recovering and his grandmother Amalia decided to send him to Cleves to convalesce in the care of his other guardian, the Elector of Brandenburg. Before he left The Hague, the Winter Queen measured his height. As she reported to her son: 'I finde both hie and Lisslotte verie much grown. My little nephue is verie inquisitive of her, he liked her verie well but she coulde not abide him. He mends strangelie and grows verie strong, you cannot imagin the witt that he has, it is not a witt of childe who is suffisant, but of a man, that doth not pretend to it, he is a verie extraordinarie childe and verie good natured.'

The adults who had observed Liselotte and William playing happily together as children were still entertaining ideas of a marriage between them. These hopes came to nothing when Liselotte's father made a greater match for her in 1672 with the widowed brother of the French King, Philippe, Duke of Orléans, the spiteful homosexual who had made his first wife, Charles II's sister Minette, so unhappy. Fortunately, Liselotte had a sharp wit and a good sense of humour.

At Cleves William went on a wild boar hunt and witnessed his first kill. Hunting was to remain a life-long passion. He also began to save up his pocket money to buy paintings. When he was fourteen, a new page named Hans Willem Bentinck entered his household. Bentinck had experienced the opposite of William's lonely childhood in a large family of brothers and sisters. He shared the Prince's tastes for art and the hunt. He was also fluent in French and William was to use him in many delicate diplomatic negotiations in the future. Bentinck became William's dearest friend for life, not hesitating to risk his own life when William, at twenty-four, contracted smallpox. Contemporaries believed that if a healthy person shared the bed of a smallpox victim, that person would draw off some of the disease, giving the sufferer a chance of recovery. William recalled that 'during sixteen days and nights I never once called out but he answered me.'

Both men survived the disease, although it weakened William's already delicate constitution. In the company of close friends such as Bentinck and in his correspondence with them – 'I am so much your friend that I feel all that happens to you as if it had happened to myself,' he wrote to Bentinck in 1665 to console him on the death of his father – William revealed a warmth and generosity that would have amazed those who found his manner cold and restrained.

When he was sixteen, William became a 'child of state'. On her deathbed, his mother had begged Charles II to look after her son, but he quickly sloughed off this responsibility. As England declared war on the Dutch Republic in 1665, it was impractical, anyway. William was furious when Johann de Witt removed the last vestiges of English influence by dismissing William's entire household, including his governor and friend, Frederick Zuylestein. Only Bentinck remained. But William was far too wise and controlled to protest for long. He set out to learn everything he could of Dutch politics from this enemy of his house, de Witt. Soon the two were on such good terms they were tennis partners. An observer remarked, 'They had better take care that the State does not become the Child of William.'

Towards the end of the war with England in 1667, Louis XIV of France staged a massive invasion of the Spanish Netherlands, claiming that he was taking towns in lieu of his wife Maria Theresa's dowry, which had not been paid. This new French aggression was alarming for the Dutch, since the Spanish Netherlands formed a barrier between them and their French neighbour. It was particularly worrying for de Witt and the Amsterdam faction, whose whole foreign policy was based on a French alliance and hostility to England. Clearly, the Franco-Dutch alliance was outmoded. But could the Dutch rely on their former foe, the English, instead? Under the auspices of Sir William Temple, who had been appointed ambassador to the States-General, a new Triple Alliance was formed between England, the United Provinces and Sweden. It was just the sort of policy that appealed to William, who felt strongly that his own and his mother's country should be allies. Sir William Temple was impressed with him:

I find him in earnest a most extreme hopeful Prince, and to speak more plainly something much better than I expected and a young man of more parts than ordinary, and of the better sort, that is, not lying in that kind of wit which is neither of use to one's self nor to anyone else, but in good plain sense, with show of application if he had business that deserved it, and that with extreme good agreeable humour and dispositions, and thus far of his way without any vice. Besides being sleepy always by ten o'clock at night, and loving hunting as much as he hates swearing, and preferring cock ale before any sort of wine ... His person, I think you know, is very good, and has much of the Princess (his mother) in it: and never any body raved so much after England, as well the language as all else that belongs to it.

In November 1670 William might have had cause to change his rosy-hued view of England when he paid his first visit to his uncle's court at Whitehall. Charles II went out of his way to make his nephew welcome, but William and his entourage were appalled at the licentiousness of the court, the venality of the courtiers, their gambling for ludicrously high stakes, drinking, fighting and swearing. After the cleanliness of Holland and the pride the Dutch took in their homes, Whitehall Palace looked squalid, shabby and filthy. The fastidious Dutch would have found the casual way in which Englishmen relieved themselves in any convenient corner of the palace and in which the King's spaniels were allowed to climb on to the dinner table and noisily chew the remains of hares, partridges and chickens highly offensive. The Dutch Prince became the victim of more cynical, sophisticated courtiers when George Villiers, Duke of Buckingham, invited him to attend a supper. The claret-loving English plied him with wine and he became so drunk he had to be restrained from breaking into the apartments of the maids of honour.

Even worse, Charles was playing a devious double game with his young nephew. Unknown to his Dutch allies and despite the Triple Alliance, Charles had already done a deal

with France by signing the Treaty of Dover with its iniqui-
tous secret clause. All his instincts were for a French alliance
and the subsidies it promised meant that he need not rely so
much on his troublesome Parliament. He had never liked the
Dutch, harbouring resentment of their treatment of him in
exile, wary of their republicanism and jealous of their commercial success.

Only with great difficulty and over time did Charles come
to understand that William was a Dutch patriot. Far from
wanting the crown that his uncle, with Louis XIV's help, was
prepared to bully a defeated Dutch nation into giving him,
William wanted only to serve his country. If the interests of
his mother's family and his country diverged, then so be it.
William would unhesitatingly choose his country. The French
ambassador in London, Colbert de Croissy, reported to Louis
that 'the King of England is much satisfied with the parts
of the Prince of Orange. But he finds him so passionate a
Dutchman and Protestant, that even although Your Majesty
had not disapproved of his trusting him with any part of the
secret, those two reasons would have hindered him.' When
William did discover his uncle's betrayal, he knew he would
never be able to trust him again.

Beyond the sphere of the rapacious and immoral court,
William made a good impression. He visited Parliament and
dined as the guest of the City of London at the Guildhall,
where his sober demeanour and dress contrasted favourably
with the extravagantly attired, dissipated courtiers the citizens
were used to. He had the opportunity to become acquainted
with leading politicians, such as Lord Halifax, Sir Thomas
Osborne – who as Earl of Danby would be so instrumental
in arranging his marriage with Mary – and Henry Bennet, Earl
of Arlington.

Arlington made the first hint that with the Queen being
childless, the Duke of York's children sickly and his duchess
grossly corpulent and unlikely to live long, William had a
good chance of some day inheriting the throne. William paid

a courtesy call on the ailing Anne Hyde, Duchess of York, his mother's former maid of honour, but it is not known if he met the eight-year-old Mary at this time. His uncles generously plied him with lavish parting gifts, but the vast debts the Stuarts owed the House of Orange from their years in exile, the recovery of which was one of the objects of the visit, remained largely unpaid.

---

The French launched their devastating attack on the Dutch Republic in 1672, which became known as the disaster year. Suspicions had only gradually been aroused of the secret alliance between France and England that facilitated this. The architect of the Triple Alliance, Sir William Temple, realised that he had been deceived, that his patron Lord Arlington had been negotiating with the French behind his back. He was recalled and the hostile Sir George Downing replaced him as English ambassador to the States-General. The English wanted to provoke an incident that would justify a declaration of war and Downing arrived with a long list of grievances.

William had hoped that the English would honour their treaty with the Dutch and not go to war. In the summer of 1671 he was writing to his good friend Lord Ossory at the English court: 'All the talk here is of the war and the great preparations that the King of France is making to attack us. I hope that the King will not abandon us, and that he stands by the treaties that he made with the States. It's in his own interests not to see us destroyed.' By the end of the year, hopes were fading. 'I beg you to tell me if you are going to be our friends or not,' he wrote. 'Everyone doubts it more and more.' Secretly, and without de Witt's knowledge, William entrusted Sir Gabriel Silvius, a former secretary of his mother's, to carry a message to his uncle in a desperate attempt to prevent war. 'If His Majesty would kindly tell me what he desires, I shall do my best to procure it,' he offered, 'in spite of Pensionary De Witt and his Cabale.' Charles did not deign to respond.

Let down by the failure of de Witt and the regents' diplomacy and betrayed by their supposed ally, England, the Dutch turned to the Prince of Orange as their only hope in the emergency. The States-General offered him the traditional offices of captain- and admiral-general, although only for a single campaign, and he hurriedly ordered the immediate conscription of every able-bodied man between eighteen and sixty. The failure of the de Witt government on the diplomatic front was matched by the dire state of the army. Louis XIV left Paris at the head of an army of 120,000 superbly trained men under the command of such seasoned commanders as Turenne, Condé and Luxembourg, bent on the destruction of 'a young Prince in poor health, who had seen neither siege nor combat, and about 25,000 wretched troops'. As the French army swallowed province after province, William and his men fell back behind Holland's own defences, the ring of sluices that as a last resort could be opened to flood the countryside in the path of the invader. Unfortunately, it had been an unusually dry summer and the advancing French complained that they were only receiving a '*demi-bain*'. They failed, however, to recognise the importance of the town of Muerden, which controlled the sluices, and did not take it.

As the crisis deepened, the twenty-one-year-old Prince was proclaimed Stadholder and captain- and admiral-general for life. Two weeks later, the French presented their peace terms. They included an enormous indemnity of 16 million guilders, the lands of Brabant and Limburg, part of Gelderland, Maastricht, and a guarantee of equality for Dutch Catholics, who represented about one-third of the population. As a final insult, an annual embassy was to be sent to Louis XIV to present him with a medal expressing Dutch gratitude for his forbearance in returning their country to the States. Considering the English had only distinguished themselves in the war by the defeat of their navy under the Duke of York at Sole Bay, their terms were almost equally harsh.

Showing how little he understood his nephew, Charles's

plan was to set him up as a puppet king, while he and Louis helped themselves to the spoils of the Republic. He sent Buckingham and Arlington to negotiate with William. They were exasperated by his stubbornness, dismissing his argument that it was not in England's interest to continue as the ally of France. Losing his temper, Buckingham said, 'It is lost. Do you not see your country is lost?' 'It is indeed in great danger,' William replied, 'but there is a sure way never to see it lost, and that is to die in the last ditch.'

Even though he had been Stadholder a mere two weeks, William convinced the States-General not to accept the dishonourable peace terms. Someone had to take the rap for the war and de Witt, whose policy of appeasement and poor management had been responsible, tendered his resignation. A barber-surgeon, William Tichelaar, had accused de Witt's brother, Cornelius, a vindictive enemy of the Prince of Orange, of conspiring to murder him. He had been arrested and tortured, but refused to confess his guilt. Johann now went to visit his brother at the prison of Gevangenpoort, where he spent some time reading the Bible to the broken man. A large hostile crowd gathered, then broke into the building and dragged the de Witts outside. In the street the people unleashed their anger and tore the brothers to pieces. William had had no cause to love the de Witts, but his failure to punish the murderers put a stain on his reputation. Caspar Fagel, a republican who would become a friend and admirer of William, now became Grand Pensionary of Holland.

By the autumn of 1672, the French were slightly less gung-ho. It rained unremittingly, and the rains turned Holland into an impenetrable bastion. 'All the roads are impassable,' Luxembourg complained, 'and nobody would dream of moving about unless he'd turned into a duck.' The Prince and his troops attacked the French remorselessly, but without any conspicuous success. A winter frost turning the floodwaters to ice enabled the French literally to skate into Holland. 'Go, my children, plunder, murder, destroy and if it be possible to commit yet greater cruelties, be not negligent therein,' Luxembourg urged. 'Let me see that I am not deceived in my choice of the flower of the King's troops.' In Amsterdam no one dared sleep and in The Hague trees were chopped down and used as barricades. A sudden thaw saved them. Luxembourg beat a hasty retreat, but not hasty enough. Many of his troops were drowned, while he himself caught a heavy cold.

William was a brilliant leader of men, courageous and ever to the fore in battle, an indefatigable campaigner who shared all the hardships of his troops, but he had had no military training. He had the sense to appoint the veteran Count Waldeck as his second-in-command. William's genius was as a diplomat rather than a military man. The best hope for the beleaguered Dutch was to weave a series of alliances against the French. In the course of 1673 William's patience, persistence and skill at the negotiating table gained Spain, the Habsburg Empire and Lorraine as allies. '*La guerre de Hollande est finie; la guerre Européenne commence*,' was the general verdict. The new alliance quickly took Bonn from the French. The tide of the war was slowly turning. Orders were sent from Paris for the French army to evacuate the United Provinces. William at only twenty-four was nominated generalissimo of the European Coalition against France.

King Charles II's selfish, misguided foreign policy had left him out in the cold. In England he and the Duke of York were facing mounting criticism. The Dutch war was unpopular and the alliance with Catholic France was regarded with growing suspicion. In the autumn of 1673 Parliament did vote subsidies to continue the war, but on the back of them forced through the Test Act. As it excluded Catholics from office, it was a thinly disguised attack on the Duke of York, whose conversion to Catholicism was now widely suspected. A few months later, despite French bribes of wine and money to selected MPs, the supply of money for the war dried up. In February 1674 the English signed the Peace of Westminster with the Dutch, in which Charles had to accept far more ignominious terms than he would have had had he presented William with fair peace terms eighteen months earlier. He must have been regretting the loss of the huge war indemnity William had been offering on that occasion.

This was not a signal for peace with France. William found the French occupation of the barrier towns of the southern Netherlands unacceptable. He was determined to continue the war until he received satisfaction on this point. Charles might have hoped to win William over and detach him from his allies by sending Lord Arlington – a bad choice, as William resented the arrogance with which he had been treated by him on the previous occasion – and William's friend Lord Ossory for talks. Ossory was to sound out the possibility of a marriage between William and his cousin, Lady Mary of York, but not actually to offer her hand.

Privately, William thought that Mary at twelve was too young and the time was not right. 'I cannot leave the battlefield nor believe that it would be agreeable for a lady to be where the battlefield is,' he told Ossory. The English King had indicated the prestige that a marriage with Mary would bring William in the courts of Europe, but William was not so sure. In many European courts, for instance, a marriage between a royal personage and a commoner, such as that between the Duke of York and Anne Hyde, would be regarded as morganatic. The children would not have the same rights of inheritance as children of parents of equal rank. If this was so, William had a stronger claim to the English crown than the Ladies Mary and Anne of York, through his mother, the eldest daughter of Charles I, who would have been next in line after her brothers Charles, James and the now dead Henry.

It was difficult for European royalty to comprehend that this was not the case in England, where the concept of morganatic marriage did not exist. Marriage was legal or it was not. The children of any marriage were legitimate with full rights of inheritance. Charles and James were disappointed that Arlington's attempts to mediate a peace failed, but they were furious that Ossory seemed to have exceeded his brief in the marriage discussions and at what they chose to regard as a snub to Lady Mary.

Relations between England and the Dutch Republic were made a little easier by the return to The Hague of Sir William Temple as ambassador, a sure sign that the English wanted to restore good relations. William dined frequently with Sir William and his wife, the former Dorothy Osborne, who was a gracious hostess. It was to Sir William that the Prince eventually turned when he was ready to discuss his thoughts on marriage, and, in particular, a marriage to Lady Mary. Walking in the gardens at Honselaersdijck in April 1676, William told Temple what he was looking for in a wife and wondered if Mary had these qualities. Temple told him that he was pleased to hear that he was considering an English match, 'that it was a great step to be nearer the crown, and in all appearance the next'. Lady Temple was about to travel to England. She would make further enquiries about the Lady Mary's character and carry two letters from William to the King and the Duke of York asking them to consider the match and for permission to visit at the end of the next military campaign.

In the autumn of 1677 William was invited to meet the King and the Duke at Newmarket. Charles had a small, ramshackle palace in Newmarket and the whole court converged on the little town for the races, hawking, cockfighting and improvised theatrical performances. The casual atmosphere at Newmarket gave Charles the opportunity to mix freely with the lowest ranks of his subjects, keeping him in touch with popular opinion in much the same way as his patronage of playhouses and taverns did in London.

Coaches had been sent to collect the Prince, who, according to Temple, 'like a hasty lover, came post from Harwich to Newmarket'. He was in such a hurry that he did not stop in Norwich for the reception that the town had prepared for him. Both Temple and Charles's chief minister, Lord Danby, were very much in favour of the match, but worried that it might founder on the King's and the Duke's insistence that William's peace terms with France must be concluded first. William was adamant. The marriage negotiations must take precedence. He would not have it said that he had sold his allies for a wife. He also surprised his uncles by his insistence on seeing the young lady first.

Back at Whitehall, William was genuinely pleased with his prospective bride, but he despaired that he was getting nowhere with his uncles on the question of the peace terms. One evening Temple found him 'in the worst humour I ever saw him'. William told him 'he regretted he had ever come into England and resolved that he would stay but two days longer, and then be gone, if the King continued in his mind of treating upon the peace before he was married.' He was clearly out of patience with his English relatives. 'It was for the King to choose how they should live henceforth,' he told Temple, 'either as the greatest friends or the greatest enemies.'

Temple hastened to speak to Charles in the morning, dreading another breach with the Dutch. To Temple's surprise, Charles immediately changed tack. He had probably been resolved on the marriage all along and judged it was not worth jeopardising it for the sake of the peace negotiations. He decided to trust William to pursue European peace – it was settled at Nijmegen in 1678 – even though he had already secured his English bride. 'I never yet was deceived in judging of a man's honesty by his looks,' he told Temple, 'and if I am not deceived in the Prince's face, he is the honestest man in the world, and I will trust him, and he shall have his wife, and you shall go immediately and tell my brother so, and that is a thing I am resolved on.'

Charles hoped to defuse opposition to his pro-French policy by the marriage of the heiress-presumptive to the Protestant Dutch Prince. It also appealed to his sense of humour to check his troublesome, Catholic brother James by imposing an ambitious, Calvinist son-in-law on him. When William and his wife Mary left Whitehall a few weeks later, William took care to write to Danby to thank him for all his work in arranging the marriage. They both hoped it would lead to a sturdy, continuing alliance between England and the Dutch Republic in William's crusade against French aggression. In fact, Louis XIV was so appalled by the marriage and by the threat of Danby's Dutch alliance that he was instrumental in the minister's disgrace and impeachment. Within the year, Charles was back in Louis's camp. If the marriage did not bring England into William's web of European alliances against the French, as he had hoped, it had given him a stake in the English crown. From now on, he needed to forge alliances with English politicians, and he was personally concerned with the fate of the monarchy.

———————

In the exclusion crisis provoked by the Duke of York's Catholicism the Earl of Shaftesbury and the Country Party, otherwise known as the Whigs, sought to advance the pretensions of the King's eldest son, the Duke of Monmouth, to the throne. They ignored or denied the fact that Monmouth was illegitimate. For all his good looks, charm and popularity, Monmouth was weak and shallow, easily manipulated by more ruthless men. Ultimately, the Tories and all right-thinking Englishmen would never agree to a bastard inheriting the crown, but what were the alternatives? The Earls of Sunderland and Halifax decided to offset Whig ambitions by bringing the Prince of Orange into prominence. To this end, they persuaded the King to despatch Henry Sidney as envoy to The Hague.

William immediately liked the handsome, urbane Sidney, inviting him to hunt and to dine with him often. This was the same Sidney who had once been such an admirer of Princess Mary's mother, the first Duchess of York, and had been banished from court by James for daring to make advances to his wife. Sidney was well connected. His sister Dorothy, Dowager Countess of Sunderland – whom as a beautiful young woman before the civil war the poet Edmund Waller had immortalised

as his Saccharissa – was the mother of Robert Spencer, second
Earl of Sunderland, one of the young 'chits' whom Charles
had now brought in as his advisers. Robert's wife Anne took
as close an interest in court politics as did her mother-in-law
and she was a close friend and correspondent of 'Beau' Sidney.
Dorothy's daughter Doll had married George Savile, Earl –
later Marquis – of Halifax, one of the cleverest politicians of
his time. As the exclusion crisis gathered momentum, Henry
Sidney kept William apprised of it. He begged William to go
to England, saying 'the monarchy was absolutely lost unless
he recovered it.'

Sunderland used his influence in the Commons to add a
clause to the Exclusion Bill to the effect that on the King's
death the crown should pass over James as if he were dead
to his elder daughter the Princess Mary. William told Sidney
that 'he thinks excluding the Duke an injustice, and he would
not advise the King to do it for all the world.' He was loath to
interfere, however, or to come to England without the King's
express permission. Frustrated by William's understandable
reluctance to let them use him in their struggle against the
Whigs, Anne, Countess of Sunderland wrote to Sidney in the
strongest terms:

Every moment shows us plainly that what you were desired to
press is more necessary, and that, if the Prince will not come, he
must never think of anything here, and he may as reasonably on
a point of conscience resolve to refuse any right that belongs to
him; for he can no more think himself accessory to this exclusion
of the Duke nor charge himself with it than I can. The thing is
already done, and his part is only to come, and prevent the
confusion which otherwise we must of necessity fall into, and,
to strengthen you with arguments, I must not omit letting you
know one thing, that the City is resolved, the moment the Bill
has passed the House of Commons, to come down and petition
the King; when it is judged what must follow! If there be nothing
to fix on, 'tis certain the Duke of Monmouth must be the King;

and if the Prince thinks it not worth going over a threshold for a kingdom, I know not why he should expect anybody should for him. The case is much changed since you were here; and a day's loss of his being here, for aught I know, may make it for ever useless to the Prince; therefore as he pleases.

William was more cautiously writing to Sir Lionel Jenkins: 'I am obliged to you for continuing to inform me of what passes in England, but I am vexed to learn with what animosity they proceed against the Duke. God bless him! And grant that the King and his Parliament may agree, without which I foresee infallibly an imminent danger for the King, the royal family, and the greatest part of Europe.'

Halifax persuaded the Lords to defeat the Bill, but presented an alternative idea of imposing limitations on a Catholic monarch. Anne Sunderland dashed off another letter to Sidney: 'Lord Halifax has undone all, and now the Prince may do as he pleases; for I believe his game has been, by his prudence and whatever you'll call it, lost – and he'll wish too late his conscience had not been so tender; but all this keep to yourself till you hear again.'

When William heard about the limitations' proposal, he was extremely worried, writing to Sir Lionel Jenkins:

I must own to you that I was much surprised to learn of mitigations of the royal authority being spoken of, in case the crown should fall to a papist. I hope that His Majesty will not incline to suffer a thing to be done so prejudicial to all the royal family: and, although they spread about that this will not take place, except with regard to a king of that religion, and would be of no consequence to kings of the Protestant religion, it must not be imagined that, if they had once taken away from the Crown such considerable prerogatives as are talked of, they would ever return again. Therefore I entreat you to represent this in my name to the King; and to beg of His Majesty, on my part, that he will not consent to a thing so prejudicial to all those who have the honour to be of his family.

When the exiled Duke and Duchess of York passed through The Hague on their way to the Spanish Netherlands, William was equally concerned at his father-in-law's bitterness towards Parliament, saying that his brother would manage better if he dissolved it. Good relations between King and Parliament were paramount, because without Parliament Charles would drift back into Louis's hands, dependent on his subsidies, which would be detrimental to Anglo-Dutch relations. To William, it was crucial to keep England out of the French pocket, to check Louis's aggression and to maintain the balance of power in Europe.

William had been busy forging closer alliances with his German neighbours and relatives. He particularly enjoyed the company of the clever and witty Sophie of Hanover, his mother's cousin, whom he had known in The Hague during his childhood. He was less keen on her son, George Ludwig, with whom he could discuss military affairs but little else. Nevertheless, George Ludwig was an honoured guest at The Hague when, as Sidney recalled, 'the Prince and Princess of Orange and the Prince of Hanover do me the honour to come to my house. They shall have music and dancing, and the best entertainment I can give them.' Such alliances would prove crucial when the time came for William to make a decisive intervention in English affairs. His fondness for Sophie also meant that William would promote her claim to the throne when it came to deciding the English Protestant succession.

Perhaps wishing to put the affairs of the kingdom in order lest he should die, the King invited William to England in July 1681, while his brother was still away in Scotland. Relations between the two men were strained, as Lord Godolphin acknowledged in a letter to William, perhaps because of the natural distrust the King felt for the ambitious young nephew waiting in the wings. Henry Sidney advised William to adopt a more conciliatory tone in his letters to the King. He also warned him that there were some who 'make him believe that

Your Highness is of the party that is most against him; that you have a constant correspondence with those (they call) his enemies; that you drive a contrary interest.' When he heard of the proposed visit James did not hesitate to add fuel to the fire, warning that the presence of the Prince of Orange would only encourage the opposition and anger Louis, who dreaded any *rapprochement* with the Dutch. No doubt the Prince would try to encourage the King to make his peace with Parliament, James opined, which meant that his exile would be prolonged indefinitely.

For all his indolence, Charles seems to have possessed great foresight. He had had the sense to have his nieces Mary and Anne brought up Protestants and to make the Protestant match between Mary and the Prince of Orange. He had discouraged the pretensions of Monmouth and officially declared him a bastard. As far as he had been able, he had made it an inevitability that William and Mary would eventually come to the crown. He could not agree to the exclusion of his brother from the throne because he believed too strongly in the principles of divine right and the hereditary succession. But James's second wife had no living children, and, by 1681, there seemed little likelihood of her producing a male heir. Perhaps he meant to convey an important message when he confided to William on this visit his opinion that if his brother ever did come to the throne, he would not last more than four years. He might have been telling William to wait upon events, to be ready to intervene when the time was right.

The visit was not considered a success. Charles was too firmly in bed with the French for William to make any headway there. And William was tactless when he accepted an invitation to dine in the City of London, which had been so vociferous in its support for Monmouth and the Whigs. On each occasion William was invited, Charles forestalled it by sending a message that his presence was required at Windsor. Although Monmouth was now in disgrace, Charles could not cease to love this errant son, and he might have shown William two seals, explaining that if he were to use one of them it was a sign that the contents of his letter were his true wishes. This, at least, was the explanation Burnet gave for William's warm reception of Monmouth at The Hague, implying that it was in accordance with Charles's covert instructions. Monmouth was his guest there in the winter of 1684–5 when William received word of King Charles's death in a terse note from James, which also conveyed the surprising news that, against all the odds, James had succeeded peaceably to his brother's throne.

———

To all outward appearances, James began by making professions of friendship, but he was already harbouring a grudge against William for what he saw as a betrayal: William's support of Monmouth. In fact, William had asked Monmouth to leave as soon as he heard of King Charles's death and he wrote protesting to the King's minister, Lord Rochester, that he had no knowledge of Monmouth's whereabouts. When Monmouth launched his rebellion, William sent Bentinck to London to offer James the aid of the Scottish regiments in the service of the Republic. He also offered to come himself to help his uncle quell the rebellion, but James declined. He had no wish to give the Prince of Orange any added lustre if he should defeat the rebels, and he could not rid himself of the suspicion that William had encouraged the rebellion in the first place.

Far from encouraging Monmouth, however, it was not in William's interests to see him snatch Mary's inheritance. If he had welcomed Monmouth at The Hague, it was to size him up, and he was reassured to find him a man of no substance. His subsequent entertainment of Monmouth was to keep him in his sight and on side. Nevertheless, he did not rest easy until the rebellion had been crushed.

William wanted good relations with his father-in-law, if only to guarantee English support in the alliance against France. But in this he was to be disappointed. Although he was by temperament, religious affiliation and conditioning as Francophile as his late brother, James had an unrealistic view of himself as the neutral arbiter of Europe. Nothing could be further from the truth. England was regarded by the rest of Europe as a bad joke, thanks to the unreliability of its foreign policy and its suspected subservience to the French. James genuinely might have wanted to be on good terms with both France and the Dutch Republic, but this was impracticable and acceptable to neither of them. James's fence-sitting left him without the French alliance when he needed it most, and guaranteed the States-General would have no hesitation in lending William its support for his intervention in English affairs.

In September 1686 James grudgingly withdrew his ambassador Bevil Skelton, who had been caught up in the unsavoury intrigue in the Princess of Orange's household, in which some of her staff had conspired to expose William's affair with Elizabeth Villiers, and replaced him with someone even more unsuitable. Ignatius White, Marquis d'Albeville, was the sort of second-rate candidate whom James felt obliged to employ because of his Catholic faith rather than any conspicuous talents in the diplomatic sphere. He came from a family of Irish Catholic adventurers, and was closely affiliated with the Jesuits at Whitehall. James entrusted this unlikely character to persuade the Prince of Orange that the Test Act was a restraint on the royal prerogative, and that it would be an advantage to William and Mary, as James's successors, if it were to be repealed.

William wrote an uncompromising reply to his father-in-law, telling him that he and Mary could under no circumstances agree to the repeal of the Act, which guaranteed the supremacy of the Church of England. If it were repealed, for instance, a Catholic King could swamp the House of Lords with new Catholic peers. Then who knew what Acts might be passed to the disadvantage of the Protestants? For good measure, William had the Pensionary of Holland, Caspar Fagel, write an official letter explaining the reasons for the Prince and Princess of Orange's objection to the repeal of the Test Act, a letter printed and distributed for general consumption in England. In February 1687 William sent over his trusted friend, Everard van Weede van Dijkvelt, to explain his reasons to James in person. James was incensed by William's refusal to compromise on this question.

Dijkvelt went on to raise a matter of crucial importance, which had been worrying William. There had been rumours that James meant to change the succession. Some of his Catholic supporters had hoped that he might be able to convert the Princess Anne to Catholicism. In this case, James might be tempted to pass over Mary and vest the crown in Anne. Failing that, a more desperate case had him declaring his marriage to Anne Hyde illegal, legitimising his son by Arabella Churchill, James FitzJames, Duke of Berwick, who had been raised a Catholic, and leaving the crown to him. None of these scenarios is likely. Having survived the exclusion crisis, James was a fervent believer in the principle of hereditary succession instilled in him by his father. Besides, he loved his daughters. He reassured Dijkvelt that he had no intention of changing the succession.

William had long been aware of the need for a constant flow of intelligence from England, but now he stepped this up. Dijkvelt's commission was to get to know men across the whole political spectrum, to make contacts, to sound out opinion. To this end he entertained lavishly and was frequently invited to dine. When he dined at the house of Charles Talbot, Earl of Shrewsbury, the guests included Lords Halifax, Danby, Devonshire, Mordaunt, Lumley, the Bishop of London and Admirals Herbert and Russell. This group continued to meet as a sort of standing committee long after Dijkvelt's visit. When Dijkvelt returned to The Hague in June 1687, he brought the first in a series of letters from prominent men, including Danby, Nottingham, Compton, Halifax, Herbert and Churchill, to William. They all professed their regard for the Prince and devotion to his interests and implied that they thought of him as their leader in opposition.

It is unlikely that William entertained any idea of armed intervention in England until the pregnancy of the Queen was officially announced on Christmas Eve, 1687. Now revolution became a real possibility. James was not going to die and leave the crown to Protestant Mary. Plans had to be made to meet the eventuality of his having a son, a Catholic who would make sure all his father's Catholic reforms stuck. In the event of James's death, the prospect of regency under Mary Beatrice and the Catholic set made Protestants wince. The consensus among the Protestants was that if Mary Beatrice did not succeed in producing a living child this time, the Jesuits would have no hesitation in inventing one. On 27 March 1688 William's old friend Danby wrote to warn him:

Many of our ladies say, that the Queen's great belly seems to grow faster than they have observed their own to do; and because it is fit Her Majesty should always have the greatest persons near her in this condition, I hope the Princess will take care that the Princess Anne may be always within call; and especially to see (when the time is near) that the midwife discharges her duty with that care which ought to be had in a case of so great concern. Our zeal here for the Protestant religion does apparently increase every day in all parts of the nation.

Danby's letter might have been one of genuine advice. On the other hand, he could have been hinting that Anne should do exactly the opposite, disappear from the scene, enabling the hoax theory to gain ground.

Whether William believed the hoax theory or not was irrelevant. He could not stand by any longer and watch Mary's inheritance put in jeopardy. If James were allowed to continue, he would destroy the monarchy. William had been invited to intervene in English affairs on previous occasions, but now he received a bombardment of letters from leading members of the opposition, pledging their support, encouraging action.

Lord Halifax, by far the cleverest, was urging caution, however. In April 1688 he wrote to the Prince with a brilliant summary of the situation: 'The irregular methods have spent themselves without effect; they have run so fast that they begin to be out of breath, and the exercise of extraordinary powers, both ecclesiastical and civil, is so far from fixing the right of them, that men are more united in objecting to them. The world is still where it was, with this only difference, that it groweth every day more averse to that which is endeavoured to be imposed upon them.'

With the failure of their policies, Halifax predicted, the Catholics looked like falling out among themselves or might have to make bridges with the Anglicans. 'Unseasonable stirrings, or anything that looketh like the Protestants being the aggressors,' Halifax warned, 'will tend to unite them, and by that means will be a disappointment to those hopes, which otherwise can hardly fail; nothing, therefore, in the present conjuncture can be more dangerous than unskilful agitators, warm men, who would be active at a wrong time, and want patience to keep their zeal from running away with them.'

A month later, Shrewsbury was writing to William expressing his regret that he would not, after all, have the opportunity to kiss the Prince's hand in Holland that summer. 'Wiser people assure me, that the jealousies of our superiors augment so fast, that such a journey would be unserviceable to you, as well as unsafe to me.' While Shrewsbury deemed it unsafe to travel abroad, at court there was such a poor attendance of the nobility that the King had very few left to serve him. The traditional link between the court and the counties was cut off leaving him isolated.

In the last days of April, Admirals Herbert and Russell and a Russell cousin did manage to visit William at his new palace of Het Loo in Gelderland to urge armed intervention. Whatever means they used to persuade him, William must have been considering it seriously because he asked his guest, the Elector of Saxony, whether he could lend him troops. On

9 May William's uncle, the Elector of Brandenburg, died, which was good news for William. Ever since the death of his wife, William's Aunt Louise, the Elector had been influenced by his second wife to support France. Now his son promised to ally with William, if only because William held out the hope of making him heir to the Orange inheritance if he did not survive the English expedition.

In his heart, William had always wanted the crown of England and felt it would be his. Now the time had come. The English visitors had left him in no doubt that the revolution would go ahead with or without him. Without him, there could be no hope of saving Mary's inheritance. England might even swing back to a republic, which might not sanction the Anglo-Dutch alliance Europe so desperately needed to quell the French and might also present a real threat to Dutch commercial interests. Mary's inheritance looked to be lost anyway if a Catholic heir, genuine or pretended, were about to be foisted on the nation. William determined to salvage what he could of Mary's rights and to secure the best out of the situation for his own country. It remained to convince Mary of what was at stake. She had to know what was going on, because if her father were dethroned it would be in her name, as she, not William, was the next heir to the throne.

Evidently, William authorised Herbert and the Russells to let the English conspirators know that if he were to receive a letter from the most prominent men in the kingdom, with the backing of others, inviting him 'to come and rescue the nation and the religion', he would act. According to Burnet, he promised that he could be ready for armed intervention by the end of September. Ostensibly, William was coming to ensure the calling of a free Parliament to reinstate English liberties. He, at least, was never in any doubt that he was coming for the crown.

It was an enormous gamble. If he played and lost, he might lose everything. But then, had he not always believed that he was a man of destiny?

# Part Two

## *The Revolution*

# 6

## *The Birth of James Francis Edward, Prince of Wales*

---

*''Tis possible it may be her child; but where one believes it, a thousand do not'*
> – Princess Anne

Princess Anne was still in Bath when she received Colonel Oglethorpe, who had been sent expressly by the King to convey news of the royal birth. As the Imperial ambassador, Hoffmann, reported to the Habsburg Emperor: 'The King told him he was not only to remit the letter but to give testimony *de visu* . . . and not without reason, for the wickedness of some people goes so far as to make them capable of accepting the idea of an imposture . . . their malice inclining them to believe that which suits their interests.' Possibly the King already suspected his beloved daughter of being among these sceptics. With the Queen's confinement safely out of the way, Anne lost no time in returning to London, all thoughts of convalescence apparently forgotten. Her uncle, Lord Clarendon, saw her at the Cockpit on the 16th, and thought she looked well. Soon after her arrival, she dashed off a letter to her sister full of hypocrisy and malice, twisting the truth to suit her preferred version of events:

> *The Cockpit, 18 June 1688*
> My dear sister can't imagine the concern and vexation I have been in, that I should be so unfortunate to be out of town when the Queen was brought to bed, for I shall never now be satisfied whether the child be true or false. It may be it is our brother, but God only knows, for she never took care to satisfy the world, or give people any demonstration of it. It is wonderful, if she had

really been with child, that nobody was suffered to feel [it] stir but Madam Mazarin and Lady Sunderland, who are people that nobody will give credit to. If out of pride she would not have let me touch [her] methinks it would have been very natural for her sometimes, when she has been undressing, to have let Mrs Robarts, as it were by chance, have seen her belly; but instead of endeavouring to give one any satisfaction, she has always been very shy both to her and me. The great bustle that was made about her lying in at Windsor, and then resolving all of a sudden to go to St James's, which is much the properest place to act such a cheat in; and Mrs Turine's [Pelegrina Turini] lying in the bedchamber that night she fell in labour, and none of the family besides being removed from Whitehall, are things that give one great cause to be suspicious. But that which to me seems the plainest thing in the world, is her being brought to bed two days after she heard of my coming to town [my being about to come back to town], and saying that the child was come at the full time, when everybody knows, by her own reckoning, that she should have gone a month longer. After all this, 'tis possible it may be her child; but where one believes it, a thousand do not. For my part, except they do give very plain demonstrations, which is almost impossible now, I shall ever be of the number of unbelievers. I don't find that people are at all disheartened, but seem all of a mind, which is a very comfortable thing at such a time as this.

Mary must have been utterly exasperated that her sister had not been present to witness the birth. How could her sister be so stupid! 'As to my sister,' Mary confided in her journal, 'she has committed an irreparable fault by her absence.' She was further annoyed by Anne's lazy reportage, which rested mainly on hearsay, in her letters. She did not hesitate to tell her so. Mary stooped pretty low herself now, when she compiled an extensive questionnaire for her sister to complete with the details of the birth gleaned from those who had been there. From Anne's vague, biased and muddled answers, and from the depositions later made by witnesses before an extraordinary meeting of the Privy Council and lodged in Chancery, we can construct a picture of the event.

---

On Saturday, 9 June 1688 Queen Mary Beatrice had been feeling restless all day. She was impatient that the workmen had still not finished at Whitehall. For months laden barges had been travelling up the Thames and delivering slabs of Italian marbles for the renovations at the palace. There was no peace. The rooms next door to the apartment she was currently occupying were still full of noise and dust. The bedchamber was unsuitable for a royal birth: it was too small and exposed to the sun, making it impossibly hot for the ordeal ahead. Windsor Castle, which she loved, had been ruled out as a suitable place for her confinement, because it was too far from London for the necessary witnesses to be present at the birth.

In early June she decided to return to St James's, the palace where she had given birth to all her other children, and gave orders for it to be prepared. A week later, she was beginning to lose patience, as it was still not ready. She sent word several times that Saturday to hurry up the preparations. 'I am determined to lie in St James's tonight even if I have to lie on the boards,' she told her women. She did not say, 'I am determined to lie in at St James's tonight', as those looking for signs of a Catholic conspiracy later asserted.

After dinner, Mary Beatrice was playing basset when word came that St James's was ready to receive her. She stayed to finish her game. It was only two days after the bishops had been sent to the Tower, and the streets had been full of ugly incidents of violence that day. It was quiet, however, when after dark a torch-lit procession carried the Queen through St James's Park in her sedan chair. The King went with her and Sidney Godolphin, her devoted Lord Chamberlain, walked beside her chair. Most of the 'family', or household, did not accompany them at this late hour.

The King, as usual, spent the night in the Queen's great bed. He rose between seven and eight that Sunday morning and went to his own quarters to dress. About a quarter of an hour after he left her, the Queen sent him word that her labour had started and to send for the witnesses. Mrs Margaret Dawson, the Protestant bedchamber woman who had attended the births of all James's children by his two wives, received word at church and immediately hurried to the Queen. This is interesting, because later those who maintained that the birth was a sham said it had been arranged to take place while the Protestant ladies were at church. Not only Mrs Dawson, however, but also many other Protestant ladies did receive word of the impending birth while they were in church and were able to make themselves available.

Mrs Dawson found Mary Beatrice huddled beside the bed shivering. Her devoted Italian bedchamber woman, Pellegrina Turini, and the midwife, Judith Wilkes, were already with her. The pallet on which the Queen might have expected to give birth had not yet been aired, so Mrs Dawson persuaded her to get back into the great bed. She sent for a warming-pan, which she and several witnesses confirmed was full of burning coals, to warm that bed. This is the only warming-pan that was introduced, and clearly it could not have contained a living baby which was 'born' unscathed two hours later. The fabrication that the Prince of Wales had been smuggled into the Queen's bed in a warming-pan was perpetrated some time after the event and was patently absurd.

The doors to the Queen's bedchamber and the antechamber were left open and the witnesses began to trickle in as word spread round St James's. The Queen Dowager, Catherine, arrived at a quarter past nine. She went up to the bed to greet her sister-in-law, then went to stand by the chimney-piece clock, where she remained throughout the confinement. James had sent for the Privy Council and these and other men who had been attending the King's levée soon entered the room. According to both King James's and Princess Anne's accounts there were present: the Lord Chancellor Jeffreys; Lord Sunderland, Lord President of the Council; Lord Arundel, the Lord Privy Seal; the Lord Chamberlain, Lord Mulgrave; the Queen's Lord Chamberlain, Sidney Godolphin; the Secretary of State, Lord Middleton; Lord Craven; Lord Huntingdon; Lord Powis; Lord Dover; Lord Peterborough; Lord Melfort; Lord Dartmouth; Sir John Ferneley; Lord Preston; Sir Nicholas Butler; the Duke of Beaufort; Lord Berkeley; Lord Murray; Lord Castlemaine – all of the Privy Council. Others included Lord Feversham, Lord Arran, Sir Stephen Fox, and Mr Griffen, 'besides pages of the backstairs and priests'. Significantly, Lord Churchill had ensured that he could not be found and asked to attend.

The women present were Lady Peterborough, Lady Bellasys, Lady Arran, Lady Tyrconnel, Lady Roscommon, Lady Sophia Bulkeley, Lady Fingal, Madame Mazarin, Madame Bouillon, Lady Powis, Lady Strickland, Lady Craven, Mrs Cran, two of the Queen Dowager's Portuguese, Mrs Bromley, Mrs Dawson, Mrs Waldegrave, Lady Wentworth and Mrs Feraine. If some of the men kept a decent distance from the bed and some Protestants such as Godolphin ostentatiously refused to watch the proceedings too closely, so that they could not later be called to testify to an authentic birth, many of the women stood as near as they could to the bed.

Whether through intention or careless omission, Anne's account makes no mention of the presence of Anne, Lady Sunderland, who had been summoned from the Chapel Royal soon after eight. She was an important witness. Married to the conniving Robert Spencer, Lord Sunderland, the Countess was loathed by Princess Anne almost as much as was the Earl. She is a 'flattering, dissembling, false woman', she told Mary. The Protestant Lady Sunderland was a close friend and correspondent of her husband's uncle, the Orangeist conspirator, Henry Sidney. The Sunderlands were also very friendly with the Churchills, which probably inflamed Anne's jealousy, and in due course the Sunderlands' son, Charles Spencer, would marry the Churchills' second daughter, Anne. Lady Sunderland took up a position beside the Queen, facing two other Protestants, Lady Arran and Lady Roscommon, on the other side of the bed. The Protestant Lady Bellasys stood near the midwife and Mrs Dawson 'stood behind a Dutch chair that the midwife sat upon to do her work'.

Anne had to admit that the curtains at the foot and the sides of the bed were kept open all the time, contradicting a scurrilous rumour that they had been closed just before the birth. James held his wife throughout her labour. In her questionnaire, Princess Mary asked her sister, 'Whether in any former labour the Queen was delivered so mysteriously, so suddenly, and with so few being called for?' to which Anne replied, 'Her labour never used to be so long.' The Queen's labour took only two hours, certainly not much longer than her previous labours, which had all been fast. Even her first labour, the birth of Katherine Laura in 1675, had been quicker than most. When her daughter Isabella was born in 1676, Mary Beatrice's labour had been so fast that the King and Queen had not arrived in time to witness the birth. And her previous confinement, the birth of Charlotte Mary in 1682, had been so speedy that not only King Charles and the Duke of York missed it, but also the nurse had not managed to arrive on time. By contrast, on this occasion there was time to call an adequate number of witnesses, and anyone who wished had access to the Queen's apartment, so that there was nothing 'mysterious' about the proceedings.

Mary Beatrice thought that her agony would go on for hours. Lady Sunderland later told the Privy Council on oath that she had felt the Queen's belly while she was in labour, for 'Her Majesty being in great pain and the midwife assuring her she would soon be deliver'd, she sayd, she aprehended the contrary, because the child lay so high, and my Lady Sunderland being next her she made her feel whereabouts it lay, which she did.'

Only two hours after the onset of labour, the pain became so excruciating that the Queen called out to the midwife, 'Oh, I die! You kill me, you kill me!' The King signalled Lord Chancellor Jeffreys to come closer. In her questionnaire, Princess Mary asked, 'Whether did any woman, besides the confidants, see the Queen's face when she was in labour? And whether she had the looks of a woman in labour?' It was only on the point of giving birth that Mary Beatrice begged her husband 'to hide her face with his head and periwig, which he did; for she said she could not be brought to bed and have so many men look on her; for all the Council stood close to the bed's feet and Lord Chancellor up on the step.'

The Queen's groans were further testimony to a genuine birth. Just before ten o'clock the child was born. Lady Sunderland had arranged for the midwife to touch her brow as a sign to the King that it was a boy. Nevertheless, as the midwife handed the baby to his nurse, Mrs Labadie, James anxiously asked her, 'What is it?' 'What Your Majesty desires,' she answered. The great majority of those present were still unaware of the child's sex. Several people heard the Queen say, 'I don't hear the child cry,' whereupon he obligingly did so. The Protestant ladies at the bedside saw everything they needed to see, as they later confirmed on oath. Lady Isabella Wentworth was one of those who verified the birth before the Privy Council, and again, fifteen years later, she repeated her testimony to Dr Hickes, the ex-Dean of Worcester, in the presence of Mrs Dawson, and signed it. She told that great sceptic Gilbert Burnet that 'she was as sure the Prince of Wales was the Queen's son, as that any of her own children were hers.' The Prince of Orange's old childhood playmate, Liselotte, Duchess of Orléans, later wrote that 'a lady not at all partial to the Queen was present at the birth and told me, for the sake of simple truth, that she saw this child still attached to the umbilical cord. She has no doubt at all that he is the Queen's son.'

Before Mrs Labadie could take the baby off to an inner room

to be washed and dressed, the King stopped her. He asked the Privy Councillors to bear witness that a child had been born. Later, they swore on oath that 'they saw the child immediately after the Queen was deliver'd, and saw it was a Prince and all the marks of being new born.' Those who saw the baby just after he was born thought he was rather black in the face, but he was soon looking normal. James was so overjoyed that he knighted the physician, Dr Waldegrave, on the spot and gave the midwife, Judith Wilkes, 500 guineas 'for her breakfast'. Such impetuosity was surely genuine. As soon as the baby was ready, he was carried through the assembled company, Lord Feversham clearing a passage through the crush with the command, 'Room for the Prince of Wales!'

Three key witnesses were absent from the birth chamber. Princess Anne was in Bath, on her own insistence and against the King's wishes, so close to the time the Queen was due to give birth. The Archbishop of Canterbury was languishing in the Tower on a charge of seditious libel, although James's enemies insisted that he had been sent there deliberately to get him out of the way for the Queen's confinement. The third key witness, Henry Hyde, Earl of Clarendon, the maternal uncle of the Princesses Mary and Anne, was attending divine service at St James's Piccadilly, this being Trinity Sunday. He had noticed that there had been a lot of whispering among the congregation, but had not known the cause until on the way home his page had told him the news. At two o'clock the thunder of guns from the Tower and the pealing of church bells announced the birth of a Prince of Wales.

It was only after he had dined that Clarendon went to court, and found the King, who had not had time to dress himself until this late hour, shaving. Even though Clarendon's nieces must now yield their place in the succession to a brother, it would never have occurred to such a loyal adherent of the Crown to question the circumstances of the birth. He seems to have been genuinely pleased for James – 'I kissed his hand and wished him joy' – while the proud father urged his former brother-in-law to go and look at the baby. He found the little prince 'asleep in his cradle, and was a very fine child to look upon'.

The child was baptised privately in his mother's bedchamber the next day in the presence of the papal nuncio, Count D'Adda, with Catholic rites. He was to be named James Francis Edward, in honour of his father, of the Queen's favourite saint, Francis Xavier, and of St Edward the Confessor, the Saxon King whom James venerated. The Pope and the Queen Dowager Catherine were godparents. A public christening and naming ceremony would be held on 15 October.

That night, the Queen awoke feeling thirsty and rang for a drink. The chambermaid who brought it to her let slip that the Prince had been extremely ill, so much so that the King had been summoned. The Queen had been sleeping and he had not wanted her disturbed. A treatment 'good for babies' had been prescribed by the physicians – they seem to have been extraordinarily ignorant and careless – and administered to the child twice by mistake. After further remedies had been applied, the baby recovered. James waited until the next day, 12 June, before writing to the Prince of Orange: 'The Queen was, God be thanked, safely delivered of a sonne on Sunday morning a little before ten; she has been very well ever since, but the child was somewhat ill last night of the wind and some gripes, but is now, blessed be God, very well again, and like to have no returns of it, and is a very strong boy.'

News of the Prince's birth had been sent immediately to all corners of the kingdom. On the day of his birth, James wrote personally to his brother-in-law the Duke of Modena, and foreign ambassadors communicated the news to their courts by special messengers. They were invited to see the baby and to visit him regularly.

Rizzini confidently reported to Modena: 'The joy is great here, and will be so in all Christendom. The King expressed his own by embracing me in a transport of joy and benignity.' Barillon told Louis XIV that the child was 'large and well made and would appear to be a nine-months baby'. The Venetian envoy saw an 'infant in the best health possible, with a good colour, a loud voice and beautiful eyes'.

Terriesi reported to Florence optimistically:

I cannot express the joy in the King's aspect, when, after giving thanks to God, he went to the Council Chamber . . . I saw the new-born Prince, and that he was beautiful, and as big and vigorous as a creature of his age could be . . . The Queen's chamber was public at the time of the birth to all ladies who chose to enter and the ante-room to all men, almost indiscriminately; so there is no fear but that both were filled with curious spectators; the Queen Dowager was present the whole time, and besides the well-affected, many of the malcontents of both sexes, so all the mischievous deceits invented by the malicious respecting a fictitious pregnancy must now be dispelled.

It was reasonable for Terriesi to suppose that the great number of witnesses attending the birth would scotch the rumours once and for all. But he underestimated the determination of James's enemies, who greeted the news of the birth with rage. As soon as it became apparent that the child was healthy and likely to live, all sorts of new, scurrilous rumours were unleashed questioning the authenticity of the Prince of Wales. Besides the original rumour that the Queen's pregnancy was a hoax, it was also claimed that she had miscarried at three, five and seven months, that a living baby had been smuggled into the Queen's bed, that the baby was born dead and another was put in its place, that a child had been born but had subsequently died and been replaced by another.

Leaving no stone unturned to justify the regime of William and Mary, Bishop Burnet's *History* includes all these possibilities. They cannot all have been true, if, indeed, any one of them was. Burnet did not go so far as to claim that the King was not the child's father, however, as some inferred. The idea of the child being an impostor quickly took hold and refused to go away. If even Princess Anne was able to suggest with impunity to her sister that the labyrinthine geography of St James's Palace made it 'much the properest place to act such a cheat in', the ignorant and credulous no doubt believed it too. The fact that there were no fewer than four doors in the Queen's bedchamber, one of them at the bed-head leading to a narrow passageway and a dressing room, and that there was only one window so that the room was dark, seemed to lend credibility to a plot. No allegation against the Catholic King and Queen was too far-fetched for the credulous rabble to believe, while those with an interest at stake were prepared to swallow any nonsense that would justify their bringing down the regime.

Some of the most valuable testimony to a genuine birth is contained in a letter written in 1699 to the Electress Sophie of Hanover by Dr Hugh Chamberlaine, the eminent man-midwife whose family invented the forceps. He told the Electress that Bishop Burnet's account was inaccurate. As a noted Whig of Huguenot extraction, the King would not have sent for Chamberlaine to attend the Queen's confinement that Sunday morning if any deception were intended. As Chamberlaine admits: 'they would never have hazarded such a secret as a supposititious child, which, had I been at home to have immediately followed the summons, I must have come time enough to have discovered, though the Queen had usually very quick labours.'

Contrary to Burnet's claim, James did summon Chamberlaine that Sunday morning, only to find he was out of town. James happened to meet Chamberlaine in St James's Park on the Monday morning and quipped that he had been absent when sent for to attend the Queen's confinement, to which Chamberlaine 'humbly replied, more warning had been necessary'. James admitted that 'they were surprised, for the Queen expected to go a fortnight longer.' Chamberlaine told the Electress that he was piqued that he had not been engaged several months earlier for the Queen's impending confinement. He admitted that 'Lady Sophia Bulkeley told me, in Her

Majesty's presence, some weeks before, that shortly there would be occasion for me; but I did not take that for sufficient orders.' Indeed, the whole business of the Queen's confinement seems to have been handled in a somewhat haphazard and careless manner, a fact not lost on Sarah Churchill who commented: 'If it was a true child, it was certainly very ill order'd.'

As usual, however, Chamberlaine offered remedies to stop the Queen's milk. Mrs Dawson and others swore before the Privy Council that they had seen milk upon the Queen's smock, but the Queen told Lady Clarendon that the baby had 'arrived without his rations'. Chamberlaine's remedies were refused, as they were not needed. Had the Queen been staging a bogus confinement, she would presumably have accepted his remedies as part of the subterfuge. Chamberlaine saw the newly born baby lying naked on his governess, Lady Powis's lap, and was of the opinion that he had been born a couple of weeks early, as had the Queen's last child.

Contrary to Princess Anne's assertion to her sister 'that the servants, from the highest to the lowest, they are all papists', at least one of those in attendance on the baby was a Protestant. Chamberlaine 'had frequent discourses with the necessary woman, who being in mighty dread of popery' sought to confide in him her worries that the 'Jesuits' were forever interfering in the nursery and that she expected to be dismissed. However, Chamberlaine continues that 'about a fortnight after the child was born, a rumour being spread through the city, that the child was suppositious, she cried, "Alas! Will they not leave the poor infant alone? I am certain no such thing as the bringing a strange child in a warming-pan could be practised without my seeing it, attending constantly in and about all the avenues of the chamber."'

Convinced by Chamberlaine's and other evidence, the Electress Sophie always maintained 'that the unfortunate young Prince was as much the child of James II as her son George was her own offspring'. Considering that it was she and her son George who were designated to inherit the crown by the 1701 Act of Settlement, this was a brave admission.

————

Prince William of Orange could not be expected to greet the news of the birth of the Prince of Wales with any enthusiasm. However, he went through the proper formalities. Prayers were ordered for the child in the Princess of Orange's chapel and William sent Count Zuylestein, his second cousin and son of his old governor, to the English court to offer his congratulations. Of course, it was an opportune moment for Zuylestein to make contact with the English conspirators and to enquire into the rumours surrounding the Prince's birth.

Princess Mary seems to have already convinced herself that there was something suspicious about the birth, as she wrote in her journal:

People thought that he [James] had risked too much before he knew if he should have a son or not, but this son appeared afterwards so suddenly that it gave cause to suspect he had played false, for it was the 8th of June, old style, that the Bishops were put in the Tower, and the 10th the Queen gave birth to a son. This was much too soon, for she lacked a month to her reckoning, even if she commenced the minute that she saw the King when he was at the cure at Bath. This circumstance, with the absence of my sister, marked something strange. But I am so strongly persuaded that if there was any deception God will not suffer that it remain a long time hidden that I am not greatly troubled, and I have rendered grace to God for the Prince and myself that neither of us is in trouble for our own proper interests, our unique care is for the church of God, but as regards that we put our confidence in Him.

Not one of the 'immortal seven' – Lords Shrewsbury, Devonshire, Danby and Lumley, the Bishop of London, Admiral Russell and Henry Sidney – was present to witness the birth of the Prince of Wales. Nevertheless, when they composed their letter of invitation to the Prince of Orange on 30 June, they reprimanded him: 'We must presume to inform Your Highness, that your compliment upon the birth of the child (which not one in a thousand here believes to be the Queen's) hath done you some injury.' They advised him that this 'false imposing' of a fictitious heir, to the injury of the Princess Mary and the nation, must be listed in William's forthcoming manifesto as one of the chief causes of his 'entering the kingdom in a hostile manner'.

After this ticking off from the seven, prayers for the infant Prince were surreptitiously dropped. The omission was soon noticed. As Hoffmann told the Emperor on 3 August: 'Yesterday I found the court not only exasperated against the Prince of Orange, but greatly afflicted, because he has suddenly forbidden the prayer which has been said in his chapel for the Prince of Wales, thus throwing suspicion on his birth, which in this kingdom (where already two-thirds of the people are of various opinions, some from wickedness, and others from established concert or credulity) must have very pernicious consequences.'

Still harbouring her suspicions about the Prince of Wales's authenticity, Mary had never been altogether happy about offering prayers for him in her chapel:

When I learnt that the Queen had given birth to a son I ordered that they should pray publicly for the child, hoping still, for the sake of the King, that it was really his son; being persuaded that, despite this, God would take care of His church. But Dr Stanley [Mary's Anglican chaplain] very much opposed these prayers, yet the Prince having told me that I was right, I persisted in having it done. However, I see now it was too precipitous, but I believed that omitting it seemed to show an aversion on my part against the poor innocent child, and it was for this reason that I would not be turned from my purpose; but I do not believe that the Prince was wrong to send Mr Zuylestein to make our compliments on this subject, for he could not do less without our putting ourselves in the wrong. But one hears every day things so strange that it is impossible to avoid having very strong suspicions. This makes me very chagrined, but, after I had consulted with the Prince, we resolved to cease to pray for the child, but it was ceased by degrees. On this M. d'Abbeville [James's ambassador at The Hague] gave me several complaints . . . I responded in very ambiguous fashion that confounded and vexed him extremely. But in the end the Prince was advised to renew the prayers for the infant.

Sincere in her religion, Mary baulked at the deception:

I avow this was against my desire, I did not wish to be guilty of dissimulation towards God. However, the Prince convinced me, saying he feared that the King would write to me in a fashion so positive that I should not be able to evade him as I had evaded his envoy. I considered then that if I once gave, under my hand, an assurance that I believed the child a son of the King, we must both, the one and the other, keep to that, and that to let the King see our defiance at the present moment would be our ruin.

If William was ruled by political considerations in the matter of the prayers, he could at least rain on the English ambassador's party to celebrate the birth of the Prince of Wales. As M. Lente, the Danish envoy at The Hague, wrote to Terriesi in London: 'no members of the court attended . . . although everybody had been invited and many had promised to come before the Prince of Orange had made it known, underhand, that they would please him by not going to the English ambassador's.' Lente concluded that: 'all this is done to throw doubt upon the birth of the Prince, and it is said the Prince of Orange repents himself of having sent an envoy to England to congratulate the King.' The party 'was very fine, well-ordered and magnificent,' he wrote, 'but nobody was there'.

Oblivious of Princess Mary's suspicions and the nature of the correspondence between her two stepdaughters, the Queen wrote a note to Mary from St James's on 6 July: 'The first moment that I have taken a pen in my hand since I was brought to bed, is this, to write to my dear LEMON.' A week later she followed this up with a note from Whitehall. 'I did not hope two months ago to have had all well over by this time,' she wrote, 'for I came a month sooner than I reckoned, which mistake I thought I could not make, counting as I used to do. If my child had not been bigger and stronger than any that ever I had, I should have thought I had come before my time.'

Much has been made of the discrepancy between the expected and actual birth dates, as seen in Mary's journal, but there can be no doubt that it is attributable to the physicians' ignorance and stupidity rather than some calculated Catholic ruse. Before long, Mary Beatrice's detractors were alleging that she could not have gone through a real confinement, because she was recovering so quickly. Indeed, on 25 June it was reported that 'the Queen is in good health, and hath been up some days, and played yesterday at cards most of the afternoon.' On 28 June she was able to receive William's Kinsman, Zuylestein, in audience. On 16 July she made her first public appearance 'at table, and in the chapel' and two days later there was a spectacular firework display on the Thames to celebrate the Queen's 'up-sitting'.

Mary Beatrice was puzzled by Mary's cool response. On 31 July she wrote a heart-rending letter telling her that she fears she is not so kind to her as she used to be:

'And the reason I have to think so is (for since I have begun I must tell you all the truth) that since I have been brought to bed, you have never once in your letters to me taken the least notice of my son, no more than if he had never been born, only in that which M. Zuylestein brought, that I look upon as a compliment that you could not avoid, though I should not have taken it so, if ever you named him afterwards.'

Puzzlement turned to hurt and on 17 August Mary Beatrice wrote from Windsor:

'Even in this last letter, by the way you speak of my son; and the formal name you call him by, I am further

confirmed in the thought I had before, that you have for
him the last indifference. The King has often told me, with
a great deal of trouble, that often as he has mentioned his
son in his letters to you, you never once answered anything
concerning him.'

Princess Mary coolly endorsed this letter, which she later
brought to England, with the ambiguous words: 'Answered
that all the King's children shall ever find as much affection
and kindness from me as can be expected from children of the
same father.'

Already inclined to believe that the Prince of Wales was
a changeling, Mary records in her journal that the eventual
return of Zuylestein from England 'brought only the confirmation of the suspicions that we already had'. Far away in
the Netherlands and dependent on the hearsay of her sister,
surrounded by James's enemies, Mary seems to have been
genuinely convinced that the child was not her brother, the true
heir to her father's throne. Thenceforth, she never betrayed the
slightest doubt that a dreadful hoax had been perpetrated on
her and the English people. But it looked as if the child would
not survive anyway.

————

When the Prince of Wales was born the decision had been
made not to put him to a wet nurse, but to feed him 'by
hand'. Barillon told the French King this practice was not
uncommon in England, infants at first being given nothing
but boiled milk and crumbs of bread, and, quite soon, more
solid food. 'One can but hope that a thing so unheard of among
all other nations will prove successful,' he added sceptically.
Later he explained to Louis: 'The reason given to justify so
extraordinary a diet is that all the Queen's children have
died of convulsions, and they believe that was caused by a
nurse's milk.'

The Prince had been born with a strong constitution, but
the small body was soon beginning to concede defeat against

so unnatural a diet. As early as 9 July, Princess Anne was writing gleefully to her sister: 'The Prince of Wales has been ill these three or four days; and if he has been as bad as some people say, I believe it will not be long before he is an Angel in Heaven.' She probably used the phrase 'Angel in Heaven' in mimicry of her stepmother. It was not until 24 July that Princess Anne answered her sister's infamous questionnaire. Perhaps taking her cue from reports of the baby's illness, Mary asked her sister, 'Is the Queen fond of it?' Anne, who nearly always referred to her brother as 'It', replied: 'The Queen forbid Lady Powis to bring the child to her before any company; but that, they say, she used to do to her other children. I dined there the other day, when they said it had been very ill of a looseness, and it really looked so; yet when she came from prayers, she went to dinner without seeing it, and after that played at comet, and did not go to it till she was put out of the pool.'

All probably fairly normal behaviour in a royal or noble household, where a queen or great lady had appearances to maintain and duties to fulfil and the children were always cared for by servants.

It is extraordinary to think that there was open access to the royal nursery at court, so that any infectious person was free to enter. Mary Beatrice had lost her first son to smallpox in 1677. Understandably, she was extremely nervous about this child being exposed to infection. Apart from the courtiers and the foreign ambassadors who had been invited to inspect the newly born infant, only a week after the Prince's birth the Lord Mayor and aldermen had to be admitted to kiss his hand. By 12 July, however, it was reported that because of the heat and the prevalence of smallpox, the King had commanded that Lady Powis admit no one to see the Prince.

Towards the end of July the King and Queen moved to Windsor, where the Prince was taken into the park every day for the air. A few days later he was established at Richmond with his household, consisting of his lady governess, the Marchioness of Powis, the under-governess, Lady Strickland, two nurses, four rockers, a laundress and a sempstress, the necessary woman and two pages of the backstairs. During the first week in August he took a turn for the worse and was extremely ill. 'Each day,' Hoffman told the Emperor, 'the Queen goes to see him, and never returns until one o'clock in the morning; after great anxiety about him yesterday, the King and Queen, who was weeping abundantly, went to Richmond this morning.' Mary Beatrice is unlikely to have been 'weeping abundantly' if the child was not hers.

All through the first week of August the child's life was despaired of. On the 6th Terriesi wrote to the Grand Duke of Tuscany that his death had been hourly expected 'from colics and other disorders occasioned by that sort of paste made of oat and barley-meal with which the doctors obstinately insisted on feeding him. Up to yesterday they had given him all the remedies to be found in the apothecaries' jars and drawers (except milk, which is not to be found there), declaring they would not give him half an hour to live if he were suckled.'

At last Mary Beatrice put her foot down. She sent to the village for a wet nurse. 'The nurse is the wife of a tile-maker, and seems a healthy woman,' Sir John Ellis told a friend, 'she came in her cloth petticoat and waistcoat, and old shoes and no stockings, but she is now rigged by degrees (that the surprise may not alter her in her duty and care), a 100 pounds per annum is already settled upon her, and two or three hundred guineas already given, which she saith that she knows not what to do with.'

Given this appropriate feeding, the little Prince was soon making a remarkable recovery. The physicians were not satisfied, however, warning the King and Queen that the breast-feeding was a sure ticket to another world. They ignored them. The Tuscan ambassador, Terriesi, shook his head in wonder at the battery of treatments to which the child had been subjected: 'It is incredible the quantity and the quality of the stuffs the doctors have poured into that little body, thirty were counted at one time on the table in his room, among them Canary wine which he was made to drink and "Dr Goddard's Drops" (nothing less than liquid fire, for if one falls on a piece of cloth, it burns a hole through it in half an hour) and other violent remedies which are now the greatest danger to be feared.' It is worth noting that Dr Goddard's Drops contained sal ammoniac, dried viper and 'the skull of a person hanged'.

The fact that James Francis Edward survived and lived to seventy-eight years of age was clearly no thanks to the doctors. Inevitably, news of his illness and being close to death triggered off a fresh crop of rumours that he had died and been replaced by another infant, even that he was the son of his wet nurse, the tile-maker's wife. Princess Anne was associated with one of the most damaging of these rumours. In the midst of the child's illness, she had sent an equerry, Colonel Sandys, to Richmond to find out what was going on. He had entered the nursery, only to be ejected by Lady Strickland. But he claimed to have had enough time to observe what he considered a dead or dying infant in the cradle. A few hours later, he reported, the King invited him to see the Prince, a perfectly healthy, lively child, playing with the fringe around his cradle. Either Sandys was telling the Princess what he suspected she wanted to hear or the wet nurse had arrived in the interim and saved the child's life.

The Prince of Wales bore a marked likeness to both his parents. Liselotte, Duchess of Orléans, who watched him grow up at the French court, observed that 'he and his mother resemble each other like two drops of water.' The German portrait painter Kneller had been commissioned to paint the infant Prince of Wales and he was always outraged at suggestions that James Francis Edward was an impostor, as he expostulated many years later:

Vat de devil! De Prince of Wales de son of de brickbat oomen? It is von lie ... I am not of his party, nor shall not be for him. I am satisfied with vat de parliament has done, but I must tell you what I am sure of, and in vat I cannot be mistaken. His fader and moder have sat to me about thirty-six times a-piece, and I know every line and bit in their faces. I could paint King James just now by memory. I say the child is so like both, that there is not a feature in his face but what belongs either to fader or moder; this I am sure of ... I cannot be mistaken; nay, the nails of his fingers are his moder's, de Queen that was.

———————

By October, there could be no doubt that invasion was imminent. James had been mortified to read in the Prince of Orange's manifesto that one of the reasons he came was to order an official enquiry into the birth of the 'pretended Prince of Wales'. James knew that he might soon be engaged in battle and decided to call an extraordinary meeting of the Privy Council, where witnesses to the birth could swear to its authenticity. If James died in battle, he wanted no dispute about the succession. His decision was understandable but foolish. By English law, if a mother and father owned a child as theirs, there could be no question of its legitimacy. The onus was on those who doubted or disputed it to prove otherwise. The diarist John Evelyn disapproved of James's action. 'This procedure was censured by some as below His Majesty to condescend to,' he wrote, 'on the talk of the people.'

James had been slow to react to the persistent rumours surrounding the birth of his son and heir. His hurt was obvious when he wrote to his cousin Sophie of Hanover on 28 September that 'they talk of my son as if he were a supposed child, they that believe such a falsity must think me the worst man in the world. I suppose they judge of me by themselves, for else they could not think me capable of so abominable a thing.'

At first, he had been incredulous that anything so public as a royal birth should be called into question, or that he should be considered so wicked as to contrive to alter the hereditary succession. How could anyone, he asked, think him so unnatural a father that 'he would debar his own daughters from the right of succeeding him, to give his kingdoms to a suppositious son?' He would rather 'die a thousand deaths, than do the least wrong to any of my children'. The Queen had even more difficulty in believing that proof of their son's authenticity was necessary, until one day, speaking to Princess Anne, she had wondered aloud how anyone could credit the absurd stories that were circulating. She was shocked when Princess Anne retorted coldly that 'it was not so much to be wonder'd at, since such persons were not present, as ought to have been there.' The Queen 'began as well as the King to suspect the worst, when his own daughter who knew so well the reality of the Queen's being with child fomented the contrary report'.

The special meeting of the Privy Council took place on 22 October. Apart from the Privy Councillors, the meeting was attended by the Queen Dowager Catherine, the Archbishop of Canterbury, all the bishops in town, the judges and eminent lawyers, the Lord Mayor and aldermen and sheriffs, as well as all those who had attended the royal birth. James addressed them:

I have call'd you together upon a very extraordinary occasion, but extraordinary diseases must have extraordinary remedys, the malicious endeavours of my enemies, have so poison'd the minds of some of my subjects, that by the reports I hear from all hands, I have reason to believe that very many do not think this son, with which God has bless'd me, to be mine, but a supposed child; but I may say, that by particular providence, scarce any prince was ever borne, where there were so many persons present.

Forty witnesses to the birth came forward to swear on oath what they had seen. No gynaecological detail was spared, and some unhygienic relics of the birth chamber were displayed as evidence. The depositions only gave the King's enemies something further to dispute. There was one notable absence from the meeting. James was anxious that Princess Anne should attend to hear what the witnesses had to say. In his memoirs, he records that the Queen had invited Anne to feel her belly, just prior to Anne's departure for Bath. He wanted Anne, therefore, to attend the meeting to 'depose her own knowledge, which (before so many witnesses of her being privy to the Queen's being with child) she durst not have disown'd'. She declined to do so, on the pretext that she was pregnant. She certainly hoodwinked her father. 'The King said the Princess would have been there,' wrote her uncle Lord Clarendon, who was there, 'but being with child, and having been subject to miscarry, it was not sage for her to go out of her chamber.'

The next day, Lord Clarendon found Princess Anne with her ladies, making jokes about what had transpired at the meeting. Anne's rather coarse sense of humour was well known. He was appalled and asked to speak to her in private, but she made an excuse that it was late and she had to go to prayers. A few days later he asked her if she had had any letters from the Princess of Orange and she denied it, telling him 'her sister never wrote to her of any of these matters.' He hesitated to speak to her two days later because she was dressing and Lady Churchill was with her. But on the last day of the month he finally managed to pin his niece down.

He told her he was 'extremely surprised and troubled the other day, to find Her Royal Highness speak so slightingly of the Prince of Wales's affairs, and to suffer her women to make their jests upon it'. She replied that surely he had heard the common rumours about him? He said that of course he had but that he gave them no credence. Anne then launched into an account of how odd the Queen's behaviour had been when she was with child. 'Is it not strange,' she mused, 'that the Queen should never (as often as I am with her, mornings and evenings) speak to me to feel her belly?' He asked if she had been invited to do so during the Queen's other pregnancies, and when she replied that she had not, her uncle asked why, then, she should have expected to do so on this occasion? 'Because of the reports,' Anne replied. 'Possibly,' her uncle said, 'she did not mind the reports.'

Anne told him that the King had certainly known of the reports, saying that 'as he has been sitting by me in my own chamber, he would speak of the idle stories that were given out, of the Queen's not being with child, laughing at them. Therefore, I cannot but wonder there was no more care taken to satisfy the world.' Clarendon asked why she had not said anything to her father. The fact that she had not done so probably meant that the King thought she gave as little credence to the reports as he had done. He warned his niece that if this were not the case, if she harboured any doubts, she must speak to the King for her own and her sister's sake. Anne said that the King would be angry if she raised the subject with him, to which Clarendon replied that she had plenty of friends who would be glad to speak to the King on her behalf. Clarendon 'begged her to consider what miseries these suppositions might entail upon the kingdom, even in case God should bless the King with more sons: I, therefore, humbly besought her to consider, and do something that the world might see Her Royal Highness was satisfied.' Anne, of course, had no intention of doing anything of the kind.

The King ordered copies of the Privy Council depositions to be presented to Princess Mary in Holland. She replied that it was not a matter for her but for Parliament to decide. James also sent the Privy Councillors to Princess Anne with copies of the depositions. She did not even glance at them. 'My lords, this was not necessary,' she told them ingenuously, 'for I have so much duty for the King, that his word must be more to me than these depositions.'

How hollow her words were, there could soon be no doubt.

# 7
## *Betrayal*

*'Let the King of a large island beware the treachery of his courtiers'*
           *– Pescatore di Milano*, last quarter of 1688

As a naval man, James II had had a particularly large weathervane erected on the roof of the Banqueting House, which was visible from his apartments at Whitehall. Always keen to know the direction of the wind to determine whether or not the boats carrying the mail from the Continent were running on time, he would have been in the habit of consulting the weathervane, but in the autumn of 1688 this became imperative. With great reluctance, James had finally swallowed the bitter pill that the intense military and naval build-up that William of Orange had been supervising for the last three months was for an invasion force to be used against him.

The whole town became fixated on the weathervane. For many weeks it remained obstinately still. While the wind blew from the west, James believed that God was with him. But many of his subjects were willing it to swing round. In a radical departure from all previous foreign invasions that had roused unified national resistance, they were praying for a 'Protestant Wind', an easterly wind that would bring the Dutch fleet across to the English coast.

The King's birthday on 14 October heralded a change. The morning was ominously quiet, without the customary salvo of guns from the Tower. 'The sun eclipsed at its rising,' John Evelyn noted with the foreboding that such phenomena aroused in the seventeenth century. 'The wind, which had been hitherto west, was east all this day,' he exulted. 'Wonderful expectation of the Dutch fleet.' Public prayers were to be read in the churches, while in the streets men were still being press-ganged into the navy.

When news of William's intentions had begun to filter through to the English court, James had found it very hard to believe that a member of his family could be plotting against him. He did not, of course, hear it from his own intelligence sources, which were poor. Louis XIV's ambassador at The Hague, Count d'Avaux, noted William's preparations very early on and believed they were intended against England. He kept Louis fully informed and he also passed on the information to Barillon in London. In late August, Louis sent the diplomat Usson de Bonrepos to England to warn James what was afoot, and to offer him French assistance should it prove necessary. James seems to have been so affronted that he had received no notice of Bonrepos's visit that he chose to disregard the warning. The papal envoy warned James on 31 August of William's intentions, but again James did not believe him. It did not help that Sunderland was ridiculing any idea of a Dutch invasion. Far from the news acting as a spur to James to step up his defences, it seems to have induced in him a profound lethargy.

Once William had definitely decided on the invasion, which he did some time in July, his main concern was security, to allay English and French suspicions until he was ready to strike. At this stage at least 200 people in England, including the seven who had issued the invitation, seem to have been aware of his intentions. John Evelyn noted in his diary as early as 10 August that 'Dr Tenison [future Archbishop of Canterbury] now told me there would suddenly be some greate thing discover'd. This was the Prince of Orange intending to come over.' It was impossible to conceal such large-scale preparations, but various feints could be employed to obscure their true intentions. In London, the States-General's ambassador, Van Citters, was to give assurances that the naval preparations were to be employed to keep the peace in the Baltic.

The fate of England was inextricably bound up with that

of Europe. In the summer of 1688 Louis XIV was planning a major European war. He had quarrelled with the Pope and the Emperor over the election of the new Archbishop of Cologne. Louis demanded the installation of his candidate, Wilhelm von Furstenburg, Bishop of Strasbourg, while the Pope and the Emperor backed the candidature of a Wittelsbach, Clement of Bavaria. Louis had the effrontery to write to Pope Innocent XI to accuse him of starting a European war if he did not withdraw support for his candidate. Louis was also using the pretext of his sister-in-law Liselotte's claim to the Palatinate to invade it. It was quite legitimate, therefore, for the Dutch to foster the impression they were merely making preparations to defend their eastern frontier. For this reason, William intended to muster his army near Nijmegen. Only very secretly, on the brink of the invasion, would his troops be shifted to the north-west coast, passing swiftly along the canal routes in a day. They would not be informed of their destination until the last possible moment.

No one could say exactly when the invasion of England would be launched. James and Louis allowed themselves to be lulled into a false sense of security. As a naval man, James did not believe that William would embark on such a hazardous venture over the storm-ridden North Sea so late in the year. Louis, too, felt that the invasion was more likely to take place in the spring of 1689. Fatally, therefore, he kept his fleet in the Mediterranean rather than deploying it in the Channel. William knew that the time to strike was now. The invitation from the seven had emphasised that speed was of the essence, since 'we shall be every day in a worse condition than we are, and less able to defend ourselves, and therefore do earnestly wish we might be so happy as to find a remedy before it be too late for us to contribute to our own deliverance.' Any delay would give James the time he needed to improve his defences. William was also aware that political concessions on James's part might cool the ardour of the conspirators, so that his chance to take the crown would be lost.

The invitation from the seven assured William that 'nineteen parts of twenty of the people throughout the kingdom' were so dissatisfied with the regime and 'desirous of a change' that he could expect huge numbers to rise in support of the invasion. They also promised that 'the greatest part of the nobility and gentry are as much dissatisfied . . . the most considerable of them would venture themselves with Your Highness at your first landing.' Their claims were wildly optimistic. James had lost the allegiance of most of his subjects, but only a small minority subscribed to the view that they should actively oppose him. He was, after all, their anointed sovereign. As for the nobility and gentry, who by now avoided James's court, they were skulking in their country houses. They would support William only if and when he was seen to be on the winning side. They did not care if he lost everything in their cause.

In these circumstances, it was as well that William determined to rely only on his own resources, to raise so great a force that he could take on James without depending on outside assistance. Never before or since has such a mighty invasion force actually been launched against England. William was leaving nothing to chance. All through the summer and early autumn he directed every aspect of the preparations with the aid of Fagel, Bentinck and Dijkvelt. William would lead the expedition himself, but at Henry Sidney's suggestion he requested the services of Count Schomberg as his second-in-command. Frederick Herman, Count Schomberg, was a German Protestant, but he had been one of Louis's most brilliant commanders and a marshal of France. He had quit in disgust after the Revocation of the Edict of Nantes in 1685, which unleashed the persecution of the Huguenots, and fled to Berlin. When he arrived in Holland, William gave him instructions on 22 July to prepare for the descent on England.

William already had at his command the core of a seasoned army, but this had to be built up to a fighting strength of 15,000 over the following three months. There were to be twenty infantry battalions, including six of the Anglo-Dutch brigade, composed of some of the English and Scottish troops that the States-General had refused to release despite James's request. Four battalions were regulars in the employ of the States-General, five were the personal troops of the House of Orange, including William's Blue Guards. There was one battalion from Brandenburg, two from Scandinavia, and two composed of French Huguenots. The cavalry consisted of fourteen Dutch regiments and one of Huguenot officers, mounted at William's expense. A motley group of English and Scottish exiles made up another regiment. Hundreds of Dutchmen worked night and day to provide food, equipment, arms and ammunition for the invasion force.

The Dutch fleet already consisted of twenty-five men-of-war and ten fireships, but twenty-four additional men-of-war were fitted out. For the transport of troops, horses, equipment and supplies, 225 additional vessels were needed. They were to carry a portable bridge, a mobile smithy, officers' baggage, a huge sum in cash and a mint, provisions such as 4 tons of tobacco, 1,600 hogsheads of beer and 50 of brandy, 10,000 pairs of boots, 300 tons of hay for several thousand horses, the Prince's personal coach and horses and the essential printing press for his propaganda. The fleet, consisting of 7,000 sailors, was to be commanded by the English defector, the disreputable but bold Arthur Herbert, and two Dutchmen, Lieutenant-Admiral Van Almonde and Admiral Evertsen.

These preparations demanded the detailed planning and delegating skills of which William had already proved himself such a master. On the diplomatic front, he also had to convince the German princes that it was in their interests to support his invasion of England and to lend troops to protect the eastern Dutch frontier in the coming European war, when he would be engaged elsewhere. The young Elector of Brandenburg, William's cousin, was at last persuaded to commit himself to William, lending 12,000 men. The Elector of Saxony would lend 6,000, the Dukes of Zell and Wolfenbuttel 4,000 and

Hesse-Cassel 3,000. These troops made their slow progress over the German plains in September.

All this time, William was kept informed of opinion in England and disseminated a steady stream of propaganda through his network of agents. D'Avaux noted that a small vessel 'very well rigged and an excellent sailor' – one of those that could cross the sea to Holland in a night – was frequently seen putting in at Maensluys at the mouth of the Meuse and suspected it was bringing intelligence. But intelligence also flowed through Van Citters at the Dutch embassy in London. It is possible that Zuylestein, after paying his compliments to the King and Queen on the birth of the Prince of Wales, returned incognito to England as one of William's principal agents. When James had requested the return in March of the English and Scottish regiments and some of the officers had obeyed his summons, a few of them, such as Colonel Sir Henry Bellasys and Aeneas Mackay, went as agents for William. In Scotland, Mackay reported to Dr William Blackadder, a gatherer of intelligence for William.

One of William's most active agents in England was James Johnston, a cousin of Gilbert Burnet. Johnston had assumed the identity of a Mr Rivers and communicated with Bentinck from Huguenot accommodation addresses in London to the same in the Netherlands. His letters looked like business correspondence, until soaked in a solution, when a cipher message written in invisible ink emerged. Every titbit of information was passed on to William, even popular lyrics being sung in the streets, such as this one about the hapless Prince of Wales:

> *Rock-a-bye baby, in the tree top*
> *When the wind blows the cradle will rock,*
> *When the bough breaks the cradle will fall,*
> *And down will come baby, cradle and all.*

Johnston understood that the key to power was through the printed word, urging William to issue a regular supply of pamphlets – including those casting aspersions on the Queen's chastity and the birth of the Prince – to keep the English engaged in his cause. 'The spirit of a people is like that of particular persons, often to be entertained by trifles,' he told his employers, 'particularly that of the English, who, like all islanders, seems to ebb and flow like the neighbouring sea.'

In late August, Jacob van Leeuwen was sent to London, posing as secretary to Van Citters, to convey military intelligence to William. Johnston returned to Holland with Henry Sidney. The latter brought a draft manifesto written by Danby for William's approval, together with a most depressing memorandum from Danby suggesting that perhaps it would be best to delay the whole enterprise until the spring. If one of the seven conspirators was getting cold feet, what hope did William have of support from the rest of the nation? He was somewhat cheered by the arrival of Russell and Shrewsbury – who put a large part of his personal fortune at William's disposal – and pressed ahead with his preparations. He ordered Fagel and Dijkvelt to rewrite the manifesto: 'It needs considerable changes,' he told them. 'You will see that by the conclusion I throw myself entirely at the mercy of a parliament.' This idea he was not prepared to encourage. Considerable care went into the presentation of the manifesto, which appeared with twin portraits of William and Mary on the masthead. Mary was to come with him to England politically and figuratively, if not physically. At the appropriate moment, 50,000 copies of the manifesto were smuggled into England and distributed. James lent his to his daughter Anne to read, although the contents can hardly have come as a surprise to her.

The month of August saw a series of letters to the Prince from English adherents, promising him their support in the event of an invasion. One of them came from John, Lord Churchill, James's lieutenant-general:

Mr Sidney will let you know how I intend to behave myself: I think it is what I owe to God and my country. My honour I take leave to put into your Royal Highness's hands, in which I think it safe. If you think there is any thing else that I ought to do, you have but to command me, and I shall pay an entire obedience to it, being resolved to die in that religion that it hath pleased almighty God to give you both the will and the power to protect. I am, with all respect, Sir, your Royal Highness's obedient servant, Churchill.

Churchill's support was important, not only because of his position in the army, but also because he was so influential, through his wife Sarah, in the household of Princess Anne at the Cockpit. He found ready allies there. The Duke of Ormonde, whose family had once been so loyal to the monarchy, had been alienated by the treatment his father had received at the hands of the Catholic Tyrconnel in Ireland. The Duke of Grafton, natural son of Charles II and Barbara Villiers, was Colonel of the First Foot Guards. Colonel John Berkeley – married to Barbara, one of the Villiers' sisters who had been brought up with the Princesses at Richmond – was the commander of a regiment of dragoons. Lord Drumlanrig was the son of the Duke of Queensberry. Lord Cornbury, son of Lord Clarendon and therefore cousin to the Princesses Mary and Anne, was Colonel of the Royal Regiment of Dragoons.

Henry Compton, Bishop of London, the former tutor of the Princesses Anne and Mary, was also closely allied with the Cockpit circle. He spent September travelling in the north of England, bringing his nephew the Earl of Northampton and others into the conspiracy. Tory plotters such as Lord Danby and his relatives linked with Whigs, such as Thomas Wharton and Charles Godfrey. The latter was married to Arabella Churchill, John's sister and James's discarded mistress.

In early September there was a diplomatic fiasco in William's favour. The French demanded from the States-General an explanation for the military and naval preparations and issued a formal warning that any act of hostility against England would be regarded as a declaration of war against France. This engendered fears that there was a secret Anglo-French pact and the States-General asked England to confirm whether this was true. At this juncture, James might have been well advised to abandon his position on the diplomatic fence and throw in his lot with Louis, but he was haunted by the fact that association with France, which had brought such opprobrium on his brother, would only add to his unpopularity. He denied that there was any understanding between England and France, adding that it was no business of France to intervene.

Rebuffed, Louis ceased to offer his beleaguered cousin any further assistance, and turned his attention to his forthcoming German war. He genuinely might have believed that the Prince of Orange was unlikely to launch an invasion against England when Europe was on the brink of a war that might threaten the Dutch Republic. On the other hand, he might have reasoned that it would be to his advantage if William did go ahead with the invasion, which would probably involve him and his army in another prolonged English civil war. For his part, William continued to believe that Louis's threats against the Rhine and the Palatinate were a feint. Surely he would not abandon James in his hour of need? If William succeeded in England, he would be able to engage its considerable resources in the European war against Louis. It seems that Louis did not think this far ahead, or believe that William would succeed in his enterprise. On 27 September, William's suspicions of a feint were dispelled. Marshal d'Humières turned the full might of the French army, 70,000 men, south-east to besiege Philippsburg and occupy a long stretch of the German frontier. The road to England lay wide open and William was free to attack unopposed by Louis.

So far, William had acted very much on his own authority. He had been able to borrow a sum of 4 million guilders from the States-General, ostensibly to boost the defences of the Republic, but he had met most of the balance of the expense of his preparations from his own pocket. As captain- and admiral-general of the Republic, he could employ the Republic's army and navy for a personal enterprise without formally involving his country in war, but permission to do so had to be sought from the States-General. William's ally, the Grand Pensionary Caspar Fagel, was a dying man, but he exerted all his considerable diplomatic skills to obtain from the States-General their support for William's enterprise.

Louis had alienated his traditional supporters in the Republic by imposing trade restrictions, particularly on Dutch herrings, which could only be imported if preserved with French salt. For once, even Amsterdam and the state of Holland were inclined to rally with the other states round the Stadholder. In a secret session of the States-General, Fagel convinced them that William needed to go to England not for the crown, but to ensure the calling of a free Parliament and to guarantee the security of the Protestant religion. He wished to restore good relations between James and his subjects, so that England might once again become a useful ally of the Republic. Permission was granted.

William employed the same platitudes in his correspondence with the Pope and the Emperor. He told the Emperor that relations between James and his people were so strained that his intervention was necessary. He assured him that he had 'not the least intention to do any hurt to his Britannic Majesty, or to those who have a right to pretend to the succession of the kingdoms, and still less to make an attempt upon the crown, or desire to appropriate it to myself'. William, who genuinely believed that no one should be persecuted for his religion, promised the Emperor that he would not 'extirpate the Roman Catholics', but rather try to give them 'liberty of conscience, and be put out of fear of being persecuted on account of their religion; and provided they exercise their religion without noise, and with modesty, that they shall not be subject to any punishment.'

By 1688 James was the only ruler in Europe who still believed that foreign policy had anything to do with religious affiliation. He could never understand why the Catholic Habsburg Emperor did not take his part, but he had alienated him by siding with Louis in the dispute over the choice of a new Archbishop of Cologne. Emperor Leopold had long been undermined in his war against the Turks – who had only just been beaten back from the walls of Vienna – by Louis's financing of them. Now, Louis's aggression on the Rhine and in the Palatinate provided the final spur for the Emperor to give William his support. Similarly, the Pope had been alarmed that James's zeal was bound to make matters worse for the Catholics in England. He was tired of James's relentless campaign to make Petre a cardinal. In his long struggle with Louis XIV, he had ample cause to feel that James supported the French King. He even adopted the same arrogant tone in his correspondence with the Vatican. Innocent XI had no problem in backing the Calvinist Prince of Orange in his enterprise against England. There was even a rumour that he had given him some financial support.

———

James remained unconvinced that William was going to attack him until well into September. On 18 and 21 September he received confirmation from his envoy the Marquis d'Albeville at The Hague that 'their goeing for England is no more a secret in these parts'. On 24 September Lord Clarendon attended the King's levée and James told him that 'the Dutch were now coming to invade England in good earnest.' Clarendon asked if he really believed that, to which James replied, 'Do I see you, my lord?' Adopting the sarcastic tone that so often betrayed him, James added, 'And now, my lord, I shall see what the Church of England men will do.' Clarendon replied stoically, 'And Your Majesty will see they will behave themselves like honest men; though they have been somewhat severely used of late.'

On 25 September James wrote his last private letter to 'my sonne, the Prince of Orange'. If he had had his suspicions of William, James refused to believe that his daughter Mary was party to the conspiracy. In mid-September he had sent his erstwhile ambassador, Bevil Skelton, to the Tower for insisting that 'the Princess of Orange's letters declaring that the armament at Holland was but for the service of the emperor of Germany, were utter deceit, as he had just been recalled from Holland, and knew it was to invade England.'

On the same day as his letter to William, James could still write to Mary: 'I see by yours of the 20th inst. that the Prince of Orange was gone to the Hague; and from thence, that he has arrived. What his business is there at this time, I do really believe you are not acquainted with, nor with the resolution he has taken, which alarms all people here very much.'

Three days later, James sounded tired and careworn as he wrote this heart-rending letter to Mary, hoping that she of all people had not betrayed him:

This evening I had yours of the 4th, from Dieren, by which I find you were then to go the Hague, being sent for by the Prince. I suppose it is to inform you of his design of coming to England, which he has been so long a contriving. I hope it will have been as great a surprise to you as it was to me, when I first heard it, being sure it is not in your nature to approve of so unjust an undertaking. I have been all this day so busy, to endeavour to be in some condition to defend myself from so unjust and unexpected an attempt, that I am almost tired, and so I shall say no more but that I shall always have as much kindness for you as you will give me leave to have.

On this same day, the Queen wrote to her stepdaughter:

I am much put to it what to say, at a time when nothing is talked of here but the Prince of Orange coming over with an army. This has been said a long time and believed by a great many, but I do protest to you I never did believe it till now very lately, that I have no possibility left of doubting it. The second part of this news I will never believe, that is that you are to come over with him; for I know you to be too good, that I don't believe you could have such a thought against the worst of fathers, much less perform it against the best, that has always been kind to you, and I believe has loved you better than all the rest of his children.

Clearly, Mary had been keeping up her correspondence with her father as a polite front, to allay his suspicions as to what was really going on. Convinced that he was the perpetrator of a Catholic conspiracy to subvert the Protestant succession, she betrayed little sympathy for his plight. James would have been cut to the heart had he been able to read Mary's journal, where she admitted that she was an accessory to her husband's intention to take her father's crown: 'The consideration of all this and the thought that my father was capable of a crime so horrible and that, humanly speaking, there was not any other means to save the Church and the State than that my husband should go to dethrone him by force, are the most afflicting reflections and would not be supportable without the assistance of God and a firm and unshakeable confidence in Him.'

Mary's inner turmoil seemed to derive more from shame at her father's perceived crime than pity for his impending downfall. As ever, she relied on God to sustain her. Careful not to betray her emotions, Mary assumed an untroubled countenance for the world, 'for I cannot talk with liberty to anyone except to the Prince, who has seen my tears and has pitied me'.

---

If James was slow to realise that he was being betrayed by his children, he could rely on few others either. The Imperial ambassador, Hoffman, already detected signs that support for James was faltering:

His soldiers are his most dangerous enemies . . . A few weeks ago orders were given to the Duke of Berwick's [James's eighteen-year-old son by Arabella Churchill] regiment to admit three or four Irish recruits into each company, which the lieutenant-colonel and five captains absolutely refused . . . upon this they were imprisoned at Windsor and cashiered by court martial (after pardon had been offered if they would retract and they had refused it); almost immediately afterwards three lieutenants and four ensigns of the same regiment resigned their commissions and a large number of soldiers deserted . . . If the King cannot depend upon these, still less can he count upon his seamen . . . who unblushingly declare they will not serve against Holland . . . It is, therefore, allowable to say that the King has against him all the clergy, all the nobility, all the people and all the army and navy, with a few exceptions, which must necessarily keep him alert on every side.

The seven had led William to believe that the army was divided, that the officers stayed only for their pay, that the soldiers hated the Catholic religion, and that huge numbers would desert. In the navy, they told him, not one in ten of the seamen was loyal. The King had been informed of a likely conspiracy in the army. The Earl of Ailesbury recalled that he and Lord Feversham had implored him to weed out the principals, namely 'the Prince of Denmark, the Dukes of Ormonde and Grafton, Lord Churchill, Mr Kirke, and Mr Trelawney'. But James hesitated to act. William was well aware that his army of 15,000 was inferior to James's strength of 40,000, although about 15,000 of these were deployed in garrisons which, as it turned out, were far removed from the action. William was depending to some extent, therefore, on the desertions and defections from the army that the conspirators were promising him.

There were indeed conspirators working against James in the army. The members of the Treason Club, a loose collection of young Whig army officers who had been followers of Monmouth, met at the Rose Tavern in Russell Street, Covent Garden. Then there was the Tangier group, composed of officers who had served in the garrison there, including Lieutenant-General John Churchill, Colonels Percy Kirke and Charles Trelawney. Thomas Langston was a member of both the Treason Club and the Tangier group and provided a useful link between the two. James had tried to create an army to serve him impartially, one that would be above politics. But he himself introduced politics into it when he conducted a survey in Lord Lichfield's regiment as to who would support the repeal of the Test Acts and penal laws. It was easy then for Thomas Langston to start a rumour that James was intending to evict all Protestant officers. The third group opposed to James, the Association of Protestant Officers, therefore came into being, determined to preserve their interests.

In the navy, officers at court were apparently complaining that their ships were not ready. With an efficiency that irritated the disaffected, Samuel Pepys at the Navy Office maintained that the ships were ready, they only needed their officers' attendance on board. The conspiracy in the navy was associated with that in the army. Some of the personnel, such as George Byng, had also served in Tangier. Much of the dissatisfaction in the navy arose from the sacking of Admiral Arthur Herbert and his replacement by the Catholic Sir Roger Strickland. Strickland nearly provoked mutiny when he had the Catholic mass celebrated aboard the flagship and James had to visit the fleet to mollify the seamen. His old friend George Legge, Lord Dartmouth, replaced Strickland. Naval officers such as George Churchill, John's brother, and Cloudesley Shovell had benefited from the patronage of Arthur Herbert, who was now commanding the invasion fleet, and were loyal to him. It was not so easy for the naval officers to conspire when they were on separate ships, however, unlike the army officers who had spent a large part of the summer together on Hounslow Heath, in easy distance of London. Dartmouth, therefore, had the navy put to sea at the earliest opportunity.

Instead of devoting all his energies to rousing the nationalistic sentiments of his subjects to resist the foreign invaders and joining his army to boost its morale, James delayed in London, making frantic political concessions that were regarded as a sign of weakness. All the policies of the last three years were reversed. He issued a proclamation in which he undertook to uphold the laws relating to Church and state – the same promise he had made on his accession and failed to keep – and to summon a free Parliament. He cancelled Bishop Compton's suspension and dissolved the hated Ecclesiastical Commission. The former lords lieutenant were restored, as were JPs and magistrates who had been sacked for refusing to co-operate in the repeal of the Test Acts and penal laws. Town charters, particularly that of the City of London, were granted in the form they had enjoyed before Charles II had started tinkering with them. The Catholic fellows James had installed at Magdalen College, Oxford were expelled and the former fellows reinstated.

The concessions prompted William to add a codicil to his manifesto asserting that 'the imperfect redress that is now offered is a plain confession of those violations of the government that we have set forth.' William's original manifesto had been careful not to blame James so much as his 'evil councillors', but James made no move to address this grievance by dismissing the Jesuit Petre and other Roman Catholics who had been invited to sit on the Privy Council. Nor did he deal with the vexed issue of the dispensing power by renouncing his claim to it. To be fair, this was not the moment to remove Roman Catholics from the army or navy, who were there by virtue of the disputed dispensing and suspending powers. Ironically, William's army contained probably as many Catholics.

James wasted an inordinate amount of time trying to reach an accommodation with the bishops and to persuade them to issue a statement condemning the impending invasion. They prevaricated. James was furious to read in William's manifesto that he was coming at the invitation of the lords temporal and spiritual. He summoned all the peers who were in London – not many since most of them were lurking in the country – and demanded which of them was party to the invitation. They all denied it or, in the case of Compton, gave an ambiguous response.

On 9 October James wrote one last pathetic letter to his beloved daughter Mary:

I had no letter from you by the last post, which you see does not hinder me from writing to you now, not knowing, certainly, what may have hindered you from doing it. I easily believe you are embarrassed how to write to me, now that the unjust design of the Prince of Orange's invading me is so public. And though I know you are a good wife, and ought to be so, yet for the same reason I must believe you will be still as good a daughter to a father that has always loved you so tenderly, and that has never done the least thing to make you doubt it. I shall say no more, and believe you very uneasy all this time, for the concern you must have for a husband and a father. You shall still find me kind to you, if you desire it.

There was no response. Mary's uncle, Lord Clarendon, noted in his diary on 16 October that he was at the King's levée: 'His Majesty told me that the Dutch troops were all embarked, and would sail with the first wind. He said he had nothing by this post from the Princess, which was the first time he had missed hearing from her of a great while.'

James would never hear from his daughter Mary again. She had made her choice, and it was with her husband, not her father.

---

In mid-October the wind changed, as Evelyn noted in his diary, and William prepared to take his leave of Mary. Over the last few months, the couple had grown closer than they had ever been. Mary had for a long time been totally devoted to William's interests, seeing him as the Protestant champion of Europe. But by now William, too, had come to appreciate how much he could rely on his wife. The evening before his departure, they had an emotional meeting in which he told her that she could depend on Count Waldeck, Pensionary Fagel and Dijkvelt if she needed any help in his absence. He advised her that in the event of his death, she should marry again – to a Protestant, of course.

Mary was so horrified by the thought of his death that it was 'as if someone had torn my heart out'. She refused to contemplate remarriage. 'I assured him that I had never loved any except himself and that I should never love another; besides that, having been married so many years without it having pleased God to bless me with a child, I believed that alone sufficient to prevent me from ever thinking of this that he proposed.' Ever the supplicant in the relationship, Mary asked his pardon for her faults and 'he replied with so much tenderness that, if it was possible, my love for him was still augmented.'

William had already made his will and the following day he addressed the States-General, thanking them for their loyalty and support. 'I have always served you faithfully and kept the welfare of this state constantly before me,' he told them. 'What God intends for me I do not know, but if I should fall, have a care for my beloved wife who always loved this country as her own.'

That afternoon, he and Mary dined together at Honselaers-dijck for the last time. Then she accompanied him as far as the river on which he was to embark to take him to Brill and his flagship, *Den Briel*. She remained in her carriage watching until William disappeared from view, then she returned to The Hague. D'Avaux observed that she was in tears. As she confided in her journal that night, she was distraught, filled with dread of what might happen to William. As in all times of emotional upset, she soon succumbed to an old kidney ailment and had to be bled.

The following day was one of public fast and prayer in the Republic. Mary noted in her journal that even the Jews observed it. Spain was one of William's allies, even though the Queen of Spain was James's niece, Marie-Louise, the daughter of his long-dead sister Henriette, Duchess of Orléans. The Spanish ambassador therefore attended a Catholic mass for the success of the enterprise. Only the French and English ambassadors conspicuously failed to observe it.

William was impatient to take advantage of the favourable wind and on 20 October the fleet finally cast off. At The Hague, d'Albeville detected a slight change in the direction of the wind, which soon veered strongly from the west. The fleet struggled north through choppy seas that by night turned into a maelstrom. It was impossible, especially for the laden transport vessels, to make any headway and the ships were scattered. Signals went out from ship to ship to head for the nearest friendly port. They limped back in twos and threes to ports along the Dutch coast, tired, seasick and dispirited. Hundreds of horses had been suffocated when the hatches had had to be closed during the storm, but there was surprisingly little other damage, only the loss of one ship. As the fleet regrouped at Hellevoetsluys, William came under pressure to change his plan. Some advocated that the warships sail first, to deal with the English fleet if necessary, and the slower transports follow separately once a landing had been secured. To his credit, William refused to deviate from his original plan. The great armada would sail as a single force.

News of the invasion fleet being thrown back on Dutch shores was greeted with joyful relief at the English court, so that it was reported that 'never place was more thronged than our drawing-room at Whitehall this evening.' The Catholics were looking immensely pleased. The King took advantage of this brief uplift in his fortunes by sacking his chief minister, Lord Sunderland. The wily politician had already been in contact with William and soon he fled to Rotterdam disguised as a woman. His dismissal came too late to do James any good and failed to anticipate that Sunderland could still be useful. Sunderland had nothing to contribute in the current situation, which was a military one, but James could have benefited from his nimble, opportunistic mind when the military game was finished and James's fate hung on a political solution.

Confined to port by the 'popish' wind for another week, William had to contain his impatience, while the inactive fleet with its thousands of men and horses to be fed could only swallow more and more money. Morale sank and sickness spread. On 1 November William invited Mary to visit him and she dashed to Brill from her sickbed. Their meeting was short and, for Mary, the second separation was even more painful than the first. The following day she attended public prayers in the town for the success of the expedition: her husband's enemies noted that the King of England's daughter had publicly given her prayers and good wishes to a task force setting out to ruin him. She climbed the 315 steps of the church tower for a final glimpse of the fleet, but was disappointed to find that she could only see the masts. At one o'clock, the fleet sailed in fine weather with a following wind.

Few had been apprised of the intended destination of the invasion force. To a large extent, it was dependent on the wind. Remembering the attack on the Medway in his brother's reign, James had strengthened his defences in the Thames estuary. William had no intention of being beholden to English conspirators such as Danby, who was planning a rising in the north, by landing in their midst. At first, however, the wind carried the fleet up the east coast of England, so that it looked as if William were indeed heading to join the northern conspirators. The wind then suddenly veered east, sending the Dutch fleet down past the mouth of the Thames – where Lord Dartmouth and the English fleet were currently confined by the adverse wind – and round through the Straits of Dover. It was William's intention to avoid an engagement with the English fleet, wanting to preserve it intact, and, indeed, when

Dartmouth did emerge from the Thames he did not pursue the Dutch or force an engagement.

As William's armada passed the Isle of Wight on 4 November hundreds of spectators lined the cliff tops and the beaches to watch its stately progress. There were so many ships that the convoy was twenty miles long. Music could be heard drifting over the water from the ships. William's flagship carried a banner inscribed with the Orange family motto, '*Je Maintiendrai*', while others carried streamers with slogans in Latin such as '*Pro libertate et religione*' and '*Pro religione protestante*'.

That day was William's thirty-eighth birthday and the eleventh anniversary of his marriage to Mary, an auspicious day to land. But it was thought preferable to proceed further along to the Devon coast. At noon on Monday, 5 November, Gunpowder Treason or Guy Fawkes's Day, the wind veered again, making a landing possible at Torbay, just short of Lord Bath's heavily garrisoned port of Plymouth. Count von Solms-Braunfels was the first to go ashore and, seeing the people were friendly, William quickly followed. Burnet dashed up to William to congratulate him. Since he had always disputed the theory of predestination with the Calvinist William, William could not resist asking him, 'What do you think of predestination now?' A service of thanksgiving was held on the beach. That night, William's personal standard incongruously flew over the fisherman's hut where he slept.

The following morning a local showed the invaders a deeply shelving bay nearby where the transports could disembark. Twenty-four hours after the fleet had dropped anchor, the disembarkation of men, horses and equipment was complete and William's army was able to start its advance on London. The people of Devon had not forgotten the terrible repercussions of Monmouth's rebellion, they still dreamed of gibbets, yet they did nothing to repel or resist the invaders. Instead, they called out their blessings to the Prince and offered him and his troops cider and apples.

If the Dutch were amazed at how filthy the English country people were and that even women and quite young girls indulged in pipe-smoking, the English were in their turn impressed at the discipline of these foreign troops. They were polite and, at William's insistence, paid for everything they needed rather than just taking it. When two of his soldiers stole a chicken, he made a terrible example of them by hanging them. If the country people were not afraid to extend a welcome, William was quietly fuming that none of the nobility or gentry, in particular none of the seven who had invited him, had welcomed him at his landing, as promised. Beacons had not been lit to alert the country to an invasion threat – as they had on the occasion of the Spanish Armada in 1588 – and news travelled slowly. It was not altogether surprising that it should take a few days to bring in the support William was expecting.

Progress was slow in pouring rain through the muddy lanes of Devon, but William made a triumphant entry into Exeter at the head of his troops. Bishop Lamplugh and the dean had fled in fear to London – James quite unaccountably rewarded Lamplugh with the vacant see of York – but the town offered no resistance. It was fair time and the people enjoyed the splendour of the unexpected military show. The occasion merited a propaganda pamphlet from the Prince's printing press: *A Letter from Exon to a Gentleman in London*. Burnet conducted a service in the cathedral where a *Te Deum* was sung and William's manifesto was read. Neither now nor at any subsequent time was there any question of William following Monmouth's example and declaring himself King. He came, he insisted, only to ensure the calling of a free Parliament to right the wrongs of the current regime. After the service Burnet shouted 'God save the Prince of Orange', but few cried 'Amen!'

In his new headquarters in the bishop's house at Exeter, William complained to Shrewsbury, who had accompanied him from Holland, that there was still no show of support for him from people of any influence or standing. Gleeful reports were reaching London of this lukewarm response to his landing. Shrewsbury assured him that no one wanted to be the first to welcome him, but if one came, the rest would follow quickly, for no one wanted to be the last either. More than a week after his arrival, William was so despondent that he was on the verge of returning to Holland and leaving the English to sort out their own problems. At this critical moment, Sir Edward Seymour of all people, a local Tory with such an inflated sense of his own importance that he would say that the Duke of Somerset belonged to *his* family, came to offer his support. The fact that he had once criticised the quality of William's champagne appeared to be forgotten.

As Shrewsbury had predicted, the trickle of adherents soon became a flood. One of the seven, Edward Russell, together with the Whig, Thomas, Lord Wharton – who claimed to have written the lyrics of 'Lillibullero', the anti-Catholic song set to a catchy tune by Purcell that accompanied James II out of three kingdoms – Lord Colchester and Lord Abingdon joined the Prince. As the King was joining his army at Salisbury Plain, reports reached William of risings in other parts of the country. Danby, as promised, had organised one in York and Lord Delamere one in Cheshire. The Earl of Devonshire raised an army in the north Midlands with headquarters at Nottingham. The Earls of Manchester, Stamford, Rutland and Chesterfield joined him. To the rear, Lord Bath surrendered Plymouth on 17 November. George Churchill came into Portsmouth, surrendered his ship, the *Newcastle*, and declared for the Prince, while his brother was still marching with the King from London to Salisbury. In early December Shrewsbury took Bristol for the Prince. It looked as if, after all, the Prince was to have the support he had been promised, although it had taken so long that William was in no mood to be gracious, which did not bode well for his future relations with his leading subjects.

James had never been the brightest or most quick-witted of men, but now the elderly man began to show alarming signs of mental disintegration. He who believed that kings were to be obeyed did not know what to do when this kingly authority proved worthless. It was as if 1642 were being replayed and his father's plight had come back to haunt him. He seemed incapable of reaching a decision about anything, and if he did, of sticking to it. Under the intense nervous strain, his stutter became noticeably worse. Occasionally, he would display a flash of his old arrogance, as when he told a delegation of peers that it would be impossible to call a free Parliament while there was a foreigner occupying the country, before dismissing them. He delayed in London until the last possible moment, fussing about the safety of the Prince of Wales. At last he decided to send the baby and some of his attendants to Portsmouth, ready for an escape to France. He made his will, leaving everything to the Queen and the Prince of Wales. He left the reins of the government in the hands of the Queen and five councillors.

Signs of treachery all around him and crumbling support, even in his beloved army and navy, contributed to James's mental decline and his lack of confidence. Lord Cornbury, his nephew, was the first to desert the King's army and go over to the enemy. When the news reached court on 15 November, Lords Churchill and Godolphin were observed to celebrate by laughing and skipping down the gallery together. Cornbury's loyal father, Lord Clarendon, was mortified at his son's defection. 'O God, that my son should be a rebel!' he moaned. 'The lord in his mercy look upon me, and enable me to support myself under this most grievous calamity.'

When Clarendon visited Princess Anne a few days later, he confessed he was so ashamed he hardly dared show his face. Tellingly, Anne replied, 'that people were so apprehensive of popery, that she believed many more of the army would do the same.' Anne had already decided on her course of action, because she wrote to the Prince of Orange on the 18th, the day after her father and her husband left town to join the army, assuring him of her support. She and the other defectors had necessarily made their concerted plans before the King left London.

James reached his camp at Sarum on the 19th, two weeks after the Prince of Orange had landed on English soil. Almost immediately, he was completely incapacitated by a heavy, persistent nosebleed, which endured for most of the time he was there. The old remedy of hanging a key down his back was applied, but nothing would stop the bleeding. Possibly it was brought on by nervous strain. In his memoir, he claimed that the nosebleed was providential, because otherwise he would have agreed to make a foray to Warminster, where he claimed Lord Churchill would have handed him over to the Prince of Orange. If that was the plan, it was not one approved by William, who had no intention of confronting his father-in-law on the battlefield or anywhere else. His policy was to avoid him. William knew James's psychology well. It is not too far-fetched to claim that he knew exactly what he was doing: driving James, through despair, to give up without a fight.

A meeting was held at the King's camp on 23 November as to what course of action to adopt. Churchill and others advocated engaging the enemy at once, whereas Louis Duras, Lord Feversham, recommended retreat. Possibly Lord Churchill resented that the French-born Feversham, rather than himself, was in command again, as he had been at the time of the Monmouth rebellion. Churchill's co-conspirator, Percy Kirke, had been arrested before they left London, but that night Churchill, Lord Grafton and Colonel Berkeley deserted to the Prince of Orange at Axminster, Churchill leaving a letter attributing his lack of loyalty to the dictates of his conscience. It is interesting to note that once their foot soldiers knew where they were going, most of them returned to the King's camp. Churchill, then, did not bring in the numbers he had promised, but the very fact of his treachery dealt a decisive blow to the King's confidence. After all, James had raised John Churchill 'from the dirt' and he was understandably stunned and hurt by his ingratitude. Schomberg greeted Churchill coolly, commenting that this was the first time, to his knowledge, that a lieutenant-general had defected in the field.

The following night the King reached Andover in the first stage of his withdrawal to London. Princess Anne's ponderous husband, George of Denmark, had greeted each betrayal with the words, '*Est-il possible?*' Now he, too, defected in the night. The next morning, James showed little sign of surprise or disappointment at his departure. 'Is "*Est-il Possible*" gone too?' he asked, in a rare show of humour. He commented in his memoir that the Prince of Denmark's defection concerned him only because he was the husband of his dearest child, whom he still believed was innocent of any part in the conspiracy, otherwise the loss was of less consequence than that of one good trooper. He gladly sent his coach and luggage after him.

By failing to engage the enemy in the west, James had lost the military advantage. The struggle would now be political rather than military. James was not good at politics, whereas the Prince of Orange was a master. William could not believe his good fortune that James seemed to be giving up without striking a blow, exactly as he had hoped. He advanced on Salisbury, following the King as he retreated towards London.

At the Earl of Pembroke's home at Wilton, William paused. Loving paintings as he did, he was entranced by the Van Dykes, particularly the one depicting the three eldest children of Charles I in those last golden days of the Stuart autocracy before the civil wars. In this family portrait he saw his uncles, the future Charles II and James II, and his mother, the second Mary Stuart. The third Mary Stuart, James's daughter, would be William's wife. The paintings were so fine that he urged his secretary, Constantyn Huygens, to go back to look at them. He had neglected to do so when he first passed because the weather was so cold. Meanwhile, William would continue to pursue his Uncle James, that child of the idealised Carolean court, even if it meant hounding him out of his kingdoms.

# 8
## Flight

'Whom then could I trust, if my own daughters had deserted me? If only my enemies had cursed me, I could have borne it'

– James II

James returned to London a broken man, but a far more devastating blow than the treachery of his nobles and army officers awaited him. At Whitehall he discovered that his beloved daughter, the Princess Anne, had defected to the enemy. She had sneaked out of the Cockpit in the night, leaving a letter of explanation for the Queen. When James arrived at the palace that dark winter afternoon, the Imperial ambassador Hoffman was struck by how ghastly he looked. News of Anne's defection subsequently left him so distraught that a lady of the court told Sir John Reresby that 'it disordered him in his understanding'. 'God help me!' he cried. 'My own children have deserted me.' Now he could think only of flight, of protecting the lives of the one person who had always been loyal, who had never let him down, Queen Mary Beatrice, and of their baby son, by sending them to safety in France. He would follow them as soon as he could.

On the morning of 27 November Lord Clarendon had been walking in Westminster Hall when there was an outcry that the Princess Anne had disappeared, no one knew where, but that 'somebody had violently carried her away.' When he went to the Cockpit, he found all the Princess's women running about hysterically. Some of them had even accosted the Queen's servants, demanding what the Catholics had done with the Princess, and burst in on the Queen herself to voice their suspicions that her priests had had the Princess murdered.

Mary Beatrice replied coolly that no doubt the Princess would reveal her whereabouts in due course.

That morning the Princess's nurse, Mrs Butts, had discovered her bed empty. Clearly she had left it in a hurry and the Princess's clothes of the previous day were strewn about the room. On the evening before Anne's disappearance, an order had come from James for the arrest of Anne's companions, Lady Churchill and Mrs Berkeley, both wives of defectors. Anne had begged the Queen to delay until the following morning. The impending arrest of her dearest Lady Churchill in no way precipitated the Princess's defection. She had been planning it for some time.

In her *Conduct* written many years later, Sarah Churchill was at pains to deny that it had been her idea for the Princess to abscond from her father's court, or, indeed, that there had been any conspiracy at all. 'It was a thing sudden and unconcerted,' she wrote, 'nor had I any share in it, farther than obeying my mistress's orders.' According to Sarah, news of the Prince of Denmark's going over to the Prince of Orange and the King's imminent return 'put the Princess into a great fright. She sent for me, told me her distress, and declared that rather than see her father she would jump out at window. This was her very expression.'

If Sarah was trying to imply that the news of the Prince of Denmark's defection came as a surprise to Anne, the evidence suggests otherwise. The Denmarks had been planning their defection for about three months, in concert with the Churchills; John Churchill had written to the Prince of Orange as early as 4 August to assure him of his support. Then there is the undeniable fact of Anne's letter of 18 November to the Prince of Orange, confirming her resolve:

Having on all occasions given you and my sister all imaginable assurances of the great friendship and kindness I have for you both, and on the subject you have now written to me I shall not trouble you with many compliments, only in short assure that you have my wishes for your good success in this so just an undertaking, and I hope the Prince [of Denmark] will soon be with you to let you see his readiness to join with you, who I am sure will do you all the service that lies in his power. He went yesterday with the King towards Salisbury, intending to go from there to you as soon as his friends thought it proper. I am not yet certain if I shall continue here or remove into the City; that shall depend on the advice my friends will give me, but wherever I am I shall be ready to show you how much I am your humble servant.

It might well have been a shock to Anne that no battle had taken place and that her father was returning to London so soon. She might even have expected her father to have been killed or captured. No wonder she panicked at the prospect of his imminent return. Later, the Prince of Denmark confided in Lord Clarendon that he was amazed the three ladies had not left the Cockpit sooner, as had been planned, *before* the men had deserted the army. As it turned out, Churchill and Berkeley left the King's camp in the early hours of 24 November and the Prince of Denmark followed twenty-four hours later. The ladies did not leave the Cockpit until two days after that, having made last-minute arrangements.

Before the orders for her arrest arrived, Sarah did admit that Anne had sent her to liaise with Bishop Compton, and it is a fair assumption that he was masterminding the operation, probably in consultation with other members of the seven such as Danby and Devonshire. As ever, Sarah's duty was to organise the Princess. In the early hours of the 27th, Anne, Sarah and Mrs Berkeley descended the backstairs leading from Anne's closet, the route by which her close-stool would ordinarily be emptied. The faithful old retainer, Mrs Dawson, slept on soundly outside Anne's locked bedchamber door. The backstairs had only recently been constructed, almost certainly with the purpose of escape in mind. It is interesting to note that a week later, with her father on the brink of losing his throne and rioting in the streets of London, Anne could coolly write to her household treasurer, Sir Benjamin Bathurst: 'I have nothing to say only to desire you to give order that the back stairs at the Cockpit may be painted that they may be dry against I come home.'

Met by Charles Sackville, Lord Dorset, outside the Cockpit, the party made their way through the darkness up to Charing Cross, laughing hysterically after Anne lost one of her high-heeled shoes in the mud. Dorset had offered his gauntlet to cover the royal foot instead. Bishop Compton was waiting in a hackney coach to drive them to his house in the City. From there, they were taken in slow stages to Nottingham, the bishop wearing military attire and brandishing a pistol to protect his Protestant Princess. 'Nor did she think herself safe,' commented Sarah, 'till she saw that she was surrounded by the Prince of Orange's friends.'

At Nottingham Lord Chesterfield noted that Anne was pretending 'that her father the King did persecute and use her ill for her religion, she being a Protestant and he a Papist'. By Anne's own admission to her uncle, Clarendon, James had never pressed her in the matter of religion. The King had merely given her some books and papers to read, but, according to Sarah Churchill, 'never came to any harshness'. Chesterfield had no reason to like James, who as Duke of York had tried to seduce his young wife, but he proved more loyal now to his anointed sovereign than did his daughter. When Anne invited him to sit on her council, Chesterfield demurred, on the grounds that he already 'had the honour to be a Privy Councillor to His Majesty her father; therefore I would be of no council for the ordering of troops which I did perceive were intended to serve against him.' Anne was highly displeased by this response.

Chesterfield was further filled with disgust when he discovered that the old Protestant Association, whose original purpose had been to bring the Catholic Mary Stuart, Queen of Scots, to her ruin, had been revived and that 'the daughter' was giving it her support. Now the association was pledged 'to destroy all the papists in England, in case the Prince of Orange should be killed or murdered by any of them'. It is possible that Anne was too stupid to draw the logical conclusion that the first heads to fall would be that of her father and stepmother, but it is equally possible that she was so bitter that she simply did not care. Chesterfield, however, drew back in horror from subscribing to the document drawn up by the Bishop of London, and many others followed his lead, 'which made the Princess Anne extremely angry'.

Anne's letter to the Queen, meanwhile, had been left behind in her bedchamber. In his memoir, James said that it never reached the Queen. But it was soon printed in the *London Gazette*, the sort of propaganda exercise that smacked of Orange conspiracy. It contradicted her previous letter to her brother-in-law in that she affected to be surprised by her husband's defection. The letter, although written in Anne's hand, was clearly composed by someone else:

*The Cockpit, 25 November 1688*

Madam,

I beg your pardon if I am so deeply affected with the surprising news of the Prince's being gone, as not to be able to see you, but to leave this paper to express my humble duty to the King and yourself; and to let you know that I am gone to absent myself to avoid the King's displeasures which I am not able to bear, either against the Prince or myself. And I shall stay at so great a distance as not to return before I hear the happy news of a reconcilement: and, as I am confident the Prince did not leave the King with any other design than to use all possible means for his preservation, so I hope you will do me the justice to believe that I am incapable of following him for any other end.

Never was anyone in such an unhappy condition, so divided between duty and affection to a father and husband; and therefore I know not what I must do, but to follow one to preserve the other. I see the general feeling of the nobility and gentry who avow to have no other end than to prevail with the King to secure their religion, which they saw so much in danger by the violent counsels of the priests; who to promote their own religion, did not care to what dangers they exposed the King. I am fully persuaded that the Prince of Orange designs the King's safety and preservation, and hope all things may be composed without more bloodshed, by calling a Parliament.

God grant a happy end to these troubles, that the King's reign may be prosperous, and that I may beg of you to continue the same favourable opinion that you have hitherto had of your most obedient daughter and servant.

An angry mob had surrounded Whitehall threatening to tear the Queen to pieces if she did not surrender the Princess Anne, but at last the discovery and the printing of the letter allayed their suspicions. James was furious when he arrived at Whitehall a few hours later to find that the hysterical accusations of Anne's servants had put the Queen's life in danger. It was not the only unpleasantness that the Queen had endured during his absence. A few days earlier she had been pulling on her glove, when she recoiled. Something had been placed inside it. Drawing out the offending item, she had found one of the pamphlets disparaging the birth of the Prince of Wales. Evidently someone had slipped into the Queen's bedchamber to put it there.

As a fond father, James could not help feeling concerned that Anne's precipitate flight might endanger her in her delicate condition. He still believed that she was pregnant, although this was a lie, another of Anne's convenient fabrications. When the Prince of Denmark admitted the sham to Anne's uncle, Lord Clarendon, a few days later, he was shocked. 'Good God! Nothing but lying and dissimulation,' he expostulated, understanding with a terrible clarity the magnitude of the deception Anne had perpetrated on her father.

Only hours after his return to London, James called a meeting of the Privy Council to ask its advice. He promised to summon a Parliament for 15 January and Jeffreys was asked to prepare the writs. Father Petre offered James the only sound advice he ever gave him: namely, not to flee. But he could see that James had already made up his mind. Without taking his leave of a king whose downfall he had done so much to engender, Petre made his escape in disguise, joining the train of the new English ambassador departing for Paris.

To buy time, James sent Lords Halifax, Godolphin and Nottingham to Hungerford a week later to open negotiations with the Prince of Orange. In reality, James had no intention of treating with his ruthless son-in-law. James was so haunted by thoughts of his father's end that reason seemed to desert him. At the very best, he knew his power as king would be severely curtailed; at worst, he imagined he would suffer the fate of some of his unfortunate predecessors and be done away with. According to Clarendon, James had already guessed that 'the Prince of Orange came for the crown, whatever he pretended; but that he would not see himself deposed; that he had read the story of Richard II.'

James's priority was to get the Queen and the Prince of Wales out of the country. The Modenese ambassador, Rizzini, who had known the Queen since her childhood, feared for her safety and was urging flight. Terriesi, the Tuscan ambassador, offered wiser counsel. He advised them to wait until they knew the mind of the Prince of Orange and the country, that they should only flee the kingdom in the last resort, and that he did not see the situation as being that desperate yet. 'I could not believe the English wished to change their legitimate King for a foreigner,' he commented astutely. He warned James that sending the Queen and the Prince to France would be a disastrous move, since his subjects had such a deep distrust of that country. If they had to flee, Flanders, in the dominions of the King of Spain, would be a more sensible option.

The loyal Lord Dartmouth at Portsmouth was also at pains to warn James of the evils that would ensue if he sent his son and heir to France. 'Pray, Sir, consider farther on this weightie point, for can the Prince's being sent to France have other prospect than the entailing a perpetuall warre upon your nation and posterity and giving France a temptation to molest, invade, nay hazard the conquest of England.' It was an uncannily accurate prediction. But even if Dartmouth had been prepared to obey instructions to send the Prince to France or return him to London by sea, it was too late to do so, as enemy ships were blockading Portsmouth harbour.

James sent orders to Lord Dover, the governor of Portsmouth, to send the child, his wet nurse and attendants back to London in the coach of his governess, Lady Powis. He was sending two regiments of cavalry under a Catholic colonel and a detachment of dragoons to meet them on the road. The party left Portsmouth at 5 a.m. on 8 December and nearly fell into the hands of the Prince of Orange's troops combing the Forest of Bere. At Southwark the people, recognising Catholic troops, attacked them. The coach and six careered on towards Whitehall, leaving its escort to defend themselves. It drew in at 3 a.m. on the morning of the 9th, the little Prince having slept through most of the ordeal.

A yacht had been hired at Gravesend to take the Queen and the Prince to France. Early on the 9th the advance party, including Lord and Lady Powis, the Queen's devoted Bolognese friend Countess Victoria Davia, her brother and a priest, Pellegrina Turini, Lord and Lady O'Brien and Sir William Waldegrave, the physician, left Whitehall. That evening, the King and Queen dined in public as usual, the Queen eating a hearty meal before her long journey, and retired to bed early. Just after midnight, the Queen's Italian wardrobe master, Riva, dressed as a common sailor, came to her apartments with her disguise, the clothes of an Italian laundress.

At two in the morning she emerged to find the King and the French Count Lauzun, who had volunteered his services to assist her escape, waiting for her. The Queen, who had never once abandoned the King in moments of danger and misfortune, threw her arms around him, begging to stay with him while their son alone went to France. James managed to persuade her to leave by assuring her that he would follow in twenty-four hours. Packets of her jewels, including the heirloom D'Este pearls and the diamond earrings given to the young bride by Louis XIV, were secreted about the persons of Riva and Lauzun.

They collected the Prince, his nurse Mrs Labadie and his wet nurse Mrs Smith and then the cloaked figures made their way out through the privy garden. They were challenged several times by the guard, to whom Riva called 'Friend' and brandished the master key. Terriesi's coach drove them through the streets of Westminster to the Horseferry Stairs. Riva had taken to duck shooting on the Surrey marshes and the boat he had hired to make the river crossings was now waiting for him. The rain was lashing down and there was a strong wind, so that the Thames was looking distinctly menacing as the party boarded the small craft, which was then buffeted across the choppy river.

At Lambeth Stairs a royal page, Dominic Dufour, was looking out for the group, who were by now soaked and shivering. Count Lauzun's coach was in the yard of the Swan Inn and he went to collect it. Meanwhile, the Queen, the two nurses and the sleeping baby tried to shelter in the shadow of St Mary's Church. With her child in her arms, Mary Beatrice was looking across the river, straining for a last glimpse of the lights of Whitehall Palace through the rain and darkness.

Someone emerged from the inn and, curious, started towards the women. Riva thought fast. He ran towards the man and knocked him to the ground, apologising profusely. Fortunately, he repaired to the inn to take care of his injuries. The party clambered into the coach, with the page Dufour insisting he come too, since by now he had recognised the Queen. There were several patrols along the road, on the lookout for escaping Catholics. At one point it looked as if they would definitely be stopped and searched when a voice called out of the darkness, 'Let us go and see, surely that is a coach full of papists', but the weather discouraged them. Twenty miles short of Gravesend, two horsemen rode up to the coach, one a royal equerry and the other Lauzun's companion, M. de St Victor, to escort it. Later, M. de St Victor would return to Whitehall to assure James the Queen had boarded safely.

Two miles outside Gravesend the King had sent three Irish sea captains to intercept the party and guide it across the marsh to a small boat that would ferry them to the waiting vessel, so as to avoid the town. As they approached the hired yacht, the advance party leaned over the sides to hurry up the 'laundress' and the others who had kept them waiting. Lauzun handed the captain 200 guineas and explained that he wanted his Catholic friends and their wives taken to France. If necessary, James had instructed the Irish sea captains to kill him if he showed any sign of surrendering to the Dutch, and to take the vessel on to France. But the captain showed no inclination for trouble. He immediately set sail and a favourable wind sent them into a raging sea.

It was the worst passage that Mary Beatrice ever experienced. She spent most of it retching into an earthenware bowl. Mrs Smith was so sick she was unable to feed the Prince, who howled with hunger. They passed so close to the English fleet in the Downs that they could hear the bells being rung for prayers. The captain cast anchor off the coast of France, not wanting to approach it at night in such a storm. At daylight on 11 December – 21 December in France – they made their landing. The captain had guessed the identity of his passengers, telling Lauzun as he indicated the screaming baby, 'I shall be right glad to set my little friend there ashore.' As he took his leave of the Queen he told her that he would probably be hanged on his return to England, but was honoured to have done her this service.

At Calais, Mary Beatrice, ever the assiduous letter-writer, immediately wrote to the French King:

Monsieur,

A poor fugitive queen, bathed in tears, has exposed herself to the greatest perils of the sea in order to seek consolation and refuge with the greatest and most generous monarch on earth ... Owing to her singular esteem for him she wishes to confide to him that which is most precious to her, in the person of the Prince of Wales, her son. He is still too young to join with her in the grateful acknowledgements that fill her heart. I have particular pleasure in the midst of all my tribulations to live at present under your protection. I am with deepest regard, Monsieur,

Your very affectionate servant and sister The Queen of England

When James did not follow immediately as he had promised, Mary Beatrice was desperate to go back to England. Instructions came from Versailles that she must be stopped at all costs and brought to Paris. Mary Beatrice might never have realised it, but she was effectively the prisoner of the King of France. She would be treated with exaggerated respect and generosity, but she and her child would never be allowed to escape Louis's clutches while their presence served his purposes. Whatever happened to the father – and for the moment France kept James's wife and son as hostages lest he be tempted to reach an accommodation with the Dutch – the son was far too valuable a tool for Louis to use against the Prince of Orange for him ever to let him go.

Mary Beatrice soon noticed that people were looking at her with pity. The news had reached Paris only four days after her arrival in France and had been kept from her. She discovered the truth by accident. James had botched his escape attempt and was William's prisoner.

On the day of the Queen's departure, James kept his Privy Council sitting very late to consider the Prince of Orange's terms. They were not unreasonable in the circumstances. He demanded that all James's remaining strongholds – the Tower of London, Portsmouth and Tilbury – be placed in neutral hands. All Catholics in civil and military offices in defiance of the Test Acts should be dismissed. William's troops must be paid out of public funds while they remained in England. When Parliament convened in January, there should be either joint occupation or mutual absence from the capital by the King and the Prince of Orange.

Even now, James could have stayed and seen this through. Contrary to his fears, there was nothing inevitable about the Prince of Orange assuming the crown. The political nation might not have rushed to his defence, but he was still their lawful, anointed sovereign, and most of them had no thoughts of removing him from the throne. Nor was there anything but his own fevered imagination to suggest he would be condemned to death. For his son's sake, James should have hung on and negotiated with his enemies. But James was incapable of compromise and he could not conceive of a world where his hopes for the Catholic religion lay in the dust and where his son had to be raised a Protestant. Determined to flee, Ireland or Scotland would have been more sensible choices than France, since both were his kingdoms and sufficiently unsettled to pose a threat to the coming regime in London.

Late into the night he wrote anguished letters to his naval and military commanders declaring his intention to withdraw from the kingdom. He asked Dartmouth to send such ships as remained loyal to Tyrconnel in Ireland, and Feversham to disband the army, so that it could not be used against him. He destroyed the writs summoning the new Parliament in his name. The faithful Lord Ailesbury waited on him in his bedchamber and begged him not to leave. James asked what was the point of staying since his daughter Anne, his army and Lord Churchill, whom he had raised from nothing and on whom he had heaped favours, had all deserted him. What hope, he asked, could he expect from others when these three had betrayed him? The hurt of their betrayal obviously went very deep: it would have been even worse if he had known of the malicious letters Anne had been writing to her sister. But more fundamental in James's mind was his conviction that God had withdrawn His favour from him. He had been judged and found wanting.

Between one and two in the morning of 11 December, James stole out of the palace and took coach for Horseferry. A boat was waiting to ferry him to Lambeth. About halfway across, James threw the Great Seal into the Thames – it was retrieved in a fisherman's catch a few months later – in order to prevent a Parliament being called in his name and in his absence. A party of horsemen was waiting for him at Lambeth. James had foolishly chosen to escape in the company of the notorious Sir Edward Hales, the Catholic officer who had brought such opprobrium on himself in 1686 by instigating the test case about the dispensing law, when the Lord Chief Justice Herbert and a packed panel of judges ruled in the King's favour. A page of the back stairs, Labadie, the groom Dick Smith and a guide accompanied them as they negotiated the rain-sodden lanes of Kent. Richard Sheldon met them with six fresh horses at Aylesford Bridge, where they took refreshment just before daylight at the Woolpack Inn.

At Elmley Ferry they found the customs-house hoy that had been hired to take them to France and went aboard. The captain said they needed to take on ballast before they could put the hoy to sea in such rough weather, and as a seaman himself James agreed. The delay meant they were left stranded by the tide off the Isle of Sheppey until eleven o'clock that night. The party had already been observed as suspicious and Sir Edward Hales, known and hated throughout Kent, had been recognised. A group of about forty men from Faversham, many of them 'priest-coddlers' looking for escaping Catholics, set off in pursuit. When they boarded the hoy, Hales futilely offered a bribe of 50 guineas to let them go. Believing that they had apprehended an escaping Jesuit, the men roughly searched the King right down to his underwear. Among a number of valuables secreted about his person, they found his coronation ring, the gold cross of St Edward and some diamond buckles they thought must be made of glass as they were so large. The leader of the boarding party gave a receipt for the confiscated valuables and then left to return to Faversham for further assistance.

Amid torrents of abuse, James and his companions were dragged off the hoy and taken to the Arms of England Inn at Faversham. Here, someone who had served in the navy recognised the King. James demanded quill and paper and wrote a number of letters, some of which he tore up. One of them was a pathetic note to Lord Feversham telling him:

I had the misfortune to be stopt att Sheerness and brought in here this day, by a rabble of seamen, fishermen and others, who still detaine me now, tho they know me . . . speke to some of my most necessary servants to come to me, & bring with them some linnen & cloathes . . . Let James Graham know I shall want some money, if he could come & bring some himself, or send some it would be but necessary those who seized me having taken all the little I had about me when they laid hands on me.

Under the stares of the fascinated crowd of townspeople who gathered, his talk became increasingly wild and disordered as the day wore on. Haunted by the fear of being murdered, he probably thought he was going to meet his end in this obscure spot. He kept muttering biblical quotations that seemed to refer to the Prince of Orange. 'For I repent that I gave my daughter unto him, for he sought to slay me.' A few minutes later, he was comparing the Prince with Herod: 'Arise, and take the young child and his mother, and flee into Egypt, and be thou there until I bring you word: for Herod will seek the young child to destroy him.'

These ruminations were interrupted by the arrival of Lord Winchelsea, the Lord Lieutenant. He could do nothing for the King but move him to the mayor's house, which offered slightly more security. The bewildered man was pushed and jostled through the narrow streets of the town to his new lodging. He was given no privacy. His host stood outside the window reading Prince William's manifesto in a loud voice and the seamen settled in the anteroom. They insisted that they would not allow anyone so much as to touch a hair of the King's head, but he was essentially their prisoner.

A Mr Napleton, a lawyer, was sent off to the Prince of Orange's headquarters to ask for instructions. According to Clarendon, William had failed to conceal his delight when he had received the news that James had escaped, so he must have been equally crestfallen to hear of his capture. When Bentinck received Napleton, Burnet asked in an exasperated voice, 'Why did you not let him go?' 'Would you have him torn in pieces by the mob?' the man replied incredulously.

James had slipped one of the letters he had frenziedly written to a loyal old seaman to take to London. He travelled there at his own expense and was kept waiting a long time outside the council chamber door at Whitehall before being admitted. James's letter explained his position and repeated rather forlornly the request he had made to Feversham for some clean clothes and cash. After it had been read aloud, there was a quarter of an hour's silence of utter embarrassment. When no one else made a move and before Halifax could dismiss the meeting, Ailesbury rose and proposed that a deputation should be sent to the King with an escort of 120 guards to bring him back to court.

Halifax was not in the best of moods since James had sent him on a fool's errand to negotiate with the Prince of Orange, knowing that he intended to flee. News of the King's departure from the capital had signalled the breakdown of law and order and a council of peers had hurriedly convened with the City authorities at the Guildhall in an effort to stem the rising tide of violence. Feversham's disbanding the army, armed but without pay, had led to 'Irish Night', when a rumour swept the capital that marauding Irish Catholics were going to murder the citizens in their beds. In reality, perfectly innocent Irish soldiers who had been left bewildered by their sudden change of circumstances were trying to beg their way back to their own country.

The rabble embarked on an orgy of destruction. Catholic chapels were looted and put on fire. Priests were in fear of their lives, some of them being hacked down, foreigners at the mercy of the mob. Many had placed their possessions in foreign embassies for safety. Now they were burned, looted or destroyed. The Spanish ambassador's residence was attacked, even though Spain was one of William's allies. The ambassador found himself cast out into the bitterly cold streets in his nightshirt, before taking refuge at Whitehall. James's memoirs, which had already survived a shipwreck, had been placed in the care of Terriesi, who risked his life getting the elaborate trunk sent off to Leghorn amidst the rioting.

At Faversham the loyal Ailesbury found the King 'sitting in a great chair, his hat on, and his beard much grown, and resembled the picture of his royal father at the pretended High Court of Justice'. Like his father, James had assumed the role of royal martyr. Shaved and changed and wearing his own periwig rather than one of black disguise, he was brought back to London by way of Rochester and Dartford, missing a message from the Prince of Orange ordering him to stay at Rochester. In one of their volatile swings of mood, the fickle populace, who had so recently been hunting Catholic targets, shouted themselves hoarse with joy as the King passed through the City. It looked like a triumph and that night the Catholics left their hiding places and returned to court. Tactless to the last, James had a Jesuit say grace before supper.

James's effusive welcome by the Londoners meant nothing. He had lost all credibility by his flight. Oblivious, he continued to act as King, calling a meeting of the Privy Council, which only eight members attended. Some had fled and others were in prison. Judge Jeffreys had been caught trying to escape and was brought before the Lord Mayor, who promptly had a stroke at the sight of him. The perpetrator of the Bloody Assizes which followed the defeat of Monmouth's Rebellion now resided in the Tower, where he was to die in January. James sent Lord Feversham to William to suggest a meeting, a move he should have made after the Salisbury débâcle. He was arrested. The arrest of the King's envoy was seen as an affront to James, a serious departure from diplomatic niceties, but William was furious that Feversham had disbanded James's army, since he had been hoping to take it over *en bloc* for use in the European war.

That night as the King undressed for bed in the almost empty palace, William's Blue Guards were observed to be creeping through St James's Park towards Whitehall. James seemed unconcerned, since he had invited William to take up residence at St James's, and anyway, by this time he was at a loss to know which were more untrustworthy, his own guards or the Prince's. During the night he was woken from a sound sleep by Lord Middleton, who told him that Lords Halifax, Shrewsbury and Delamere wanted to see him. They had a warrant signed by William for his removal to Ham House. James demurred that Ham would be cold and damp, since the Duchess of Lauderdale was in Scotland for the winter. He suggested Rochester as an alternative and after his emissaries consulted William, who was at Syon House just outside London, this was readily agreed.

When James descended the palace stairs to his barge for the last time on the morning of 18 December, Halifax, curt in his embarrassment, and the ever gracious Shrewsbury accompanied him. A crowd of loyal nobility and foreign ministers were there to see him off. Many of them were in tears and Ailesbury observed that 'such a melancholy farewell was never seen.' A large detachment of Dutch guards would accompany the prisoner to Rochester. It was the day of the changeover. At four o'clock that afternoon hundreds of people wearing orange ribbons and waving oranges on sticks, who had been standing for hours in the pouring rain to greet him, were disappointed to find that William had already arrived at St James's Palace. His coach had slipped through the park so as to avoid them. Even though he was not yet king, William had no time for the outward trappings of monarchy, nor any of the Stuart charm that had so endeared Charles II to his subjects.

After a triumphant entry on 15 December into the Anglican stronghold of Oxford with Compton at her side and a huge following, Princess Anne and her husband returned to town the day after her father departed. She showed no remorse for his misfortune. William immediately went to the Cockpit to pay the Denmarks his respects. Even though they had served his purpose and his use for them was almost at an end, William was careful to observe the polite formalities. Anne greeted him wearing his colours of orange and green, with her whole household wearing orange ribbons like a party badge. An eye-witness was horrified to observe: 'King James was carried down the river in a most tempestuous evening, not without actual danger; and while her poor old father was thus exposed to danger, an actual prisoner under a guard of Dutchmen, at that very moment his daughter, the Princess Anne of Denmark, with her great favourite, Lady Churchill, both covered in orange ribbons, went in one of his coaches, attended by his guards, triumphant to the playhouse.'

The royal prisoner stayed at Rochester for four nights in the home of Sir Richard Head, which backed on to the River Medway. Although Dutch guards were posted at the front of the house, James noticed that there were none on the riverside. His brother-in-law Clarendon had sent a message warning him that while his enemies wanted him to flee the kingdom, his friends dreaded it. While James remained in England, he was King *de facto*. If he left, he could only be considered King *de jure*. But James had already made up his mind. He told Ailesbury: 'If I do not retire I shall certainly be sent to the Tower, and no king ever went out of that place but to his grave.'

On the evening of 23 December James's son by Arabella Churchill, the Duke of Berwick, who unlike his legitimate royal half-sisters had remained conspicuously loyal to his father, came to join him. He brought five blank passports and the two men talked for some time. After midnight James, his son Berwick and a few companions made their way to a small boat lying on the river, while the Dutch guards looked the other way. It carried them to the yacht *Henrietta*, which took them through stormy seas to the French coast. A French frigate was on the lookout and brought the party into Ambleteuse two days later, Christmas Day in England. It was just one year since the official announcement of Queen Mary Beatrice's pregnancy.

James had left behind in his Rochester prison a farewell document. He said that he was going to seek foreign aid to help him regain his throne, promising that he would not make use of it to overthrow the Protestant religion or the laws of the land. He ended by reproaching the English people for deserting him. James's flight was tantamount to his quitting the throne, or, at least, this is what his enemies would infer from it. Until this moment, he still had a large body of supporters, enough to back him if he had shown any inclination to negotiate a sensible settlement. His flight left the position of these supporters untenable, cutting the ground from under them.

When news of King James's escape reached court, Princess Anne 'was not in the least moved, but called for cards, and was as merry as she used to be'. Clarendon reproved her for this, to which she replied that 'it was true she did call for cards then, because she was accustomed to play, and that she never loved to do anything that looked like an affected constraint.' 'And does your Royal Highness think that showing some trouble for the King your father's misfortunes could be interpreted as an affected constraint?' he asked in exasperation. 'Such behaviour lessens you much in the opinion of the world,' he warned her, 'and even in that of your father's enemies.' He might as well not have bothered remonstrating with his obstinate niece, because as he was pained to observe, 'she was not one jot moved.'

In contrast to such filial ingratitude were the dignity and loyalty of her stepmother, Mary Beatrice, who was winning nothing but admiration at the French court. Even Louis, who was probably half in love with her, was impressed. 'Now that is how a queen *ought* to behave,' he told his courtiers. When he brought the tired and broken James to her at the palace of St Germain-en-Laye, she seemed to forget that they had just lost her personal fortune and three kingdoms. 'My God,' she exclaimed, 'I am the happiest woman in the world!' The French courtiers watched in amazement as the King of England threw etiquette to the winds, publicly kissed his wife and held her in a long embrace.

# 9
## The Takeover

*'If you are crowned while I and the Prince of Wales are living, the curses of an angry father will fall on you, as well as those of a God who commands obedience to parents'*

– James II to Mary of Orange

At noon on 13 February 1689 a crowd waited in the torrential rain outside the Banqueting House at Whitehall. Only a few of them would have witnessed the occasion forty years ago almost to the day when the public executioner had held up the dripping head of the king-martyr Charles I and displayed it to the spectators. While women fainted and the crowd groaned, the more intrepid had crept forward surreptitiously to soak pieces of material in the royal blood. Most of them had been present in recent weeks, however, standing outside the Parliament at Westminster and shouting to those deliberating within that they wanted the Protestant William and his wife Mary for King and Queen. Now the crowd had the satisfaction of knowing that the couple were to be offered the crown as joint sovereigns.

As they arrived at the imposing Banqueting House, William would have looked diminutive next to Mary, who with her height and statuesque figure towered over most of her contemporaries. They walked through the ranks of the assembled Houses of Parliament and members of the nobility to take their places on chairs beneath the canopy of state. Above them, the candlelight illuminated Rubens's magnificent painted ceiling depicting the Stuart ideal of kingship: their great-grandfather, James I, exchanging his earthly crown for a more glorious one in heaven. A few feet from where they were sitting, their grandfather, Charles I, had stepped out of the window on to the scaffold specially erected for his execution. Reiterating the message from Rubens's allegory, Charles's last words before the axe had fallen were to become synonymous with his martyrdom: 'I go from a corruptible to an incorruptible crown.' No longer aspiring to the divine status of their predecessors, God's representatives on earth, William and Mary were to receive their crowns not from God but from Parliament.

Lord Halifax and Speaker Powle advanced towards them and asked if they would accept the crown as joint sovereigns. The Prince held on to the Princess's hand and answered in a few words for both of them. She merely curtsied. William took care to answer *before* the reading of the Declaration of Rights, since it defined the boundaries of royal power and he did not wish it to be thought he was accepting the crown on conditions. He had already read the document and had been relieved to find that it was not more swingeing. It addressed the grievances that had arisen in James's reign, such as his misuse of the dispensing and suspending power, the fact that he had had a standing army in peacetime without the consent of Parliament, interfered with the judiciary, attempted to pack Parliament, and had punished his subjects – the bishops – for petitioning him. When her father's many faults were read out, Mary bowed her head, looking troubled.

It was the first time since her arrival in London the previous day that she had shown what was considered to be the correct demeanour. Courtiers who already resented the Dutch usurper had looked forward to Mary's coming. At least she was an English princess, a Stuart born and bred in England, and would know how royalty should behave. Unlike her dour husband, they knew her to be gracious, charming, lively and gregarious. They thronged to Whitehall to see her, only to be shocked by the manner in which she entered her father's palace. 'She came into Whitehall, jolly as to a wedding, seeming quite transported with joy,' noted John Evelyn reprovingly. Surely this was not how the daughter of a dethroned king should act when taking possession of his palace?

After meeting her sister at Greenwich, Princess Anne had accompanied her in the royal barge to Whitehall and led her to the refurbished apartments of her stepmother, Mary Beatrice, facing the Privy Garden. Not only had Mary been installed in the same apartment, but also the same bed her stepmother had shared with James. 'She ran about it, looking into every closet and conveniency, and turning up the quilts of the beds, just as people do at an inn, with no sort of concern in her appearance,' Sarah Churchill commented scathingly. Sarah, of course, was to be Mary's enemy and she would be sure never to say anything kind about her in her *Conduct* written many years after the event, although her next words were reasonable enough. 'I thought this strange and unbecoming conduct; for whatever necessity there was of deposing of King James, he was still her father, who had been lately driven from that very chamber, and from that bed; and if she felt no tenderness, I thought, at least, she might have felt grave, or even pensively sad, at so melancholy a reverse of fortune.' Not, of course, that her friend Princess Anne was displaying any of these emotions.

Mary's affected gaiety, verging on hysteria, continued the next day, the day of the ceremony at the Banqueting House. 'She rose early in the morning,' Evelyn heard from a relative who was waiting on her, 'and in her undress, before her women were up, went about from room to room, to see the convenience of Whitehall.' Not only was Mary taking possession of her father's palace, but also of his personal property and that of her stepmother. There had been time to ship Mary Beatrice's coach and horses and her coachman – Watt Dormer, who had once served Cromwell in the same capacity – to France, but James was not so lucky. Subsequently, John Evelyn was disgusted to find that Mary kept all Mary Beatrice's possessions. He noted several items of value that had belonged to the exiled Queen, including a cabinet of silver filigree, 'which, in my opinion, should have been generously sent to her'. James sent his loyal servant Mr Hayes with a request for his clothes and other personal items, a request which Lord Clarendon was pained to see was completely ignored.

Admiring Mary as he did, Gilbert Burnet was perplexed by her behaviour. 'She put on an air of gaiety when she came to Whitehall. I confess I was one of those who censured her in my thoughts. I thought a little more seriousness had done as well when she came into her father's palace, and was to be set on his throne the next day.' As Burnet 'had never seen the least indecency in any part of her deportment before, which made this appear to me so extraordinary', he asked Mary to explain it. She told him that 'the letters which had been writ to her had obliged her to put on a cheerfulness', but that she had noticed the raised eyebrows and frowns of disapproval. She had clearly gone too far, as it was not a part that came naturally to her. William was adamant that they would not be apologetic for the overthrow of James's regime, but his instructions to his ever obedient wife had struck the wrong note and she knew it.

A glance at Mary's journal reveals that she felt anything but cheerful at the prospect of assuming her father's crown. She did not want it. She had spent Christmas and New Year alone in Holland, in an agonised frame of mind. She had given up cards and dancing, 'which had been to me one of the prettiest pleasures in the world.' Her delight at William's success – she heard it from others, since it was a long time before he wrote to her – was blighted by her concern for her father. She was glad to hear that James had escaped with his life. Any guilt she might have felt was outweighed by her steadfast belief that she was acting for God and His Church, although she regretted the necessity of having to take the crown. She confided in her journal that 'I had been only for a Regency, and wished for nothing else', but she was bound to play her part in William's plans. She dreaded the prospect of being Queen, knowing 'my heart is not made for a kingdom and my inclination leads me to a retired quiet life', but the fact that William would now be King 'lessened the pain, but not the trouble of what I am like to endure'.

When William had eventually summoned her, she was grieved to leave Holland, the country that had become so dear to her, where she had been happy. 'Yet when I saw England, my native country, which long absence had made me a stranger to, I felt a secret joy, which doubtless proceeded from a natural sympathy, but that was soon checked with the consideration of my father's misfortunes, which came immediately to mind.' She was filled with happiness at the prospect of seeing William again, and 'the thoughts that I should see my husband owned as the deliverer of my country, made me vain; but, alas, poor mortal! thought I then, from whom has he delivered it but from my father!'

After Mary's arrival at Whitehall, husband and wife met in private. Mary was appalled to see the toll the recent months had taken on William's health. He was thin and coughing blood. They shed tears of joy at their reunion and tears of sorrow that it should have been in England rather than their beloved Holland. They regretted 'the loss of the liberty we had left behind and were sensible we should never enjoy here'. Already feeling the bounds of constraint, they dried their tears and emerged to begin their new life in England.

---

In the weeks since James's departure from his army at Salisbury, William had been plunged into the cauldron of English politics. The experience had confirmed him in his loathing of the English ruling class, their selfishness, their deviousness, their lack of principle and their endless deliberations. The only Englishman he liked and trusted was Henry Sidney, whose company he enjoyed. He held most of the smooth courtiers and politicians in contempt, not least for the way they had betrayed their late master. They liked him no better.

His triumph over James had quickly turned sour. Determined not to be in any way beholden to the English, William took no trouble to win their favour or court popularity, while his stilted English probably made him sound brusquer than he meant to be.

He was too stern, reserved and serious for their taste, although his handsome Dutch page, Arnold Joost van Keppel, told Lord Churchill's aide-de-camp that William was extremely merry and loquacious when sharing a bottle of jinever with his compatriots. The latent xenophobia of the English was roused by his obvious preference for his Dutch friends – men such as Hans Willem Bentinck – with whom he would be closeted for hours. Indeed, it was very difficult to gain access to William, who was at all times surrounded and protected by his Dutch coterie. At table, he broke with custom, too. Only his Dutch friends were invited to dine with him, while English nobles such as Lord Churchill, standing silently behind his chair, were completely ignored.

At the ceremony at the Banqueting House, John Evelyn was surprised that William and Mary – especially Mary – expressed no reluctance or apology in assuming her father's crown. He thought that she should have shown regret that her father's mismanagement had 'forced the nation to so extraordinary a proceeding'. It would have been a mark in her favour, he thought, and consistent with her reputation for piety. It would also have been more in accord with 'her husband's first declaration, that there was no intention of deposing the king, only of succouring the nation'.

Evelyn expressed a common concern, a feeling that events had somehow moved too fast and that matters had not turned out as expected. Few realised that William had intended to take the crown all along. They believed his manifesto, which said that he came only to guarantee the calling of a free Parliament, which everyone agreed was the only remedy for the ills that had arisen under James's rule. As far as most people were concerned, James was still their rightful sovereign, even if he had been a disaster. For them, there had never been any question of deposing him, only of forcing him to rule according to the laws of the land. When William ended up with the crown, many felt that they had been duped.

To give William his due, he had not snatched the crown by pressing the military advantage as previous usurpers such as Henry VII had done on the battlefield. Even though London was occupied by Dutch troops, William was adamant that he would fulfil the promise made in his manifesto to call a free Parliament to resolve the nation's constitutional difficulties. And this he had done. Weeks of wrangling as to whether James had forfeited his crown by leaving the kingdom followed. The Whigs believed he had 'abdicated' and left the throne 'vacant'. The Tories argued that this implied a conscious renunciation on James's part, which they felt he had not done. Anyway, 'abdication' was a term unknown to English law. The Whigs were so bold as to state that James had broken the original contract between king and people. Rubbish, said the Tories, there was no contract between king and people. The King could do no wrong.

As the Tories could not bring themselves to accept that James was no longer king, they promoted the idea of regency, as if James were a minor or a lunatic, incapable of exercising kingly power. Tories such as the Hyde brothers felt it left the option open for an eventual restoration, the thought of which appalled William. Regency could only work if James and his son were under lock and key, not living abroad under the patronage of Louis XIV. And what would happen once James died, as he might at any time? William made it quite clear that he would not accept the position of regent and that if James were invited to return, he would leave. Having invested so much in this enterprise, William wanted life tenure at least.

Even if the question of James could be disposed of on the grounds that he had quit, there was still that of the Prince of Wales to be considered. William's manifesto had promised a parliamentary enquiry into the disputed birth. As early as 24

December, Clarendon had raised the matter in a meeting with other peers, only to have the Whig Lord Wharton splutter apoplectically, 'My lord, I did not expect at this time of day, to hear anybody mention that child, who was called the Prince of Wales. Indeed I did not; and I hope we shall hear no more of him.' While it was convenient to believe that the child was a changeling, he could not be dismissed so easily. One MP observed that there was not only James II, 'but a little one beyond the sea too, that will pretend', while another referred to 'a pretended brat beyond the sea, whom you cannot put aside'.

A parliamentary enquiry into the birth was launched, but quickly dropped on the dubious grounds that since the child was in France it was impossible to establish the truth. In his memoirs, James noted that when Danby was asked why 'nothing was done to satisfy the world in a thing of that importance', he replied that 'the more they examined into it the more proof they found of the reality of the Prince's being born of the Queen.' By this time, however, the calumnies had served the Prince of Orange's purpose and he had no further use for them. It is probable that William personally entertained no doubts as to the authenticity of the Prince of Wales. His friend Bentinck was later to confirm: 'That they neither questioned his legitimacy, nor were concerned about it, for that his master being now in possession of the throne, was resolved to keep it while he lived, and cared not who it went to when he was gone.' William was careful not to disabuse Mary, however, who went to her grave believing that the child was not her half-brother.

The Commons resolved the problem of the Prince of Wales with a bold statement, perhaps the most radical measure of this session. It proposed that 'it hath been found, by experience, to be inconsistent with the safety and welfare of this Protestant kingdom to be governed by a popish prince.' Unlike other nations where the religion of the ruler determined that of the people, in England that of the people would determine that of the ruler. Catholics were barred from the throne. The principle that the Whig members of the Exclusion Parliaments had fought so hard to put on the statute book had at last been accepted. The Tories had allowed Catholic James, the rightful hereditary heir, his chance, and he had let them down. At one stroke both Houses of Parliament agreed to set aside the claims of James and his son on the grounds of their religion and of any other Catholic heirs to the throne. Given the disastrous consequences of the marriages of recent Stuart sovereigns to Catholic consorts, specifically Henrietta Maria and Mary Beatrice, it was also resolved that no monarch or heir to the throne might marry a Catholic either.

The Tory Lord Danby, who had been one of the 'immortal seven' and had led the northern rising against James, had not anticipated James's departure. He had hoped to force him to agree a settlement. Since he had gone, however, Danby championed the rights of Mary as the Protestant heiress next in line. Mary would be Queen in her own right. William, however, had no intention of being his wife's 'gentleman usher' or of holding 'anything by the apron strings'. Even if he were to accept the role of Mary's consort, what would happen to him in the event of her death? Anne was next in line and she might make an alliance with the French, leaving William out in the cold again. William had heard enough. He summoned Danby, Shrewsbury and Halifax and told them in no uncertain terms that he would accept nothing dependent on the life of another or on 'the will of a woman'. If Mary alone were to be made Queen, he could give them no further 'assistance in the settlement of the nation, but will return to my own country'.

By this time it was obvious that William aimed for the crown and nothing less. It was only after Danby wrote personally to Mary and she replied that she would not think of taking the crown except jointly with her husband, however, that the deadlock was resolved. 'I am the Prince's wife,' she wrote, 'and would never be any other than what should be in conjunction with him; I shall take it extreme unkindly, if any, under the pretence of their care for me, should set up a divided interest between me and the Prince.' The English politicians were perplexed. Clearly she must be either a very good or a very stupid woman. The Prince must have exercised some 'conjugal impositions' on 'the most complying wife in the world'. If William died before her – and he looked so ill, he could not be long for this world – they looked forward to running the government with Mary as a charming but pliant figurehead.

William realised that if he did not force a decision the English would talk and argue for ever. They were oblivious to the growing crisis in Europe. At the beginning of February he let it be known that unless he were offered the crown 'he would go back to Holland, and meddle no more in their affairs'. He would accept a joint monarchy with his wife, but only if the 'sole and full exercise of the regal power' was vested in him. Mary would have the title of Queen only. She would not have the sword of state carried before her as her sovereign predecessors had done.

The ultimatum concentrated minds wonderfully. As Halifax wisely acknowledged, if no one knew what to do with William, they did not know what to do without him either.

Those, mainly Tory, peers who could not overcome their objections were persuaded to stay away when the vote was put to the Upper House, so that the minority prepared to offer the crown jointly to William and Mary suddenly became a majority. The House of Commons was predominantly Whig and found little difficulty in swallowing a resolution for what amounted to an elective monarchy.

If William was to have the crown for life, there remained the problem of Princess Anne, who was next in line after the childless Mary. William realised that he would need to offer a sop to her Tory Anglican supporters. A compromise was reached whereby Anne would succeed William, but that any children she might have would succeed to the crown before any that William might have by a second marriage. There is no doubt that Anne resented yielding her place in the succession to the 'Dutch Abortion', as she called her brother-in-law, and she did so grudgingly. By January 1689 Anne really was pregnant and assured her uncle, Clarendon, that she would 'never consent to anything that should be to the prejudice of herself or her children'. She did not stir herself sufficiently to make her views public, however, but as usual confined her disapproval to carping behind closed doors, much to the annoyance of Clarendon, who had ventured to speak in her support.

'Now I am sensible of the error I committed in leaving my father and making myself of a party with the Prince, who puts by my right,' she complained. It seems that the Churchills had decided that their interests would be best served by supporting the proposed settlement, particularly as Sarah noted that all the leading men were in favour of it, and so persuaded Anne to comply with the plan to give her brother-in-law precedence. It did not stop Sarah inflaming Anne's jealousy and resentment of William to such a pitch that the antagonism would soon become an open breach.

These were the arguments that had filled the weeks and provided the backdrop to the ceremony at the Banqueting House on 13 February. As the trumpets sounded, the proclamation was announced to those inside the great hall that William III and Mary II were sovereign King and Queen of England, France and Ireland – the traditional titles of English monarchs since the Middle Ages. Accompanied by the pealing of bells, the beating of drums and the firing of cannon, the heralds then threaded their way through the crowd waiting outside in the streets as they repeated the proclamation throughout Westminster and the City. The rabble might roar its approval for the moment, but among more reflective minds there was uneasiness at the enormity of what had been done. The acclamation for William and Mary's sovereignty was by no means universal. It remained to be seen if they would survive, or whether James would succeed in making a comeback.

That evening, there was a great gathering at court. Everyone had come to pay their respects to the new monarchs or to satisfy their curiosity. A young lady of the Russell family wrote:

At night, I went to court with my lady Devonshire, and kissed the Queen's hands, and the King's also. There was a world of bonfires and candles in almost every house, which looked extreme pretty. The King is wonderfully admired for his great wisdom and prudence. He is a man of no presence, but looks very homely at first sight: yet, if one looks long at him, he has something in his face both wise and good. As for the Queen, she is really altogether very handsome; her face is agreeable, and her motions extremely graceful and fine. She is tall, but not so tall as the last Queen. Her room is mighty full of company, as you may guess.

It was at this first drawing room that, with the meticulous attention to rules of precedence exhibited by her otherwise dull mind, Anne objected that her low stool had been placed too near the Queen's chair of state. It was within the shadow of the canopy of state, which it ought not to be. She insisted it be removed to a correct distance from her sister's place.

Such evenings were torture for William. The heat emanating from the press of bodies crowded into the drawing room and the smoke from the wax candles and the coal fires all conspired to suffocate him and bring on his asthma. He soon persuaded Mary to encourage cards rather than conversation. Now he could make a brief appearance before disappearing into his closet. Evelyn noted the change:

Within a night or two she sat down to basset, as the Queen her predecessor had done. She smiled upon all, and talked to every body, so that no change seemed to have taken place at court as to queens, save that infinite throngs of people came to see her, and that she went to our prayers. Her demeanour was censured by many. She seems to be of a good temper, and that she takes nothing to heart; while the prince, her husband, has a thoughtful countenance, is wonderfully serious and silent, and seems to treat all persons alike gravely, and to be very intent on his affairs.

Not everyone flocked to Mary's court or was welcome there. Her uncles Clarendon and Rochester bemoaned their nieces' lack of filial duty and, loyal to James, could not approve of the new regime. Clarendon had taken refuge at his country house, while his wife ventured a visit to court. 'My wife,' he wrote, 'had some discourse with the new Queen on Thursday [14 February], who told her she was much dissatisfied with me and asked angrily, "What, pray, has *he* to do with the succession?"' Lady Clarendon assured Mary that her uncle was acting for her and her sister's true interest. Would she receive him at court? Mary replied, 'I have nothing to do to forbid any body coming to the withdrawing-room, but I shall not speak in private to him.' Mary's other uncle, Rochester, had been permitted to kiss the hands of William and Mary in public, but had not been admitted to a private audience. Mary also refused to see Rochester's daughters, little girls of seven and eight years old, because of their father's stance. She could never forgive anyone who had crossed William. Less entrenched than his brother, however, Rochester later took the oaths to the new monarchs and resumed a role in court and politics.

As a devoted daughter of the Anglican Church, Mary craved the blessing of William Sancroft, Archbishop of Canterbury and the approval of the clergy. Had she not supported the cause of the seven bishops against her father? Surely the archbishop would appreciate that one of the purposes of William's intervention had been to rescue the Anglican Church from her father's encroachments? On the afternoon of the ceremony at the Banqueting House, she sent two of her chaplains to request the archbishop's blessing and to discover his attitude to the new regime. They were also to find out if prayers were still being said at Lambeth for James and his son. They were. When the archbishop's chaplain had asked him that morning what royal personages to pray for in the Ash Wednesday service, the archbishop had replied, 'I have no new instructions to give you.' So his position was clear. Archbishop Sancroft was a man of principle. He might have had his differences with James, but he was his anointed sovereign to whom he had given his oath of allegiance. 'Tell your princess,' he now told Mary's messengers, 'first to ask her father's blessing; without that, mine would be useless.'

The upshot of the Primate's principled stand was that it was very difficult to find anyone to officiate at William and Mary's coronation on 11 April 1689. Sancroft refused either to crown them or to take the oath of allegiance. As a result, four of the bishops who had been sent to the Tower by James and hundreds of the clergy left their livings rather than take the oath of allegiance to the new monarchs. They were called non-jurors. Predictably, Henry Compton, Bishop of London, was willing to crown the new sovereigns. His part in the overthrow of James meant that he was not rewarded with the see of Canterbury when it became vacant, however. That honour went to a truly good man of God, John Tillotson, whom William later described as one of the best men he had ever known. William's creature, Gilbert Burnet, was raised to the see of Salisbury.

On the coronation morning, just as William and Mary were dressing, news came of James's landing in Ireland with French troops. It blighted the day. Worse, a letter addressed to Mary from her father was timed to arrive just prior to her leaving for the abbey: 'Hitherto, I have been willing to overlook what has been done, and thought your obedience to your husband and compliance to the nation might have prevailed. But your being crowned is in your own power; if you do it while I and the Prince of Wales are living, the curses of an angry father will fall on you, as well as those of a God who commands obedience to parents.'

There is no record of Mary's response, but she must have been shaken. The Tory Lord Nottingham, appropriately known as Don Dismallo because of his dark, serious look, had brought the letter and said that William declared that 'he had done nothing but by her advice, and with her approbation.'

It was also on this occasion that the Jacobites reported that Mary turned on William saying that 'if her father regained his authority, her husband might thank himself, for letting him go as he did.' There is no evidence that she actually said this – indeed, it is totally out of character – but it was reported to James, who never forgave her. Henceforth, he compared his elder daughter to Tullia, the Roman princess who had driven her chariot over her father's body. James spent the morning of the coronation deploring the disloyalty of his daughters to Lloyd, one of his gentlemen of the bedchamber. He could not decide which of his daughters had behaved worse. 'Both bitches, by God!' Lloyd had declared, before leaving the room. The upsetting news of James's landing in Ireland delayed the ceremony by a couple of hours.

A similar message was sent to Princess Anne. She turned to her faithful bedchamber woman, Mrs Dawson, and once again questioned her about the birth of the Prince of Wales. Could he be her brother? Mrs Dawson had already made her evidence clear to Princess Anne, who had wilfully ignored the truth, and now she repeated that there could be no doubt that the Prince of Wales was the son of Mary of Modena. 'He is, Madam, as surely your brother, the son of King James and of his Queen, as you are the daughter of the late Duchess of York,' she told her, reminding her that it was she who had seen both of them born. The truth was not something Anne wished to acknowledge to her sister and brother-in-law. The whole edifice had been built on her lies – lies which, of course, she could never admit to the world.

On the eve of the coronation, William had rewarded his supporters with new honours. Foreigners such as the Prince of Denmark and Bentinck received English peerages as Duke of Cumberland and Earl of Portland respectively, while his kinsman Count Zuylestein became Earl of Rochford. Of the 'immortal seven', Shrewsbury and Devonshire received dukedoms, Danby became Marquis of Caermarthen, Henry Sidney Earl of Romney, Lord Lumley Earl of Scarborough,

Admiral Russell Earl of Orford and Admiral Herbert Earl of Torrington. John Churchill became Earl of Marlborough.

Of the rest of the nobility, there was a poor showing at the coronation at Westminster Abbey. 'Much of the splendour of the ceremony was abated by the absence of divers who should have contributed to it,' Evelyn wrote, 'There were but five bishops and four judges; no more had taken the oaths. Several noblemen and great ladies were absent.' Some of them stayed away out of principle, while others hesitated to show themselves, fearing that James's arrival in Ireland heralded his return. Offence was also taken at the coronation medal showing the English oak broken and replaced by an orange tree with the words, 'Instead of acorns, golden oranges'.

It was the first and only time that both King and Queen were invested with the sword, sceptre and orb. William was impatient and contemptuous of what he considered an old 'popish' ceremony, although the new monarchs took a new oath, 'to maintain the Protestant religion as established by law' and to govern 'according to the statutes in Parliament agreed on and the laws and customs of the same'. Nor was he going to have any truck with the Stuart kings' mystical practice of touching for the King's Evil. When later his subjects appealed to him to touch their afflicted faces and necks to cure the scrofula, he told them, 'God give you better health and more sense!'

When the moment came at the coronation to offer up gold coins to the Church, William and Mary found they had no money. In all the panic arising from the news of James's landing in Ireland, it had been forgotten. There was an awkward pause before Danby stepped forward with 20 golden guineas. Bishop Burnet followed with a sermon in which the Queen's father was obliquely criticised. This is surprising in view of the fact that William later warned Danby never to criticise James in front of Mary. Halifax had done so and she had been furious. She would not hear her father maligned by her subjects.

After the ceremony, Mary looked hot and oppressed by the weight of jewels she was carrying. Anne commiserated, only to be slapped down by her elder sister, who retorted, 'A crown, sister, is not so heavy as it appears.' Clearly, she was beginning to find Anne as irritating as did her husband, who could not stand her. The banquet that followed was running late and it was dusk when, according to custom, the King and Queen's champion rode into Westminster Hall and threw down his gauntlet as a challenge to anyone who disputed the title of the new monarchs. There was an embarrassed silence, as the guests could not see the gauntlet in the fading light. No one took it up.

———————

Mary was at first very popular as Queen. She had all the social skills her husband lacked. If the nobility could not easily resort to William, they felt that they could approach the Queen for favours. But it soon became apparent that she would do nothing without referring to her husband. What was the point of a queen who could grant no favours? Gradually, they drifted away and left her alone.

It came as something of a relief to Mary. In her journal she complains that 'I was come into a noisy world full of vanity.' It was not the life of peaceful meditation she had become used to in Holland. Mary had gone to public prayers four times a day there. In London she had 'hardly leisure to go twice, and that in such a crowd, with so much formality and little devotion'. She was in despair that 'I could not make people mind the Sunday more.' She was appalled at the immorality, pugnacity, rough manners, swearing and drunkenness, and lack of religious devotion of her new subjects. This behaviour was endemic in all classes. It was an age that still believed that a nation's sins could bring down God's wrath, hence the proclamations for days of public fast and prayer to allay it. Mary wrote in her journal that she was surprised 'to see so little devotion in a people so lately in such eminent danger'. She issued numerous proclamations to reform manners, but her efforts collapsed in ridicule when parish constables resorted to confiscating pies that poor people had brought to cook shops to be heated while they attended church on Sundays, the day of rest.

Increasingly, Mary found herself lonely and isolated. 'I found myself here very much neglected, little respected, censured by all, commended by none,' she wrote. This was particularly true once William began to spend every spring and summer on campaign overseas. In her whole six-year reign, they spent only the equivalent of three together. Elizabeth Villiers had returned to England and was still very much part of William's life, although he was discreet about the affair. Mary knew she could not trust her sister, who was so much under the influence of Sarah Churchill, whom Mary neither liked nor trusted. Mary's old friendship with Frances Apsley, her dearest Aurelia, had petered out. Frances was now Lady Bathurst, her husband a member of Princess Anne's household, and she had necessarily moved into Anne's circle. Mary kept up a correspondence with her father's cousin, Sophie of Hanover, whom William greatly respected, and her Dutch friend, Madame d'Obdam. In England she had no one in whom she could confide her troubles, although she was very fond of Lady Derby, her groom of the stole.

At court and elsewhere she was subjected to insult for her disloyalty to her father. When her father's ex-mistress Catherine Sedley, Countess of Dorchester, told friends that she was going to court, she was warned that Mary would treat her 'on no higher a foot than her father's daughter', to which Catherine replied, 'Then I will treat her like her mother's.' When Mary duly acknowledged her coolly, Catherine retorted, 'Why so proud, Madam? For if I broke one commandment with your father, you broke another in coming here.'

Mary eagerly went to the theatre to watch a performance of Dryden's *Spanish Friar*, which her father had banned because it ridiculed the Catholic Church. Unfortunately, she had not read the play beforehand, so that she was unprepared for the whole audience turning round to stare at her while the following dialogue took place:

How now! What means this show?

'Tis a procession.
The Queen is going to the Cathedral,
To pray for our success against the Moors.

Very good: she usurps the throne: keeps the old King
In prison; and at the same time is praying for a blessing:
O religion and roguery, how they go together!

Mary could only cover her face with her fan. It was worse in the fourth act: 'A crown usurped, a distaff on the throne . . .' was followed by 'What title has this Queen but lawless force? And force must pull her down.' Under the accusing stares of her subjects, Mary called for her hooded cloak, but she knew she could not leave, even though those in the pit had now totally turned their backs on the stage and were watching her reactions. The play was taken off next day by royal command. Needless to say, Shakespeare's *King Lear* would not be staged in this reign.

William and Mary contributed to the gradual decline of court life – which had begun with her Catholic father – by their withdrawal from Whitehall. Mary would still attend the Chapel Royal and organise a ball for the King's birthday and occasionally dine in public at Whitehall, but William flatly refused to live there. It was too hazardous for his health to remain in London, with its polluted skies and fogs. Whitehall itself was damp, dirty and uncomfortable, squalid in comparison with the couple's Dutch houses. Soon after their arrival they had discovered Hampton Court and fallen in love with it. This would be their home. The old Tudor palace of Cardinal Wolsey would be pulled down, all but the great hall, and a magnificent new European palace on the model of Versailles built in its place. Sir Christopher Wren was called in to design it.

The English, who thought nothing of wasting their fortunes on outward appearance and gambling, groaned at the expense. Whitehall and St James's had been good enough for previous monarchs, so why not for the Dutch usurper? Wren's plans had to be modified. Now, a new building with apartments for the King and Queen would be added to the old. These apartments, when they were ready, offered less access to the monarchs than had been the case in previous royal residences. The King and Queen might be approached only as they passed through the public rooms and corridors to their private apartments. Pending the completion of the works, Wren transformed an old Tudor gatehouse on the river into a Water Gallery for the Queen, providing temporary accommodation for her, complete with her own marble bathroom with hot and cold running water – a great novelty. Mary could reach Hampton Court from Whitehall by river in a couple of hours and spent many happy hours in her Water Gallery discussing the details of her new palace with Wren.

As there were so many complaints about the inaccessibility of Hampton Court – 'people here being naturally lazy' – with the King only coming in to Whitehall once or twice a week for council meetings, William paid Lord Nottingham 18,000 guineas for his country house in Kensington. Again, Wren would convert this 'sweet villa' into something resembling a palace, although William and Mary always called it Kensington House. Until it was ready, they would rent Holland House from the Rich family to be closer to London. Wren found the Queen an exacting employer, although he acknowledged she was a lady of exquisite taste. Several times a week she would walk to Kensington from Whitehall, striding across the parks with her architect by her side, to check progress. He had to work at such a pace that there were two major accidents in which workmen lost their lives.

Other than these unfortunate episodes, which Mary believed were God's judgement on her impatience, the renovations of Hampton Court and Kensington were Mary's greatest pleasures, taking her away from the cares of state and the backbiting of the court. In these homes, the Queen's subjects could admire her talent for embroidery in her bed curtains, the new printed calicoes imported from the East, and the large collection of blue and white Delftware and porcelain from China she had heaped on Grinling Gibbons's tiered shelves and chimney-pieces. Together with her introduction of pug dogs and the concept of keeping a goldfish as a pet, she set an enduring national trend for chintz and blue and white china.

Loving art as he did, William would extract the best of the royal collection from Whitehall – the Raphaels, the Holbeins, the Titians, the Rembrandts, the Lelys – to hang in his new homes. Following the example of her mother, Anne Hyde, who had patronised Lely, the Queen commissioned Kneller to paint the 'beauties' of her court, which would hang initially in her Water Gallery, but later in the King's dining room at Hampton Court. Unfortunately, Mary equated beauty with virtue and the result was far inferior to the luscious feminine beauty depicted in the earlier Lely paintings. The plain Catherine Sedley was quick to pose the question, 'Madam, if the King was to ask for the portraits of all the wits in his court, would not the rest think he called them fools?'

One of William's physicians in Holland had told him that gardening was therapeutic. It was certainly a hobby that afforded husband and wife enormous pleasure and gave them a respite from government. Mary threw herself into planning the gardens at both Hampton Court and Kensington. Daniel Defoe had once seen her walk past looking truly animated as she discussed with Wren the laying of the foundations of the gardens at Kensington: it was as if, he said, she was conscious that she would only have a few years to enjoy them. At Hampton Court long gravel walks and avenues of trees were complemented by canals and fountains, which William planned with the Huguenot designer Daniel Marot. Exotic plants and trees were located and brought back from far-flung corners of the world and thrived in new hothouses.

Orange trees in tubs punctuated the courtyards, while rows of neat box marked the boundaries of the lawns. Mary had rediscovered something of the serenity of the domesticated existence she had enjoyed in Holland.

––––––––––

In the spring of 1690 William was glad to leave London to take up arms against James in Ireland. A military campaign came as a relief after the squabbles he was caught up in among the English politicians. He had tried to share the spoils of victory between Whigs and Tories, although he personally preferred the Tories, but two-party government meant mayhem. The Whig majority in the Commons was peeved at the King's preference for the Tories. They were also determined not to make the same mistake they had with James II by granting revenue for life. Frequent parliaments must be called if the King wanted a regular income. As a result, William and the royal household would be chronically short of money, although the creation of the Bank of England and the national debt in 1694 would at least help finance the European war. This was just as well since the English, who had wallowed in civilian sloth for so long, had no concept of the cost of modern warfare and begrudged paying for it. The King retained his prerogatives to call and dissolve Parliament and to wage war, but it was the need to call Parliament frequently to vote supplies for the war that guaranteed the post-Revolution government of King-in-Parliament.

William was irritated that the Declaration of Rights, clipping the wings of the monarchy, had been placed on the statute book as the Bill of Rights. His desire for religious toleration had been rebuffed. From the moment of his arrival in England, William had been anxious to tamp down the worst manifestations of anti-Catholicism. He had assured the Emperor that he would use his best endeavours to do this, but Parliament refused to comply by introducing any kinder legislation for the Catholics. All William could do was exercise his prerogative to refuse to enforce the penal laws. As for the Dissenters, James had been in discussions with the Anglican hierarchy about once more embracing the Presbyterians within the Established Church and extending toleration to the rest. Now, the Anglicans retracted. The Toleration Act of 1689 allowed freedom of worship to Protestant Dissenters, but they were still excluded from office by the Corporation Act of 1661 and the Test Act of 1673. They could, of course, circumvent these by taking the sacrament in the Anglican Church occasionally, giving rise to what Daniel Defoe was to describe as the scandal of 'occasional conformity'.

William had at last realised his ambition to bring England into the European war on the side of the allies, which he had been trying to do since his marriage to Mary in 1677. On William's arrival in London in December, James's close confidant, the French ambassador Paul Barillon, had been given twenty-four hours to leave. War had been declared on France in May 1689. Before he could return to the European battlefield, however, William had to settle the British Isles. When offering William and Mary the English crown, Halifax had known that the Scots would have to make their own decision. The Convention Parliament sitting in Edinburgh offered them the crown of Scotland on 11 April 1689. Thenceforth, William called himself King of Great Britain, although it would be another eighteen years before the union he favoured became a political reality. James had many supporters in the Highlands, who were able to defeat a small force William had sent to Scotland at Killiecrankie in July. Their leader, Viscount Dundee, was killed in the battle, however, and for the moment opposition to the new regime melted away. If James had landed in Scotland, as he wanted to do, rather than Ireland, there was a good chance that he would have been able to muster sufficient support to launch an attack on England.

The Irish saw James as a means of breaking the connection with England, while the French put him there to keep William away from the European battlefield. Given his empirical,

non-ideological approach to politics, William had put out
feelers to James's man in Ireland, Lord Tyrconnel, whereby
in return for their submission Irish Catholics would be granted
toleration. This would have been a sensible solution and
avoided much bloodshed. The talks came to nothing, however, and William had no option but military intervention.
He decided to go there himself to confront James without
further delay. He took the Prince of Denmark with him, no
doubt to ensure Anne's loyalty while he was away, although
he could not bring himself to offer boring George a place in
his coach.

He left Mary in charge in his absence. She was a firm believer
that 'women should not meddle in government' – which she
had never done until now – and her only concern was that
she 'should not make a foolish figure in the world'. She so
underestimated her own abilities that she later told Sophie of
Hanover: 'a woman is but a very useless and helpless creature
at all times, especially in times of war and difficulty. I find by
my own sad experience, that an old English inclination to the
love and honour of the nation signifies nothing in a woman's
heart without a man's head and hands.'

She had a council of Whigs and Tories of varying degrees
of loyalty, who thought that they would be able to take
advantage of the inexperienced woman. They soon learned
otherwise. Mary proved an astute judge of character. She
referred all major decisions to William, sitting up late into
the night straining her eyesight in the candlelight to write him
long letters, which routinely ended with her protestations of
love: 'Farewell, I will trouble you with no more, but only desire
you, whatever happens, to love me as I shall you to death' and
'Loving you with a passion which cannot end but with my life'
and 'Adieu, do but love me, and I can bear any thing'.

In an emergency there was no time to consult William and
here Mary acted courageously and decisively. There was a
traitor in the council and she suspected it was Lord Mordaunt,
betraying secrets to France. The revelation of his treachery

came to her from an anonymous source in letters written in lemon juice, only visible when held up to a flame. Soon the French fleet was in the Channel. Admiral Herbert was showing a marked reluctance to engage the enemy, but 'lay drinking and treating his friends'. Mary was about to relieve him of his command when he engaged the French off Beachy Head. But he let the Dutch do all the fighting, keeping the English fleet to the rear and then retreating to the Thames. Mary was mortified, writing to the Dutch government to give her personal apology. Herbert, now Lord Torrington, was flung into the Tower.

With the French victory and the removal of most of William's troops to Ireland came the threat of invasion. The French were working with James's supporters – the Jacobites – in England, some of whom were receiving sums of money from Mary Beatrice. Mary ordered the imprisonment of all suspected leading Jacobites, including her uncle, Clarendon. She suspected her aunt, the Queen Dowager Catherine, whom she had never liked, of intriguing against her. A report reached Lord Nottingham of a plot to kill Mary. A lady and a gentleman with a Scottish accent had been overheard after dark in Birdcage Walk planning the assassination of the Queen as she went into chapel, 'when she had but few gentlemen with her and her sixpenny beggars, with their petitions'. Later, a fire at Whitehall, which Mary escaped in her nightclothes, could well have been another attempt to kill her. Out of the darkness, as the Queen and her ladies watched the licking flames, the Jacobite Sir John Fenwick shouted insults at her. When the French attacked Teignmouth in Devon, however, the whole country rallied round the Queen in outrage.

Although she was rapidly gaining the love of her people through her dedication, her piety and her goodness, Mary's health was suffering under the strain of it all. Her day began at six, when she was woken with tea – one of her expensive indulgences – and she then spent two hours reading and writing. Prayers were said at eight, followed by business for four or five hours until dinner. There were cards and public receptions from four until seven. Evening prayers and supper over, she would attend to her private correspondence until midnight or the early hours of the morning. She went to sleep in the knowledge that she might be woken at any hour to deal with a national emergency. Through all this, she told William that 'I must grin when my heart is ready to break, and talk when my heart is so oppress'd I can scarce breathe.'

When her face became stiff and swollen, leeches were applied behind her ears. She could neither sleep nor eat. Unfortunately, Mary was the type for whom stress meant weight gain. She had always dreaded becoming fat, perhaps remembering how gross her mother had become, but she had gained a double chin and a considerable amount of weight since returning to England. At just under six feet tall, Mary had a large frame, a generous but well-proportioned figure, and a waist, certainly by her early thirties, of twenty-eight inches. She was a large woman by modern standards, but huge compared with her contemporaries. She had always enjoyed walking, but now she would do so vigorously in an effort to keep her weight down. 'I go to Kensington as often as I can for air,' she told William, 'but then I can never be quite alone; neither can I complain, that would be some ease; but I have nobody whose humour and circumstances agrees with mine enough to speak my mind freely to. Besides, I must hear of business, which being a thing I am so new in, and so unfit for, does but break my brains the more, and not ease my heart.'

On top of all this, she was distraught with worry about William. 'The concern for his dear person who was so ill in health when he went from hence, the toil and fatigue he was like to endure, the ill air of the country he was going, his humour when I knew he would expose himself to all dangers,' consumed her. In fact, William's health usually improved on campaign, the outdoor exercise being beneficial. There was also the underlying dread: 'the cruel thought that my husband and my father would fight in person against each other, and if either should have perished in the action, how terrible it must have been to me.'

William landed at Carrickfergus in June 1690 with 44,000 men. His foreign troops were shocked at the state of the country, the poverty and backwardness. The people were in a wretched condition, unhealthy, dirty, starving and dressed in rags. James's French soldiers had been burning and pillaging, just as on the Continent they were currently turning the fertile Palatinate into a desert, but the Protestant citizens of Londonderry in Ulster had held their besieged town. William gave chase to James's constantly retreating army. At last he caught up with it near Drogheda on the River Boyne. As William rode fearlessly up and down encouraging his troops, his garter star was visible to the French, who took aim. The shot grazed his shoulder but did no serious damage. Thinking they had killed him, a message was sent to Paris, where there were celebrations burning William's effigy in the streets. A few hours later William rode before his troops again, waving his sword in his right arm to show that he was still able to fight.

Next day, William was in the thick of the battle, while James watched from a hilltop. The veteran military commander Count Schomberg was killed. James's inexperienced Irish troops ran away. The French fought on, but it was hopeless. Seeing that the victory was to be William's, James fled, not stopping until he reached Dublin. 'Madam,' he told Frances, Lady Tyrconnel, 'your countrymen have run away.' 'If they have, Sire,' this sister of Sarah Churchill retorted, 'Your Majesty seems to have won the race.' At Kinsale he took ship for France, never to set foot in any of his kingdoms again.

On the battlefield, women were already scavenging, stripping the dead of all their possessions. They set up a market there and then to sell the stolen propety. A Dutch soldier writing to his wife told her he had not been able to believe his eyes at the savagery with which the English had treated the Irish and the French, not least the English showing their contempt for the Irish by running over their bodies with their carriages.

When news of William's victory at the Boyne reached Mary, she was filled with joy and relief. Evidently she believed her father was his prisoner, because she wrote: 'I know I need not beg you to let him be taken care of, for I am confident you will for your own sake. Yet add that to all your kindness, and, for my sake, let people know you would have no hurt come to his person.'

After the Irish campaign, Mary had to find out from the *Utrecht Courant* that William had promised the States-General that he would return to the United Provinces almost immediately. He meant to stay in London only two weeks. Mary was frustrated that they had so little time alone together. 'Ladies who before kept away in consideration of my business, now came in crowds, believing I had nothing to do but chat with them.' Soon she was left alone again with all the cares of government on her shoulders. The only compensation was that Shrewsbury, the one politician she trusted, had now consented to serve as one of her advisers, at least for a while. Shrewsbury, whose mother Anna Maria Brudenell had notoriously been the lover of the second Duke of Buckingham and had watched him fatally wound Shrewsbury's father in a duel, tended to spend long periods away from court nursing his health.

Known as the 'King of Hearts', Shrewsbury seems to have been in love with Mary. She was observed to blush and tremble whenever she saw the handsome courtier, who gossips were convinced would ask for her hand in the event of William's death. There is no question, however, that she was ever anything but totally faithful to William, even though he was breaking her heart by handing out James's Irish lands to his mistress, Elizabeth Villiers, rather than setting up the schools she wanted for 'the poor Irish'.

James's defeat in Ireland did nothing to reduce the Jacobite threat. Lord Preston and one of James's former secretaries, John Ashton, took advantage of William's absence to plan a rising on a large scale. They were seized, tried and sentenced to death. Mary signed the warrant for Ashton's execution in great distress, since she had known him from her childhood. Many appeals were made to Mary to spare Preston's life. Knowing Mary's love of children, his family went so far as to place his small daughter in the Queen's closet. When Mary found her there staring up at the portrait of James II, the child was primed to say, 'I am reflecting how hard it is that my father should be put to death for loving your father.' Preston tried to bargain for his life by naming his co-conspirators, implicating Danby, Dorset and Devonshire, who were found to be guilty of nothing more than indiscretion. William, who wanted all his English subjects to put the past behind them, destroyed the evidence against them, earning their everlasting gratitude.

After his resounding defeat in Ireland, James had received a cool reception in France. Louis had been so furious that he had not been able to bring himself to greet his royal cousin until several days after his return. The initial sympathy felt for him had long given way to exasperation. Louis's courtiers found James a crashing bore. 'When one listens to him,' drawled Madame de Sévigné, 'one realises why he is here.' Liselotte, who had never had any time for fools, wrote to her aunt, Sophie of Hanover: 'The more I see of this King, the more excuses I find for the Prince of Orange, and the more admirable I think he is.'

Nevertheless, in the New Year of 1692 a French force of 20,000 men gathered at La Hogue, on the Cherbourg peninsula, where James joined them with a contingent of Irish soldiers. A new invasion scare swept England, putting fresh heart into the Jacobites. There was a plot afoot to seize Mary on her father's landing. She was sure that she would be murdered. There were fears of disloyalty in the navy, which Mary addressed by appealing directly to her officers, expressing her complete confidence in them. At the same time, she went to Hyde Park to review the few troops – those whom William had not taken to Europe – who were left to defend the country.

At this moment, James unwittingly came to her aid. He

issued a declaration, promising that on his restoration he would continue much as before, and listing hundreds of names on whom his vengeance would fall. It was so ludicrous that the Jacobites hurriedly sought to publish a toned-down version, but Mary was too quick for them. Showing that she had learned a great deal from William about the value of propaganda, she promptly had James's declaration printed and distributed, with her own comments on it.

When an Anglo-Dutch fleet under Admiral Russell and Lieutenant-Admiral Van Almonde won a great victory at La Hogue, a grateful Mary immediately despatched £38,000 for distribution among her seamen. The unfinished royal palace at Greenwich, she promised, would be transformed into a hospital for sick and disabled seamen. Wren's services were again in demand. Mary's popularity among her people soared. Her only regret, as she confided in her journal, was that she did not order a public thanksgiving to God straight away. She was waiting for news of William's victory at Steinkirk, but instead he was defeated with terrible losses. 'Will should have knotted,' was the English people's verdict, referring to Mary's new hobby of tying linen threads into knots to keep her agitated hands occupied, 'and Moll gone to Flanders.'

Even James realised that La Hogue spelled the end of his hopes. 'My unlucky star has made its influence felt over the arms of Your Majesty,' he wrote to the long-suffering Louis, 'always victorious until they battled for me. I beg you not to take any more interest in a prince so unhappy.' Louis needed little encouragement to do just that.

But James had one more card to play. He gave his blessing to a French plot to assassinate William in Flanders. 'I have been informed of the business,' he told the assassin Grandval when he came to St Germain. 'If you and your companions do me this service, you shall never want.'

Grandval, however, was betrayed and seized as soon as he set foot in Flanders. He confessed, revealing that James had given his approval to the plan, and was executed.

Sensational trials like this one were among the popular reading of the day, but Mary was in a dilemma about authorising its printing. She shrank from publicising what she regarded as her own shame: 'that he who I dare no more name father was consenting to the barbarous murder of my husband.' She knew that the knowledge of it would afflict her for the rest of her life. 'I was ashamed to look any body in the face. I fancied I should be pointed at as the daughter of one who was capable of such things, and the people would believe I might by nature have as ill inclinations. I lamented his sin and his shame.'

As ever, Mary was concerned with William's reaction. She feared that her father's intention to kill him 'might lessen my husband's kindness for me'. Mary soon confided in her journal her relief that this was not the case. William did not blame her for her father's actions and his love for her had not diminished. Whatever that love amounted to, William had never been able to give Mary all the emotional support she so desperately needed. But he was all she had. She had lost her father. And it looked as if she had lost her sister, too.

# Part Three

*Consequences*

# 10
## The Quarrel

*'In all this I see the hand of God, and look on our disagreeing as a punishment upon us for the irregularity by us committed upon the revolution'*

– Mary II

Once their father was dethroned and cast out, it was not long before the fragile unity of the protagonists began to disintegrate. William loathed his sister-in-law, saying that if he had been married to her rather than her sister, he would have been the unhappiest man in the world. For her part, Anne hated her brother-in-law, referring to him in her letters to Sarah Churchill, now Lady Marlborough, as Caliban, the Monster and the Dutch Abortion. The two sisters, Mary and Anne, had grown apart since their girlhood. They had loved each other then, in spite of occasional sibling jealousies, but now they were women with very different personalities. Mary's husband had usurped Anne's place in the succession and, what's more, he treated her husband, the kindly but ineffectual George, with scant respect.

It was not guilt over their dispossessed father and brother that tore the sisters apart. Ostensibly, it was petty quarrels over lodgings and money, which developed into something more serious when Anne's loyalty and that of her friends the Marlboroughs was called into question. After an initial show of respect for the new Queen, her sister, Anne resorted to the aggrieved sulking, the disobedience and obstinacy, with occasional flashes of malice and hypocrisy, that had characterised her relations with her long-suffering father and stepmother, even if they had been slow to realise it.

Both Anne and Sarah were quarrelsome. Anne might have

been lazy and passive, but she seems to have had a jealous temperament, one that easily took umbrage. She would then nurse her grievance and bear a grudge against the person who had perpetrated it. Sarah was quick-witted, impatient and had no time for fools; her fiery temper was legendary and her sharp tongue made her many enemies. She possessed a strong sense of what was right and wrong and would not hesitate to fight for someone she felt was wronged, as, for instance, her mistress Princess Anne during the years of William and Mary's reign. Perhaps because she was so fearlessly outspoken, Sarah was never popular, and in the course of her long life she managed to quarrel with just about every member of her family. She did not like William, probably realising that here was one man she would not be able to influence, and in her *Conduct* she denigrated Mary, whom nearly everyone came to love and admire.

As William told Halifax at the outset, the Marlboroughs would not be able to dominate him and his wife as they did the Prince and Princess of Denmark. On the contrary, William considered Marlborough 'assuming' and could never bring himself to trust a man who had deserted his sovereign in the field. Sarah was peeved that her husband was not being accorded by William the honours and promotions she felt he deserved. She had a weapon to hand that could be used against William and Mary in the person of Anne, who at this stage was completely under her influence. What might have been a dull existence with a passive husband was made vibrant and exciting for Anne by the presence of Sarah, whom she adored. It was easy for Sarah to fan the flames of Anne's incipient jealousy of her sister and resentment of her brother-in-law and, once there was an open breach, keep it that way, so that the sisters never spoke to each other again.

Of course, in her *Conduct* Sarah was careful to exonerate herself from any part in the royal quarrel. She put it down to the difference in temperament between the sisters. 'Mary soon grew weary of anybody who would not talk a great deal,'

James was mortified that anyone should question the legitimacy of his son (*inset*). Kneller, who had painted James Francis Edward, as well as James II and Mary Beatrice many times, could identify features the boy had inherited from each of his parents.

Playing cards were useful in disseminating news of momentous events and propaganda.

| VI ♡ | ◇ QUEEN | KING ♡ |
|---|---|---|

The Prince of Orange going into Exeter.

The King going to Salisbury

The ould Oxford Regiment of Horse with 4 more, first left the King and went to the Prince.

| ◇ KNAVE | X | KNAVE ◇ |
|---|---|---|

The King coming from Salisbury the Armie following in hast the Enemy not being near.

The Lord Dartmouth refusing to carey yᵉ Child over to France he returns to Whithalle

The Queen and child and father Peters going away in the night

| I ♡ | II ♡ | VII ♡ |
|---|---|---|

The King leaving London about three a Clock in the Morning in his barge

The King and with 2 more are stoped by rude seamen being in an hoy by the Isle of Shipey.

The Prince of Orange coming to Sᵗ Iameses is received with great Ioy.

William, Duke of Gloucester, seen here with his friend Peter Bathurst, was suffering from hydrocephalus. His Welsh servant noted that it was very difficult to find a periwig to fit the child's enlarged head.

After her return to England in 1689, Mary II developed a double
chin and gained weight. Unfortunately, the fashions of the 1690s
did not suit her, but that did not hinder her from indulging in the
fine clothes she loved and buying white gloves by the dozen. She
found the fan useful to hide her face on the occasion when Dryden's
play, *The Spanish Friar*, implicitly criticised her and the whole
audience turned round to stare at her in the royal box.

Sarah Churchill, later Duchess of Marlborough (*right*), and Barbara
Berkeley, later Lady Fitzharding, sneaked out of the Cockpit with Princess
Anne, when she deserted her father in December 1688. The three were
friends from childhood, but later Anne and Sarah quarrelled bitterly.

Born the posthumous son of Prince William II of Orange into a chamber shrouded in deepest mourning, King William III's hooked nose and gaunt features are thrown into relief here by the candlelight as he neared the end of his life. Tubercular and asthmatic, he could not abide London's smoke-polluted air and crowded drawing rooms.

Queen Anne looking triumphant in coronation robes. Only thirty-seven when she came to the throne, seventeen pregnancies in as many years, massive weight gain, gout and possibly arthritis meant that she was virtually an invalid.

James Francis Edward led a tragic, wasted life. His birthright denied by his half-sisters, Mary II and Anne, his whole life was spent in a hopeless quest to recover his father's crown. He bears a striking resemblance in this portrait to his mother, Mary Beatrice, as seen in Verelst's portrait of her in her riding habit.

she wrote, 'and the Princess Anne was so silent, that she rarely spoke excepting to ask a question.' Quite hypocritically, Sarah claimed that she did everything she could to stop Anne quarrelling with her sister. 'It was impossible for any body to labour more than I did to keep the two sisters in perfect unison and friendship, thinking it best for them not to quarrel when their true interest and safety were jointly concerned to support the revolution.' If this was the case, Sarah failed miserably, and she was not given to failure.

Everyone went to court in hopes of wielding influence and in pursuit of employment and financial gain, but among the most sought-after perquisites were lodgings at Whitehall. The very best lodgings, after the newly refurbished apartments occupied by Mary, were those of the late Charles II's mistress, the Duchess of Portsmouth, who had returned to her native France. William agreed that Anne might occupy these apartments. She then pushed her luck and asked for the adjoining apartments as well for her servants. Mary prevaricated. Those rooms had been promised to Lord Devonshire and she would have to consult him. Anne sulkily retorted that 'whichever way *he* decided, *she* would not take the Earl of Devonshire's leavings.' She held on to the Duchess's prized apartments, even though she soon found them too uncomfortably close to her sister's.

Anne then demanded the palace of Richmond, saying that she 'had loved it in her infancy, and the air agreed with her'. In all the years since, she had rarely shown any inclination to be at Richmond and she must have known that her late governess Lady Villiers's interest in the palace had reverted to her daughter, Katherine Puissars, who refused to give it up. Katherine was probably encouraged to make a stand by her sister, Elizabeth Villiers, William's mistress, who was already daggers drawn with Sarah Marlborough.

By this time, Anne had retired to Hampton Court to await the outcome of her seventh pregnancy. She was so monstrously swollen that John Evelyn suspected that it would 'prove a tympane onely'. On 24 July 1689, however, Anne's political importance soared with the birth of a son. 'This morning, about four o'clock,' the *London Gazette* announced, 'Her Royal Highness the Princess Anne of Denmark was safely delivered of a son, at Hampton Court. Queen Mary was present the whole time, about three hours; and the King, with most of the persons of quality about the court, came into Her Royal Highness's bedchamber before she was delivered. Her Royal Highness and the young prince are very well, to the great satisfaction of Their Majesties and the joy of the whole court, as it will, doubtless, be of the whole kingdom.' Not only was Anne next in line to the throne after William and Mary, but now she was the mother of the heir to the dynasty. He was baptised William Henry after the King, and William and Mary stood sponsors, proclaiming him Duke of Gloucester the same day.

At his birth, Anne's son was described as a 'brave lively-like boy', but within weeks he suffered convulsion fits so severe that the physicians despaired of his life. Mary, who doted on the child as if he were her own, looked on his illness as 'the righteous judgement of God upon our unhappy family and these sinful nations', and prayed fervently for his recovery. The arrival of a new wet nurse, a Quakeress named Mrs Pack, seemed to sort out the immediate problems. Anne anxiously fussed over him, moving his household to Campden House near Kensington gravel pits because of its purer air. Here he would be taken out every afternoon in dry weather in his miniature coach with horses 'no larger than a good mastiff', led by his coachman, Dick Drury.

The relationship between the monarch and the heir to the throne is often fraught, not least because the heir becomes the focus of the opposition. It was disconcerting for Mary to learn, therefore, 'how my sister was making parties to get a revenue settled'. It was noted that Sidney, Lord Godolphin – whom Anne and Sarah referred to affectionately as Mr Montgomery in their correspondence – frequented the Cockpit far more often than he paid his respects to the Queen. Godolphin was Lord of the Treasury and it was probably from him that Anne heard the disturbing news that William, when examining expenditure, had been 'astonished to think how it was possible for the Princess Anne to spend her revenue of thirty thousand pounds per annum'. In fact, Anne had never managed to live within her income. Her indulgent father had more than once paid her gambling debts and she had been angry that he had denied her the extra £10,000 a year she had been demanding, quite unfairly blaming Mary Beatrice.

Now Anne's friends in the House of Commons – the Tories and high churchmen – were asking for her to receive an allowance of £70,000 a year. For the heir to the throne to receive a parliamentary grant outside the monarch's gift was unprecedented. It would make Anne, who had a better claim to the throne than William, dangerously independent. Anne probably reasoned that it was equally unprecedented for the heir to the throne to yield her place in the succession to another, as she had done for William. Mary was furious at what she saw as an insult to William by Anne's going behind their backs to appeal to Parliament for an independent income, and taxed her sister with the matter when she came to court. 'What was the meaning of the proceedings in the House of Commons?' she asked. Anne replied that 'She heard her friends there wished to move that she had some settlement.' 'Friends?' Mary replied imperiously. 'Pray, what friends have you but the King and me?' The younger sister, stung by this jibe, poured out her feelings to Lady Marlborough, who redoubled her efforts on Anne's behalf.

The sum of £70,000 was excessive for the Princess and her household, even if she was heir to the throne and the mother of a son. It was understandable that Anne wanted some independence from her brother-in-law since, with the exception of the gifts he lavished on his Dutch favourites, William was not generous by nature. Anne was probably right not to trust him. For instance, when William obtained James's

Irish estates, he did not accord either of James's daughters their share. He was also to let down Prince George by asking him to yield certain mortgages in Denmark as part of a peace treaty on the understanding that he would be compensated in England. George had to agree a substantial cut in order to get anything at all and wait until 1699 to receive payment.

William sent the personable Lord Shrewsbury to the Cockpit to reason with Anne. He promised her an income of £50,000 a year from the royal revenues and also the settlement of her current debts 'if she would desist from soliciting Parliament'. Shrewsbury first appealed to Lord Marlborough, who begged to be left out of it. His wife was 'like a mad woman', he told Shrewsbury, and would by no means listen to reason. She said that 'the Princess would retire if her friends would not assist her.' The indomitable Sarah told Shrewsbury that William's offer was all very well, but it would be of no use to the Princess if William chose to break his word. When Shrewsbury put his arguments to the Princess, she repeated mechanically that 'Since that affair is now before the Commons, it must take its course' and 'the business is now gone so far that I think it reasonable to see what my friends can do for me.'

Just before Christmas William and Mary suffered a humiliating defeat when the Commons voted Anne £50,000 a year. William decided to make the best of the situation and responded very graciously to the House, and he advised Mary to let the matter drop. But Mary was outraged by this snub to William and tackled her sister directly when she next came to court. In what way had the King been unkind to her and when had he ever broken his word? she demanded. Anne forbore to mention her grievance that William had usurped her right to the throne. Nor, on a more mundane note, did she hark back to the occasion during her pregnancy when William had eaten the whole dish of fresh peas – a rare treat – at dinner, while Anne had longed for them so much she had not been able to take her eyes off them. Similarly, Sarah noted that when he received a dish of fruit, William would always select the best for himself and offer Anne the worst peach and grapes. She refused to admit she was in the wrong in approaching the Commons without the King and Queen's knowledge and, as ever when confronted by her more articulate elder sister, took refuge in a sulky silence.

All over Christmas and into the New Year of 1690 the coldness continued between the sisters, Anne failing to pay her respects to the Queen over this period. William, who 'thought it an ungenerous thing to fall out with a woman', went to visit Anne to tell her so, but she merely replied that he would never have cause to fall out with her. The successful outcome of Anne's soliciting the Commons, which she had done on Lady Marlborough's advice, made her even more devoted and grateful to her favourite. Sarah, however, was disappointed that the sum fell so far short of what the Princess had been seeking and asked Lord Rochester's advice as to whether Anne should be satisfied with £50,000 or try to get more. Rochester replied that 'he did not only think she should be satisfy'd with that but that she should have taken it any way the King & Queen pleased.'

---

Early in 1690 Mary confided sadly in her journal her fears that the revolution government was threatened by a party that had formed for her father – the Jacobites – a second party that was in favour of a republic, and 'I have reason to fear that my sister forms a third.' Mary was extremely troubled at the continuing coldness between her sister and herself and would like to have spoken to her, but she 'saw plainly that she was so absolutely governed by Lady Marlborough that it was to no purpose'. Not only was Anne's attitude hurtful to Mary, it was also disloyal. Left alone to govern an unstable country under threat of invasion, Mary needed her sister's support. Instead, Anne was heading a party against her, finding 'fault in everything that was done' and 'doing in little things contrary to what I did'.

One of Anne's grievances was William's ill-disguised contempt for her husband. Prince George was an amiable nonentity, as Charles II had long ago recognised, but Anne was
devoted to him. William had made him especially unwelcome
on the Irish expedition of 1690. He had not invited him to ride
in his coach with Bentinck, leaving him to tag along with the
rest of the army, and he had neglected to invite him to dine at
his table. According to Sarah, he took as little notice of him as
'if he had been a page of the backstairs', a point that she no
doubt impressed on Anne, who was hurt for her husband. In
the following year, therefore, George and Anne resolved that
he would seek glory elsewhere. He would serve as a volunteer
in the navy. When George told William of this scheme, on
the eve of William's departure for Flanders in January 1691,
he made no comment. George might have been a bumbling
fool, but in his youth in Scandinavia he had been considered
courageous in the field, and William wanted to take no chances
that he would win any laurels in his war.

He left it to the Queen to deter the hapless George from
going to sea. Her first inclination was to persuade Anne to
ask her husband to change his plans. She hesitated to approach
her sister directly, however. The coldness between them still
persisted and since the disappointment of her eighth pregnancy
in October 1690, when a daughter named Mary had died
within two hours of her birth, Anne had become increasingly
morose and sullen. Mary decided to broach the subject using
Lady Marlborough as an intermediary. Sarah refused to offer
any assistance in the matter and sat back to await the inevitable
escalation of the sisters' quarrel. In exasperation, Mary sent
Lord Nottingham to forbid the Prince from going to sea.
Unfortunately, George's luggage was already stowed aboard
and now he had to go through the humiliation of retrieving
it. Caring little for any embarrassment they had caused the
government by George's unwanted volunteering, Anne was
so mortified on her husband's behalf that 'the two sisters
quarrelled terribly.' As Mary said, it gave her 'the pretence

to raile, and so in discontent go to Tunbridge'.

A far more serious threat to the new regime was posed by Marlborough's growing disenchantment. He was dangerous because of his influence in the army and his wife's control over Princess Anne. William had not only rewarded him for his part in the Revolution with an earldom, but made him a Privy Councillor and gave him a court appointment as a gentleman of the bedchamber at £1,000 a year. Besides this, he was a lieutenant-general in the army. But Marlborough was dissatisfied. William knew he was a good soldier, but he did not trust him enough to offer him the command he craved. Nor did he give him the lucrative post of Master of the Ordnance. That went to William's favourite, Henry Sidney. Above all, Marlborough made no secret of his resentment that William surrounded himself by Dutchmen, giving them all the best commands in the army and showering them with English and Irish lands. He was so vociferous in his complaints that it must have been calculated.

Calculated, too, was Marlborough's *rapprochement* with James. In January 1691 both Marlborough and Godolphin made contact with the Jacobite agent, Henry Bulkeley. On a personal level, Godolphin had been in contact with St Germain all along, because he was romantically attached to Mary Beatrice and frequently sent her presents from London. Marlborough was playing the role of penitent and he asked another Jacobite, Colonel Sackville, 'to go to the King [James] and acquaint him with his sincere repentance, or to intercede for mercy, that he was ready to redeem his apostasy with the hazard of utter ruin, his crimes appearing so horrid to him that he could neither eat nor sleep'. He said he was willing to leave wife and home in James's cause – which surely must have raised James's suspicions. As earnest of his sincerity, he gave them vital information about the composition and intended disposal of William's military and naval forces. He even offered to bring over the English troops in Flanders, although when James did later request this Marlborough declined to do so.

No matter how much he might resent the new regime, Marlborough could surely not be seriously entertaining the idea of James's restoration. It is more likely he was playing a double game. It might have been inspired by the threat of William adopting James's and Mary Beatrice's infant son, James Francis Edward, as his heir. No European royal, including William, gave any credence to the allegation of the child's being a changeling. This resolution was being urged on William by the Emperor Leopold and was suggested from time to time by Sophie, Electress of Hanover. As the next Protestant heir after Princess Anne and her son, Sophie had the most to gain from the current arrangement, but advocated the reinstatement of James Francis Edward because she was convinced that it was his right as the true hereditary heir to his father's throne. Probably unknown to Mary, William was prepared to give the idea of adopting the boy serious consideration, the only obstacle being the implacable opposition of his parents.

It was enough of a threat to worry the Cockpit circle and one that had to be counterchecked. By holding out the prospect of a Jacobite restoration, Marlborough felt he could keep St Germain at bay, while protecting the interests of Princess Anne. The Jacobites were encouraged to believe that the Princess looked favourably on a restoration, that she sympathised with her brother and might facilitate his way to the crown when the time was right. To make this more convincing, the Marlboroughs persuaded Anne to write a letter of penitence to her father:

*1 December 1691*

I have been very desirous of some safe opportunity to make you a sincere and humble offer of my duty and submission to you, and to beg that you will be assured that I am both truly concerned for the misfortune of your condition and sensible, as I ought to be, of my own unhappiness. As to what you may think I have contributed to it, if wishes could recall what is past, I had long since redeemed my fault. I am sensible it would have been a great relief to me if I could have found means to acquaint you earlier with my repentant thoughts, but I hope they may find the advantage of coming late, of being less suspected of insincerity than perhaps they would have been at any time before.

It will be a great addition to the ease I propose to my own mind by this plain confession if I am so happy as to find that it brings any real satisfaction to yours, and that you are as indulgent and easy to receive my humble submissions as I am to make them, in a free, disinterested acknowledgement of my fault, for no other end but to deserve and receive your pardon.

I have had a great mind to beg you to make one compliment for me, but fearing the expressions which would be properest for me to make use of might be perhaps the least convenient for a letter, I must content myself at present with hoping the bearer will make a compliment for me to the Queen.

The letter was delivered to James eight months after the date it bears. The Jacobite post was more efficient than this. It is tempting to think that William might have intercepted the letter, but there is no firm evidence that he knew of it and Mary never mentions it in her journal. The letter might have been backdated to look as if it had been written and sent before the English naval victory at La Hogue, which took place in May 1692. Whether or not James detected that the phrasing of the letter betrayed that someone other than his daughter had composed it, he was not inclined to believe its sincerity. His Jacobite supporters were warned that 'being solicited to pardon his son and daughter, the Prince and Princess of Denmark, he could never have a good opinion of them or put any confidence in them.' The Jacobites were cynical enough to realise that if Marlborough effected an overthrow of William's government he would put Anne, not her father James or her brother James Francis Edward, in his place.

With his excellent network of spies in the Jacobite camp and elsewhere, William was already well acquainted with what was going on in Princess Anne's household, through Barbara Berkeley, now Lady Fitzharding, who was Elizabeth Villiers's sister. Like all the Villiers, she hated their relations, the Churchills. Anne had received an anonymous letter warning her that Lady Fitzharding was spying on her and a few months later was warning Sarah to be on her guard against her: 'for I doubt she is a jade and there is too much reason to believe she has not been so sincere as she ought, I am sure she hates your faithful Mrs Morley [Anne], and remember none of her family were ever good for anything.'

William understood that his English subjects felt the need to take out an insurance policy with St Germain, but Marlborough's perfidy was too dangerous to tolerate. Not only was he in correspondence with the exiled King and being insubordinate and threatening to turn the army against its Dutch commanders, but he and his wife were also alienating Princess Anne from the King and Queen. Marlborough's move to persuade Parliament to expel all Dutchmen from the King's service was the last straw. Many of these men, such as Bentinck who had left a beloved, dying wife to accompany William on his expedition to England, had left their homes and risked everything for William and he was not going to abandon them. On 20 January 1692 William struck. That morning at the King's levée Marlborough, in his capacity as gentleman of the bedchamber, handed the King his shirt, which was received in silence. Afterwards, William despatched Nottingham to inform Marlborough that he was to sell all his offices and leave the court.

His dismissal was a sensation. Evelyn could only speculate that it was because the avaricious Marlborough had been enriching himself by taking bribes. No one knew the real cause and William and Mary had no wish to publish the extent of his treachery. William told one MP that Marlborough had treated him in such a way that if he were a private gentleman he would have challenged him to a duel. It was left to everyone's imagination to fill in the details, or to think that William and Mary were acting unreasonably. It was this that Princess Anne was able to capitalise on.

————

Marlborough's disgrace should have been the end of the affair as far as Princess Anne was concerned, but unfortunately it was only the beginning. Two weeks after Marlborough's dismissal, Anne committed a flagrant breach of etiquette by arriving at court with Lady Marlborough in tow. Obsessed as she was with court etiquette, Anne must have understood the enormity of what she was doing. She was deliberately insulting the King and Queen. Sarah, too, must have known that as the wife of a disgraced man she should not have appeared at court. As her sister was now entering the final weeks of her ninth pregnancy, Mary decided not to risk a scene by saying anything that evening, but the next day she sent her a letter putting her case in the strongest terms:

*Kensington, Friday, 5 February*
Having something to say to you which I know will not be very pleasing, I choose rather to write it first, being unwilling to surprise you, though I think what I am going to tell you should not, if you give yourself time to think, that never any body was suffered to live at court in Lord Marlborough's circumstances. I need not repeat the cause he has given the King to do what he has done, nor his [William's] unwillingness at all times to come to extremities, though people do deserve it.

I hope you do me the justice to believe it is much against my will that I now tell you that, after this, it is very unfit that Lady Marlborough should stay with you, since that gives her husband so just a pretence of being where he should not. I think I might have expected you should have spoke to me of it; and the King and I, both believing it, made us stay thus long [by 'it' Mary meant Sarah's dismissal from Anne's household, which as a courtesy to the King and Queen she should have effected]. But seeing you

[were] so far from it that you brought Lady Marlborough hither last night, makes us resolve to put it off no longer, but tell you she must not stay, and that I have all the reason imaginable to look upon your bringing her as the strangest thing that ever was done. Nor could all my kindness for you (which is always ready to turn all you do the best way), at any other time, have hindered me from showing you so that moment, but I considered your condition, and that made me master myself so far as not to take notice of it then.

But now I must tell you, it was very unkind in a sister, would have been very uncivil in an equal; and I need not say I have more to claim, which, though my kindness would never make me exact, yet, when I see the use you would make of it, I must tell you I know what is due to me, and expect to have it from you. 'Tis upon that account I tell you plainly, Lady Marlborough must not continue with you, in the circumstances her lord is.

I know this will be uneasy to you, and I am sorry for it, for I have all the real kindness imaginable for you; and as I ever have, so will always do my part to live with you as sisters ought; that is, not only like so near relations, but like friends, and as such I did think to write to you. For I would have made myself believe your kindness for her [Sarah] made you at first forget what you should have for the King and me, and resolved to put you in mind of it myself, neither of us being willing to come to harsher ways; but the sight of Lady Marlborough having changed my thoughts, does naturally alter my style. And since by that I see how little you seem to consider what, even in common civility, you owe us, I have told it you plainly, but, withal, assure you that, let me have never so much reason to take any thing ill of you, my kindness is so great that I can pass over most things, and live with you as becomes us. And I desire to do so merely from that motive, for I do love you as my sister, and nothing but yourself can make me do otherwise; and that is the reason I choose to write this rather than tell it to you, that you may overcome your first thoughts. And when you have well considered, you will find that, though the thing be hard (which I again assure you I am sorry for), yet it is not unreasonable, but what has ever been practised, and what yourself would do were you Queen in my place.

I will end this with once more desiring you to consider the matter impartially, and take time for it. I do not desire an answer presently, because I would not have you give a rash one. I shall come to your drawing room tomorrow before you play, because you know why I cannot make one [she did not want to sit down at the basset table with Lady Marlborough]. At some other time we shall reason the business calmly, which I will willingly do, or any thing else that may show it shall never be my fault if we do not live kindly together. Nor will I ever be other, by choice, than Your truly loving and affectionate sister, M.R.

On receipt of this letter, Anne ignored her sister's advice to give it some calm reflection. Clearly, she did not feel any obligation to obey the Queen's orders, in marked contrast to her own father's unquestioning obedience to Charles II, and her obstinate nature would not allow her to dismiss one of her servants at the Queen's request. If it came to a choice between her sister and her dear Lady Marlborough, she would choose the latter. The phrasing of the letter she fired off the day after she received the Queen's is not characteristic and one imagines her penning it with Sarah dictating over her shoulder:

*The Cockpit, 6 February 1692*
Your Majesty was in the right to think that your letter would be very surprising to me; for you must needs be sensible enough of the kindness I have for my Lady Marlborough, to know that a command from you to part from her must be the greatest mortification in the world to me, and, indeed, of such a nature, as I might well have hoped your kindness to me would have always prevented. I am satisfied she cannot have been guilty of any fault to you, and it would be extremely to her advantage if I could here repeat every word that ever she had said to me of you

in her whole life. I confess it is no small addition to my trouble to find the want of Your Majesty's kindness to me on this occasion, since I am sure I have always endeavoured to deserve it by all the actions of my life.

Your care of my present condition is extremely obliging, and if you could be pleased to add to it so far as, upon my account, to recall your severe command (as I must beg to call it in a manner so tender to me, and so little reasonable, as I think, to be imposed on me, that you would scarce require it from the meanest of your subjects), I should ever acknowledge it as a very agreeable mark of your kindness to me. And as I must freely own, that as I think this proceeding can be for no other intent than to give me a very sensible mortification, so there is no misery that I cannot readily resolve to suffer rather than the thoughts of parting with her.

If, after all this that I have said, I must still find myself so unhappy as to be pressed on this matter, yet Your Majesty may be assured that, as my past actions have given the greatest testimony of my respect both for the King and you, so it shall always be my endeavour, wherever I am, to preserve it carefully for the time to come as becomes

Your Majesty's very affectionate sister and servant, Anne

Anne summoned her uncle, Lord Rochester, to the Cockpit and asked him to present her letter to the Queen. Having perused its contents, he flatly refused to do so. Rochester had warned James not to sanction his daughter's employment of the trouble-making Sarah Churchill at the outset, and he cannot have relished the consequences of James's indulgence in giving in to his daughter's pleading as he watched Sarah exacerbate the quarrel between his two nieces. Anne used another messenger to convey the letter to her sister. On Rochester's advice, Mary then sent Lord Nottingham to the Cockpit requesting the removal of Lady Marlborough. Again, Anne stood on her rights, claiming that the Cockpit was her own private property, given to her and her heirs in perpetuity by King Charles II, and that it was not part of the court at Whitehall. Mary was adamant and Anne retaliated with a sarcastic letter:

*The Cockpit, 8 February 1692*

I am very sorry to find that all I have said myself, and my Lord Rochester for me, has not had effect enough to keep Your Majesty from persisting in a resolution, which you are satisfied must be so great a mortification to me as, to avoid it, I shall be obliged to retire, and deprive myself of the satisfaction of living where I might have frequent opportunities of assuring you of that duty and respect which I always have been, and shall be desirous to pay you, upon all occasions.

My only consolation in this extremity is, that not having done any thing in all my life to deserve your unkindness, I hope I shall not be long under the necessity of absenting myself from you, the thought of which is so uneasy to me, that I find myself too much indisposed to give Your Majesty any further trouble at this time.

As she had in the past under her father's regime, Anne determined to appear as the injured party. There had been no request whatsoever for *her* to leave the Cockpit, but now she posed as a distressed woman being driven from her home when she was on the brink of giving birth. To many, the Queen's behaviour seemed unreasonable, as they had no idea what all the fuss was about. William and Mary were maintaining a discreet silence about Marlborough's perfidy, and it is probable that they did not know that Anne had written to her father. So it seemed to some that the Queen's sister was being persecuted for no good reason. It suited Anne to appear the martyr.

With an income of £50,000 a year, there was no danger of Anne being homeless. For the immediate future and probably to win the sympathy of the aristocracy, she asked the Duke and Duchess of Somerset for the loan of Syon House, on the Thames at Isleworth, and they acceded to this request, despite William's displeasure. Before she left the Cockpit on 19 February, Anne presented herself at court for a final interview with her sister, who, according to Sarah, remained 'as insensible as a statue'. At the same time, the Dutch guards failed to salute Prince George in the park, prompting one of Anne's anti-Dutch remarks, so typical of the Cockpit circle. 'I cannot believe it was their Dutch breeding alone without Dutch orders that made them do it because they never omitted it before,' she told Sarah, 'these things are so far from vexing either ye Prince or me that they really please us extremely.' With the removal of the Denmarks to Syon, there followed a decree for the removal of their guards, which was especially disconcerting at this time of economic and social disruption when so many highwaymen roamed the roads.

Before he left for the Continent in March, William sent a message to Syon requesting the removal of Lady Marlborough from Anne's household, but he was ignored. To mend the breach in the royal family, Sarah should have done the decent thing and resigned from Anne's service, but she was determined not to lose her hold over the Princess. The Dutch envoy in London, L'Hermitage, said that when Sarah's friends urged her to resign, she 'responded that she knew the Princess perfectly; if she [Sarah] was separated from her for only two weeks, she would be gone forever; and she hopes to maintain herself in the Princess's favour as long as possible.' Sarah probably recalled the occasion in the Richmond days when Anne was swearing undying love for Mrs Mary Cornwallis. Only weeks after the loved one had left the household, Anne had eradicated her from her mind. In another echo of the Richmond childhood, Anne was protesting to Sarah that 'I am more yours than can be exprest & had rather live in a cottage with you than reigne empresse of ye world with out you.'

Any intimations from Sarah that she might resign were met with a panicked response from Anne: 'Mrs Freeman . . . must give me leave to tell her, if she should ever be so cruel to leave her faithful Mrs Morley, she will rob her of all the joy and quiet of her life; for if that day should come, I could never enjoy a happy minute, and I swear to you I would shut myself up and never see a creature.' Anne protests that Sarah is not the cause of her falling out with the King and Queen. 'It would have been so, however, for the monster is capable of doing nothing but injustice, therefore rest satisfied you are no ways the cause, and let me beg once more, for God's sake, that you would never mention parting more; no, nor so much as think of it.'

Anne was even prepared to forgo part of her revenue rather than lose Sarah, and assured Sarah that Prince George was in total agreement with her. 'Can you think either of us so wretched that for the sake of twenty thousand pound, and to be tormented from morning to night with flattering knaves and fools, we would forsake those we have such obligations to, and that we are certain we are the occasion of all their misfortunes?' she wrote. Showing how much she hated her brother-in-law she continued:

Besides, can you believe we would ever truckle to that monster who from the first moment of his coming used us at that rate as we are sensible he has done, and that all the world can witness, that will not let their interest weigh more with them than their reason. But suppose I did submit, and that the King could change his nature so much as to use me with humanity, how would all reasonable people despise me? How would that Dutch abortive laugh at me and please himself with having got the better? And which is more, how would my conscience reproach me for having sacrificed it, my honour, reputation and all the substantial comforts of this life for transitory interest, which even to those who make it their idol, can never afford any real satisfaction, much less to a virtuous mind? No, my dear Mrs Freeman, never believe your faithful Mrs Morley will ever submit. She can wait with patience for a sunshine day, and if she does not live to see it, yet she hopes England will flourish again.

———

On 17 April 1692 Anne gave birth to a son, who was immediately baptised George and died one hour later. She had sent Sir Benjamin Bathurst to warn the Queen that she was in labour and 'much worse than she us'd to be', but Mary did not come until it was all over. She was under enormous pressure, governing alone in William's absence, worried by conspiracies at home and the threat of invasion from abroad. When she arrived at Anne's bedside, she found Anne weak and exhausted, but hardly at death's door. Something about her sister's selfish and righteous attitude when the country was in such danger snapped the slender threads of Mary's control.

According to Sarah, who was not present during the Queen's visit but heard about it from Anne, Mary 'never asked how she did, nor expressed the least concern for her condition, nor so much as took her by the hand'. She addressed Anne much more sharply than she surely meant. 'I have made the first step by coming to you, and I now expect you should make the next by removing my Lady Marlborough.'

'I have never disobeyed you but in that one particular,' Anne replied, 'which I hope will some time or other appear as unreasonable to you as it does to me.'

Mary stood up and left the house, escorted to her carriage by Prince George, to whom she repeated her request that Lady Marlborough be told to leave her sister's service. By the time she reached Whitehall she had simmered down sufficiently to regret her outburst. 'She trembled, and looked as white as the sheets,' she told Lady Derby remorsefully when recounting the scene with her sister.

Not only did Anne refuse to obey her sister's order to dismiss Lady Marlborough, but also showed she had no intention of returning to court by arranging to lease Berkeley House in Piccadilly from Lord Berkeley in exchange for the Cockpit. Berkeley House would not be ready for her occupation for some months yet, but Mary did not hesitate to retaliate for this latest show of defiance. She issued formal orders that anyone who visited the Princess would not be received at court.

By this time, Mary was at her wits' end, struggling to muster the forces to withstand James's imminent invasion while scotching Jacobite conspiracies at home. Her sister's behaviour was another tax on her energies and a continuing source of sadness. The revelation of a plot to overthrow the government implicated Lord Marlborough, who was immediately sent to the Tower. Perhaps fearing her own arrest and that they would be prevented from seeing each other, Anne dashed off a letter to Sarah:

*Syon, May, 1692*

I hear Lord Marlborough is sent to the Tower, and though I am certain they have nothing against him, and expected by your letter it would be so, yet I was struck when I was told it, for methinks it is a dismal thing to have one's friends sent to that place. I have a thousand melancholy thoughts, and cannot help fearing they should hinder you from coming to me, though how they can do that, without making you a prisoner, I cannot imagine. I am just told by pretty good hands that as soon as the wind turns westerly there will be a guard set upon the Prince and me. If you hear there is any such thing designed, and that 'tis easy to you, pray let me see you before the wind changes, for afterwards one does not know whether they will let one have opportunities of speaking to one another. But let them do what they please, nothing shall ever vex me, so I can have the satisfaction of seeing dear Mrs Freeman; and I swear I would live on bread and water, between four walls, with her, without repining; for as long as you continue kind, nothing can ever be a real mortification to your faithful Mrs Morley, who wishes she may never enjoy a moment's happiness, in this world or the next, if she ever prove false to you.

Mary might well have been aware that Anne had received the Jacobite Lady Ailesbury at Syon, who came to warn her that James's invasion force only waited for a favourable wind and that 5,000 troops would carry her to her father. Now was the time to redeem her past disloyalty to her father by flying to his side as soon as he landed. Anne feigned interest but was prevaricating. When Lord Ailesbury visited her after the French defeat at La Hogue, she told him, 'It is not a proper time for you and I to talk of that matter any further.'

On 20 May, a month after she had given birth, Anne wrote to Mary that 'I have now, God be thanked, recovered my strength well enough to go abroad.' She continued in a deceptively meek tone:

And though my duty and inclination would both lead me to wait upon Your Majesty as soon as I am able to do it, yet I have of late had the misfortune of being so much under Your Majesty's displeasure as to apprehend there may be hard constructions made upon anything I either do or not do with the most respectful intentions. And I am in doubt whether the same arguments that have prevailed with Your Majesty to forbid people showing their usual respects to me may not be carried so much farther as not to permit me to pay my duty to you. That, I acknowledge, would be a great increase of affliction to me, and nothing but Your Majesty's own command shall ever willingly make me submit to it. For whatever reason I may think in my own mind I have to complain of being hardly used, yet I will strive to hide it as much as possible. And though I will not pretend to live at the Cockpit, unless you would be so kind as to make it easy for me, yet wherever I am, I will endeavour always to give the constant marks of duty and respect which I have in my heart for Your Majesty.

Anne chose Dr Edward Stillingfleet, Bishop of Worcester, to convey this missive, which he believed to be a genuine attempt at reconciliation, to her sister. As the letter did not make any promise of Anne's acquiescence to the Queen's request for the dismissal of Lady Marlborough, it brought the predictable response from Mary:

I have received yours by the Bishop of Worcester, and have little to say to it, since you cannot but know that as I never use compliments, so now they cannot serve. 'Tis none of my fault that we live at this distance, and I have endeavoured to show my willingness to do otherwise; and I will do no more. Don't give yourself any unnecessary trouble [in coming to court], for be assured, 'tis not words can make us live together as we ought. You know what I required of you; and now I tell you, if you doubted it before, that I cannot change my mind but expect to be complied with, or you must not wonder if I doubt of your kindness. You can give me no other marks that will satisfy me. Nor can I put any other construction upon your actions than what all the world must do that sees them. These things don't hinder me being very glad to hear you are so well and wishing you may continue so, and that you may yet, while 'tis in your power, oblige me to be your affectionate sister, Marie R.

It was just the sort of response Anne expected. She wrote triumphantly to Sarah, quickly passing over the matter of the death of Sarah's small son with the words: 'I am very sensibly touched with the misfortune that my dear Mrs Freeman has had of losing her son, knowing very well what it is to lose a child; but she knowing my heart so well and how great a share I bear in all her concerns, I will not say any more on this subject for fear of renewing her passion too much', before alighting on the real business:

The Bishop brought me the Queen's letter early this morning, and by that little he said he did not seem so well satisfied with her as he was yesterday. He has promised to bear me witness that I have made all the advances that were reasonable. And I confess, *I think the more it is told about that I would have waited on the Queen, but that she refused seeing me, it is the better*; and therefore I will not scruple saying it to anybody when it comes my way.

Anne was evidently sending a copy of the Queen's letter

to Sarah. 'I don't send the original for fear any accident may happen to the bearer,' she told her, 'for I love to keep such letters by me for my own justification.' In spite of her assurance to the Queen in her letter of 20 May that 'For whatever reason I may think in my own mind I have to complain of being hardly used, yet I will strive to hide it as much as possible', Anne's letter to Sarah makes it clear she was intending to do the opposite. She wanted it made public that she had tried to effect a reconciliation and been rebuffed, that she was the injured party, cast out by the Dutch usurper and her unreasonable sister. As she continued smugly in her letter to Sarah: 'Sure never anybody was used so by a sister! But I thank God I have nothing to reproach myself withal in this business, but the more I think of all that has passed, the better I am satisfied. And if I had done otherwise, I should have deserved to have been the scorn of the world, and to be trampled upon as much as my enemies would have me.'

To goad Mary further, Anne sent Lady Fitzharding to the Queen. Had she perhaps, in her weakness and suffering after her recent childbirth trauma, mistaken the Queen's order? Did she really expect her to dismiss Lady Marlborough? Completely exasperated, Mary told Lady Fitzharding, 'My sister has not mistaken me, I never will see her upon any other terms than parting with Lady Marlborough – not for a time, but for ever! I am the Queen,' she exclaimed, 'and I will be obeyed!' Lady Fitzharding had never seen Mary so angry.

It soon transpired that the Jacobite plot involving Marlborough was a fabrication of Robert Young's, a disciple of Titus Oates, to whom William in a lapse of good judgement had granted a pension. Marlborough was released from the Tower on an appeal of habeas corpus on 15 June, prompting another sour comment from Anne: 'it is a comfort they cannot keep Lord Marlborough in the Tower longer than the end of the term; and I hope, when Parliament sits, care will be taken that people may not be clapped up for nothing, or else there will be no living in quiet for anybody but insolent Dutch and sneaking, mercenary Englishmen.' All Mary could do to show her displeasure was to strike Marlborough's name off the list of Privy Councillors, together with the two others who had raised his bail, Halifax and Shrewsbury.

Anne, meanwhile, ignored the advice of some of her more well disposed 'family' to send her sister her compliments on the great victory at La Hogue. Mary's 'arbitrary letter' received that morning gave her all the excuse she needed for neglecting this basic civility to her sister and sovereign.

———————

Through the early summer of 1692 Anne was embroiled in petty disputes with Lady Berkeley over the house in Piccadilly. 'I was yesterday at Berkeley House, which I like very well, but my Lady looked so mightily out of humour that I did not go into all the garrets nor the wings as I intended,' she complained to Sarah, 'and until she goes out of the house it will be impossible to order anything or see it at one's ease; and when she will be pleased to move, God knows.'

Anne intended to spend August and September in Bath, despite the non-appearance of 'Lady Charlotte', the term she used for menstruation, indicating that she might be pregnant again. 'I have not yet seen Lady Charlotte,' she confided to Sarah, 'which I wonder very much at for I used to be very regular & I cannot fancy she has taken her leave for nine months because since my first three children I have never bred so soon.' Normally, pregnancy would have deterred her from hazarding such a long journey on rough roads, but this time she was determined to ignore the risk.

She was less sanguine, however, about taking her son with her. At three, the little Duke of Gloucester was neither speaking nor walking and a mother's instinct must have told Anne that something was wrong. She knew he was not the most prepossessing child to look at, but she always referred to him fondly as 'my boy'. As she told Sarah on this occasion:

The Lady [Fitzharding, the child's governess] that has now such a mind to go to the Bath has, I fancy, spoke to Dr Radcliffe to persuade me to carry my boy hither, for yesterday, without my asking him anything about it, he said I might have the child at a house within three mile of the Bath, for it would be more for my satisfaction than to leave him behind me, and the journey could do him no harm. If I were sure these were his own thoughts, and that the journey was not too great for my boy, I should be mightily tempted to carry him, but since Campden House agrees so well with him, and that there is so much reason to believe people consider their own satisfaction more than mine or than they do the child's good, I think I had better be from him five or six weeks, than run the hazard of his meeting with an accident that one may have cause to repent one's whole life.

No doubt Mary would be pleased to have the child stay in Kensington, rather than accompanying his parents to Bath. Even though she and her sister were not on speaking terms, she continued to make a fuss of her nephew. Sometimes she would send one of her bedchamber women to pay her compliments to the boy and enquire after his health. On these occasions, the Queen's messenger would studiously ignore Princess Anne, according to Sarah taking no more notice of her than if she had been a rocker if she should happen to be in her son's nursery during the visit. Mary would also buy the child toys – he had a favourite toyshop in Cannon Street – not failing to record what she had given him in the *London Gazette*.

While she was spoiling her nephew, however, Mary's ostracism of his mother continued. At Bath the Lord Mayor – a tallow-chandler, Sarah wrote disgustedly – and corporation received orders not to show Princess Anne 'the same respect and ceremony as has been usually paid to the royal family'. Returning to London in October and at last taking up residence in Berkeley House, where she would live for the next three years, Anne found that the minister at St James's Piccadilly had been forbidden to place the text of his sermon on her cushion, the normal courtesy afforded royalty. One day the two sisters passed in the street in their coaches but refused to acknowledge each other. Only Prince George tried to keep up some civility, escorting Mary from the Council Chamber into dinner and asking William if he might come to pay him his compliments on his birthday, a request that William readily granted. George had been urged to try to heal the breach by his brother, the King of Denmark.

Anne remained obstinately opposed to any *rapprochement*, but she could not refuse the King and Queen access to her son. Her advisers warned her that it was important to keep the child firmly in the royal eye, lest William be tempted to accept James Francis Edward as his heir as part of peace terms with France. In June 1692 the exiled Queen Mary Beatrice had given birth to another child, Louise Marie, whom James called La Consolatrice, the child sent to comfort them in their exile. He had invited Mary and Anne and other prominent English ladies to attend his wife's confinement, assuring them of Louis's promise of a safe passage in and out of France. They declined to attend. It was hardly feasible for them to do so, anyway, as Anne was still recovering from childbirth herself and Mary was running the country in William's absence. Even if doubts could be entertained about the reality of the birth of James's son, there could be none about Princess Louise Marie, whose birth was witnessed by all the most prominent members of the French court, as well as the wife of the Danish ambassador. Neither Mary nor Anne is recorded as ever referring to this undoubted sister.

So the little Duke of Gloucester was frequently sent to visit the King and Queen, who were both fond of him. The fact that there was something amiss was becoming more apparent as the child grew older. 'Although he was so active and lively, yet could he not go up and down stairs without help, nor raise himself when down,' his devoted Welsh servant, Jenkin Lewis, wrote, 'which made people conclude it was occasioned by the over-care of the ladies about him.' The child's head seemed to be swollen, in that 'his hat was big enough for most men; which made it difficult to fit his head with a peruke.'

If his mother was not admitted to the royal presence, the child at least could be coached to make pertinent remarks. He loved 'drums and arms and stories of war' and had his own little troop of boys armed with wooden swords and muskets at Kensington, whom he drilled before the King and Queen, pausing to tell Mary that his mama had once had guards, but now had none. From being late to talk, by his fifth year he sounded precocious, politely telling Mary when she wanted to give him one of her exotic birds, 'Madam, I will not rob you of it.' On asking what the carpenters were doing at Kensington and being told by Mary that they were mending the gallery so that it would not fall, he replied, 'Let it fall, let it fall, and then you will scamper away to London.' When Lord Berkeley interrupted him to pay his compliments while he was playing with his model ship, the child sighed in exasperation, 'Who would be a prince!'

By the winter of 1694, it looked as if Mary would outlive her consumptive, asthmatic husband and perhaps even her sister, who had given birth to a stillborn son earlier in the year and already believed herself to be pregnant again. An almost constant state of pregnancy and failure to produce a living child other than her one delicate son were taking a terrible toll of Anne's health and making her increasingly morose. Perhaps she was beginning to doubt that her 'sunshine day' would ever come. But then fate took a hand, moving with that stealth and swiftness that made disease so dreadful to Anne and her contemporaries.

# 11

## *An Untimely Death*

*'Go, see now this cursed woman, and bury her, for she is
a king's daughter'*

> – text chosen by a Jacobite for a sermon after
> Mary's death

On the night of 21 December 1694 the candles burned
until they spluttered to extinction in Queen Mary's closet
at Kensington, being replaced by the cold grey fingers of a
winter dawn. In the stillness of the night there was a rustling
as papers were sifted, the cracking sound of parchment as it
was unfolded and read, a pause while long-ago endearments,
promises, disappointments and confessions, plans and instructions, accounts of battles and negotiations were remembered.
Letters recalling adolescent passions at Richmond and the more
sober professions of a restrained husband merged with those
expressing a father's love and concern followed by his angry
remonstrations. Together with the year's journal and a devout
woman's papers of meditation they were resolutely torn and
fed to the fire's hungry flames, which shot up in a burst of
energy.

Mary had been in low spirits ever since William had
announced his plans to leave for the Continent again in
the New Year. The strain and loneliness as she struggled
to manage alone in his absence year after year had worn her
down. As she wrote to a Dutch friend, Madame d'Obdam,
that summer, she was only thirty-two but beginning to look
stout and old before her time. There was no one in England
in whom she could confide her feelings. Besides William, the
one person to whom she might have looked for understanding

was her sister, Anne, but the two had not seen or spoken to each other for two years now, an enduring sadness for Mary. William's imminent departure depressed Mary unutterably. Once so vivacious, she seemed to have lost the will to live.

She had been feeling unwell for some days. She was chilled then feverish, she had a headache and she ached. Perhaps it was just a winter chill. It was certainly cold enough, the sky leaden and threatening snow. She had not called for the physicians, but dosed herself with her usual remedies. Yesterday, she had even felt well enough to go out. But this morning she had awoken feeling really ill, and by the evening she had noticed what she had always dreaded: a rash on her shoulders and arms, the telltale sign of smallpox. As she had done before leaving Holland in 1689 and again under threat of French invasion in 1692, Mary was putting her affairs in order. Ever prepared for death, morbidly so, Mary knew it had come to claim her.

First she sorted her papers, burning some and preserving others. Then she puzzled over her accounts, not for the first time trying to make the figures tally. She was endearing in her earnestness. Her account book is punctuated with notes for the Prince apologising for her mistakes and appealing to him to pay her debts in the event of her death. Ever conscious that death might be imminent, Mary had written as early as December 1687: 'I find heer 817.14 [guilders] to much I am sure it must be by my mistake but where it ly I cannot find I beg ye Prince to pardon this & all othere my mistakes if he happens to look over this book after my death I own it was carlessnes at first & lazynes now made me guilty of this mistake, but I promise for ye future if I live more exactness & care.'

She worried about her debts, promising in 1688: 'I hope the Prince will pardon all the faults in these accounts & forgive the depts [sic] I have made, if god give me life I shall pay them as fast as I can, if not I hope the Prince will let non be wrongd for my follys.'

There were bills for Richard Beauvoir the jeweller and Thomas Tompion the watchmaker, Godfrey Pole the perfumer and Solomons de Medina for Indian goods. Extravagances such as yards of brightly coloured silks and satins, black velvet, gold and silver lace, white gloves ordered by the dozen, silk stockings, fans, ribbons, blue and white porcelain jars and tea at three guineas a pound were easily balanced by her many acts of charity. She had endowed William and Mary College in the colony of Virginia and supported ministers in New England. She gave generously to the Society of the French Gentlewomen at The Hague and to the Huguenot refugees in London. She gave sums to 'a poor woman at Hampton Court' and 'for Mrs Miller a blind woman'. She had made herself responsible for the upkeep of a little boy and girl boarded with a woman in Kensington. Just recently, these orphans had received 'for cutting the boys hair & new combs 5s 6d', 'apothecarys bill when the boy was sick 8s', '2 pair of gloves & new ribin for the girls cap 7s', 'a cosy winter coat twelve shillings'. Meticulous about paying her debts, Mary left instructions for the few she owed to be paid, her charities to be continued, and that her servants were to be looked after – obligations that her husband, in his profound grief after her death, would honour.

There was no need to catalogue her extensive collection of jewellery, since she had already done so a few months previously. The jewellery represented some of the joys of her life, as well as some of the sorrows of her family. Mary loved pearls, particularly the necklace that had belonged to William's grandmother, Amalia, which she wore in all her portraits after her marriage. The single baroque pearl earring that her grandfather Charles I had worn on the scaffold and that had passed to his eldest daughter, the Princess of Orange, was in her collection. A large, exquisitely cut rose-diamond pendant hanging from a lover's knot of small diamonds bore testimony to William's love in the inscription on the back and their intertwined initials.

The Little Sancy was the most spectacular of Mary's diamonds. It had belonged to Mary's great-grandmother, Marie de Medici, who had sold it to William's grandfather. Mary's mother-in-law, Mary Stuart, had pawned it to raise money for her brother, the exiled Charles II, who had declined to retrieve it for William once he was restored to the throne. It had taken William many years to buy it back. To Mary, the most precious of her jewels was the ruby ring William had given her on her marriage. She was no longer wearing it. During the summer, the stone had fallen out, which Mary saw as a very bad omen, and once it was repaired she had wrapped the ring in a paper, writing that it 'was the first thing he ever did give me' and put it away safely.

In a paper not found until months later, Mary wrote that she did not want her body to go through the usual ritual of being opened after her death. She asked that her funeral be simple. She had always disliked pomp and ceremony in religious services and wrote that she did not want any 'extraordinary expense' the country could not afford in the straitened circumstances of the war.

Finally, Mary picked up her quill for the last time to write a letter to her husband. In it, she alluded to a relationship that had ruined her happiness in this world and was endangering his hopes of the world to come. No name was mentioned; probably only the recipient understood to whom she was referring, and one can only speculate that the unnamed person was Elizabeth Villiers. The letter was secreted in a drawer of her desk.

It was easier to die, Mary reflected, if one had no children to tie one to this world. For years she had hoped that God would bless her with children, until she had become resigned to the fact that it was not to be. 'If I had had children,' she wrote in her journal three years before her death, 'I should have been in pain for them, that is why I regard the lack of children as a mark that the Lord wills that I be more detached from this world and readier when it pleases Him to call me to himself.'

As day broke on 22 December, Mary emerged from her closet, ready to face what God had planned for her.

————

A royal death was just as public a spectacle as a royal birth. As Mary lay in the great four-poster bed that stood in the middle of her bedchamber at Kensington, the physicians gathered round, fussing and arguing about the diagnosis. The rash led most of them to pronounce smallpox. The King was urgently summoned from Westminster, shocked and fearful that the terrible disease that had killed both his parents had now struck his wife. In one of those thoughtful gestures so typical of her, Mary gave permission for all members of her household who had not had the disease to withdraw immediately. William arrived, begging her not to leave him, while the clergy and courtiers filed in to the bedchamber and the antechamber to pray, watch and wait as the disease took its course.

William had a camp bed placed beside his wife's bed, so that he could stay beside her day and night. He forced himself to stop coughing, so that when Mary awoke suddenly in the night she asked where he had gone. The next day, William retired briefly to his closet, where he gave vent to his despair in the presence of Bishop Burnet. He burst into tears and cried that there was no hope of saving the Queen, and that, 'from being the most happy, he was now going to be the most miserable, creature on earth.' William was usually so restrained; Burnet had never seen him so distraught. His love for Mary and his attachment to her evidently went much deeper than anyone had ever guessed. 'He said, during the whole course of their marriage, he had never known one single fault in her: there was a worth in her that nobody knew besides himself.'

On Christmas Day, congregations wept and prayed for her in the churches, but Mary seemed to rally. The rash had disappeared, prompting the physicians to think that it was only measles after all. William wrote to one of his cousins: 'You can believe what a condition I am in, loving her as I do.

You know what it is to have a good wife. If I should lose her, I shall have done with the world.' All hopes of recovery were dashed when that evening the physicians declared that they had been mistaken, the pus-filled spots had merely turned inward, leaving Mary's skin as clear as glass. It was a very bad sign. As a crowd gathered in the bitterly cold weather in the park outside waiting for news and the bedchamber filled with more weeping courtiers, Mary asked faintly, 'Why are you crying? I am not very bad.'

Probably because he was a Jacobite, the eminent Dr Radcliffe was not called in until the 27th, when he said there was no hope of saving the patient. The torments to which the nine physicians had subjected her – bleeding, purging, blistering and 'scarifying' her forehead with hot irons – had all been useless.

The physicians took William aside, telling him that Mary should be told to prepare for death. The new Archbishop of Canterbury, Thomas Tenison, who had replaced the good Archbishop Tillotson whose death in November had so upset Mary, approached the bedside. Realising what he was trying to tell her, Mary answered weakly, 'I believe I shall now soon die, and I thank God, I have from my youth learned a true doctrine that repentance is not to be put off to a deathbed.'

Mary and her contemporaries knew all about the art of preparing for a good death. Death was ever present in every home, rich and poor, whether taking mothers in childbed or snatching their infants or making the sort of swift visitation in diseases for which there was no known cure. Death came so suddenly that it was wise always to be prepared for it. Mary had read Charles Drelincourt's *A Christian Defence against the Fears of Death* several times, and there were many other similar books that she probably studied. She had long been prepared for death, often expected it and even welcomed it. 'For herself,' Archbishop Tenison noted, 'she seem'd neither to fear death, nor to covet life.'

Archbishop Tenison took up his place beside the dying

woman's bed. Eventually, she motioned him to sit. She asked for the Collect in the Communion of the Sick, as well as other prayers, to be read to her several times a day. Occasionally, Mary dozed off until, rousing herself from one of these slumbers, she said, 'Others have need to pray for me, seeing I am so little able to pray for myself.' In all these deathbed preparations, there does not seem to have been any mention made of Mary's father, nor is she known to have expressed any remorse for her part in his downfall. She was such an assiduous examiner of her conscience throughout her life, that had she felt she had wronged her father she would surely have confessed it now. But Mary seems to have gone to her death genuinely convinced that her father had tried to foist a changeling on the nation to perpetuate his Catholic religion.

Nevertheless, the non-juror Ken, who had been Mary's chaplain during her early days in Holland and had surrendered the bishopric of Bath and Wells for refusing to take the oath of allegiance to William and Mary, remonstrated with the archbishop for failing to coax an admission of guilt and repentance from the dying woman: 'I therefore challenge you to answer before God and the world, Did you know of no weighty matter which ought to have troubled this Princess's conscience, tho' at present she seem'd not to have felt it, and for which, you ought to have mov'd her to a special confession, in order to absolution?' his letter demanded. 'Were you satisfied, that she was in charity with all the world? Did you know of no enmity between her and her father, of no variance between her and her sister?'

Surely, he wrote, the Revolution had not been effected without wrongs done for which penitence must be shown and God's forgiveness sought? Was the archbishop so hungry for court favour that he had failed in his duty to the dying woman? It was 'no offence against the government,' Ken wrote, 'to have persuaded a dying daughter to have bestowed one compassionate prayer on her afflicted father, had he been never so unnatural, tho' the case was here quite contrary, for he was one of the tenderest fathers in the world'.

Ken's conclusion was that Mary had disobeyed the fifth commandment, Honour thy father and thy mother, and that as a consequence her life was cut short. 'I hope the surviving Princess will consider, and take warning, and repent,' he added ominously, 'lest God be provoked, to cut her life as short as her sister's.'

─────────

As all hopes of Mary's recovery diminished, William lost control and broke into passionate weeping that amazed the onlookers, who had always known him to be so cold and reserved. Mary begged him not to make her suffer the pangs of death and parting more than she was already doing, and to take care of himself for the country's sake. Spiritually, she was already removed from the world, even from the person she had loved most. He was carried fainting from the crowded room.

Mary asked the archbishop to pray with her and read the psalms while she prepared for communion, which she took with all the bishops present. She had worried that she would not be able to swallow the bread, but managed to do so. She refused any further medicine with the words, 'I have but a little time to live, and would spend it a better way.' She drifted in and out of sleep and delirium while prayers continued around her. Suddenly she beckoned Tenison nearer, telling him that a popish nurse was hiding behind the screen at the head of the bed. He assured her that no one was there. 'Look again! Dr Radcliffe has put a popish nurse upon me, and she is always listening to what is said about me – that woman is a great nuisance to me . . .'

In her feverish dreams Mary was back in her girlhood when her sister Anne had smallpox and their chaplain worried that she was left alone with a Catholic nurse. The shameful secret of her parents' conversion to the Catholic religion, her mother's dying without the rites of the Anglican Church and the hideous deathbed scene she had not been allowed to attend, all rose up to haunt her. Only strangers surrounded her now, crowding the room, watching her die. The ministers, the great ladies, the scurrying servants and necessary women, the physicians and clergymen, they cannot all have had immunity from smallpox. While they attended the passing of a queen from one world to the next in the suffocating, stinking room, their periwigs and gowns, their caps and robes and aprons, the cloths with which they mopped the sick woman's face and body, must have harboured the organisms of a highly contagious disease.

Every day her sister Anne had sent a message asking for news of her, although Mary was probably unaware of this. Anne believed herself to be pregnant and so much in danger of miscarrying that she would not go up and down stairs, spending most of her time lying on a couch. But she had had smallpox and sent a message to her sister that she would run any hazard to have the pleasure of seeing her.

Probably those attending the Queen warded off Anne's enquiries because they did not want the sick woman disturbed or upset. Lady Marlborough was determined to see another slight intended for Princess Anne. Nor did she soften her opinion with the passage of time, because when she wrote her *Conduct* she still did not have a kind word to say for the dying woman. The Queen's groom of the stole, Lady Derby, wrote to Sarah to thank the Princess for her kind message, but asked her to defer her visit, 'it being thought necessary to keep the Queen as quiet as possible'. She added a postscript saying, 'Pray, Madam, present my humble duty to the Princess', which made Sarah 'conclude more than if the College of Physicians had told it me that the disease was mortal'.

Even now, Lady Marlborough could not let it go. She was convinced that the Princess was not invited to the Queen's bedside so as 'to leave room for continuing the quarrel, in case the Queen should chance to recover, or for reconciliation with the King, if that should be thought convenient, in case of the Queen's death'. In reality, Mary was way beyond such worldly concerns. 'How this conduct to a sister could suit with the character of a devout Queen,' Sarah fumed, 'I am at a loss to know.'

It was only when Anne sent Barbara, Lady Fitzharding, a friend of the royal sisters from their Richmond days, and she was bold enough to force her way through the crush to Mary's bedside, that Mary would have known of her sister's concern. But it was too late. Mary was beyond coherent speech, maybe even understanding. She nodded vaguely in acknowledgement and muttered, 'Thanks'. She would never be reconciled with her sister now, while Lady Fitzharding returned to Berkeley House with news of the Queen's vague response, which Sarah contrived to translate for posterity as 'no answer but a cold thanks'.

Soon after midnight on the 28th, William returned to his wife's bedside. He was crying and knew he would not have the chance to say goodbye to her properly now, because she was unconscious. The archbishop continued to read psalms beside the comatose woman. Earlier, in her last lucid moments, she had told him about the letter she had written for William and left in her desk. She asked the archbishop to look for it after her death and take it to her husband. At a quarter to one in the morning of the 28th, Mary passed from unconsciousness into death. The tolling bells announced her passing to her sorrowing subjects waiting in the park and throughout Westminster and the City, where life had come to a standstill.

———

After the Queen's death, William shut himself up in his chamber, seeing no one. So great was his grief that courtiers feared his own death must be imminent. For days his faithful secretary Huygens waited outside, in case his royal master might have a letter to deliver. William's former page Arnold Joost van Keppel, whose blond good looks and joviality would win him the earldom of Albemarle, lost patience with him. The

King was not to be disturbed. He would emerge when he was ready. Go away! He would speak to no one.

Oblivious of her instructions, still tucked away in the drawer of her desk, the embalmers had gone to work on the dead Queen's body. Her heart had been removed, placed in a violet velvet box and, together with her entrails, placed in the Stuart vault of King Henry VII's chapel at Westminster. A bill from Dr Harel, her apothecary, specified:

For perfumed sparadrape, to make cerecloth to wrap the body in, and to line the coffin; for rich gummes and spices, to stuff the body, and to fill up the urne [where the heart and entrails were enclosed]; for Indian balsam, rectifyed spirrits of wine tinctured with gummes and spices, and a stronge aromatized lixivium to wash the body with; for rich damask powder to fill the coffin, and for all other materialls for embalminge the body of the High and Mighty Princess Mary, Queen of England, Scotland, France, and Ireland etc. As also for the spices and damask powders to be putt between the two coffins, with the perfumes for the cambers [chambers]; altogether £200 os od.

This was the dawning age of the funeral business and no expense or treatment was to be spared the dead Queen. She would have been horrified to learn that the full pomp and ceremony of her state funeral was to cost the country £100,000. A lock of her rich brown hair was cut off to be made into a mourning memento for her grief-stricken husband. The court and the country were plunged into deepest mourning, everyone swathed in black. No jewels, nor anything shiny, could be worn, which might attract the spirit of the dead one back to earth. All looking-glasses and pictures were covered for the same reason. The body of the Queen was taken from Kensington to Whitehall, hung with yard after yard of black cloth, where it was to lie in her bedchamber until the route to the Banqueting House, where it was to lie in state, could be made ready with black-covered walkways. Sir Christopher Wren was busy preparing an elaborate catafalque, under which the Queen's body would rest, at Westminster Abbey.

Unable to bear the sound of hammering as black cloth was hung in the rooms at Kensington, William removed to a house overlooking Richmond Park. Here, during her childhood, Mary had romped with her sister Anne and the Villiers' girls. She had sent her dwarf drawing master, Mr Gibson, scurrying off with letter after letter to her beloved Frances Apsley. She had dreamed of love, laughed and gossiped and whispered with the other girls, stood in her new manteau while concealing a letter behind her back as her governess had asked what she was doing in her closet on such a lovely, sunny day. And now she was dead at only thirty-two.

When the news of Mary's death reached France, the Modenese envoy Rizzini dashed off a letter to his master:

The news will have reached you of the death of the Princess of Orange [as she was still referred to by those who did not recognise the regime] of putrid smallpox after three days' illness . . . That Princess, young, beautiful, and reputed the delight of a rebellious people, is suddenly become a frightful spectacle, and a subject for their bitter tears. She was a daughter who sinned against the commonest and most indispensable law of Nature ordained by God – that of honouring her parents . . .

James refused to mourn a daughter who had long been dead to him. There was every reason to believe that she had died impenitent. It was an additional affliction to him, he said, to see 'a child he loved so tenderly persevere to her death in such a signal state of disobedience and disloyalty'. In his memoirs, he wrote that he 'heard his poor daughter had been so deluded, as to declare at her death, that her conscience no ways troubled her, that if she had done anything which the world might blame her for, it was with the advice of the most learned men of her church who were to answer for it, not she; this made the King cry out, O miserable way of arguing so fatal both to the deceiver and those that suffer themselves to be deceiv'd.'

He forbade his court at St Germain to go into mourning and asked Louis XIV to issue the same instructions at
Versailles. Disgusted, some of the French nobility ignored
him and donned mourning out of respect for the Prince and
Princess of Orange, to whom they were related. If James and
the Jacobites thought that Mary's death would give them the
chance to seize the throne, they were sadly mistaken. The
English drew together in grief, rallying round William in his
terrible loss. They had grown to love the Queen and mourned
her passing as they might one of their own families.

The death of the Queen brought reconciliation between
William and her sister. Lord Sunderland had lost no time
insinuating himself into William's favour. Indeed, James's dismissed minister had been in correspondence with William even
before James's fall and his return to England was gradually
followed by his reinstatement in government. William thought
highly of him, though he could never trust him. Sunderland
had acquired political maturity and more circumspection. 'The
King must be sarved,' he would drawl. The Sunderlands and
their great friends the Marlboroughs probably spent many
hours at Althorp discussing their royal masters and how they
could retain their grip on power. Lady Sunderland knew that
the Prince of Wales was no changeling, she had witnessed his
birth, and she must have banished any doubts on this score
from the Marlboroughs' minds. Sarah would have heard the
same from her sister Frances, Lady Tyrconnel, who had been
one of the witnesses at his birth. Nevertheless, there could be
no going back to James II.

Princess Anne was where the future lay. Only William's
frail life now stood between her and the throne. Sunderland
considered it essential for the rift in the royal family to be
mended and Mary's death offered an opportunity. Much
against Sarah's wishes, Sunderland and Marlborough persuaded Anne to write a letter of condolence to William as the
first step in the process of reconciliation. Having spent so many
years out in the cold, Anne was now more inclined to be guided

by the men's cool and considered counsel than Sarah's wild impetuosity. She obediently wrote to her brother-in-law:

> *Berkeley House, 28 December 1694*
>
> I beg Your Majesty's favourable acceptance of my sincere and hearty sorrow for your great affliction in the loss of the Queen. And I do assure Your Majesty I am as sensibly touched with this sad misfortune as if I had never been so unhappy as to have fallen into her displeasure. It is my earnest desire Your Majesty would give me leave to wait upon you, as soon as it can be without inconveniency to you and without danger of increasing your affliction, that I may have an opportunity myself not only of repeating this, but of assuring Your Majesty of my real intentions to omit no occasion of giving you constant proofs of my sincere respect and concern for your person and interest, as becomes, sir, Your Majesty's most affectionate sister and servant, Anne.

William could never like his sister-in-law, but he was disinclined to carry on a quarrel that had been kept alive by the sisters in their pride and obstinacy. He could not afford to be at loggerheads with his heir, who, when all was said and done, had a stronger claim to the throne than he did. The Archbishop of Canterbury had been closeted with the King in his grief. He had had the unenviable task of presenting William with Mary's letter, in which she probably referred to Elizabeth Villiers. In his grief and shame, William agreed to break with Elizabeth. He paid her handsomely. She received property worth £30,000 a year including, to Princess Anne's indignation, Irish estates that had been given to James when he was Duke of York, which, by right, should have passed to her. And he found her a husband in the Duke of Hamilton's younger son, George, whom he created Earl of Orkney. Given her wit and intelligence, it is not surprising that 'Squinting Betty' became a great hostess. In one of George I's receptions, she encountered two other 'fallen' ladies, Louise de Kéroualle, Duchess of Portsmouth, and Catherine Sedley, Countess of

Dorchester. Catherine could not resist making one of her most famous quips: 'Who would have thought that we three whores should meet here?'

The archbishop also urged William's reconciliation with his sister-in-law and William sent him to talk to Anne early in the New Year. A few days later, Anne's guards were restored to her and on 13 January William received her at Kensington. Anne was so grossly swollen that she had to be carried into the palace and up the stairs to the presence chamber in her sedan chair. William received her kindly. She told him in faltering tones that she was truly sorry for his loss and he replied that he was much concerned for hers. They could hardly speak for their pent-up tears and withdrew for nearly an hour into the privacy of William's closet, where they both wept.

As his heir, William immediately gave Anne her old childhood home of St James's Palace as her official residence. Here, William said, she could keep court 'as if she were a crowned head'. Even before she had moved from Berkeley House and prior to the Queen's funeral, courtiers were flocking to pay their compliments to the rising star. One courtier remarked loudly, 'I hope Your Highness will remember that I came to wait upon you, when none of this company did.' As a further mark of William's goodwill, he gave his sister-in-law nearly all his wife's jewels. It cut no ice with Sarah, who was in no hurry to be reconciled with 'Caliban'.

Anne's son, the five-year-old Duke of Gloucester, remained in the cleaner air of Campden House in Kensington. Overhearing the servants speaking of the Queen his aunt's death, the strange child muttered, 'Oh, be doleful!'

---

From 21 February, members of the public were admitted to the Banqueting House to pay their last respects to the late Queen. Even though it was so cold that the Thames had frozen, they took up their positions in the snow from six in the morning, being admitted only from noon until five.

They found the inside of the Banqueting House ablaze with candles. Twelve gentlemen-at-arms stood on either side of the empty throne. The Queen lay with her hands crossed over her breast on draperies of purple velvet fringed with gold. At her head were the crown of state, the sceptre and the orb, at her feet the sword and the shield. At each corner of the open coffin stood one of her ladies swathed in deepest mourning, relieved by others every half an hour. In an alcove behind curtains of purple velvet inscribed with the Orange family motto, '*Je Maintiendrai*', William mourned in private, his deep grief kept concealed from the curiosity of his subjects. So great was the press of people that some were turned away and pickpockets did a roaring trade.

The state funeral took place on 5 March, when the bells of the parish churches tolled all over England. There had been a squabble at the palace, the Queen's favourite lady, her groom of the stole Lady Derby, demanding her rights to take possession of the furniture and rich draperies in her dead mistress's rooms. A distracted William acceded to her wishes, but she could not be chief mourner. Princess Anne was too indisposed to play that part, as was Lady Ailesbury, the descendant of King Henry VIII's sister, Mary, Duchess of Suffolk. The honour of chief mourner at the late Queen's funeral went to the next highest lady in the land, Elizabeth, Duchess of Somerset, the Percy heiress.

Three hundred poor women led the funeral cortège, followed by the officers of Mary's household, her chaplains, the Lord Mayor and aldermen of London, and Sir Christopher Wren, Surveyor-General of the Works. It was appropriate he was here. As a public tribute to Mary, William had decided to press on with Wren's building of the Greenwich Hospital for Sick and Disabled Seamen, a project that had been so close to Mary's heart. For the first time ever, members of both Houses of Parliament, all 500 of them, attended a royal funeral. The Great Seal of William and Mary had been broken on her death, but a new one depicting William alone quickly replaced it. Parliament was usually dissolved on the monarch's death, but this was a dual monarchy and it continued to sit.

Preceded by the banners of England, Wales, Scotland, Ireland, France and Chester, Mary's master of the horse, Lord Villiers, led her favourite mount. The Queen's coffin was carried in an open chariot drawn by eight horses, a man leading each of them. Six peers acted as pallbearers. One of the Queen's bedchamber women rode at each end of the chariot, guarding the body. The Duchess of Somerset, as chief mourner, followed behind the chariot, with the Lord Privy Seal, Lord Pembroke, and the Lord President of the Council, the Duke of Leeds – who as Lord Danby had arranged Mary's marriage – on either side of her. The Duchess's long mourning train was carried by the Duchesses of St Albans and Southampton. Eighteen peeresses, six ladies of the bedchamber, six maids of honour and six women of the bedchamber brought up the rear.

As they wound their way from the Banqueting House by way of Whitehall Palace to Westminster Abbey, the ladies' trains dragged in the snow and remained wet while they sat in the chilly stone edifice through the long funeral service. Henry Purcell, who had been employed as singer and organist in the Chapel Royal and at Westminster Abbey for most of his life and who had composed many celebratory odes for Mary on happier occasions, had composed the music. The Queen's Funeral March with its repeated muffled strokes was followed by the Canzona and then his new choral setting of 'Thou knowest, Lord, the secrets of our hearts, shut not thy merciful ears unto our prayers, but spare us, Lord most holy . . .', before the measured tones of the Funeral March were resumed.

The Archbishop of Canterbury took the opportunity to reprimand the congregation for their sinful lives. The Queen's untimely death was a sign of God's anger because her people had ignored her many proclamations for the Reformation of Manners: 'A sparrow falls not to the ground without God's providence, much less a crowned head. God has guided and ordered this affair as he does all things, most suitable to his own justice. He is righteous, but we have been wicked.' The English had not been sufficiently grateful for their recent delivery from popish tyranny. They had continued to lead immoral lives, to drink and fight and swear, despite the Queen's constant urgings to reform and show more devotion to God. Just as a sinful people had brought God's wrath on themselves in the form of plague and fire thirty years earlier, now they had lost a good and pious Queen through their failure to heed her advice or follow her example.

In France, James criticised Tenison's funeral sermon extolling his daughter's virtues. He complained that 'she was canonised for a sort of parricide, by usurping her father's throne, and sending him together with the Queen and the Prince her brother to be vagabonds in the world.' Only the generosity of a neighbouring monarch had succoured them, while 'their own subjects and even children had lost all compassion and duty.' He despaired now too that his younger daughter, Anne, would never 'return to her duty'. He saw that she preferred to be reconciled with her brother-in-law, who had usurped her right to the crown, rather than with her own father.

After the service, the coffin was lowered into the Stuart vault. The only other occupant was Mary's uncle, the loose-living King Charles II, who had joked and laughed his way through her fraught wedding and bedding ceremonies. In a vault close by lay her great-great-grandmother, the first Mary Stuart, the beheaded Queen of Scots, after whom she had been named; her mother-in-law, the second Mary Stuart, who had died of smallpox at Christmas 1660; her godfather, Prince Rupert; her mother, the commoner Anne Hyde; and innumerable royal infants, the progeny of her mother, her stepmother and her still living sister Anne. Their duty to their royal mistress severed by death, Mary's household officers broke their white staves and threw them and their keys of office into the vault. Then Mary was shut into the impenetrable darkness as it was sealed.

Chilled to the bone, the mourners returned to their homes, their long trains and tired feet dragging in the melting snow as the premature darkness of a winter afternoon descended on the town.

# 12

## The Succession

---

*'He bid me find means to let you know that he forgave
you from the bottom of his heart ... he gave you his
last blessing, and prayed God to convert your heart, and
confirm you in the resolution of repairing to his son, the
wrongs done to himself'*

– Queen Mary Beatrice to Princess Anne on the death of
James II

With the death of Mary, the widowed William III suddenly
became one of Europe's most eligible bachelors again. In his
mid-forties, asthmatic, tubercular, frail and stooped, the King-
Stadholder was nevertheless considered a catch by a whole
bevy of European princesses and their ambitious mothers.
William could see the sense of providing a Protestant heir
to succeed to the thrones of England and Scotland if Anne or
her son died without heirs, and, more immediately, an heir for
the House of Orange who might one day become Stadholder
in his place.

Whether William was capable of fathering a son, of course,
was a moot point. He had had no children by Mary. This
might be explained by the fact that an infection, incurred after
her first and only pregnancy ended in miscarriage, rendered
her sterile. Or it might, as Mary's 'mam' Mrs Langford
always asserted, have been owing to the fact that William
did not give Mary any reason to expect a child. Mrs Langford
would have waited on her mistress intimately. She would
have been in a good position to know what transpired in
the marriage bed. The fact that Mary never ceased to hope
for a child, as she confided in her journal, might be attributed

to her ignorance and innocence. Apart from Mary, William's mistress, Elizabeth Villiers, bore him no children during a relationship lasting many years. Yet once she was married to the Earl of Orkney in 1695 when she was about thirty-eight – well into middle age by the standards of the time – she bore him three children in quick succession. A question mark therefore hangs over William's virility.

The second problem was that William does not appear to have liked women very much. His mother had been emotionally cold and distant and had died when he was only ten years old. His grandmother Amalia had been domineering. He had been brought up in an almost exclusively male household. As he matured, it was apparent that women attracted his attention only if they were clever and witty. It was these qualities that drew him to Elizabeth Villiers, whose company and conversation he so much enjoyed. How sexual their relationship was, we cannot know. Mary was in another category. At first horrified by the emotional demands his young wife was making of him, William grew to love Mary for her gentleness, her compliance as a wife, her good taste and charm. He could never show a woman the warmth he revealed in his letters to his closest male friends. He had been cold and reserved with Mary through much of their marriage, perhaps unconsciously discouraging the emotional outpourings that were so much part of her nature, but she had won whatever love he had to offer by her loyalty and devotion to his cause.

Ladies at the English court, accustomed to the appreciative glances and lascivious attentions of Charles II and his brother James, were peeved that William completely ignored them. As the intensely feminine Mary understood, William had always preferred the company of his male companions. Those friends – Henry Sidney, Lord Romney; Thomas Butler, Lord Ossory; Charles Talbot, Lord Shrewsbury; the Prince of Vaudemont, as well as Portland and Keppel – were all handsome, urbane, sophisticated, able and intelligent. These were the qualities William found attractive in men. He had spent at least half of virtually every year of his adult life on the campaign field. At home, he would spend hours hunting and relax by spending the evenings talking and drinking with his male friends. The ceremony and diversions of the English court – drawing rooms, cards, balls, complimenting the ladies and unctuous flattery – as well as the playhouse all bored him.

The attention that another man might have spent on women, William lavished on his male favourites, in particular on Arnold Joost van Keppel, whom he created Earl of Albemarle in January 1697. The fortunes of the handsome page had been promoted by Elizabeth Villiers, to confound her brother-in-law, William's lifelong friend, Hans Willem Bentinck, Earl of Portland. She hated Portland because he had always disapproved of her illicit relationship with William. Portland had also made many enemies at court. The English nobility resented him as a serious, rather pompous Dutchman, who was always closeted with the King, assuming what they felt was their rightful place. They were outraged that William had squandered on this Dutch interloper huge tracts of English lands – he had tried to give him the greatest part of Wales, but had to back down in the face of objections – and lucrative offices, making him the richest man in the country.

While Portland took the brunt of it, Keppel escaped much of this xenophobic prejudice, because he was cheerful, amusing and knew the art of pleasing. Shrewsbury summed up the English courtiers' attitude when Keppel was sent to him with a message from the King: 'This young man brings and carries a message well, but Portland is so dull an animal, that he can neither fetch nor carry.' The fact that he was 'beautiful in his person, open and free in his conversation, very expensive in his manner of living', could drink with the best of them and easily adopted the dandified ways of the fops made Keppel acceptable at court. If, as Sarah Marlborough complained, he was impudent and haughty, these were traits the English nobility also understood.

Even before Mary's death, Portland was losing ground to

Keppel. William was showing an obvious preference for the handsome young man, nineteen years his junior, while his old friend Portland was becoming just a bit of a bore. In the wake of Mary's death, William took to the bottle and his physicians were seriously worried about the prodigious amount he was drinking. Only Keppel seemed to be able to bring any cheer to the devastated widower. William found relief from his loneliness in Keppel's light-hearted, sympathetic company and in his kindness. It was probably a mistake to make Keppel his secretary, because the frivolous young man hated any drudgery, and the two would sit chatting for hours while the letters awaiting the royal signature piled up unheeded. It was obvious to Portland that he was being ousted from William's confidence and affections and he seethed with jealousy.

Two months after Keppel was created Earl of Albemarle, Portland resigned all his posts at court. William was devastated and wrote begging him to reconsider. 'I don't know how I restrained myself from coming to see you in your apartments. Nothing is left me but to beg you, by all the ties that should be dearest to you, to change this pernicious decision and I feel sure that if you retain the least affection for me you will not refuse this prayer, however hard it may seem to you.' He begged him at least to stay on for another year. Glowing in this proof that William still cared for him, Portland backed down. He accompanied William to Holland in the spring, only to find that Albemarle was more in William's favour than ever and not afraid to treat Portland with 'impertinence'. He repeated his intention to resign and retreated to stay with the Prince of Vaudemont in Brussels, where he nursed his hurt and grievance.

It was the Prince's unhappy task to try to effect reconciliation between his two friends, a task not helped by Portland's next letter to William, the contents of which came as a profound shock. He told William that it was not only the way Albemarle treated him that was coming between them, but also that 'Sire, it is your honour which I have at heart.'

He now came to the nub of the problem. 'The kindness which Your Majesty has for a young man, and the way in which you seem to authorise his liberties and impertinences make the world say things that I am ashamed to hear.' Dancing round the subject and forbearing to use the contemporary word 'sodomy', Portland assured William that he believed him 'as far removed as any man in the world' from 'these things'. However, the 'malicious gossip' was not only heard in London but also in The Hague and in the army, 'tarnishing a reputation which has never before been subject to such accusation'. He begged William not to take what he was telling him amiss or to resent his frankness, but 'if it is fitting from anyone, is fitting from a man who loves you as I do'.

William was flabbergasted. 'It has so much astonished me that I hardly know where I am,' he replied. 'If I did not love you as much as I do, and I were not so strongly convinced of your good intentions I could not take it other than ill, and perhaps any man other than myself could only put a very bad interpretation on it.' He could not resist adding that Portland's decision to leave his service would add to the rumours and speculation. He promised to do anything to stop 'such horrible calumnies': anything, that is, but remove the source of the problem, Albemarle's constant presence at his side. 'It seems to me very extraordinary,' he complained, 'that it should be impossible to have esteem and regard for a young man without it being criminal.'

Whether the homosexual allegations were a figment of Portland's imagination, derived from his hurt and jealousy and fuelled by idle gossip, or contained an element of truth, his audacious letter to William had the opposite effect to what he had hoped. William made no attempt to deny the allegations. Perhaps he felt they were beneath contempt and did not feel he had to justify himself. Or perhaps they were true. It might have been no accident that Sir John Vanbrugh's *The Relapse, or Virtue in Danger*, a play whose homosexual allusions caused a sensation, appeared at this time when there was so much gossip surrounding William and his favourite. Albemarle was certainly very like the effeminate fop who played the leading character. William probably knew that Albemarle had at least one mistress and was known for his promiscuity and 'vices', as Sarah Marlborough described them, but it made no difference to their relationship.

If William had ever entertained homosexual feelings for Portland, the latter was unaware of them. Homosexuality filled him with repugnance. But the fact that even such a close friend of thirty-three years' standing as Portland could harbour suspicions of William's sexuality might be significant. Burnet tells us ambiguously that William 'had no vice but one sort, in which he was very cautious and secret'. Elizabeth Villiers's friend, Jonathan Swift, disagreed with Burnet. 'It was of two sorts – male and female – in the former he was neither cautious nor secret.' Scorning to let gossip interfere with a relationship he had come to depend on, William continued to spend hours alone with Albemarle, fuelling speculation as to its nature. Perhaps it was the platonic love of a lonely, ageing man for a beautiful and vigorous youth, or the love of a doting father for the son he never had, or perhaps it was sexual. We shall never know.

At the French court, rumours of William's homosexual inclinations caused no great surprise. His enemies at St Germain seized on them with alacrity. His childhood playmate, Liselotte, had always made oblique allusions to William's sexuality – or lack of it – and later wrote that 'The King is said to have been in love with Albemarle as with a woman, and they say he used to kiss his hands before all the court.' Such overt displays of affection were more typical of William and Liselotte's great-grandfather James I with George Villiers, the first Duke of Buckingham, than William's with Albemarle. An avid and highly amusing gossip, Liselotte was not always entirely accurate. She took homosexuality in her stride. After all, she was married to Louis XIV's brother, the effeminate Philippe, Duke of Orléans, who with his homosexual cronies had made the life of his first wife, Charles's and James's sister Minette, such a misery.

It was Liselotte, herself once earmarked as a bride for William, who was now anxious to promote her daughter, the twenty-year-old Elizabeth Charlotte, as a prospective bride for him. At Versailles, the German-born Liselotte's admiration for William had grown in direct proportion to her growing awareness of James's stupidity. By 1696 both France and the allies were exhausted by the war and groping towards a peace. Perhaps Elizabeth Charlotte of Orléans might be 'a bird of peace accompanied with happiness'? Liselotte had her Danish lady-in-waiting write to Portland to sound him out. His reply was not encouraging and he was right to think that such a marriage would never be acceptable.

Not only were the English confirmed in their suspicion and distrust of France, the national enemy, but Elizabeth Charlotte would have to change her religion, since the 1689 Bill of Rights forbade the monarch, or any heir to the throne, to marry a Roman Catholic. His Most Christian Majesty the King of France would be most unlikely to agree to his niece's conversion to Protestantism – he had, after all, driven all his Protestant subjects from France – and her marriage to the Calvinist William. Liselotte, who had had to convert to Catholicism to marry 'Monsieur', complained, 'I find that religion spoils a great many things in this world, as my daughter at this moment cannot marry King William.'

Ruling out the Catholic Bourbon princess, a list of the most eligible 'princesses of marriageable age and of the Protestant or Lutheran religion' was compiled by Portland. It included the Princess Royal of Sweden, Hedwig Sophie, a petite fifteen-year-old; the Princess Royal of Denmark, Sophie Hedwig, 'eighteen, tall, of excellent disposition, well-bred and graced with the best qualities of her sex', Lutheran; Sophie Charlotte of Hesse-Cassel, sixteen, 'well endowed both in mind and body, of moderate height, of a gentle and kindly disposition and of the Reformed religion'; the twenty-five-year-old Marie-

Elisabeth of Saxe-Eysenach, 'with a striking appearance and charming temper', Lutheran; and another Marie-Elisabeth, a twenty-year-old princess of the Holstein-Gotorp family. In spite of her extreme youth – she was only fourteen – a match with Louise Dorothea Sophie, daughter of William's cousin and ally Friedrich of Brandenburg, made most sense in dynastic terms. An alliance between the most important of the German states – one that would soon become the kingdom of Prussia – and England and the Dutch Republic made a lot of sense. Reluctantly, William felt that he should at least take a look at the girl.

In September 1696 William travelled to meet the Elector and his family at their house, Moylandt, in Cleves. Portland and Keppel accompanied him. The usual courtly nonsense applied as to who should sit on the only armchair in the room. As soon as the Elector took his leave, protocol dictated that William could sit in the armchair. The Electress sat on her bed, while Portland and Keppel were allotted stools. Everyone else including the Princess who was under scrutiny had to stand, while the company settled down to five hours of card-playing. His kind nature and gallantry prompted Keppel to abandon protocol and bring out another stool for Princess Louise, insisting that she sit down.

William was scrupulously kind and polite to the girl, but he was not impressed. It would be difficult to find another royal wife as beautiful and charming as Mary, but this girl came nowhere close. She was tall and thin with a figure as flat as cardboard. She was apparently well read, but showed not a jot of humour. In such a dull court, where the English noticed with disdain that the women were badly dressed, the Princess appeared gauche and her manner was not considered pleasing. She would cut a poor figure at the English court. As Matthew Prior reported to Shrewsbury: 'The Princess is not ugly, but disagreeable; a tall miss at a boarding school, with a straggy [sic] lean neck, very pale, and a great lover, I fancy, of chalk and tobacco pipes.'

That evening William dined with the Princess and her mother, with Keppel valiantly helping the conversation along. Too much wine was sloshed into large glasses, so that everyone quickly became drunk. Portland spent the evening talking politely with the Elector. The visit had been planned to last several days, but next morning, after a church sermon and a stroll with his cousin, William and his party took their leave and repaired to Het Loo, the gracious house that held so many memories of Mary. The jilted Princess and her mother returned to Berlin. Perhaps she was disappointed. Certainly, William's English subjects were disappointed. 'Have the people then forgot the Queen so soon?' he exclaimed. 'Well, if they have, I have not.' On the anniversary of her death, he would shut himself up all day, refusing to see anyone, passing the time in prayer and meditation. He had never wanted to remarry anyway. Perhaps now there could be an end to the whole wretched business.

———

The ongoing war between William's old and new favourites, Portland and Albemarle, reached a brief lull when William sent Portland as his first official ambassador to Paris after the conclusion of the Peace of Rijswijk ending the nine years' war in the autumn of 1697. The oversensitive Portland was convinced that this was a ruse to get him out of the way, but he must have been mollified by the reception he received in France. The French regarded Portland in a completely different light than did the xenophobic English. Here was a man of the world, a suave cosmopolitan, with courtly manners, plenty of experience of diplomacy, a grasp of languages and a comprehensive understanding of the European situation. No Englishman could have played this delicate part so well at this particular time and Portland was immensely popular in Paris, where he kept his embassy in grand style. Even Louis XIV thought highly of him, so much so that he was permitted to hold the candlestick at the royal couchée.

News of the peace was greeted with joy and relief in England. The stock of the Bank of England – only three years old – shot up from 84 to 97. When William entered London in triumph on 16 November 1697, his popularity was at an all-time high. It was not a situation that would last long. The predictable backlash against the war and European involvement meant that the general election in the summer of 1698 returned a strongly Tory House of Commons. Always suspicious of the Whig magnates and the Whig money-making interest in the City, who were largely in favour of William's policies, these Tory squires represented the landed interest. They had little understanding or patience with William's European outlook and the new-fangled financial stratagems and burden of debt that the war entailed.

They lost no time in voting to reduce William's carefully built-up, disciplined and experienced army to a mere 7,000 men. Typical of their 'Little England' mentality, they voted that only native-born Englishmen might serve in the army and all foreign troops, including William's devoted Blue Guards, were to leave the country. William was in such despair that he seriously considered abdicating. How could the English be so short-sighted as to leave themselves so vulnerable, he wondered. 'It's impossible to credit the serene indifference with which they consider events outside their own country,' he wrote to the Dutch Raadspensionary, Antonius Heinsius, in exasperation.

The Peace of Rijswijk had won him important concessions. Not only had France lost much of its conquered territory, but Louis XIV had been forced to recognise William as King of England and his principality of Orange had at last been returned to him. As luck would have it, James and Mary Beatrice had just arrived at Fontainebleau for their autumn stay with the French monarch when news of the peace reached him. He was intensely embarrassed that he had had to recognise William's sovereignty and everyone present during the visit of the exiled King and Queen tried hard not to mention the peace that was occupying all their minds. In the course of the peace negotiations, James had been offered the crown of Poland, made vacant by the death of John Sobieski, as a sop to his pride. With his usual obduracy, James replied that the covenant between him and his people was indissoluble, that he could not accept the allegiance of another nation without violating his duties to his own.

In the same vein, an attempt to include a secret clause in the peace treaty, to the effect that William III would recognise the Prince of Wales as his heir, provided he were left in quiet possession of the throne during his lifetime, came to nothing. James flatly refused to consider such a proposal when Louis raised it. According to James's bastard son, the Duke of Berwick, Mary Beatrice exclaimed, 'I would rather see my son, dear as he is to me, dead at my feet, than allow him to become a party to his father's injuries.' James told Louis that he could bear the usurpation of the Prince of Orange with Christian patience, but not that 'his own child should be a complice to his unjust dethronement'. The crown was his by divine right. No earthly power could alter that or the order of succession. Berwick thought they were extremely foolish to dismiss the idea and with the benefit of hindsight, it was certainly one of the best opportunities there was ever to be of a Stuart restoration.

So mortified was Louis by the concessions he had made to William that he stubbornly refused to carry out William's demand that the exiled Stuarts be sent away from St Germain, perhaps as far as Avignon. William could not countenance the presence of the intriguing Jacobite court so close to England. Another Jacobite conspiracy to assassinate him had been foiled in 1696, and he could not allow this situation to continue. On the understanding that they were to be banished from the French court, William had agreed to pay Mary Beatrice's allowance of £50,000 a year, according to the terms of her marriage contract. Parliament authorised the payment of the money to the treasury, but the refusal of the Stuarts to leave St Germain gave William the perfect excuse to pocket the money.

Out of curiosity, many Englishmen seized the opportunity afforded by the peace to visit Paris. With his usual acerbic pen, Matthew Prior noted of James: 'the old bully is lean, worn, and rev'led, not unlike Neal the projector; the Queen looks very melancholy but well enough, their equipages are all very ragged and contemptible.' Everyone wanted to see the 'pretended' Prince of Wales, but he only appeared once at chapel with his sister, Louise Marie. He was a beautiful boy, as Liselotte attested: 'It is impossible to see him without falling in love with him. He has such a charming disposition I think that in time he will become a great king, although he is only nine years old.' She could not resist adding, 'I am sure that already he would rule better than his father.'

The hard-won European peace was soon in jeopardy. In Spain, the inbred, degenerate, childless Carlos II was close to death, begging the question of the disposal of his vast empire. To allow it to be passed as a whole either to France or the Habsburg Empire would upset the crucial balance of power in Europe. Louis, of course, had his greedy eyes on the Spanish inheritance. His late wife, Maria Theresa, had been the sister of the dying monarch. On her marriage, she had renounced her claims to the Spanish throne, both for herself and for her descendants, but Louis argued that the renunciation was invalid since her dowry had never been paid. It was logical that the Dauphin should inherit. The Habsburg Emperor had his own candidates in mind: either his son Charles, by his third marriage, or his grandson through his first marriage, the six-year-old Electoral Prince of Bavaria. Carlos II himself favoured the latter. William was anxious that neither of these great powers carried off the whole prize without making concessions to the other.

Portland's embassy ended in the spring of 1699, when he returned to London to find that Albemarle had moved into his old apartments adjoining the King's at Kensington.

It was the last straw. He announced his intention to retire immediately. William wrote sadly to Heinsius: 'I had done everything within reason to give the Earl of Portland satisfaction, but a blind jealousy has prevailed above all that ought to be precious to him.' It was only with the greatest difficulty that William persuaded him to continue negotiations with the new French ambassador in London, Count Tallard, for the partitioning of the Spanish Empire. The plan to place the young Electoral Prince of Bavaria on the Spanish throne had been disappointed in January 1699 by his death in mysterious circumstances. Now negotiations had to begin anew for a second partition treaty that would give Spain and the bulk of its dominions to Archduke Charles and the Spanish possessions in Italy to the Dauphin in compensation. But before the expected demise of the moribund Carlos in Madrid, a sudden death in England threw the plans for the Protestant succession into jeopardy again.

---

On 24 July 1700, the eleventh birthday of Princess Anne's precious only son, William, Duke of Gloucester, was celebrated at Windsor Castle. An elaborate banquet was followed by dancing, at which the child 'overheated' himself, while in the evening he viewed a spectacular firework display from the ramparts. That night he was put to bed complaining of a sore throat and chills, while his devoted mother tended him anxiously. Two days later he developed a fever, then fell into delirium. The physicians were unsure of the diagnosis. Possibly it was smallpox, but no rash had appeared. The child was 'bled, blistered and cup't, tho' to no purpose'. When Dr Radcliffe turned up, he demanded who had bled the patient. It meant, he said, that there was nothing he could do for him. They had killed him. On the morning of 30 July, the boy died.

The Marlboroughs were visiting the Sunderlands at Althorp when the Prince fell sick, and as Marlborough was his governor, he was hurriedly summoned to the deathbed. In her agony at the loss of her only child, Anne shut herself up in her rooms, where only Lady Marlborough was permitted to attend her. The day after his death, an autopsy was carried out on Gloucester's body, during which 'the head was opened, and out of the first and second ventricles of the cerebrum were taken about four ounces and halfe of limpid humour.' The child had been suffering from hydrocephalus, water on the brain, accounting for his difficulty with balance and climbing stairs, although there had as yet been no sign of mental impairment, but this was not the immediate cause of his death. The usual rituals of disembowelling and embalming were carried out.

Once the child's corpse was ready, it was removed at night in a torch-lit procession to London, led by Lord Marlborough. At Old Palace Yard, Westminster, it was carried into the Prince's lodgings, which were 'hung with black cloth, floor'd with bays, and furnisht with wax-lights', where it lay in state, surrounded by the gentlemen of his household. So great was the crush of people to view the body of Princess Anne's only son and heir that the Lord Chamberlain gave orders that no one might do so if they were not dressed in mourning. Another torch-lit procession accompanied the body on the night of 9 August to Westminster Abbey, where the last of Princess Anne's ill-fated progeny was laid to rest in the Queen of Scots' vault. His household officers broke their white staves and threw them into the open vault and departed.

Anne never recovered from the loss of her only son. Henceforth, she would always sign her letters to Sarah, 'Your poor unfortunate faithful Morley'. Her ambition to produce an heir to the throne had cost her her health long before the child's death. In the spring of 1695 the eminent physician Dr John Radcliffe had declared that she was suffering from a false or 'hysterical' pregnancy. She was so furious at his diagnosis that she dismissed him, but by June it was only too obvious that he had been right. As early as 1692, she had been suffering severely from 'rheumatism'. The next summer, she told Lady Marlborough that 'ye uneasiness that stiring gives me now' was considerable. In the course of the following year she was finding it increasingly difficult to climb stairs, she was lame and could hardly straighten her legs. She was frequently in pain. Contemporaries would come to describe her condition vaguely as 'the gout', but in the first instance it seems much more likely that one of her many pregnancies had triggered off rheumatoid arthritis.

In spite of her condition, by the close of 1695 Anne was pregnant again. She miscarried a daughter in February 1696. Around this time, the discovery of the Jacobite plot to assassinate William led to the formation of an association to avenge his death, similar to the one formed by the northern conspirators whom Anne had joined in 1688. All Anne's household swore to uphold the oath the association demanded. Provision was also made for Parliament to sit in the event of William's murder, ensuring Anne's smooth accession to the throne. Nevertheless, in James's memoirs it is claimed that in 1696 Anne wrote to him 'to know whether he would pleas to permit her to accept it [the crown] should the Prince of Orange dye, and it be offer'd to her'. She promised to 'make restitution when opportunities should serve'. This was strange, indeed, while Gloucester was still alive to succeed her and she had hopes of more children. St Germain might be forgiven for viewing her request with cynicism. Did she really expect them to believe that she would return the crown to her father or her brother when the time was right? James refused her request on the principle that 'he was not for permitting ill that good might come of it'.

In the autumn of 1696 Anne again miscarried a son in the sixth month of her thirteenth pregnancy. Six months later she miscarried again. At the end of that same year, 1697, she suffered another miscarriage, too early to tell the sex of the child. The following autumn she miscarried at six months, a boy whom the surgeons reckoned had been dead inside her for several days. Towards the end of January 1700 she was 'within six weeks of her time' when she lost another male child, although he might have been dead inside her for a month.

Of her seventeen pregnancies in seventeen years of marriage, including one set of twins, Gloucester was the only surviving child. After his death, the Prince and Princess of Denmark continued to hope that more children would be born to them, but in fact Anne was never to conceive again.

In her terrible grief, Anne apparently turned immediately to her father. Certainly the court at St Germain was apprised of the young Duke's death before the official news of it reached Versailles. A suggestion has been made that it was now that Anne asked her father's permission to succeed William, promising that she would ensure her brother's succession after her, but the sources are vague and unreliable. There seems to be every reason to believe that Anne made this proposal to her father at some point, either before or possibly some time after Gloucester's death. It was probably a continuation of the policy begun by Marlborough and Godolphin in 1691 to fob off St Germain while serving Anne's interests.

Immediately after her son's death, however, it is more likely that Anne's letter was a spontaneous outpouring of grief, telling her father that his grandson was dead. One might absolve Anne of any selfish political motive in writing to her father on this occasion. Through her many early miscarriages and the deaths of her children, her father had always been there to comfort her. No doubt feeling bereft as the last surviving member of the Stuart family in England, it was natural Anne would turn to her father now.

As the Duke of Gloucester was considered too young and innocent to be implicated 'in the crime of rebellion and usurpation of his grandfather' – indeed, he did not even know he had a grandfather and an uncle in France – the decision was easily taken to order the French court into mourning as 'a mark of respect due to his rank'. Rizzini optimistically speculated that 'the Prince of Wales is freed from the most formidable rival he had, and were it not for the point of religion, he would perhaps be proclaimed at once, on condition of leaving the usurper in possession for his lifetime.'

The eyes of Europe were now locked on the English succession. At Het Loo for the summer, William was stunned by the death of the heir. Even though he had had his differences with the mother, he had been very fond of the boy, whom he had invested with the Garter on his seventh birthday. He had recently given the little Duke Mary's apartment near his own at Kensington, where he had frequently watched him reviewing his boy soldiers. William had been touched by the child's promise to devote his troops to his service.

The reconciliation between William and Anne had only been superficial. She acted as his official hostess at court functions, going to a touching amount of effort to please him. William would give a ball for Anne's birthday and she would repay the compliment by doing the same for him. William and the Denmarks would sometimes dine together with every appearance of family unity and civility. But there was always an underlying friction. There had been disagreements with Anne when in 1698 Gloucester had reached the age at which his own male household was established.

Anne had been gratified that Marlborough had been appointed governor to her son. It confirmed his return to royal favour, a recognition at last of his talents, especially when William told him, 'My lord, teach him but to know what you are, and my nephew cannot want for accomplishments.' But she was less than happy that Burnet was made his preceptor. And when William promised that she might appoint the more junior servants and then forgot and appointed them himself, leaving her in the embarrassing position of not being able to fulfil the promises she had made to those she had selected, she was furious.

Reminded of his promise, William lost his temper and shouted, 'She shall not be Queen before her time!' It was Albemarle who intervened to smooth things over, taking Anne's list to Holland and persuading William to agree to most of the appointments. As ever between William and Anne, there was also the vexed problem of money. Parliament had voted £50,000 a year for the upkeep of Gloucester and his household, only for William to hand over £15,000 and pocket the rest. Anne had to make up the difference, leaving her in financial straits.

On hearing the news of Gloucester's death, William locked himself into his chamber to mourn and to write a letter of sympathy to his grieving sister-in-law: 'I do not believe it necessary to use many words to tell you of the surprise and sorrow with which I learned of the death of the Duke of Gloucester. It is so great a loss for me and for all England that my heart is pierced with affliction, I assure you that on this occasion and on any other I shall be glad to give you any marks of my friendship.'

Obviously something had to be done, and soon, to declare the order of the English succession in statute. The 1689 Bill of Rights had already declared that no Roman Catholic might succeed to the throne. As long as the exiled King James and Queen Mary Beatrice's son, James Francis Edward, commonly called the 'pretended Prince of Wales' or 'the Pretender' by everyone in England except the Jacobites, clung to the Catholic faith, he was excluded from the line of succession to his father's throne. The myth surrounding his birth, the assumption that he was a changeling, had not been dispelled among his father's former subjects. Although there could be no suspicion about the birth of his sister, Louise Marie, born in 1692, she too was excluded from the succession on religious grounds.

The same applied to other Catholic heirs. Of the two daughters of Charles I's late daughter, Henriette Anne, Duchess of Orléans – whose nursery at St Cloud Princess Anne had briefly shared during her childhood – the elder, Marie-Louise, the first wife of Carlos II of Spain, had died childless. The younger, Anne-Marie, had married Victor Amadeus II of Savoy, a man who threw his enemies into boiling oil. The English definitely did not like the sound of him. Anne-Marie's elder daughter was to marry back into the French royal family, becoming the mother of Louis XV, while her younger daughter would marry Philippe of Anjou, future King of Spain. There were also three sons.

Of the thirteen children of Charles I's sister, Elizabeth of Bohemia, her second son, Charles Louis, Elector Palatine, had produced two legitimate children, of whom only Liselotte survived. She had had to change her religion when she married Philippe, Duke of Orléans, which ruled her and her two children, Philippe and Elizabeth Charlotte, out of the English succession. The Queen of Bohemia's next son, Prince Rupert, had ended his days in London living with the actress Peg Hughes, by whom he had a daughter, Ruperta, but she was illegitimate. Elizabeth's only other married son, Edward, had converted to Rome when he married Anne Gonzaga, by whom he had two daughters, both Catholics. The elder, Benedicta, wife of the late John Frederick of Brunswick-Lüneburg, was mother to two girls, Catholics who had married Mary Beatrice's uncle Rinaldo D'Este, Duke of Modena, and the Emperor Joseph respectively. Only the twelfth child of the Queen of Bohemia, Sophie, widow of Ernst August of Brunswick-Lüneburg, Elector of Hanover, was a Protestant. In 1700 she was a sprightly seventy years of age and still had four sons living, of whom the eldest, George Ludwig, erstwhile suitor to Princess Anne, was undoubtedly Protestant.

William had frequently corresponded with Sophie, whom he had known since his childhood when she had lived at The Hague with her mother, and met her from time to time either in the Dutch Republic or in her home territory. She was extremely reluctant to take the English crown. She had written to William shortly after he had been offered the crown to congratulate him, while at the same time telling him: 'I lament King James, who honoured me with his friendship' and she believed firmly in the hereditary right of James Francis Edward to succeed his father. But on the other hand she wanted to uphold the Protestant religion and she was ambitious for her family. William had been keen to nominate Sophie and her heirs in the line of succession in the Bill of Rights in

1689, but as Princess Anne gave birth to Gloucester that year, it was not thought necessary to specify who should succeed them.

At that time, Princess Anne had been consulted about the choice of Sophie as next in line after herself and her heirs and she seems to have been perfectly happy about it. After all, it was an arrangement that excluded her brother, James Francis Edward, who, as the only legitimate son of their father King James II, had the right to take precedence over her – a mere daughter. By denying her brother's right, maintaining the lies she had perpetrated about his birth, she could ensure her own succession. Her security could only be bolstered if the Hanover relatives were promised some stake in the crown in the future.

In October 1700 William invited Sophie and her daughter, Sophie Dorothea, to Het Loo for talks. He was keen to draw Hanover into his network of alliances, and only too happy to promise Sophie Dorothea that he would support her husband Frederick William of Brandenburg's assumption of the title King of Prussia. More to the point, William succeeded in persuading Sophie to accept the English inheritance.

When she heard the news, Liselotte wrote one of her exuberant letters to her beloved Aunt Sophie:

The Princess of Denmark is said to drink so heavily that her body is quite burnt up. She will never have any living children, and King William's health is so delicate he can't live long. So you will soon sit on your grandfather's throne, and I shall be overjoyed, much more pleased than if it had been my children and myself, because I love my dearest *tante* more than anyone; when the time comes I will send you a compliment as wide as it is long, and stick 'Your Majesty' all over it, although for the time being I shan't write any compliments, for you are now what you always were: the one person in all the world worthy of being a great queen. Now I am happy to be here and Catholic, so that there is no obstacle between you and the crown.

When William made plans to bring Sophie's grandson, the

Electoral Prince George August to England, Princess Anne
scotched them by announcing she was pregnant. It was another
pretence, but Anne, ever fixated on her own survival and
interests, had no intention of having a rival in the wings just
when the crown was about to be hers.

———————

No sooner was William back in England than on 1 November
he received an express from Paris telling him that Carlos II had
died. Ignoring the Second Partition Treaty which presumed to
decide Spain's destiny, Carlos left everything to Philippe, Duke
of Anjou, second son of the Dauphin. Louis XIV hesitated for
just a moment. Should he adhere to the terms of the treaty,
which he had signed, or should he accept what was offered for
his grandson? The temptation was just too great. He accepted
and presented the sixteen-year-old to the Spanish ambassador
and the whole court as King Philip V of Spain.

Alarming reports reached London and Vienna that the
Spanish Regency Council intended to invite Louis XIV to
govern Spain during the rest of his grandson's minority.
Worse, Louis was making flamboyant remarks to the effect
that the Pyrenees had ceased to exist and that he saw no reason
why his grandson's acceptance of the crown of Spain should
necessitate a renunciation of his rights to that of France. The
Emperor was certainly not going to accept this situation and
William was alarmed that the French immediately moved to
occupy the fortresses in the Spanish Netherlands that had acted
as a barrier between the French and the Dutch. All his adult
life he had laboured to preserve this barrier. Now, it looked
as if his life's work was to be swept aside at a stroke.

Europe moved inexorably towards war. In England, instead
of applying themselves to the impending danger and the curb-
ing of French expansionism, the Lords moved to impeach the
hapless Portland for his role in negotiating the Second Partition
Treaty. The Tory majority in the House of Commons fell on
the Dutchman like dogs over a bone. Only in June did they give

their full attention to the question of the succession. On the 12th the King gave his assent to the Act of Settlement, which stipulated that the English crown should pass after Anne to Sophie of Hanover, granddaughter of James I, and her heirs being Protestant.

But members were taking no chances with future foreign monarchs. Showing how much they resented William's foreign favourites and frequent excursions to his own country, the Act stipulated that the monarch must not leave the country without Parliament's permission or involve England in foreign wars in defence of territories not belonging to England. No foreigner might hold office or a place of trust, either civil or military, under the Crown or sit in Parliament, or have any grant of land from the Crown. Office-holders or those in receipt of a royal pension could not be members of the House of Commons. No pardon under the Great Seal might be given to someone impeached by the Commons. Finally, the monarch had to take communion in the Church of England. It was all grossly insulting to William and a greater curtailment of the royal prerogative than any of the clauses in the Bill of Rights, but he was feeling too old and tired and concerned about the European situation to do anything about it.

In July he returned to The Hague, taking the Earl of Marlborough with him. William was too great a man to allow past differences to impede him now. He knew that he would not see out this new conflict. Marlborough, as the husband of Anne's friend and confidante Sarah, would be the most powerful man in her government. He had the skills needed to take his place both as military commander and at the negotiating table. William appointed him Ambassador Extraordinary to succeed him as leader of the coalition against France. Delegates at The Hague were shocked at William's appearance. Added to his usual pulmonary problems, he was suffering from oedema. His physicians would wrap his grossly swollen legs in hot flannel to bring him some relief. Exhausted, he left Marlborough at The Hague and retired to Het Loo, where he followed events from a distance.

The new Grand Alliance resolved that the crowns of France and Spain should never be united. The aim was to secure the Spanish possessions in Italy and the southern Netherlands for the Emperor. The Dutch would provide an army of 120,000 men, the Emperor 90,000 and the English 40,000. Other princes were to be invited to join them. Any lingering hopes that Louis might be brought to his senses and negotiate a more equitable division of the Spanish inheritance were firmly squashed by an event that now took place at St Germain.

James II had been unwell for some months. In March he had been at mass when, appropriately, as the words of the anthem were sung, 'Remember, O Lord, what is come upon us: consider, and behold our approach. Our inheritance is turned to strangers, our houses to aliens', he fainted. The following month he took the waters at Bourbon and felt a little better. A slight stroke in July left his right side partly paralysed. He had spent a great deal of time in his last years doing penance for his sins at the monastery of La Trappe and he did not slacken now. Liselotte wickedly noted that he spent so many hours on his knees praying that he was in danger of doing himself an injury. Indeed, it was while he was at prayer that he suddenly keeled over unconscious, having suffered a second stroke.

On his deathbed, James told his weeping wife, 'Think of it, Madam, I am going to be happy!' He had already impressed on his twelve-year-old son to remain true to the Catholic faith but to be tolerant of others in the matter of religion, never to force a man's conscience. He urged his little daughter always to follow her mother's example. He told God that he forgave his three great enemies – the Emperor, the Prince of Orange and his own daughter, the Princess Anne of Denmark – from the bottom of his heart.

Visiting his dying cousin, Louis XIV was moved to pity by Mary Beatrice's tears and entreaties to recognise her son as King of England. Louis called a council to decide the matter, only to find that his ministers were all opposed, as it contravened the Peace of Rijswijk. Louis argued that he had only recognised William as King *de facto*, whereas James's son would be King *de jure*. His ministers knew that such hair-splitting would cut no ice with William. Only Louis himself, out of sentiment and affection for the luckless James and his lovely wife, the Dauphin and the princes of the blood were in favour of proclaiming James's son and heir king. In the background, Louis's morganatic wife, Madame de Maintenon, whom Mary Beatrice had always taken care to cultivate, was urging him to do right by the boy. Against all sage advice, when James expired peacefully on Friday afternoon, 16 September 1701, Louis had the thirteen-year-old James Francis Edward proclaimed King James III of England and VIII of Scotland before the whole court.

William was dining with several German princes and English lords at Het Loo when he heard this news. He was so angry at Louis's flagrant renunciation of the agreement he had made in the Peace of Rijswijk that he went red and pulled his hat down to hide his face. He immediately ordered his ambassador, Lord Manchester, to leave Paris and the French ambassador in London to be expelled. There could be no question now that war was imminent, while in England there was so much popular indignation that the King of France should presume to interfere in their affairs that William instantly gained all the support he had spent so many months trying to win through persuasion. Parliament would vote all the necessary supplies for the war, and popular disgust at its recent xenophobia was exemplified by the fact that Daniel Defoe's pamphlet, *The True-Born Englishman*, became an instant bestseller.

William was not so petty as to extend to James the insult the latter had meted out to his daughter, Mary, by refusing to don mourning. As a king, William assumed violet mourning. However, it was to be only partial 'as for a relation: persons of quality not to put their liveries into mourning.' Anne was very angry when she received these instructions, because she had already assumed full mourning and had to take down the black cloth from her apartments at St James's. 'I am out of all patience when I think I must do so monstrous a thing as not to put my lodgings in mourning for my father,' she told Godolphin, complaining of 'the ill natured, cruel proceeding of Mr Caliban'.

Anne's rare show of sentiment for her father might have been inspired by the moving letter she had received from Mary Beatrice, written a few days after James's death:

I think myself indispensably obliged to defer no longer the acquainting you with a message which the best of men, as well as the best of fathers, has left with me for you. Some few days before his death, he bid me find means to let you know that he forgave you from the bottom of his heart, and prayed God to do so too, that he gave you his last blessing, and prayed God to convert your heart, and confirm you in the resolution of repairing to his son the wrongs done to himself; to which I shall only add, that I join my prayers to his herein with all my heart, and that I shall make it my business to inspire to the young man who is left to my care, the sentiments of his father, for better no man can have.

According to *The Life of James II*: 'There is no doubt but that the Princess of Denmark was moved with this letter, she had for a long time been (or pretended to be) in a disposition of making some reparation for past injuries.' The letter implies that Anne had indeed made promises to her father James concerning her brother, James Francis Edward, promises that Mary Beatrice as regent during her son's minority had every hope of seeing fulfilled. She had never really grasped the world's cynicism and still tended to believe the lies she was told. No one knew better than Anne how to dissemble, so that it is extremely unlikely that her promises were genuine. All that is certain is that ambition got the better of her when the crown at last fell within her grasp.

Towards the end of February 1702 the King was trying out a new horse, Sorrel, at Hampton Court, when it suddenly stumbled on a mole-hill, throwing him. William had broken his collarbone. His surgeon, Dr Ronjat, set it, but instead of staying still for a few days, William insisted on making the bone-jolting journey in his coach to Kensington that same evening, with predictable results. The bones had to be set again.

A man in good health would have been able to take such an injury in his stride, but William was almost certainly suffering from tuberculosis as well as a range of other complaints. It was soon observed that William's bones were not knitting together as they should and that there was swelling extending from the injured shoulder down the right arm to the hand. He tried to continue business as usual, urging that the Abjuration Bill excluding the Catholic James Francis Edward, the 'Pretender', from the throne should be made ready for his signature as quickly as possible. The Commons were also discussing the possibility of a union of England and Scotland, essential if the Stuarts' original kingdom were not to fall into the hands of the 'Pretender' and the Jacobites. There was no guarantee as yet that Scotland would make provision for the Hanoverian succession.

Strolling along the gallery at Kensington admiring his pictures, William soon felt tired and sat down to rest. He fell asleep in front of an open window, but fearing his peevish temper no one dared to wake him. Soon he was coughing and feverish. He took to his bed but was unable to sleep and turned away all food and drink. The physicians hovered round, prescribing an array of useless remedies. Only the quinine given for his fever is likely to have brought him some relief.

Albemarle returned in haste from The Hague on the morning of 7 March, but when he told the King how well the discussions with the allies were going, William showed little interest.

'*Je tire vers ma fin*,' he told the favourite. He gave him the keys to his cabinet, saying he knew what to do. For a while William's physician, Gorvaert Bidloo, held him in his arms, since he could not sleep lying down. Then the pages arranged the pillows to prop him up. At five in the morning of the 8th, Tenison, Archbishop of Canterbury, and Burnet came to give him the sacrament.

It was only at the last moment that Portland arrived at the bedside. Some said that Albemarle had been keeping him out, others that the servant despatched to his home at Windsor to fetch him lost his way in the dark. By this time, William had lost the power of speech. Instead he took the hand of his old friend – the friend who as a young man had risked death from smallpox to save William's life – and carried it to his heart. With that, he died.

When the dead King was undressed, it was found that he was wearing Mary's precious ring and a lock of her hair on a black ribbon close to his heart. He had not ceased to love her.

As the sun came up on the new day, Bishop Burnet dashed to St James's to be the first to tell Anne that she was now Queen. She assumed full mourning, telling everyone that the black was for her father; only the violet trimming was for William. According to her orders, the mourning for the dead King would be cursory and cease on her coronation, which was fixed for 23 April, the same day as her father's seventeen years earlier. Prince George was chief mourner at William's funeral, which took place on 12 April at Westminster Abbey privately at midnight, so simple that Burnet complained it was 'scarce decent'. William had cared nothing for pomp and ceremony anyway. He would probably have preferred to be laid to rest in Holland, but here he would lie beside Mary in the Stuart vault. Albemarle was said to be incoherent with grief.

Anne had spent some of the months before her accession reading English history and she now appropriated Elizabeth I's motto, *Semper Eadem* – Always the Same. Trading on her English birth, she told her subjects in her mellifluous voice: 'As

I know my own heart to be entirely English, I can very sincerely assure you there is not anything you can expect or desire from me which I shall not be ready to do for the happiness and prosperity of England.' It was her uncle Lord Rochester's idea to stress her English birth, to please the Tories, but for Anne it had the added advantage of distinguishing her from Mary Beatrice and her children being brought up in France, as well as her unpopular dead brother-in-law.

Carried to her coronation in an open chair, enormously overweight and virtually an invalid at thirty-seven, Anne could congratulate herself that she had survived to see this day. She had wanted the crown for herself and for her children. She had betrayed her father, cast doubts on her brother's birth, quarrelled with her sister, resented her brother-in-law, lied and dissimulated, ruined her health to provide an heir to the crown. Now she had no children and she had ignored her brother's right, despite promises made to her father. But she had the crown. She would be the mother of her people. She was greeted in a huge wave of popularity.

Only the Jacobites hoped and planned for a better day. Meanwhile, they had cause to think kindly of the mole who had upset William's horse and proposed a new toast: 'To the little gentleman in black velvet!'

# 13
## Broken Promises

*'Though I can never abandon, but with my life, my own just right . . . yet I am most desirous rather to owe to you the recovery of it. It is for you that a work so just and glorious is reserved. The voice of God and nature calls you to it; the promises you made to the King our father enjoin it'*

– James III and VIII, otherwise known as the Pretender,
to Queen Anne

On the morning of Friday, 30 July 1714 Queen Anne felt well enough to get up and have her hair combed. She had been sick in the night, but this morning there was a meeting of her Privy Council, who, since Whitehall Palace had burned to the ground in 1698, had no choice but to come all the way out to Kensington for it. Anne, always assiduous in fulfilling her duties, was determined to attend the meeting, even though her council was quarrelling so bitterly that after a late-night sitting recently she had spent the night in her bedchamber sobbing.

She went to check the time. The clock loomed huge in front of her. She stared at it transfixed. Mrs Dawson, the bedchamber woman who had served her faithfully for forty-nine years and her mother before her, asked cheerfully what was so fascinating about the clock. Anne made no response but turned to her with 'a dying look', at which Mrs Dawson shouted for help. The physicians on duty dashed to the scene and, judging that the Queen had had a stroke, shaved her head and let blood. She came to herself again, but a little after nine she had a second stroke. She was sitting speechless and motionless in the chair, surrounded by physicians and anxious attendants, when the first of the Privy Councillors arrived. She stared fixedly at him, giving no sign of recognition. Clearly, the Queen was in no condition to attend the meeting, whose deliberations now took on a new urgency.

The Queen's condition was one that her third physician, Sir David Hamilton, had dreaded and done everything he could for the last three years to avert. His aim had been to keep her quiet, suspecting that 'the translation of the gouty humour from the knee and the foot, first upon the nerves and then upon the brain' would bring on her death. Any disquiet or agitation would set off this process. There had been plenty of agitation, however, not just recently over the vexed question of the succession and the matter of a member of the Hanoverian family taking up residence in England, but almost from the outset of the Queen's reign. She who had been determined to steer a middle course, to be kept 'out of ye power of ye mercyless men of both partys', she who had wanted only the good of her people, had found herself like a storm-tossed ship buffeted in the fierce seas of party warfare.

None of it was helped by the fact that her dearest Sarah, who had been her prop and her fiercest supporter against her father, her sister and her brother-in-law, had turned into a fearful monster. Mrs Freeman had taken her prized frankness a little too far, showing Anne none of the deference she believed was a Stuart monarch's due. Sarah had harangued her, tried to cajole then drive her into the arms of a party she found abhorrent, insulted her in public, bullied her in private, threatened her with blackmail, even made obscene suggestions about her relationship with a bedchamber woman. Anne had become scared of her, trying desperately to avoid her, though thankfully she did not come to court very often.

She could not avoid a bombardment of letters, however, letters which after the break between them Sarah continued to write to Sir David Hamilton, knowing the physician would read them to her. Anne had wanted to get rid of the importunate Duchess for a long time, but for as long as

Lord Marlborough had been essential for the propagation of the war it had not been possible to dismiss his wife. Only in 1710 did the opportunity finally arise and even then the Queen remained uneasy, because Sarah was threatening to publish the thousand or so letters she had written her through their long relationship – letters that would embarrass her and damn her in the eyes of the world. There was nothing the Queen could do to stop her except, as Sir David Hamilton advised, not provoke the woman who had become as volatile as a volcano.

It had all seemed so hopeful back in the spring of 1702 when Anne's 'sunshine day' had come. Then she had felt secure in the friendship of her dearest Mr and Mrs Freeman and Mr Montgomery. She had been able to give Sarah, her beloved Mrs Freeman, the most prized offices at court: groom of the stole, mistress of the robes and keeper of the privy purse. Mr Freeman had immediately received the Garter William had denied him and she had been able to elevate him to the dukedom of Marlborough after his great victory at Blenheim in 1704. Mr Montgomery – Sidney, Lord Godolphin – had become her Lord Treasurer, her chief minister, and his steady support and tireless work had been such a comfort to her. And, of course, her beloved husband Prince George – Mr Morley – she had placed at the head of the Admiralty, although it was Marlborough's brother, Admiral George Churchill, who did all the work. Still timid and unsure of herself but encouraged that she had such firm, devoted friends to help her, Anne had written to her dear Mrs Freeman: 'As for your poor unfortunate faithful Morley . . . if you should ever forsake me, I would have nothing more to do with the world, but make another abdication, for what is a crown when ye support of it is gone, I never will forsake your dear self, Mr Freeman nor Mr Montgomery, but always be your constant faithful servant, & we four must never part, till death mows us down with his impartial hand.'

Later, she had told Mr Montgomery, 'As long as I live, it

370

shall be my endeavour to make my country and my friends easy.'

Nothing was more liable to upset the Queen than division and strife among her people. As party warfare between Whig and Tory reached a new intensity, Anne had tried to steer a middle way. Like her brother-in-law before her, she had believed it was her prerogative to choose her ministers. She could not know that party government was the way of the future, inevitable, when the majority returned to the House of Commons, Whig or Tory, would determine the party of the ministers serving the monarch. Only then would the electorate have the government they had voted for.

Anne's natural inclination lay with the Tories, who had been such firm supporters of the monarchy and her beloved Anglican Church. But she could not condone the extreme High Church Tories, men such as Lord Nottingham and her uncle, Lord Rochester, any more than she could the extremists of the other party, the Whig Junto. Rochester had never been able to make any headway with his niece; he had always been frustrated in his attempts by Sarah, and when he refused to take up the office the Queen had given him in Ireland, Anne had no hesitation in dismissing him. It was the final break with her mother's family.

Anne determined to form a mixed ministry of moderates, at first with her dear friends Marlborough and Godolphin, who were Tories, and Robert Harley, who with his nonconformist, Parliamentarian background, had come from the Whigs. And, of course, they all agreed the propagation of the war was essential. With Lord Marlborough leader of the Grand Alliance and captain-general of the allied forces, it was Godolphin's job at the treasury to ensure that the army received its pay and supplies, for Marlborough was adamant that his men operate in the best conditions. Not for his troops the lack of food and boots, pay and medical attention that the poor French foot soldiers had to endure.

The war! The wretched war! It had stretched on and on.

God had blessed England with great victories, at Blenheim, Ramillies, Oudenarde, even Malplaquet, and each time Queen Anne had gone in procession through cheering crowds to Sir Christopher Wren's magnificent new cathedral, St Paul's, to give thanks to God. But increasingly she had wondered, 'When will this bloodshed ever cease?' The country had become divided between those who wanted to continue the war, among them those Whigs making money from it, and those who wanted peace. The cry 'No peace without Spain!' which both parties had agreed at the outset, had become unfeasible. When Louis sued for peace after the terrible winter of 1708, it was quite obvious that the allies' terms were impossible to meet. He could not unseat his grandson from the Spanish throne, even if he wanted to. Philip V was adamant he would remain King of Spain and Louis was not about to wage war on his own grandson. Why should Charles of Austria have everything and Philip nothing? Its treasury so empty that Louis had to have the silver furniture in the Hall of Mirrors at Versailles melted down, its people dying of famine, France resolved to fight on, while Marlborough and the allies moved ever closer to its frontiers.

Relegated to the sidelines by the Whigs who perpetrated the war, the more extreme Tories asked who cared who sat on the throne of Spain? That was a European problem, nothing to do with England. But England was no longer the insignificant offshore island whose monarch depended on subsidies from Louis XIV. Thanks to William III's lifelong battle to curb the power and ambition of France, England was a nation to be reckoned with, in a position to decide the fate of Europe, to influence the balance of power. And, ironically, it was Harley and his new Tory allies, after a Tory landslide in the election of 1710 and the fall of Marlborough and the Whigs, who entered into secret talks with the French to end the war. 'Perfidious Albion' would sell out its allies. Anne had known nothing of these secret talks at first, but in due course she had wholeheartedly supported the move towards peace.

It helped that Emperor Joseph I died in the spring of 1711, leaving the sprawling Austro-Hungarian Empire to his brother Charles. Clearly, Charles could not now be King of Spain. A year later, there was a series of deaths in the French royal family. A measles epidemic wiped out the Grand Dauphin, his son and elder grandson. Only a sickly child of two remained as Louis's heir, while his grandson, Philip V, in Spain voluntarily renounced his claim to the French throne. It was easy then for Britain to agree he should retain Spain and the Indies, in exchange for extensive commercial advantages which would make it a great commercial power, far superior to her Dutch neighbour. Britain won the Asiento, the exclusive right to import slaves from Africa into the King of Spain's dominions in South America and the Indies, one of the foundations of its future wealth.

---

The prolonged war and party strife had agitated the Queen, much to her physicians' concern. But nothing upset her more than the disagreements with Mrs Freeman. It seems the friendship had been under threat right from the beginning of the reign, Anne later telling her erstwhile favourite: 'it has not been my fault that we have lived in ye manner we have done ever since I came to the crown.' Even before that, there had been a hurtful incident that had bruised the friendship. Anne had sent her bedchamber woman, Abigail Hill, to fetch her gloves. Anne had been standing just outside the door when she had heard Abigail's gentle enquiry, her hesitant appeal to Lady Marlborough, who had picked up the Queen's gloves by mistake. Then the searing words, 'Have I taken something belonging to that disagreeable person?' and the contempt as she threw them on the floor for Abigail, the poor relation she had brought to court as one of Anne's serving women, to pick up. Neither Anne nor Abigail had ever spoken of the incident, bound together in silence by mutual embarrassment.

In truth, Sarah had had her fill of court life long ago. As

young as fourteen, when she had been maid of honour to the Duchess of York for two years, she had become disenchanted with it, but then she had met John Churchill, whose career was so bound up with the Duke of York, and they had married. As Sarah's children had grown older, she had wanted to be at home with them. Totally uneducated in her youth, Sarah had discovered an interest in books, particularly the classics, and liked nothing better than to stay at her house at St Albans surrounded by her growing family and reading. The contrast of life in Princess Anne's household, hemmed into stuffy rooms with her royal mistress, still producing children when Sarah had finished with all that, more often than not sick, her talk dull and routine tedious, she found increasingly irksome.

There was to be no escape for Sarah. Anne had always been generous and as soon as she became Queen she heaped lucrative offices on her favourite, offices that necessitated her constant presence at court about the royal person. Her elder daughters, Lady Henrietta, who had married Godolphin's son Francis, and Lady Anne, who had married Lord Sunderland's son Charles Spencer, had each received generous dowries from Anne and now became ladies of the bedchamber.

But Sarah begrudged time spent at court and became increasingly impatient with the Queen. Contrary to what people thought, that the shy and reticent Queen was merely the puppet of the Marlboroughs, Sarah knew that Anne had always been her own person. She was tenacious and independent, with her own ideas and all her father's obstinacy. With the impatience of a quick-witted person at someone slow and stubborn, Sarah became increasingly frustrated by Anne's dogged refusal to fall in with her wishes in the matter of party politics. It was an ongoing struggle that was to wreck their friendship and bring Sarah's husband's career to an ignominious end.

Unlike her husband whose veneration for the monarchy inclined him towards the Tories, Sarah was a fierce and determined Whig. She knew the Queen had 'imbibed the most unconquerable prejudices' against the Whigs from her earliest years. The granddaughter of Charles I and Lord Chancellor Clarendon believed the Whigs to be the enemies of the monarchy 'and had been taught to look upon them all as rank republicans, and as always in readiness to rebel'.

'I can not help being extremely concerned, you are so partial to ye Whigs,' Anne protested to her friend, 'because I would never have you and your poor unfortunate faithful Morley differ in opinion in ye least thing . . . I know the principles of ye Church of England and I know those of ye Whigs, and it is that, and no other reason which makes me think as I do of ye last.'

It was the death of the Marlboroughs' only surviving son and heir, John, Lord Blandford, in February 1703 of smallpox at Cambridge University that widened the incipient breach between Mrs Morley and Mrs Freeman. Sarah was inconsolable and became a virtual recluse either at St Albans or at Windsor Lodge, the house in the Great Park that the Queen had given her for life. Anne knew what it was to lose a son and offered to come to comfort Sarah, pleading that 'ye unfortunate ought to come to ye unfortunate.' She was rebuffed and withdrew, hurt and confused. Sarah's absence from court now became prolonged, but she was soon bombarding the Queen with long letters packed with political argument. It might be that Blandford's death coincided with the onset of the menopause for Sarah, who in the immediate aftermath of her bereavement had cause to think she was pregnant again, only to be disappointed. Certainly from this time on she became more wildly impetuous, strident, out of control.

While Marlborough and Godolphin treated the Queen with deference and submission, Sarah let no such inhibitions affect her. She failed to see that the frank, open discussion that had been encouraged between a princess and her friend was inappropriate between a queen and a subject. Gaining in confidence all the time, Anne was only too aware of what was due to her as Queen. She was sufficiently convinced of her majesty, the mystical nature of her sovereignty, to revive the custom of touching for the Evil, the last English monarch to do so, even though she knew she owed her position to Parliament rather than divine right. In the spring of 1706 she wrote to Sarah, ordering the medals that were given out at the ceremony: 'I desire you would order 200 pieces more of Healing Gold, for I intend (and it please God) when I come from Windsor to touch as many poor people as I can before the hot weather comes. I do that business now in the Banqueting House, which I like very well, that being a very cool room, and the doing of it there keeps my own house sweet and free from crowds.'

But Sarah was impatient with the idea of sovereignty and the awe and respect it should be accorded. She had never had much time for royalty, having witnessed at first hand their all-too-human faults and weaknesses. She was tactless and insensitive not to acknowledge that there must be a subtle shift in the relationship between the Queen and herself now. She took at face value Anne's polite insistence: 'I beg my dear Mrs Freeman would banish that hard thought out of her head that I can ever be displeased at anything that comes from you, for sure I must be void of all reason if I were not sensible that there can not be a greater mark of kindness than telling one every thing freely, it is what has always been my request to you to do, & I do again beg you would continue that goodness to your poor unfortunate faithful Morley.'

No one knew better than Sarah how greatly Anne feared her brother, James Francis Edward, whom she had not seen since his infancy. Not only did he have a better claim to the throne than she did, as their late father's only legitimate son, but he was a living reminder of Anne's betrayal of her father, and of the lies and duplicity she had used to oust both of them from the throne. Sarah tried to convince Anne that the Tories were all secret Jacobites at heart. Anne was too level-headed to accept such a generalisation:

I own I can not have that good opinion of some sort of people that you have, nor that ill one of others, & let the Whigs brag never so much of their great services to their country & of their numbers, I believe the revolution had never been, nor the succession settl'd as it is now, if the Church party had not joyned with them, & why those people that agreed with them in these two things should all now he branded with ye name of Jacobite I can't imagine, have they not great stakes as well as them, & that if they had neither conscience nor honour would prevail with them not to give into what would be for their destruction, sure ye same argument will hold for both Whig & Tory. I do not deny but there are some for ye P. of Wales, but that number, I believe is very small, & I dare say there are millions that are call'd Jacobites, that abhor their principles as much as I do.

She refused to give way to Sarah's arguments, telling her:

I can not help thanking my dear Mrs Freeman for ye letter she sent me last night, because I'm sure she means it out of kindness to me, but I will not go about answering any part of it, finding you are so fixed in ye good opinion you have of some, & ye ill opinion you have of other people, that it is to no manner of purpose to argue any thing with you, therefore shall leave it to providence & time to convince you of ye mistakes you are in several things.

Sarah did not know her own strength. She should have let the matter drop, put politics to one side in her dealings with the Queen, who still wanted to maintain their friendship. Instead, she took offence at the Queen's refusal to heed her political advice and had no hesitation in making her feelings known. 'I must confess it is no small mortification to me,' Anne complained, 'that differences of opinion should make you cold to your poor unfortunate faithful Morley, & hinder you from coming to me, for whatever you say I can never take it ill, knowing as I have said already, that you mean it kindly.'

When the High Church Tories introduced the Occasional Conformity Bill as a means to undermine the Toleration Act of 1689, suppress the Dissenters and snub the Whigs, Sarah rushed to the defence of the Whigs and to press her arguments on the Queen, who replied: 'I must own to you that I never cared to mention anything on this subject to you because I knew you would not be of my mind, but since you have given me this occasion, I can't forbear saying that I see nothing like persecution in this Bill, you may think this is a notion Lord Nottingham has put in my head, but upon my word it is my own thought.' She begged she 'would never let differences of opinion hinder us from living together as we used to do'.

Just as she resisted the Whig extremists, Anne had no intention of being intimidated by the High Church Tories. Loyal daughter of the Anglican Church as she was, in the final resort she could not support their Occasional Conformity Bill, which infuriated them. She was just as fervent an Anglican as she had ever been and cared deeply for her Church. Had she not chosen as the text for her coronation sermon, 'Kings shall be your Nursing Fathers and Queens your Nursing Mothers'? She had yielded her income from first fruits and tenths – Queen Anne's Bounty – to support the poor parish clergy, and later she would have Nicholas Hawksmoor build new churches in London's sprawling suburbs, so that her people would not be won over to dissent. Her actions did much to counteract Tory propaganda. She did not need Tories such as Lord Nottingham nor, indeed, Whigs such as the Duchess of Marlborough to tell her where her duty lay.

By the spring of 1704 Sarah's good friend Lord Godolphin was telling her that 'you should not abuse that great indulgence of Mrs Morley' by being absent from court so often. It was becoming apparent to Sarah that she was losing her hold over the Queen. In letter after letter Anne protested that she still felt the same about Sarah, her feelings had not changed. It did not occur to Sarah that it was her self-destructiveness that was ruining the relationship, that matters might still be mended if she bothered to attend court and was less obstreperous. She was convinced that someone was influencing the Queen against her, but who? It did not take Sarah long to ferret out the self-effacing, mouse-like Abigail Hill, her own poor relation.

She had done everything for this girl, taken her and her siblings into her own household, found them positions at court, Abigail as a bedchamber woman, Alice a laundress, the brother Jack a page to Prince George. The other son she had clothed and put in school. And now the wretched girl had insinuated herself into the Queen's confidence, prompted by the sly Robert Harley, a man Sarah had never liked or trusted. Robert was Abigail's cousin on her father's side, but, unlike Sarah, he had done nothing for her when her father had died leaving his family in want. It was only when Harley had been trying to find a direct channel to the Queen that he had taken notice of the bedchamber woman and remembered their kinship.

The Queen had once found Sarah so exciting, so vibrant, with such bold confidence. For someone as shy and taciturn as Anne, it had been thrilling to watch her favourite in action. But now all that energy seemed to be turned against her old friend. Sarah had become a bully, unpitying as she bombarded the Queen with letters of complaint, lectured her endlessly about the merits of the Whigs, as good as told her over and over again she was too stupid to make her own decisions. But here she was wrong. She would have done better to listen to Anne when she told her, 'I must own I have ye same opinion of Whig & Tory that ever I had, I know their principles very well, & when I know my self to be in ye right, nothing can make me alter mine.'

Sarah had failed to take account of the fact that the Queen was now almost an invalid, even though in the summer of 1703 Anne had told her she was so lame she could hardly cross the room except with two sticks. This meant that the court was duller than ever and that the Queen was virtually isolated, prey to anyone who could infiltrate the bedchamber. She was in a pitiable condition. When the Scottish representatives who had come to England to discuss the Union had called on her at Kensington, Sir John Clerk of Penicuik was aghast at the sight that met him: 'Her Majesty was labouring under a fit of the gout, and in extreme pain and agony, and on this occasion everything about her was much in the same disorder as about the meanest of her subjects. Her face, which was red and spotted, was rendered something frightful by her negligent dress, and the foot affected was tied up with a pultis and some nasty bandages.'

Next time he visited, the 'despicable' situation had not improved:

The poor lady, as I saw her twice before, was again under a severe fit of the gout, ill dressed, blotted in her countenance, and surrounded with plaisters, cataplasisms, and dirty-like rags ... I believe she was not displeased to see any body, for no court attenders ever came near her. All the incence and adoration offered at courts were to her ministers, particularly the Earl of Godolphin, her chief minister, and the two secretaries of state, her palace of Kensington, where she commonly resided, was a perfect solitude, as I had occasion to observe several times. I never saw any body attending there but some of her guards in the outer rooms, with one at most of the gentlemen of her bedchamber. Her frequent fits of sickness, and the distance of the place from London, did not admit of what are commonly called drawing-room nights, so that I had many occasions to think that few houses in England belonging to persons of quality were kept in a more private way than the Queen's royal palace of Kensington.

No wonder the Queen had basked in Abigail's soothing presence, as she ministered to some of the worst excesses of the royal maladies, performing intimate tasks that would have been beneath Sarah as a peeress and that she would have found disgusting. Sir John Clerk's description seems to indicate that Anne was indeed suffering from the gout, 'in extreme pain and agony', although her previous incapacity sounded more like a form of arthritis. There would be intervals when she was blessedly free of it, such as when Jonathan Swift described her at Windsor 'hunting the stag till four this afternoon . . . she drove in her chaise above forty miles.' Anne could no longer ride, but she was not deterred from hunting 'in a chaise with one horse, which she drives herself, and drives furiously, like Jehu, and is a mighty hunter, like Nimrod'. More often than not, however, she was in pain and discomfort. Abigail was always there with a kind word, a dish of tea and a pleasant tune on the harpsichord, quiet and unassuming in contrast to the strident, volatile Duchess.

Sarah was absent from court writing the Queen querulous letters through most of 1704. By November, Anne had virtually given up on her old friend. As she wrote sadly to Godolphin: 'I agree that all Lady Marlborough's unkindness proceeds from ye real concern she has for my good, but I can't hope as you do, that she will ever be easy with me again. I quite despair of it now, which is no small mortification to me, however I will ever be ye same, & ready on all occasions to do her all ye service that lies in my poor power.'

Fortunately for Anne, some of Sarah's energies were drawn into her running battles with Sir John Vanbrugh over the construction of Blenheim, the palace being built at the nation's expense in the royal park at Woodstock, which the Queen had so generously given the victor of that great battle. Far from being grateful, Sarah hated the house from the start.

———

Matters took a turn for the worse when a Whig majority was returned to the Commons in the election of 1705. Now the Whig Junto, the extremists, demanded that one of their own have a ministerial position. Thinking that as the Marlboroughs' son-in-law he would have the best chance of being accepted, their chosen candidate was Charles Spencer, Earl of Sunderland, that angry young man who had been calling for a republic. Anne had loathed his parents, Robert, second Earl of Sunderland – who had died in 1702 – and his countess, Anne, and she loathed the son. She bitterly resented Whig attempts to foist him on her, and, more particularly, she resented the fact that the once moderate Marlborough and Godolphin were pressurising her to fall in with the plan. The war could not be continued, they argued, without Whig support, so that some concessions had to be made to the party.

Everyone recognised that the succession was Anne's vulnerable point and they did not hesitate to needle her on the matter for political advantage. The High Church Tories had been in correspondence with the Dowager Electress Sophie and were threatening to invite her to England. The Tory goal was to disrupt relations between the two courts and to rupture the Grand Alliance, as Sophie's son, the Elector George Ludwig, was only too aware. He had no wish to see either his mother or his son, the Electoral Prince George August, living in England, where they would be forced into opposition to the Queen.

Any speculation that Anne had a lingering feeling of guilt towards her brother and intended to restore him to the throne after her death was idle. She was not given to family sentiment, as her past behaviour towards her father and sister made only too apparent. There was never any question in her mind that her Catholic brother had to be excluded because of the threat he posed to the Protestant religion, and the same applied to his sister, Louise Marie, who was to die when she was only twenty. Even after the Whigs exposed the fiction of the warming-pan story at the Sacheverell trial in 1710, Anne found it convenient to equivocate, maintaining a pretence of doubt, even to Sarah, that 'she was not sure the Prince of Wales was her brother.' She would never let her guard down on this matter. Later, when Sir David Hamilton told her that he did not believe the Prince of Wales to be genuine, Anne 'received this with cheerfulness, and by asking me several questions about the thing'.

Anne's instinct for self-preservation meant that she regarded the Hanoverian succession as her surest weapon against James Francis Edward, who, if he had any right whatsoever, should be on the throne in her place. One of the reasons she had been so much in favour of the Union with Scotland was to guarantee the Hanoverian succession. But Anne, perhaps remembering too well the trouble she had caused her own sister and brother-in-law when she was heir to the throne, had no wish to see her successor setting up a rival court in England, the focus and instrument of the opposition. Selfish to the end, desiring only national unity, Anne's personal policy was to keep any successor out of the kingdom during her lifetime.

While Marlborough and Godolphin were pressurising Anne to take Sunderland as the price of the Whigs quashing the Tories' intended invitation to Sophie, Sarah suspected that the Queen's resistance to her son-in-law's appointment was owing to someone's prompting in the background. Marlborough demurred, telling his wife, 'You know that I have often disputes with you concerning the Queen, and by what I have always observed that when she thinks herself in the right, she needs no advice to help her to be very firm and positive.'

In August 1706 Godolphin threatened to resign if the Queen refused to accede to the Junto's demands, a prospect that alarmed her, as she was not yet ready to part with him. In desperation, she turned to Robert Harley for advice and he sent her the following memo:

> Nothing will satisfie them.
>
> If so much pressed now to take him in, when most think him unfit, will it be possible to part with him when he appears to be so.
>
> All power is given them.
>
> Those that press it must be delivered from the engagements or terrors they are under. If you stop now, it will make you better served and observed by all sides, it is gone so far it will be too late hereafter – everybody will worship the idol party that is set up. Balance the good and the evil of taking him or keeping him out.

It did not take Sarah long to pitch in on Sunderland's behalf, writing to the Queen: 'Your security and the nations is my chief wish, and I beg of God almighty as earnestly as I shall do for his pardon at my last hour, that Mr and Mrs Morley may see their errors as to this *notion* before it is too late, but considering how little impression any thing makes that comes from your faithful Freeman, I have troubled you too much & I beg your pardon for it.'

Unfortunately, Anne misread *notion* for *nation* and was mortally offended. She did not reply and Sarah fired off another letter complaining of 'Your Majesty's great indifferency and contempt in taking no notice of my last letter'.

It went against all Anne's instincts to give in, as she told Godolphin:

All I desire is my liberty in encouraging & employing all those that concur faithfully in my service whether they are call'd Whigs or Torys, not to be tyed to one, not to ye other, for if I should be so unfortunate as to fall into ye hands of either, I shall look upon my self tho I have the name of Queen, to be in reality but their slave, which as it will be my personal ruin, so it will be ye destroying of all government ... Why for God's sake, must I who have no interest, no end, no thought but for ye good of my country, be made so miserable as to be brought into ye power of one set of men, & why may I not be trusted, since I mean nothing but what is equally for ye good of all my subjects?

Sarah now went too far, telling the Queen: 'I desire you wd reflect whether you have never heard that the greatest misfortunes that ever happen'd to any of your family has not been occasion'd by having ill advises & an obstinacy in their tempers that is very unaccountable.'

Anne replied coolly: 'It would be more pleasing whenever you are pleased to let me have the satisfaction of hearing from you, if you would write in ye stile you used to do, & why it was altered I can't imagine for I'm sure I never gave no cause for it ... I have nothing more to add at present but that as unkind as you are to your poor unfortunate faithful

Morley, I will ever be with all truth & tenderness my dear Mrs Freeman's.'

Anne had to back down in the matter of Sunderland in order to secure the necessary supplies for the war, but it meant that Marlborough and Godolphin had forfeited her unquestioning allegiance. They had failed to protect her from the extreme Whigs. As the erstwhile moderates Marlborough and Godolphin were drawn inexorably towards the Whigs, who supported the war effort, their former colleague Robert Harley was moving towards the Tories. And the Tories retained their influence in the Queen's bedchamber. Anne's favourite physician, Dr John Arbuthnot, was a High Tory and the bedchamber woman, Abigail Hill, was also a Tory. They had constant access to the invalid.

Sarah's fury knew no bounds when she discovered Abigail had married, in the summer of 1707, Samuel Masham, the eighth son of an impoverished baronet, without any reference to herself. He was an insignificant man, she sneered, 'always making low bows to everybody, and ready to skip to open a door'. Worse, the Queen was party to the secret marriage. Sarah imagined she had found the conspiracy she had suspected all along:

I discovered that my cousin was become an absolute favourite; that the Queen herself was present at her marriage in Dr Arbuthnot's lodgings, at which time the Queen called for a round sum out of the privy purse [2,000 guineas, which she probably gave Abigail as a dowry]; that Mrs Masham came often to the Queen when the Prince was asleep, and was generally two hours every day in private with her: and I like wise then discovered beyond all dispute Mr Harley's correspondence and interest at court by means of this woman.

When Sarah taxed the Queen with her duplicity over the marriage, Anne shrugged it off. 'I have a hundred times bid Masham to tell it to you, and she would not.'

A showdown, in which Marlborough and Godolphin

threatened to resign rather than work with Harley, led to Harley's dismissal. He had failed to muster sufficient support. And now Marlborough and Godolphin were able to play the Jacobite card, knowing Anne's fear of her brother's pretensions. Popular dissatisfaction in Scotland with the Union of 1707 and the loss of its national independence made it ripe for Jacobite revolt. With his back against the wall in Europe, Louis XIV saw his opportunity in the spring of 1708. James Francis Edward, now twenty years of age, was to lead an expedition to link up with the Jacobites in Scotland. With the sort of misfortune that had always dogged his father, no sooner had the young man arrived at Le Havre than he came down with measles. His physicians forbade him to sail. By the time he did so a week later, an Anglo-Dutch fleet had been mustered in the Channel and hung on the tail of the French ships as they approached the Scottish coast. As no signals were to be seen from the Jacobite rebels on shore, the unhappy James returned home an ignominious failure.

When the Whigs inevitably triumphed at the next election, Marlborough had no hesitation in telling Anne that 'the greatest part of the party' – the Tories – had known of or supported the Pretender's invasion attempt and that only the Whigs could guarantee her security. Godolphin was now using the threat of the Electoral Prince's coming to England as a means to induce the Queen to accept more Whigs in her government.

She was adamant when she told Marlborough: 'if this matter should be brought into Parliament, whoever proposed it whether Whig or Tory, I should look upon neither of them as my friends nor could never make any invitation neither to the young man, nor his father, nor grandmother . . . it being a thing I can not bear to have any successor here tho it were but for a week.'

The Queen's opinion of her once kind and gentle Lord Marlborough took a further knock when he wrote to Sarah after his victory at Oudenarde: 'I do, and you must, give thanks to God for his goodness in protecting and making me the instrument of so much happiness to the Queen and the nation, *if she will please to make use of it.*' The letter was written in confidence to his wife, of course, but Sarah could not resist sending it to the Queen. She immediately seized on the phrase and wrote to Marlborough asking, 'what is ye use you would have me make & then I will tell you my thoughts very freely & sincerely.'

Her letter crossed with one from him, leaving her in no doubt that he had gone over totally to the Whigs. He advised her 'to have no more resentments to any particular person or party [meaning his son-in-law, Sunderland, and the Whigs], but to make of such as will carry on this just war with vigour, which is the only way to preserve our religion and liberties, and the crown upon your head'.

———

Jealous of the bedchamber woman who she felt had usurped her place as the Queen's confidante, Sarah's behaviour now became outrageous. She made a rare appearance at court towards the end of July 1708, bringing with her a scurrilous verse, probably written by Arthur Maynwaring, an unsavoury associate of the Whigs who had assumed a regrettable influence over her. She could not wait to show the libel to the Queen:

> *When as Queen Anne of great Renown*
> *Great Britain's Scepter sway'd,*
> *Besides the Church, she dearly lov'd*
> *A Dirty Chamber-Maid.*
>
> *O! Abigail that was her Name*
> *She stich'd and starch'd full well,*
> *But how she pierc'd this Royal Heart,*
> *No Mortal Man can tell.*

> *However, for sweet service done*
> *And Causes of great Weight,*
> *Her Royal Mistress made her, Oh!*
> *A Minister of State.*
>
> *Her Secretary she was not*
> *Because she could not write*
> *But had the Conduct and the Care*
> *Of some dark Deeds at Night.*

Anne must have been horrified, but, not content to leave it at that, the Duchess followed it up with a letter in which she accused the Queen of lesbian tendencies:

And tho Your Majesty was pleased to desire me not to speak any more of her [Abigail], which I know to be her own request & what would be of great advantage to all her designs if she could obtain it, yet I must humbly beg pardon if I cannot obey that command, the rather because I remember you said at the same time of all things in this world, you valued most your reputation, which I confess surpris'd me very much, that Your Majesty should so soon mention that word after having discover'd so great a passion for such a woman, for sure there can be no great reputation in a thing so strange & unaccountable, to say no more of it, nor can I think the having no inclination for any but of one's own sex is enough to maintain such a character as I wish may still be yours.

The Queen never forgave Sarah for this. Unfortunately, a few weeks later the Duchess was to accompany her to St Paul's for the thanksgiving service for the victory at Oudenarde. Anne had spent most of the summer at Windsor, nursing Prince George, whose asthma was now so bad that he could not have long to live. The journey to Kensington was hot and uncomfortable and by the time the Queen reached St James's, she had no inclination to don the heavy jewels which Sarah, as groom of the stole, had laid out for her to wear in the victory procession. It was not until they were in their coach and on the way that Sarah noticed the absence of the jewels. Absurdly, she attributed this to Abigail's influence and harangued the Queen the whole way to St Paul's. When they arrived, the Queen paused to say something and Sarah immediately stopped her with a loud 'Be quiet!' before shocked onlookers.

Even Sarah might have had cause to realise she had over-stepped the bounds of decorum, but remained unrepentant. She sent the Queen another letter from Marlborough in which he despaired, 'I am so tired of what I hear, and what I think must happen in England' that he would take the first oppor-tunity to retire. 'I must be in some manner answerable for the actions of the Queen,' he continued, 'who is noways governed by anything I can say or do.' Sarah could not resist slipping in a sarcastic note of her own, saying, 'Your Majesty chose a very wrong day to mortify me, when you were just going to return thanks for a victory obtained by Lord Marlborough.'

Anne's response was cold: 'After the commands you gave me on the thanksgiving day of not answering you, I shou'd not have troubled you with these lines, but to return the D. of Marlborough's letter safe into your hands, & for the same reason do not say anything to that nor to yours which enclosed it.'

Lady Marlborough was the last person the Queen would have wanted near her when her beloved husband and best friend for quarter of a century, Prince George, lay dying at Kensington that October, but Sarah realised that it would look bad if she neglected to be there. She rushed to the bedside to find the Queen kissing her dying husband, which she continued to do after he had expired. Naturally, Anne wanted to stay beside him, but Sarah was determined she leave the dismal scene behind and accompany her to St James's. Anne pointed to her watch, telling Sarah that when the hand reached a certain hour she might come to her, but until then she insisted on being left alone with her husband. She also asked for Masham to be sent to her, a request that Sarah completely ignored, supposedly because of how it might look.

At the appointed time, the bereaved woman was hustled

out of the palace by Sarah, clutching her arm in a vice-like grip, as if she were her prisoner. Alice Hill darted forward to give the Queen her hood. Then Dr Arbuthnot and Abigail emerged in their path. Sarah was enraged that: 'at the sight of that charming lady, as her arm was upon mine, which she had leaned upon, I found she had strength to bend down towards Mrs Masham like a sail, and in passing by, went some steps more than was necessary, to be nearer her; and when that cruel touch was over, of going by her with me, she turned about in a little passage room and gave orders about her dogs and a strong box.'

At St James's Sarah, who seemed to mock the Queen's grief, noticed that she ate two hearty meals. She received Godolphin to discuss the funeral arrangements. Pathetically, the Queen later went alone to Sarah's apartments, only to find that she was not there. It seems that she had accomplished her mission in extracting Anne from Kensington and what she imagined to be Abigail's influence and had lost interest. Dazed with shock and grief at the loss of her husband, Anne had just remembered a small detail and was reduced to leaving a note:

I scratched twice at dear Mrs Freeman's door, as soon as lord treasurer went from me, in hopes to have spoke one more word to him before he was gone; but nobody hearing me, I wrote this, not caring to send what I had to say by word of mouth; which was, to desire him, that when he sends his orders to Kensington, he would give directions there may be a great many yeomen of the guard to carry the Prince's dear body, that it may not be let fall, the great stairs being very steep and slippery.

Disparaging the Queen's sorrow, Sarah thought it extraordinary that she had asked Godolphin to check the Stuart vault at Westminster Abbey to ensure that if the Prince was laid to rest there, there would be enough space beside him for Anne. She also removed the Prince's portrait from the Queen's bedchamber at Kensington, on the pretext that 'I thought she loved him, & if she had been like other people 'tis terrible to see a picture while the affliction is just upon one.' It was tortuous for Anne, who wrote to Sarah: 'I can not end this without begging you once more for God sake to let the dear picture you have of mine, be put into my bedchamber for I can not be without it any longer.'

By Christmas the Duchess had left the court again, but continued to needle the Queen from afar. She asked for some vacant rooms at St James's to expand her apartments and when the Queen refused, Sarah asked that they might repeat their conversation publicly, confident that it would be thought strange 'that after the service Lord M. had done her, she would not give him a miserable hole to make him a clean way to his lodgings'.

Absent for so much of the time overseas, Marlborough could only know at second hand what was going on. Unwisely, he allowed himself to be drawn into his wife's quarrel and wrote to the Queen 'hoping that in time you will be sensible of the long and faithful service of Lady M. and that God will bless you with the opening of your eyes', to which Anne replied reasonably:

You seem to be dissatisfied with my behaviour to the Duchess of Marlborough. I do not love complaining, but it is impossible to help saying on this occasion, I believe no body was ever so used by a friend as I have been by her ever since my coming to ye crown. I desire nothing but that she would leave off teasing & tormenting me & behave herself with the decency she ought both to her friend & Queen, & this I hope you will make her do . . . I shall end this letter as you did yours to me, wishing both your eyes & the Duchess of Marlborough's may be opened & that you may ever be happy.

The impeachment of Dr Henry Sacheverell, the crypto-Jacobite who had preached an incendiary sermon attacking the Revolution settlement and the Hanoverian succession – indeed, questioning by what right Anne sat on the throne – by the Whigs united the fragmented Tory Party against the government. By 1710 the war had become very unpopular and Marlborough was being blamed for prolonging it for private profit. The opposition was in agreement that the Queen should be rescued from the tyranny of the Marlborough family and that England should get out of the war. Lord Shrewsbury, although a personal friend of Marlborough's, moved into opposition to the Whig ministry and was frequently in consultation with the Queen.

Angry that the Queen had refused to make him captain-general for life and finding that appointments in the army – notably a promotion for Abigail Masham's brother Jack Hill – were being made without reference to him, Marlborough complained to the Queen: 'I can't help but think the nation wou'd be of opinion that I have deserv'd better than to be made a sacrifice to the unreasonable passion of a bedchamber woman.' He was determined to demand the Queen either dismiss Abigail or accept his resignation, but was deterred from going so far when he found that his friends did not support him. Instead, he asked permission to retire if Hill were given the regiment. Anne withheld Hill's appointment.

Sarah had not finished with the Queen yet. She was determined to enforce a confrontation 'to vindicate myself'. The Queen told her to put her thoughts in writing, but ignoring this, Sarah sent her a message: 'If this afternoon be not convenient, I will come every day, and wait till you please to allow me to speak to you. And one thing more I assure Your Majesty which is, that what I have to say will have no consequence either in obliging you to answer or to see me oftner hereafter than will be easy to you.'

The last interview between the two women took place that same afternoon at Kensington. Sarah told her 'there is a thousand lies made of me' and that people had been telling the Queen 'severall things . . . that I have said of you, that I am no more capable of than I am of killing my children'. To this Anne replied, 'There is without doubt many lies told.'

Sarah begged the Queen to tell her 'what you have heard that I might be able to clear my self in any thing in which I was wronged', to which Anne replied mechanically, 'You said you desired no answer, & I shall give you none.' Sarah started to cry and, seeing that she was getting nowhere with the Queen, who kept repeating her answer like a mantra, took her leave, saying, 'God would punish her either in this world, or in the next for what she had done to her this day.' As Anne later told Sir David Hamilton: 'it was very hard passing a sentence upon any body, for that was a thing between God and themselves.'

After pausing in the gallery to wipe away her tears, Sarah thought of something else she wanted to tell the Queen and 'I went back again to the closet & scratch'd at the door,' which the Queen opened herself. Sarah said she would take care not to be at Windsor Lodge next time the Queen came to the castle, to which Anne replied that she was perfectly easy about her coming to the castle. It was said only to placate the Duchess. Anne had no intention of seeing her again if she could help it and, indeed, this was the last time the two women, who had once enjoyed such a passionate friendship, were ever to meet.

The Queen might have rid herself of the presence of Lady Marlborough, but she could not dismiss her from her offices while her husband's presence was deemed essential to the war. Nor had she freed herself from the Marlborough family. Lord Sunderland had always been obnoxious to her, never more so than when he attempted to raise the question of Abigail Masham in Parliament, demanding her dismissal. Anne was incandescent with rage. She was no more inclined to bow to pressure to dismiss one of her servants now than she had been in the late Queen her sister's time, when Lady Marlborough's dismissal was being demanded. Marlborough was convinced that Sunderland was being singled out solely because he was his son-in-law and 'in order to make it impossible for me with honour to continue at the head of this glorious army'. Anne told Godolphin in no uncertain terms:

It is true indeed that ye turning a son-in-law out of his office may be a mortification to the Duke of Marlborough, but must the fate of Europe depend on that, and must he be gratified in all his desires, and I not in so reasonable a thing as parting with a man who I took into my service with all ye uneasiness imaginable & whose behaviour to me has been so ever since, & who I must add is I believe obnoxious to all people except a few.

Ignoring her husband's advice *not* to write to the Queen any more, Sarah warned Anne that the dismissal of their son-in-law would provoke Marlborough's resignation. It was now that she threatened to publish the Queen's letters to her, letters containing such protestations as 'I wish I may never see the face of Heaven if ever I consent to part with you' and 'I wish I may never enjoy happiness in this world or the next, for Christ Jesus sake do not leave me.' Obviously, they would cause an international sensation. As Anne told Sir David Hamilton: 'when people are fond of one another, they say many things . . . they would not desire the world to know.'

Aware that anything she told Hamilton would be reported back to Anne, Sarah informed him of her intention to publish the letters. She said 'that she took more pleasure in justifying herself, than Your Majesty did in wearing your crown, and that she wondered that when Your Majesty was so much in her power, you should treat her so.'

The Duchess had plenty of new grievances against the Queen to add to her ongoing resentment of Abigail Masham. She was saddened that her dear friend Lord Godolphin had been dismissed as Lord Treasurer in August 1710. Anne did not even give him a personal interview, but sent a message asking him to break his staff of office, 'which I believe will be easier for both of us'. In an age of corruption, Godolphin left office a poor man and the Queen never paid him the pension she had promised.

Sarah was also angry that Anne refused to honour her original promise to give her offices to her daughters after she retired. Anne had no intention of continuing the Marlborough hold by promoting the daughters in their mother's place, not least because she had grown to dislike them. 'The one is cunning and dangerous to be in the family,' she said of 'the little Whig' Anne Sunderland, while 'the other silly and imprudent, and lost her reputation', she pronounced on Henrietta Godolphin, who was indeed mixing with strange company. She dismissed the third daughter, Mary, Duchess of Montagu, as being 'just like her mother'. As for what she had promised, she told Hamilton, 'persons may promise, and yet upon occurrences change.'

When Marlborough returned to England, he was very angry to hear of his wife's behaviour to the Queen, of whom he had always been fond. Sarah was still threatening that 'such things are in my power that . . . might lose a crown', when relief came from a most unexpected quarter. As one of the key allies, George of Hanover let it be known that Marlborough must stay to see the war out, but that the Duchess should leave the Queen's service. She had no option but to submit. In a final desperate attempt to save his wife's positions, Marlborough carried a letter of humble apology from the Duchess to the Queen. Anne would not relent. That night, Sarah threw her key of office at her husband, who next day returned it to the Queen.

---

In the spring of 1711 Sarah was vacating her apartments at St James's and asked if she might store her furniture at the palace, pending the completion of Marlborough House, which was being built on a slice of land that had once been the private royal garden. She used Lord Shrewsbury as an intermediary and Anne replied that the Duchess could rent storage space for 10s a week. Furious, Sarah removed all portable fixtures from her apartments, down to the mantelpieces and doorknobs. In retaliation, Anne ordered a temporary halt to the construction of Blenheim, angrily saying 'that she would not build the Duke a house when the Duchess was pulling hers to pieces'.

Elizabeth, Duchess of Somerset – the Percy heiress who had offered Anne a refuge at Syon and been chief mourner at Queen Mary's funeral – had inherited Sarah's offices as groom of the stole and first lady of the bedchamber. Sir David Hamilton was pleased to note that this Duchess 'is of the first quality and in that respect suitable to you. She seems to converse with a courteous calmness which makes her the more suitable to Your Majesty's temper.' The Queen could only agree and so soothing did she find the Duchess's company that she insisted on retaining her despite her husband's being a fierce Whig.

There is no question that while Anne treated Lady Somerset as a friend and equal, she continued to regard Abigail as a servant, even though she obtained Sarah's office of keeper of the privy purse. Lady Marlborough's accusations of a close relationship between the Queen and the bedchamber woman were absurd, because Anne Stuart could never regard her as her social equal. This explains why she held out for so long before agreeing to give Samuel Masham a peerage – part of a bid to expand the Tory presence in the Upper House after Marlborough's dismissal at the end of 1711. As a peeress, she said, Abigail could not be expected to carry out the menial tasks she was used to about the Queen's person. Only when she had Abigail's assurance that she would continue to perform these duties did her husband get his peerage.

Marlborough had been on the brink of invading France when the Tories Harley, now Lord Oxford, and Henry St John, Viscount Bolingbroke, had embarked on their secret peace talks through the Jacobite Earl of Jersey and the Abbé Gaultier. It might be said that they saved Paris, which would almost certainly have fallen if Marlborough had been allowed to continue the war. They went so far as to encourage the pretensions of the Pretender, although they did not make it sufficiently clear at the outset that they could raise the matter of his restoration in Parliament only if he was prepared to change his religion, which he was not. The 'Jacobite peace' fuelled speculation that Anne was secretly in favour of her brother succeeding her. Not only did James Francis Edward receive this impression, but also he was convinced that Anne had made such a promise to their father. In May 1711 he wrote to the sister who had not seen him since he was a babe in arms:

You may be assured, Madam, that though I can never abandon, but with my life, my own just right, which you know is unalterably settled by the most fundamental laws of the land, yet I am most desirous rather to owe to you, than to any living, the recovery of it. It is for you that a work so just and glorious is reserved. The voice of God and nature calls you to it; the promises you made to the King our father enjoin it; the preservation of our family, the preventing of unnatural wars require it; and the public good and welfare of our country recommend it to you, to rescue it from present and future evils, which must, to the latest posterity, involve the nation in blood and confusion, till the succession be again settled in the right line.

The violence and ambition of the enemies of our family, and of the monarchy, have too long kept at distance those who, by all the obligations of nature and duty, ought to be more firmly united ... The natural affection I bear you, and that the King our father had for you, till his last breath; the consideration of our mutual interest, honour and safety, and the duty I owe to God and my country, are the true motives that persuade me to write to you, and to do all that is possible for me to come to a present union with you.

Your own good nature, Madam, and your natural affection to a brother, from whom you never received any injury, cannot but incline your heart to do him justice; and, as it is in your power, I cannot doubt your good inclinations.

He received no response and, in fact, his plea fell on deaf ears. Anne had never had any time for family sentiment. Lady

Marlborough was probably right when she said 'she was very hard'. Anne had no intention of upsetting the Hanoverian settlement, which guaranteed her security. When Sir David Hamilton repeated the rumours to her in the autumn of 1712 that 'things looked as though the Pretender was designed and all in places who are for him', Anne replied, 'O fye, there is no such thing. Do you think I am a child, and to be imposed upon?' In the spring of 1714 she assured the bishops that her zeal for the Church of England and the liberties of the nation was unimpaired. She added impassively that she did not recognise the Pretender for her brother, and that she could hardly do for him what she had not done for her own father.

As committed as Anne to the Hanoverian succession, Shrewsbury intervened decisively to insist on the banishment from France of James Francis Edward as a condition of the peace. He was exiled to Bar-le-Duc in the duchy of Lorraine, a guest of Liselotte's daughter Elizabeth Charlotte, whose husband the Duke of Lorraine rebuffed further attempts to hound him out of there too. At first Anne refused to endorse the hysteria the Whigs were generating over the Pretender by issuing a proclamation against him. But Bolingbroke, knowing he had gone too far in the Jacobite direction and fearing for his own future once it was clear that the Hanoverian succession was inevitable, convinced her otherwise and on 21 June 1714 Anne issued a proclamation offering a £5,000 reward for the apprehension of the Pretender should he ever set foot in the three kingdoms. The Commons immediately voted to improve the offer to £100,000, to which Anne responded 'that the hearty concern they shew'd in it, for the Protestant succession, was very agreeable to her'. It was the final betrayal of the pledge she had made to her father.

No sooner was the war ended by the Peace of Utrecht between Britain, the Dutch Republic and France at the end of March 1713 than the clamour revived for a member of the Hanoverian family to live in England. Both the Dowager

Electress Sophie and her son George were demanding not just the invitation, but also a civil list allowance for Sophie, and the Pretender's expulsion from Lorraine. The Queen fired off letters to all three of them, the Dowager Electress, her son and her grandson, telling them in no uncertain terms that their presence would not be welcome, that it would lead to disturbances among her subjects and put the succession of their family in jeopardy. Anne had never shared the friendship with Sophie that Sophie had enjoyed with her sister Mary. Anne's relations with Hanover had always been courteous, if cool. The harshness of her letter came as such a disagreeable shock to the eighty-four-year-old Sophie that it is said to have brought on her death within days of receiving it. When Sir David Hamilton asked Anne if she was affected by the Electress's death, she shrugged indifferently, telling him 'that the Princess Sophia was chipping-porridge [a matter of no importance] it would neither give her more ease, nor more uneasiness'.

———

Only two months later, Anne too was slipping out of the world. After her second stroke on 30 July, her ministers had been anxious that her former Lord Treasurer, Oxford – whom she had dismissed for his ineptitude in relations with Hanover, his lateness for appointments, and his being so frequently drunk that she seldom understood what he said – should be replaced immediately. There was no time now to await the arrival of the Duke of Marlborough from his self-imposed exile. Under the terms of the Regency Act, Oxford might still claim to hold office after the Queen's death if another appointment were not made. A successor had to be found fast. All were agreed that Lord Shrewsbury was the most suitable choice and he came to the Queen's bedside to receive the staff of office. Taking it from her Lord Chancellor, she handed it to Shrewsbury. When Shrewsbury asked if she knew him, she nodded. He wasted no time in sending a messenger to Hanover, to tell her successor that she could not possibly live and to urge his hasty departure for England.

After her second stroke, Anne could only say 'Yes' and 'No', so that it was obviously Jacobite propaganda that she had been heard to mutter, 'My brother, my poor brother.' Nor could she have made 'a sort of confession' regarding her brother to John Robinson, Bishop of London. Just as she had never shown her brother James Francis Edward any affection in life, she said nothing about him on her deathbed. Nor was anything relating to him found among her papers. A packet found under her pillow, which the Jacobites claimed was a secret will, nominating James Francis Edward as her successor, or correspondence from him, was burned unopened after her death. As it was being consumed by the flames, an observer noticed that the writing was in French and in a large, schoolboy hand. More likely letters from Prince George than from a brother whose handwriting could never be described as large and clear.

Dr Arbuthnot was of the opinion that the Queen's life was cut short by the troubles with which she had had to contend. 'I believe sleep was never more welcome to a weary traveller,' he told Jonathan Swift, 'than death was to her.' It came so suddenly on the morning of 1 August 1714 that the forty-nine-year-old Queen, perhaps unlike her more mystical sister unwilling to confront her mortality until it was too late, had not had time to sign her will. She had given £2,000 to the poor and divided her jewellery between her favourite, the Duchess of Somerset, and her only surviving first cousin, Anne-Marie, Duchess of Savoy, with whom she had briefly shared a nursery at St Cloud. Nothing at all was left to James Francis Edward. That would have been an admission of kinship, and Anne, who had had to become a self-protective survivor from her earliest childhood, was not going to do that, to expose her own lies and deceit, even on her deathbed.

It was irrelevant anyway, as the will was unsigned. George of Hanover, her erstwhile suitor, would honour the bequest of £2,000 to the poor, even though his lawyers advised him he had no obligation to do so, but not the gifts of jewellery to the Duchesses of Somerset and Savoy.

Nor was Anne able to receive the sacrament. She expressed no deathbed repentance for her behaviour towards her father, her stepmother or her siblings. As ever bent on her own survival, she had done nothing once she came to power to make restitution to her brother, as it seems she had promised her father she would do. On the contrary, she had declared him an outlaw with a price on his head. Probably she had never had any intention of restoring the crown to him and by the time she lay on her deathbed it was far too late to undo the wrongs of the past. She had not earned the forgiveness her father had given her on his deathbed.

Her father King James lay unburied. Cast out of his kingdoms, dying in exile, his coffin still waited above ground in the Church of the English Benedictines in rue St Jacques, Paris, beside that of his daughter, the Princess Louise Marie, who had died of smallpox in 1712. The coffins were to remain there until James's posterity regained the crowns of England and Scotland and the position to which they had been appointed by God, theirs by divine right, when they would be transferred to Westminster Abbey for burial. It was a call that never came. Instead, the luckless James's earthly remains fell victim to the fury of the *sans-culottes* as the French Revolution of 1789 swept away the old regime.

As they had demonstrated in the so-called Glorious Revolution of 1688 in England, James's daughters by the commoner Anne Hyde had a far greater sense of political reality than he did. Each of them in her own way had been a remarkable queen. They had done what they believed was right for their kingdoms and the Protestant religion, in which they had been indoctrinated from their childhood. They had presided over the painful transition from the turbulence of the seventeenth to the stability of the eighteenth century, heralding a more tolerant society, an age of booming commerce when Great Britain finally took its place as a great power in the world.

Neither of them had expressed remorse for her part in her father's downfall, earning them the epithet 'ungrateful daughters'. Perhaps they felt the end justified the means. Anne more than Mary knew what lies and duplicity had been employed to end their father's Catholic tyranny. If she felt guilt or remorse, she never admitted it. Self-contained to the end, Anne, the last of the Stuart monarchs, took her secrets to the grave, as she was laid beside her beloved husband and the rest of her dynasty.

# Notes

*Full bibliographical details are given on pp. 435–42*

## Prologue

Accounts of King James's flight and capture are in Clarke, vol. ii, pp.251–78; Ailesbury, vol. i, pp.194–226; Turner, pp.444–9; BM Add. MSS 32095. It was Lord Ailesbury who saw him sitting in a great chair and made the comparison with his father, King Charles I, at his trial, Ailesbury, vol. i, p.209. The fact that London was given over to the mob is recorded in Clarke, vol. ii, pp.256–9. James asks the question in his memoirs how anyone could seriously believe he would debar his daughters from the throne just to put a changeling in their place, Clarke, vol. ii, pp.193, 202. We know that the nobility and gentry were skulking in their country houses from *Ellis Correspondence*, vol. ii, p.235 and Haile, p.199. The Imperial ambassador noted that James had raised Churchill 'from the dirt' in Haile, p.212. W.A. Speck makes the point that James saw defeat as a sign that God had withdrawn His favour in *Reluctant Revolutionaries*, p.121. Lord Dartmouth's letter advising James against sending his son to France is in Dalrymple, vol. ii, Appendices, Appendix Part 1, p.329. News of Anne's desertion left James 'disorder'd in his wits', Reresby, p.550. James told his brother-in-law Henry Clarendon that he suspected William came for the crown, Clarendon, *Diary*, vol. ii, p.194. Pepys describes James playing with the child Mary in his *Diary*, 12 September 1664, vol. ii, p.166.

Something of James's state of mind when he is captured by the 'seamen and rabble' is contained in a letter he wrote to Lord Feversham, pathetically asking for clean clothes and cash, Althorp Papers BL Loan, Saville Papers/Revolution Papers C8 Add.75366. Professor Miller emphasises the point that James saw all opposition as subversive and republican in *James II*, p.12. Speck makes the point about James's mental instability, p.71, and the likelihood he was suffering from a nervous breakdown, p.118. We know that James often dwelled on the fate of fallen kings because during the exclusion crisis he wrote to his brother, Charles II: 'Remember Edward II, Richard II and the King our father', Miller, *James II*, p.98. He makes a similar remark to his brother-in-law, Clarendon, *Diary*, vol.ii, p.212. We know James feared for his life from a remark he made to Ailesbury, vol.i, p.224.

## Chapter 1 Queen Mary Beatrice

p.11    'It is strange to see.' Clarendon, *Diary*, vol.ii, p.156.

p.11    The description of how the Queen spent her time at Bath is in a letter by Terriesi, Haile, p.167.

p.12    'There is a strong hope'. Ibid., pp.172–3.

p.13    'the Orangists, therefore'. Ibid., p.174.

p.13    'No words can express'. Ibid., p.173.

p.13    'afflicted at hearing'. Ibid., p.174.

p.14    'it is strange to see'. Clarendon, *Diary*, vol.ii, p.156.

p.14    When Parliament got wind of. Its dissatisfaction is described in a letter by Colbert de Croissy, Haile, p.35.

p.15    'The Princess Mary of Este'. Ibid., p.19.

p.16    Peterborough's rebuff. Ibid., p.18.

p.16    'Ever since it reached'. Ibid., p.21.

p.17    'Sire, you will find'. Ibid., p.25.

p.17    'Then I am a married man' Russel, Lady Rachel. *Some Account of the Life of Rachel Wriothesley, Lady Russell*, p.7.

p.18    his little red morocco-bound notebook. This is known as the Family Note Book of James, Duke of York. In it he recorded in his own hand the births and deaths of his children by Anne Hyde, her death, his subsequent marriage to Mary of Modena and the births and deaths of three of their children. James noted that he and Princess Mary of Modena were 'married & bedded' at Dover. The notebook is in the Royal Library at Windsor Castle (RC IN 1006014) and I quote from it by kind permission of Her Majesty Queen Elizabeth II.

p.18    Prince Rinaldo D'Este, was impressed. He described the scene in a letter to his nephew. Haile, p.42.

p.19    the King's favourite spaniels. Evelyn, *Diary*, 4 February 1685, vol.ii, p.207.

p.19    'not to permit any stragling'. Dutton, p.136.

p.20    the sour and childless Queen Catherine . . . Somerset House.

Noted in the journal of Codebo, the Duchess of Modena's private secretary. Haile, p.42.

p.22    she liked to divert herself 'with the Princesses'. Ibid., p.52.

p.22    Mary Beatrice had received a far superior. Ibid., p.18.

p.23    She invited Italian musicians. Ibid., p.48. John Evelyn described the Italian Opera's first performance in London, *Diary*, 5 January 1673–4, vol.ii, p.95.

p.23    'The Duchess of York succeeds marvellously'. Haile, p.42.

p.23    at least a few of the Italians. Ibid., pp.43–4.

p.24    Among her four maids of honour. Her English household is listed in *Anglia Notitiae*, 1676.

p.24    Edward Coleman. Haile, p.49.

p.24    £5,000 a year pin money. Mentioned in a letter by the Marquis of Montecuccoli, Ibid., p.54.

p.25    'so firm and steady'. Ibid., p.44.

p.25    she had sat up until midnight playing ombre. The description of how she spent the time leading up to her confinement is contained in a letter from the Marquis Cattaneo to the Duke of Modena, Ibid., pp.51–2.

p.26    the Duchess quickly had her child baptised. Ibid., p.52.

p.26    'You were a witness'. Ibid., p.55.

p.26    'the Prince of Orange arrived'. Ibid., p.63.

p.27    'I am much grieved'. Ibid., p.64.

p.27    'make haste, lest'. Lake, 4 November 1677, p.6.

p.27    'to the infinite griefe'. Evelyn, *Diary*, 30 March 1676, vol.ii, p.110.

p.28    'The people of London'. Haile, p.66.

p.28    'instead of using a coal leafe'. Lake, 12 December 1677, p.15.

p.28    'great as was my joy'. Haile, p.67.

p.28    Waller . . . pen a verse in her copy of Tasso. Ibid., p.46.

p.29    'Many people believe'. Ibid., p.68.

p.29    'The King has prorogued Parliament'. Ibid., p.72.

p.29    'so satisfied with her journey'. Dalrymple, vol.ii, Appendices, p.202.

p.31    'Affairs here are getting'. Haile, p.75.

p.31    'I am much afflicted'. Ibid., p.76

p.31    'constrained by necessity'. Ibid., p.78.

p.32    'Their Royal Highnesses'. Ibid., p.81.

p.33    'Tomorrow I leave for'. Ibid., p.82.

p.34    'She is very tall'. Ibid., p.88.

p.34    'even with the hazard'. Clarke, vol.i, p.574.

p.35    'O Dio! How things'. Haile, p.100.

p.35    'one of the dearest things'. Ibid., p.102.

p.36    'But I console myself'. Ibid., p.103.

p.37    'all passing so quickly'. Terriesi's description, ibid., p.109.

p.37    The Duke's enemies. Barillon to Louis XIV, ibid., p.109.

p.38    'Pray follow my example'. Ibid., p.127.

p.38    'her outward affability'. Evelyn, *Diary*, 13 July 1686, vol.ii, p.254.

p.38    'So artificially did this young Italian'. Burnet, *History*, p.244.

p.39    'The Queen, you must know'. Brown, p.30.

p.39    John Evelyn noticed that a court ball. Evelyn, *Diary*, 14 October 1686, vol.ii, p.256.

p.39    'All ladies of quality'. Brown, p.31.

p.39    The whole tone of court life. Evelyn, *Diary*, 14 December 1685, vol.ii, p.211.

p.40    the Italian tenor, Cifaccio. Ibid., 30 January 1687, vol.ii, p.259. He heard Cifaccio again when Samuel Pepys prevailed on him to sing at a small private concert, despite the fact that the tenor was 'proudly conceited' and 'disdaining to show his talent to any but princes'. Ibid., 19 April 1687, vol.ii, p.263.

p.40    'I could not have believed'. Ibid., 29 December 1686, vol.ii, p.258.

p.40    Mary Beatrice's wan appearance . . . two sons by Arabella Churchill. The situation is described in a letter by Terriesi, Haile, p.136.

p.41    'none of the most virtuous, but a wit'. Evelyn, *Diary*, 19 June 1673, vol.ii, p.89.

p.41    'It cannot be my beauty'. Jesse, *Reign of the Stuarts*, vol.iii, p.76.

p.41    'Passed the Privie Seal'. Evelyn, *Diary*, 19 January 1685–6, vol.ii, p.247.

p.41    'She loves her husband'. Barillon's letters of 31 January and 3 February 1686 to Louis XIV about the unfolding scandal are in Haile, p.142.

p.42    a pew reserved at St Ann's Church. *Ellis Correspondence*, vol.i, p.92.

p.42    'One thing I must say'. Bathurst, p.31.

p.43    The Queen was touched. Letter to William of Orange, 21 August 1687, Haile, p.163. William Frederick of Nassau,

Count Zuylestein, was the son of William's former governor.

p.44 And the spirit of Love. *A Collection of the Newest and Most Ingenious Poems, etc*; Hopkirk, p.29.

p.44 'Undone, undone'. Burnet, *History*, p.477.

p.44 Mrs Bromley, burst in. Described in a letter by Terriesi, 11 May 1688, Haile, p.180.

p.44 'I was soundly frightened'. Haile, p.181.

p.45 'all things about her person'. Burnet, *History*, p.476.

p.45 his daughter Anne regularly attended the Queen's toilette. Clarke, vol.ii p.200.

p.45 'went so far in desiring'. Burnet, *History*, p.476.

p.45 'For, methinks, if it'. 20 March 1688, Brown, p.35.

p.45 Queen once struck her in the face with a glove. Boyer, p.2.

p.45 Her pride was her downfall. Burnet, *History*, p.476.

## Chapter 2 Princess Anne of Denmark

p.47 'I can't help thinking Mansell's'. 14 March 1688, Brown, p.34.

p.47 all the maternal figures . . . were destined to leave her. Gregg emphasises this point, *Queen Anne*, p.8.

p.49 He said that he would rather she was the Duke's whore. Edward Clarendon, vol.i, pp.377–81.

p.49 the girl had taken physick. Letter from Elizabeth of Bohemia to Charles, Elector Palatine, 20 December 1660, Elizabeth, Queen of Bohemia, p.331.

p.50 one of the coldest days in living memory. Pepys, *Diary*, 6 February 1665, vol.ii, p.209.

p.50 Charles, Duke of Cambridge, whose birth. Pepys noted in his *Diary* on 6 May 1661 that the Yorks 'are not much troubled at it', vol.i, p.182.

p.50 'I am very glad to hear'. Bryant, p.181.

p.52 the Duchess intense jealousy. Pepys, *Diary*, 15 May 1663, vol.i, p.419.

p.52 'he hath come out of his wife's bed'. Ibid., 23 June 1667, vol.iii, p.166.

p.52 amassing jewels for herself. Ibid., 27 January 1667–8, vol.iii, p.358.

p.52 Lord Southesk had purposely contracted a venereal disease. Burnet, *History*, p.154.

p.53    The bedchamber woman, Mrs Dawson. BM Add. MSS 26657.

p.53    James, Duke of Cambridge ... covered with spots. Pepys, *Diary*, 30 April 1667, vol.iii, p.118.

p.54    Both the Duke's sons ... gravely ill. Ibid., 14 May 1667, vol.iii, pp.126–7.

p.54    'The King and Queen and the Duke'. Ibid., vol.iii, p.250.

p.55    dined alone in melancholy mood. Ibid., 3 September 1667, vol.iii, p.240.

p.56    'That she would bring'. Coke, *Court and State of England*, vol.iii, p.116.

p.57    'a violent Church of England man'. Clarke, vol.i, p.453.

p.57    'Truth, truth,' Anne replied. Burnet, *History*, p.207.

p.58    'The Duchess dead, a princess'. Evelyn, *Life of Mrs Godolphin*, p.13.

p.59    'we had used to play together'. Marlborough, *Memoirs*, p.7.

p.60    'ignorant of everything but'. Marlborough, *Private Correspondence*, vol.ii, p.146.

p.60    'I must tell you that I abhor'. 29 April 1686, Brown, p.16.

p.61    'When they were children'. Quoted in Gregg, *Queen Anne*, p.7.

p.62    'Deare Semandra, none deserves'. 22 September 1679, Bathurst Papers, BL Loan 57/71 719B, 66; Brown, p.6.

p.62    'all covered in jewels'. Evelyn, *Diary*, 15 December 1674, vol.ii, p.99.

p.64    'This week hath produced'. Lake, p.1.

p.64    'was a very busy, zealous Roman Catholic'. Ibid., p.7.

p.64    'The Duke visited her every day'. Ibid., p.12.

p.65    'appear'd to bear very'. Ibid.

p.65    'I find you weare mightely'. Bathurst Papers, BL Loan 57/71 719B, 64–5.

p.66    'I was to see a ball'. Ibid., 64.

p.66    'All the people heare'. Ibid., 65; Brown, p.5.

p.67    'Limonade cinemont water'. Ibid., 66; Ibid., p.6.

p.67    'All the fine churches'. Ibid., Ibid.

p.67    'Duke of Hanover is coming'. Russell, *Some Account of the Life of*, 17 September 1680, pp.44–5.

p.68    'not liking her person'. Coke, *Court and State of England*, vol.ii, p.118.

p.68    John Sheffield, Lord Mulgrave. He later married Anne's illegitimate half-sister, Catherine Darnley, daughter of James, Duke of York and Catherine Sedley.

p.69 'If I coud love you better'. Bathurst Papers, BL Loan 57/69 719B, p.95.

p.70 'he had the Danish countenance'. Evelyn, *Diary*, 25 July 1683, vol.ii, p.184.

p.70 'I have tried him drunk'. Quoted in Gregg, *Queen Anne*, p.35.

p.70 'Walk with me, hunt'. Hibbert, p.27; Bryant, p.338.

p.71 'a great jarr, or vessel'. Butler, p.52.

p.71 'I must now inform you'. Bathurst, p.164.

p.71 'You may believe twas'. Ibid., p.174.

p.72 'The Duke of York came in just'. Brown, p.12.

p.72 'My frank, open temper'. Marlborough, *Memoirs*, pp.10–11.

p.73 'looked like a madwoman'. Ibid., p.8.

p.73 'We talk here of going to tea'. Quoted in Bucholz, p.17.

p.74 'trifling fashions, rules of. Marlborough, *Private Correspondence*, vol.ii, p.120.

p.74 'I believe you will be sorry to hear'. Bathurst, p.180.

p.74 the Jesuits had poisoned her uncle. Gregg, *Queen Anne*, p.37.

p.75 'Ye Queen sent me'. Ibid., p.48.

p.75 'She pretends to have a great deal'. Brown, p.31.

p.76 'Nobody has yet said anything'. Ibid., p.16.

p.76 'I am of your opinion'. Ibid., p.17.

p.76 'You must know there was never grace'. Anne to Mary, 29 December 1686, Ibid., pp.20–1.

p.77 'I have always forgot to thank'. Anne to Mary, 10 January 1697, Ibid., p.22.

p.77 dance called the riggadoon. Anne to Mary, 11 April 1687, Ibid., p.28.

p.77 'all consumed, but the younger'. Lady Russell to Dr Fitzwilliam, Russell, *Letters*, p.103.

p.77 'The good Princess has taken'. Ibid.

p.78 'So that it is plain'. Anne to Mary, 13 March 1687, Brown, p.25.

p.78 'Everybody knows how often'. Ibid.

p.79 'because I am not used to'. Ibid.

p.79 'to suffer all extremities'. Letter from John Churchill to William of Orange, 17 May 1687, quoted in Gregg, *Queen Anne*, p.49.

p.79 'Pray don't let anybody'. Brown, p.27.

p.80 'I have now very little to say'. Ibid., p.34.

p.81   'the rumour among the women'. Clarendon, *Diary*, 14 April 1688, p.169.

p.81   'pressed her to go to the Bath'. Burnet, *History*, p.477.

p.82   he was a kind and indulgent father. Burnet, Ibid., p.457.

p.82   'Madam, I think you will be brought to bed'. Clarke, vol.ii, p.329.


## Chapter 3 *Princess Mary of Orange*

p.83   'And though I know you are a good wife'. Strickland, vol. x (1847), p.378.

p.83   Mr Gibson. Princess Mary refers to Mr Gibson carrying her letters to and from Frances Apsley several times in their correspondence, Bathurst Papers, BL Loan 57/69 719B, 59, 64.

p.84   'just like an ordinary'. Pepys, *Diary*, 12 September 1664, vol.ii, p.166.

p.84   She was particularly galled. Anthony Hamilton, pp.328–32.

p.85   'This Duchess was a very handsom'. Reresby, 5 August 1665, p.55.

p.85   'gone over to his pleasures'. Pepys, *Diary*, 13 May 1666, vol.ii, p.471.

p.86   Mr Gibson. His wife was a dwarf, too, but they had nine normal-sized children. Edmund Waller wrote a poem, 'The Marriage of the Dwarfs', for the Gibsons' wedding day, reproduced in *Selected Poems of Abraham Cowley, Edmund Waller and John Oldham* (Penguin, 1998).

p.86   'I did see the young Duchess'. Pepys, *Diary*, 2 March 1669, vol.iv, p.143.

p.86   A courtier joked. Anthony Hamilton, p.329.

p.87   'If I had any nuse'. Bathurst Papers, BL Loan 57/69 719B, 76.

p.87   'Tho St Jeames'. Ibid., 175.

p.87   'Dr D. Mrs.' Ibid., 75.

p.88   'It is very trew'. Ibid., 175; Bathurst, p.38.

p.88   'new croe quil pen'. Ibid., 75; Ibid., p.32.

p.89   'Why dear cruel'. Ibid., 58; Ibid., p.46.

p.89   'Who can imagin'. Ibid., 168–9; Ibid., p.51.

p.90   'I have stil the marks'. Ibid., 181–2; Ibid., pp.54–5.

p.90   'What can I say more'. Ibid., 163; Ibid., p.60.

p.91   'if I shoud dy'. Ibid., 183; Ibid., p.62.

p.91   'Sunday too a cloke'. Ibid., 158–9; Ibid., pp.63–4.

p.92    'it was much against his will'. Clarke, vol. i, p.503.

p.92    'be content with a cotage'. Bathurst Papers, BL Loan 57/69 719B, 173; Bathurst, p.66.

p.94    'if he should meet with one'. Anon, *Royal Diary*, p.27; Grew, p.21.

p.95    'she wept all that afternoon'. Lake, 21 October 1677, p.1.

p.95    'If you do not come'. Bathurst Papers, BL Loan 57/69 719B, 52; Bathurst, p.78.

p.96    'Gather it up'. Lake, p.6.

p.96    gone to bed in his woollen drawers. Orléans, 11 January 1678, p.32.

p.97    'Now, nephew to your work'. Lake, p.6.

p.97    'he was a very fond husband'. Zee, p.124.

p.97    wearing all her new jewels. Lake, 15–16 November 1677, p.9.

p.98    'Yes, Madam, but you'. Ibid., 19 November 1677, p.10.

p.98    'the pore dear distresed bab'. Bathurst Papers, BL Loan 57/69 719B, 189; Bathurst, p.43.

p.98    her great love for the little Lady Isabella. Quoted in Chapman, p.99.

p.99    had played games of ninepins. Anthony Hamilton, p.192.

p.100   'Are you noble?' Zee, p.129.

p.102   William kicked the altar step. Grew, p.49.

p.103   she would entertain him with light chatter. Anon, *Royal Book*, 50

p.103   'the princess was grown somewhat fat'. Lake, 9 January 1677–8, p.22.

p.103   'Synce it was my hard'. Bathurst Papers, BL Loan 57/69 719B, 190; Bathurst, pp.82–3.

p.104   'a very tender parting'. Henry Clarendon, *Correspondence*, 22 February/4 March 1677–8, vol.i, pp.11–12.

p.104   'I suppose you know'. Bathurst, pp.88–9.

p.105   'pray let her be carefuller'. Dalrymple, vol.ii, Appendices, p.155.

p.105   'I would hardly give me'. Bathurst, p.91.

p.106   'I was very glad to see'. Dalrymple, vol.ii, Appendices, p.202.

p.106   'no further hope of a child'. Haile, p.82.

p.107   'I am exceedingly glad'. Dalrymple, vol.ii, Appendices, p.216.

p.108   'And let the Prince flatter'. Ibid., vol.iii, Appendix, p.57.

p.108   'Nobody could understand'. Chapman, p.115.

p.109   He awarded Mary no allowance. Burnet, *History*, p.439.

p.III 'Your Honour may be astonished'. Strickland, vol.x (1847), p.333.

p.II2 'when what is past'. Bathurst, p.189.

p.II2 'The only thing I ever asked'. Zee, p.209.

p.II3 'to express their real concern'. Strickland, vol.x (1847), p.371.

p.II3 'I found her reasons as strange'. Bowen, p.116.

p.II4 'I have found nothing'. Ibid.

p.II4 'It gave me an astonishing'. Burnet, *History*, pp.458–60.

p.II4 books on history and divinity. Ibid., p.439.

p.II5 'She had great knowledge'. Ibid.

p.II5 'She knew little of'. Ibid., p.440.

p.II5 'she did not know that the laws'. Ibid.

p.II6 'always in very dubious'. Bowen, p.117.

p.II6 'in a manner so assured'. Ibid.

p.II7 'I rendered thanks'. Ibid.

p.II7 'This it has pleased the Lord'. Ibid.

p.II7 'Besides the interest'. Ibid.

p.II7 'so that even if I see a son'. Ibid., p.118.

p.II7 In this time I received'. Ibid., p.123; Baxter, p.226.

## *Chapter 4 King James II*

p.II9 'He was bred with high notions'. Burnet, *History*, p.114.

p.II9 it did not do for a king to be weak . . . meet opposition with force. This point is emphasised by Professor Miller in *James II*, p.II.

p.I20 the King . . . was permitted . . . deathbed admonitions. Ibid., p.4.

p.I20 James had already been planning his escape. Ibid.

p.I2I 'Remember Edward II'. Letter from James to Charles. Ibid., p.98.

p.I22 'I have found staying with the Queen of England'. Quoted in Turner, p.22.

p.I22 the happiest years of his life. Miller, *James II*, p.16.

p.I22 The army's firm structure . . . appealed to his authoritarian nature. Ibid., p.58.

p.I23 ever obedient to his brother's wishes. Ibid., p.4.

p.I24 'She indeed shew'd both her wit'. Clarke, vol.i, pp.387–8.

p.I24 so many new beauties ripe for seduction. Anthony Hamilton, p.190.

p.I25 not strength but weakness. Miller, *James II*, p.35.

p.125 'the King could see things'. Burnet, *History*, p.114.

p.125 He had no patience with opposition. A point made very strongly by Miller, *James II*, p.12.

p.126 James confessed to Charles that he and Anne. Clarke, vol.i, pp.387–8.

p.126 James's 'family', his servants, took exception to him marrying a commoner. Ibid.

p.126 James had taken to visiting her bed. Edward Clarendon, *Life*, vol.i, p.382.

p.127 'to prevent, with her authority'. Ibid., p.384.

p.127 boon companions . . . Anne's sexual favours. Anthony Hamilton, pp.192–3.

p.127 'for having placed his affection so'. Edward Clarendon, *Life*, vol.i, p.387.

p.127 the indignity of being interrogated. Ibid., p.389.

p.127 she expressed her regret. Ibid., p.392.

p.127 Seeing the game was up. Ibid.

p.127 'he must drink as he had brewed'. Burnet, *History*, p.114.

p.127 a respect that soon became very sincere. Anthony Hamilton, p.194.

p.128 he lost no time in being unfaithful. Ibid., p.195.

p.128 'He was perpetually in one amour'. Burnet, *History*, p.114.

p.128 Lord Chesterfield removed his. Pepys, *Diary*, 5 January 1662–3, vol.i, p.370; ibid., 19 January 1662–3, vol.i, p.375.

p.128 Maids of honour . . . which of them the Duke would 'ogle' next. Anthony Hamilton, p.268.

p.128 'The Duke of York is in all things'. Pepys, *Diary*, 30 October 1668, vol. iv, p.42.

p.128 ferocious hunting. Ibid., 22 June 1663, vol.ii, p.8; 8 August 1666, vol.ii, p.428. Miller makes the point that for James it was a substitute for war, *James II*, p.43.

p.129 'began a method of sending pages'. Burnet, *History*, p.115.

p.129 spending in excess of £60,000 a year. Pepys, *Diary*, 23 June 1667, vol.iii, p.166.

p.129 Although she liked to preside. Ibid., 28 January 1667–8, vol.iii, p.358.

p.130 garden at Whitehall. Pepys, *Diary*, 28 August 1667, vol.iii, p.230; Edward Clarendon, *Life*, vol.iii, p.291.

p.131 'more sensibly touched in his'. Clarke, vol.i, pp.440–1.

p.131 in simplistic terms: black or white, right or wrong. Miller, *James II*, p.12.

p.131  James tried to persuade a Jesuit. Clarke, vol.i, pp.440–1.

p.131  Charles's confession . . . he was a Catholic at heart and wished to convert. Miller makes the point that Charles's promise to declare himself a Catholic may have been sincere at first but soon became a bargaining device, Miller, *James II*, p.61.

p.132  Primed by Foxe's *Book of Martyrs* . . . the Catholics would do anything. Ibid., pp.66–7.

p.132  'the treachery and malice of the Popish Faction'. Quoted in Speck, p.168.

p.133  James might have been foolish . . . to the Duke of Buckingham. Miller, *James II*, p.64.

p.134  he could not play the fool a second time. Ibid., p.71.

p.135  'My brother will lose his throne for his principles'. Turner, p.458.

p.136  'Your wives prostituted to the lust of. Quoted in Speck, p.169; Miller, *Popery and Politics in England*, p.75.

p.137  'young Crofts is lawful son to the King'. Pepys, *Diary*, 27 October 1662, vol.i, p.340.

p.137  'he lov'd the Duke of Monmouth'. Clarke, vol.i, p.490.

p.137  Monmouth was not Charles's son, but a by-blow of Robert Sidney. James writes of Lucy Walter: 'and after her being with the King she prov'd so soon with child and came so near in time, that the world had cause to doubt whose child it was', Clarke, vol.i, p.492.

p.138  'in my mind all things tend to a republick'. Dalrymple, vol.ii, Appendices, p.217.

p.138  'You see how violently my enemies'. James to William of Orange, 14 May 1679, ibid., p.218.

p.138  'so that except His Majesty begin to behave'. James to William of Orange, 1 June 1679, ibid.

p.139  'I find you hunt almost every day'. Turner, p.196.

p.140  'Pray, once and for all'. Ibid., p.209; Hay, p.48.

p.141  'You are a man of conscience'. Ibid.

p.141  'that except he became a Protestant'. Turner, p.210.

p.141  'that then his case was more desperate'. Ibid.

p.141  Lord Dartmouth asked pointedly if the box. Dalrymple, vol.ii, Appendices, Appendix Part 1, p.68.

p.143  'The King walked about with a small train'. Turner, p.222.

p.143  Charles lay on his deathbed. The scene is described by Barillon in a letter to Louis XIV and reproduced in Turner, pp.224–8.

p.143  James saw kingship as a sacred trust. Miller, *James II*, p.124.

p.144 'restless and violent, that he could not hold'. Burnet, *History*, p.374.

p.144 'My lord, your father would have gone further'. Ibid., p.435.

p.144 'if ever he changed his religion'. Ibid.

p.144 When James said that he intended to 'establish' the Catholic. Miller makes the point he wanted to see them on an equal footing with Protestants, *James II*, p.126.

p.145 win many converts for Rome. Ibid., p.127.

p.146 James was disgusted at the abject behaviour. He expressed it in a letter to William of Orange, 14 July 1685, Dalrymple, vol.ii, Appendices, Appendix Part 1, p.134.

p.146 'the best way to engage me'. Clarke, vol.ii, p.15; Miller, *James II*, p.136.

p.147 the dispensing power . . . against the spirit of the constitution. Miller, *James II*, p.165.

p.147 'The Kings of England'. Carswell, p.148.

p.149 'You have not dealt with me like gentlemen'. Ibid., p.170.

p.149 James's dealings with the Vatican were no less tactless. Ibid., pp.73–4.

p.149 unwilling to take no for an answer. Ibid., pp.153–4.

p.151 'Do you not know I am above the law'. Burnet, *History*, p.455.

p.152 'as was sadly experienced by the horrid rebellion'. Quoted in Miller, *James II*, p.165.

p.152 'Trade he had much at heart'. Quoted in Speck, p.205.

p.156 'This is a standard of rebellion'. Miller, *James II*, p.185.

p.156 An increasingly nervous Sunderland urged him to drop the case. Kenyon, *Robert Spencer*, p.201.

p.156 James was determined not to make his father's mistake . . . show weakness before his enemies. Miller emphasises this characteristic of James, *James II*, p.11.

p.156 'If this be once'. Speck, p.143.

p.157 London went mad with joy . . . bonfires were lit all over town. *Ellis Correspondence*, 3 July 1688, vol.ii, pp.11–12.

p.158 As he confided to William in a separate letter. Letter from Sidney to William, 30 June 1688, Sidney, vol.ii, pp.269–71.

## Chapter 5 Prince William of Orange

p.159 'You will all find the Prince of Orange'. Henry Clarendon, *Diary*, vol.ii, p.194.

p.159　stunned with grief and shock. Elizabeth of Bohemia to the Elector Palatine, 6/16 November 1650, *Letters*, p.179.

p.161　Even Mary's relatives. Kroll, pp.34–5.

p.162　'Who is the lady with the furious'. Kroll, p.96; Strickland, vol.x (1847), p.256.

p.162　'My little nephue'. Elizabeth of Bohemia to Sir Edward Nicholas, 1/10 January 1655, Elizabeth, Queen of Bohemia, p.227.

p.162　'You are so partially'. Zee, p.19.

p.162　Mary saw Stuart and Orange. Miller, *James II*, p.8.

p.163　'a little world in themselves'. Zee, p.21.

p.164　William sat beside his other uncle. There is a print of this dinner in the Rijksmuseum, Amsterdam.

p.164　'a very prettie boy'. Pepys, *Diary*, vol.i, p.61.

p.164　'the being who is dearest'. Zee, p.27.

p.165　'I finde both hie and Lisslotte'. Elizabeth of Bohemia to the Elector Palatine, 1/11 April 1661, Elizabeth, Queen of Bohemia, p.342.

p.165　'during sixteen days and'. Quoted in Zee, p.100.

p.166　his mother had begged Charles II. Elizabeth of Bohemia to the Elector Palatine, 10/17 January 1661, Elizabeth, Queen of Bohemia, p.334.

p.166　'They had better take care'. Zee, p.40.

p.167　'I find him in earnest'. Courtenay, vol.i, p.285.

p.168　'the King of England is much satisfied with the parts'. Dalrymple, vol.i, p.47.

p.169　'All the talk here is of the war'. Zee, p.63.

p.169　'I beg you to tell me'. Ibid.

p.169　'If His Majesty would kindly'. Ibid.

p.170　'a young Prince in poor health'. Ibid., p.67.

p.171　'It is lost. Do you'. Ibid., p.72.

p.171　'All the roads are impassable'. Ibid., p.80.

p.171　'Go, my children, plunder'. Ibid., p.81.

p.173　'I cannot leave the battlefield'. Ibid., p.94.

p.174　'it was a great step to be nearer'. Courtenay, vol.i, p.468; Grew, p.21.

p.174　'like a hasty lover'. Courtenay, vol.i, p.114.

p.175　'in the worst humour I'. Coke, p.210.

p.175　'It was for the King'. Ibid.

p.175　'I never yet was deceived'. Courtenay, vol.i, p.504.

p.177　the young 'chits'. Sidney Godolphin, of whom Charles II said, 'he is never in the way and never out of it', was another of the 'chits'.

p.177 'the monarchy was absolutely lost unless'. Sidney, vol.ii, p.70.

p.177 'he thinks excluding the Duke an injustice'. Ibid., p.120.

p.177 'Every moment shows us plainly'. Ibid., pp.122-3.

p.178 'I am obliged to you for continuing to inform me'. Ibid., pp.126-7.

p.178 'Lord Halifax has undone all'. Ibid., p.125.

p.178 'I must own to you that I was much surprised to learn of mitigations'. Ibid., p.139.

p.179 'the Prince and Princess of Orange and the Prince of Hanover'. Ibid., p.146.

p.179 as Lord Godolphin acknowledged. Ibid., pp.209-12.

p.179 Henry Sidney advised William to adopt. Ibid., pp.212-19.

p.179 'make him believe that Your Highness'. Ibid., pp.212-13.

p.180 The visit was not considered a success. Ibid., p.220.

p.181 William's warm reception of Monmouth. Burnet, *History*, p.374.

p.183 Dijkvelt's commission . . . he entertained lavishly. *Ellis Correspondence*, 10 May 1687, p.289.

p.184 'Many of our ladies say'. Dalrymple, vol.ii, Appendices, Appendix Part 1, p.216.

p.185 'The irregular methods have spent'. Ibid., pp.219-22.

p.185 'Unseasonable stirrings, or anything'. Ibid.

p.185 'Wiser people assure me'. Ibid., p.225.

p.185 he asked his guest, the Elector of Saxony. Baxter, p.225.

p.186 The English visitors had left him in no doubt. Ibid., p.231.

p.186 She had to know what was going on. Ibid., p.226.

p.186 'to come and rescue the nation'. Ibid., p.225.

p.186 According to Burnet. Burnet, *History*, p.474.

## Chapter 6 *The Birth of James Francis Edward, Prince of Wales*

p.189 ''Tis possible it'. Brown, p.124.

p.189 'The King told him'. Haile, p.189.

p.189 Lord Clarendon . . . thought she looked well. Henry Clarendon, *Diary*, vol.ii, p.178.

p.189 'My dear sister can't imagine'. Brown, pp.37-8.

p.190 'As to my sister'. Bowen, p.124.

p.191   The bedchamber ... small and exposed to the sun. As described in a letter from Count D'Adda to the Cardinal Secretary of State, 1/11 June 1688, Haile, p.183.

p.191   Windsor Castle ... ruled out. Ibid. According to a letter from Lady Russell to Dr Fitzwilliam, dated 6 April 1688, Windsor had been ruled out as early as April: 'They speak as if the Queen's going to Windsor began to be doubtful', Russell, *Letters*, p.134.

p.191   'I am determined to lie in ... boards'. Boyer, p.3; Oman, p.108; Hopkirk, p.125.

p.191   Mary Beatrice was playing basset. Letter from Terriesi, Haile, p.187.

p.192   Mrs Dawson found Mary Beatrice. Anne to Mary, 24 July 1688, Brown, p.42.

p.192   She sent for a warming-pan. Brown, p.43; Clarke, vol.ii, p.200.

p.192   The fabrication ... perpetrated some time after. Fuller, *A Plain Proof of the True Father and Mother of the Pretended Prince of Wales*, made full use of the warming-pan story.

p.192   The Queen Dowager. Anne's letter to Mary of 24 July records the time of her arrival and where she stood, Brown, p.41.

p.193   According to Princess Anne's account. Anne to Mary, 24 July 1688, Brown, pp.39–43.

p.194   Mrs Dawson 'stood behind'. Brown, p.41.

p.194   Anne had to admit that the curtains. Ibid.

p.194   In her questionnaire. The full questionnaire and Anne's answers are reproduced in Dalrymple, vol.ii, Appendices, Appendix Part 1, pp.305–10, Chapman, *Mary II*, 263–66.

p.194   to which Anne replied. Brown, pp.39–43.

p.194   'Her Majesty being in great pain'. Clarke, vol.ii, p.199.

p.195   The King signalled Lord Chancellor. Brown, p.40.

p.195   'to hide her face'. Ibid.

p.195   'a lady not at all partial to the Queen'. Orléans, 20 May 1706, p.123.

p.196   He asked the Privy Councillors to bear witness. Brown, p.40; Clarke, vol.ii, p.199.

p.196   Judith Wilkes, 500 guineas. Hoffman to the Emperor, 11 June 1688, Haile, p.189.

p.196   He had noticed that there had been a lot of whispering. Henry Clarendon, *Diary*, 10 June 1688, vol.ii, p.176.

p.196   Clarendon went to court. Ibid.

p.197   'a very fine child to look upon'. Ibid.

p.197   'The Queen was, God be thanked'. Dalrymple, vol.ii, Appendices, Appendix Part 1, p.293.

p.197   'The joy is great here'. Haile, p.187.

p.198   'I cannot express the joy'. Ibid.

p.199   'much the properest place'. Anne to Mary, 18 June 1688, Brown, p.37.

p.199   Chamberlaine admits: 'they would never'. Dalrymple, vol.ii, Appendices, Appendix Part 1, pp.311–13.

p.200   'If it was a true child'. Althorp Papers, BL Loan, D11, *An Account of the Undeserv'd Treatment etc*, 1.

p.200   'the servants, from the highest'. Brown, p.42.

p.200   Chamberlaine 'had frequent discourses'. Dalrymple, vol.ii, Appendices, Appendix Part 1, pp.311–13.

p.200   'that the unfortunate young Prince'. Chapman, *Privileged Persons*, pp.169, 171.

p.201   'People thought that he had risked too much'. Bowen, p.124.

p.202   'We must presume to inform Your Highness'. Dalrymple, vol.ii, Appendices, Appendix Part 1, pp.228–31.

p.202   'Yesterday I found the court'. Haile, p.195.

p.202   'When I learnt that the Queen had given birth'. Bowen, p.125.

p.203   'I avow this was against my desire'. Ibid.

p.203   'no members of the court attended'. Haile, p.193.

p.203   'The first moment that I have taken a pen'. Ibid., p.191.

p.204   'I did not hope two months'. Ibid.

p.204   'the Queen is in good health'. Ellis to John Mey, 25 June 1688, *Ellis Correspondence*, vol.i, p.380; Haile, p.193.

p.204   a spectacular firework display. Evelyn, *Diary*, 17 July 1688, vol.ii, p.274.

p.204   'And the reason I have to think so'. Haile, p.192.

p.204   'Even in this last letter'. Ibid.

p.205   'Answered that all the King's children'. Ibid.

p.205   'brought only the confirmation'. Bowen, p.126.

p.205   'One can but hope'. Haile, p.189; Hopkirk, p.130.

p.205   'so extraordinary a diet'. Hopkirk, p.131.

p.206   'The Prince of Wales . . . Angel in Heaven'. Anne to Mary, 9 July 1688, Brown, p.38.

p.206   'The Queen forbid Lady'. Ibid, p.42.

p.206   park every day for the air. *Ellis Correspondence*, 26 July 1688, vol.ii, p.70.

p.207   'Each day the Queen goes'. Haile, p.195.

p.207    'from colics and other'. Ibid.

p.207    'The nurse is the wife'. *Ellis Correspondence*, 9 August 1688, vol.ii, p.115; William Chiffinch to the Duke of Newcastle, HMC Portland, 159.

p.208    'It is incredible the quantity'. Terriesi to the Grand Duke of Tuscany, 13/23 August 1688, Haile, p.196.

p.208    'he and his mother resemble each'. Orléans, p.123.

p.209    'Vat de devil!' Oman, p.114; Hopkirk, p.136.

p.209    'This procedure was censured'. Haile, p.202.

p.209    'they talk of my son'. James II to Electress Sophie of Hanover, 28 September 1688, Doebner, p.71.

p.210    'he would debar his own daughters'. Clarke, vol.ii, pp.193, 202.

p.210    'it was not so much to be wonder'd at'. Ibid., p.197.

p.210    The Queen 'began as well as the King'. Ibid.

p.210    'I have call'd you together'. Ibid., p.198.

p.211    In his memoirs . . . Anne to feel her belly. Ibid., p.202.

p.211    'depose her own knowledge'. Ibid.

p.211    'The King said the Princess'. Henry Clarendon, *Diary*, vol.ii, p.196.

p.211    Clarendon found Princess Anne with her ladies. Ibid.

p.211    'her sister never wrote to her'. Ibid., p.197.

p.211    'extremely surprised and troubled'. Ibid., p.198.

p.211    'Is it not strange'. Ibid.

p.211    'Because of the reports'. Ibid.

p.212    'as he has been sitting'. Ibid.

p.212    He warned his niece. Ibid.

p.212    'begged her to consider'. Ibid.

p.212    'My lords, this was'. Ibid., p.199; Clarke, vol.ii, p.202.

## Chapter 7 Betrayal

p.213    'Let the King of a'. Hopkirk, p.138; Haile, p.214.

p.213    many . . . were praying for a 'Protestant Wind'. Speck, p.85.

p.213    'The sun eclipsed'. Evelyn, *Diary*, 14 October 1688, vol.ii, p.279.

p.214    press-ganged into the navy. Men were being press-ganged up to 27 October, according to Carswell, p.167.

p.214    his own intelligence sources. Speck refers to the incompetence of his intelligence service, p.71.

p.214    the papal envoy. Speck, p.80.

p.214 'Dr Tenison now told'. Evelyn, *Diary*, 10 August 1688, vol.ii, p.275.

p.215 The invitation from the seven. The letter is reproduced in full in Dalrymple, vol.iii, pp.228–31.

p.216 nobility and gentry . . . avoided James's court. *Ellis Correspondence*, vol.ii, p.235; Hoffman to the Emperor, 8 October 1688, Haile, p.199.

p.216 claims were wildly optimistic. Speck, p.73.

p.216 only a small minority. Ibid.

p.216 at Henry Sidney's suggestion. Dalrymple, vol.ii, Appendices, Appendix Part 1, p.231.

p.218 'very well rigged and'. Childs, p.160.

p.218 Aeneas Mackay . . . Blackadder. Ibid., pp.145–6.

p.218 Rock-a-bye baby. Quoted in Zee, p.237.

p.219 'The spirit of a people'. Carswell, pp.132–3.

p.219 'It needs considerable changes'. Ibid., p.160.

p.220 'Mr Sidney will let you know'. Dalrymple, vol.ii, Appendices, Appendix Part 1, pp.239, 299; Speck, p.219.

p.221 another prolonged English civil war. Speck, p.77.

p.222 He told the Emperor. Dalrymple, vol.ii, Appendices, Appendix Part 1, pp.256–7.

p.223 James remained unconvinced . . . September. Speck, p.80.

p.223 'their goeing for England'. Ibid, p.81.

p.223 Clarendon . . . 'used of late'. Henry Clarendon, *Diary*, vol.ii, p.189.

p.224 'the Princess of Orange's letters'. Strickland, vol.vii (1866), p.146.

p.224 'I see by yours of the 20th. Ibid., p.147.

p.224 'This evening I had yours of the 4th,. Ibid.

p.224 'I am much put to it what to say'. Haile, p.197.

p.225 'The consideration of all this'. Baxter, p.227.

p.225 'seen my tears and has pitied me'. Bowen, p.126.

p.225 'His soldiers are his most dangerous'. Haile, p.198.

p.226 The Earl of Ailesbury recalled. Childs, p.142.

p.226 Treason Club . . . Tangier group. Ibid., pp.156–7.

p.227 Lichfield's regiment. Ibid., p.158.

p.227 summer together on Hounslow. Ibid.

p.228 'the imperfect redress'. Speck, p.84.

p.229 'I had no letter from you'. Strickland, vol.vii (1866), p.148.

p.229 'His Majesty told me that the Dutch troops'. Henry Clarendon, *Diary*, vol.ii, p.194.

p.230　'I assured him that I had never loved'. Zee, p.249; Bowen, p.129.

p.230　'he replied with so much tenderness'. Bowen, p.129.

p.230　'I have always served you'. Zee, p.249.

p.230　She was in tears. D'Albeville also observed her crying. Strickland, vol.vii (1866), p.162.

p.231　even the Jews observed it. Bowen, p.130.

p.231　William came under pressure to change his plan. Carswell, p.178.

p.231　'never place was more thronged'. *Ellis Correspondence*, vol.ii, p.253.

p.232　She climbed the 315 steps. Bowen, p.133.

p.233　when Dartmouth did emerge from the Thames. HMC Dartmouth, vol.iii, pp.59–69.

p.233　'What do you think of predestination now?'. Carswell, p.184.

p.236　'O God! That my son'. Henry Clarendon, *Diary*, vol.ii, p.204.

p.236　'that people were so apprehensive of popery'. Ibid., p.205.

p.237　assuring him of her support. Brown, p.43.

p.237　the nosebleed was providential. Henry Clarendon, *Diary*, vol.ii, p.212.

p.237　His policy was to avoid him. Carswell, p.195.

p.238　'from the dirt'. Hoffman to the Emperor, 29 November/9 December 1688, Haile, p.212.

p.238　Schomberg greeted Churchill coolly. Lediard, vol.i, p.81.

p.238　'Is "*Est-il-Possible*" gone?' Carswell, p.198.

p.238　husband of his dearest child. Strickland, vol.vii (1866), p.168.

p.239　Constantin Huygens. This is the son of William's grandmother's secretary, who had devised the programme for William's education.


## Chapter 8 Flight

p.240　'Whom then could I trust?' Grew, p.181.

p.240　'it disordered him in his'. Reresby, p.550. The court lady was probably Eleanor, wife of Sir Thomas Oglethorpe.

p.240　'God help me!'. Zee, p.258.

p.240　'somebody had violently carried'. Henry Clarendon, *Diary*, vol.ii, p.207.

p.241　Sarah's *Conduct* is incorporated in Marlborough, Sarah, Duchess of, *Memoirs*.

p.241　'It was a thing sudden'. Marlborough, *Memoirs*, p.14.

p.241　'put the Princess into'. Ibid., p.12.

p.241 'Having on all occasions'. Brown, p.43.

p.242 liaise with Bishop Compton. Marlborough, *Memoirs*, p.12.

p.242 In the early hours. Ibid., p.13; Strickland, vol.vii (1866), pp.168–70.

p.243 'I have nothing to say'. Brown, p.45.

p.243 Dorset had offered his gauntlet. Strickland, vol.vii (1866), pp.168–70.

p.243 'Nor did she think'. Marlborough, *Memoirs*, p.13.

p.243 pretending 'that her father'. Strickland, vol. vii (1866), pp.170–2.

p.243 'never came to any harshness'. Althorp Papers, BL Loan, D11, *An Account of the Undeserv'd Ill Treatment, etc*, 1.

p.243 'had the honour to be'. Ibid.

p.243 the old Protestant Association. Ibid.

p.244 'which made the Princess Anne'. Ibid.

p.244 James said that it never reached. Clarke, vol.ii, p.227.

p.244 'Madam, I beg your'. Brown, p.44.

p.245 James was furious. Clarke, vol.ii, pp.226–7; Strickland, vol.vii (1866), p.173.

p.245 she had been pulling on. Count D'Adda mentions this episode in a letter to the Cardinal Secretary of State, Haile, p.212.

p.245 'Good God! Nothing but'. Henry Clarendon, *Diary*, vol.ii, p.216.

p.246 'the Prince of Orange came'. Ibid., p.212.

p.246 'I could not believe the English'. Letter from Terriesi to Tuscan Secretary of State, Haile, p.215.

p.247 'Pray, Sir, consider farther'. Dalrymple, vol. ii, Appendices, Appendix Part I, p.329.

p.248 At two in the morning. Riva wrote a detailed account of the Queen's escape, BM Add. Mss Eg 1677; Haile, pp.217–20; Clarke, vol. ii, pp.244–7.

p.250 'Monsieur, A poor fugitive queen'. Haile, p.221.

p.251 He asked . . . Feversham to disband the army. HMC Hamilton, p.113.

p.251 James asked what was the point of staying. Ailesbury, vol.i, p.195.

p.252 God had withdrawn His favour. Speck, p.121.

p.252 James's escape, capture and return to London, and final escape are described in Clarke, vol.ii, pp.251–78; Ailesbury, vol.i, pp.194–226; Turner, pp.444–9.

p.253 'I had the misfortune'. James to Feversham, 12 December

1688, Althorp Papers, BL Loan, Saville Papers/Revolution Papers C8 Add. 75366.

p.254    According to Clarendon. *Diary*, vol.ii, p.224.

p.254    'Why did you not let him go?' Burnet, *History*, p.506; Ailesbury, vol.i, p.201.

p.254    there was a quarter of an hour's silence. Ailesbury, vol.i, p.201.

p.255    The rabble embarked on an orgy. Clarke, vol.ii, pp.256–9; Speck, p.89.

p.255    James's memoirs ... Terriesi. Terriesi got the memoirs off safely to Leghorn and they eventually reached James in France. Clarke, vol.ii, p.242. The original manuscript was burned during the French Revolution, but fortunately several copies had been taken.

p.255    'sitting in a great chair'. Ailesbury, vol.i, p.209.

p.255    Catholics left their hiding places. Burnet *History*, p.506.

p.255    He had lost all credibility. Hoffman said, 'whether he goes or stays, he will never be but the shadow of a king', Haile, p.224.

p.256    William's Blue Guards. Letter from Hoffman to the Emperor, 27 December 1688, Haile, p.224.

p.256    he was woken from a sound sleep. Burnet, *History*, p.507; Clarke, vol.ii, p.265.

p.256    When James descended the palace stairs. Jesse, *Court of England*, vol.i, p.90; Evelyn, *Diary*, 18 December 1688, vol.ii, p.283; Ailesbury, vol.i, p.218.

p.257    His coach had slipped through the park. Burnet, *History*, p.507.

p.257    'King James was carried down the river'. Strickland, vol.vii (1866), p.179.

p.258    'If I do not retire'. Ailesbury, vol.i, p.224.

p.258    a farewell document. Clarke, vol.ii, pp.273–5; Oman, p.147.

p.258    cutting the ground from under them. Speck, p.118.

p.258    'was not in the least moved'. Henry Clarendon, *Diary*, vol.ii, pp.249–50.

p.259    'she was not one jot'. Ibid.

p.259    her personal fortune. The information that 'her lands at Monti should be sold to help the King with money' is in a letter from Count D'Adda to the Cardinal Secretary of State, 26 November 1688, Haile, p.209. In his will, James – always meticulous about money – requested that in the event of his son's restoration this sum be repaid her.

p.259   'My God,' she. Haile, p.225.

p.259   French courtiers watched in amazement. They were shocked that he embraced his wife in public, according to the Marquis D'Angeau's Journal. Hopkirk, p.165.

## Chapter 9 The Takeover

p.260   'If you are crowned'. A copy of the letter was found among the papers of Lord Nottingham. Dalrymple, vol.ii, Appendices, Appendix Part 2, p.15.

p.261   *before* the reading of the Declaration. Speck, pp.113–14.

p.261   'She came into Whitehall'. Evelyn, *Diary*, vol.ii, pp.289–90.

p.262   'She ran about it'. Marlborough, *Memoirs*, p.19.

p.262   'I thought this strange'. Ibid.

p.262   'She rose early in the'. Evelyn, *Diary*, vol.ii, pp.289–90.

p.262   He noted several items. Ibid., 13 July 1693, vol.ii, p.322.

p.263   'She put on an air'. Burnet, *History*, p.523.

p.263   She had given up cards. Doebner, p.5.

p.263   concern for her father. Ibid.

p.263   'I had been only for a Regency'. Ibid., p.11.

p.264   'Yet when I saw England'. Ibid., p.10.

p.264   appalled to see the toll . . . William's health. Ibid.

p.264   tears of joy . . . sorrow. Ibid.

p.264   'the loss of the liberty'. Ibid.

p.265   'forced the nation'. Evelyn, *Diary*, vol.ii, p.289.

p.266   adamant . . . to call a free Parliament. Speck, p.90.

p.266   Weeks of wrangling. Described in great detail in Speck.

p.267   Clarendon had raised the matter. Henry Clarendon, *Diary*, vol.ii, p.235.

p.267   dropped on the dubious grounds. Speck, p.102.

p.267   'nothing was done to'. Clarke, vol.ii, p.201.

p.267   'That they neither questioned'. Ibid., p.312.

p.268   'holding anything by the apron'. Speck, p.108; Strickland, vol.x (1947), p.414.

p.268   'I am the Prince's wife'. Strickland, vol.x (1947), p.414.

p.269   The ultimatum concentrated minds. Speck, p.108.

p.270   'never consent to anything'. Henry Clarendon, *Diary*, pp.249–50.

p.270   'Now I am sensible'. Strickland, vol.vii (1866), p.184.

p.271   'At night, I went to court'. Ibid., p.197.

p.271   Anne objected that her low stool. Ibid., p.198.

p.271   'Within a night or two'. Evelyn, *Diary*, vol.ii, p.289.

p.272   'My wife,' he wrote. Henry Clarendon, *Diary*, vol.ii, pp.263–4.

p.272   little girls of seven. Strickland, vol.vii (1866), p.200.

p.273   'Tell your princess'. Clarke, vol.ii, p.270.

p.273   'Hitherto, I have been willing'. Dalrymple, vol.ii, Appendices, Appendix Part 2, p.15; Strickland, vol.vii (1866), p.203.

p.274   'if her father regained his authority'. Clarke, vol.ii, p.328.

p.274   'Both bitches, by God!'. Chapman, *Mary II*, p.172.

p.274   'He is, Madam, as surely'. Clarke, vol.ii, p.329.

p.275   'Much of the splendour'. Evelyn, *Diary*, 11 April 1689, vol.ii, pp.292–3.

p.275   never to criticise James. Dalrymple, vol.ii, Appendices, Appendix Part 2, p.169.

p.276   'A crown, sister'. Strickland, vol.vii (1866), p.211.

p.276   'I was come into a noisy world'. Doebner, p.11.

p.276   'to see so little devotion'. Ibid.

p.277   'I found myself here'. Ibid., p.14.

p.277   Catherine Sedley . . . 'coming here'. Chapman, *Mary II*, p.183.

p.277   to watch a performance of Dryden's. Ibid.

p.280   'Madam, if the King'. Ibid., p.217.

p.280   Daniel Defoe. Defoe, p.345.

p.283   'women should not meddle . . . foolish figure'. Doebner, pp.22–3.

p.283   'A woman is but a very'. Letter from Queen Mary II to Electress Sophie of Hanover, 19/29 December 1693, Doebner, pp.107–9.

p.283   'Farewell, I will trouble . . . bear anything'. Bowen, pp.181, 189, 201, 206.

p.285   'I must grin when'. Bowen, p.222.

p.285   Mary's size. There is a waxwork funeral effigy of her on display in the museum at Westminster Abbey. This would have been made soon after her death to inform or remind her subjects what she had looked like in life and was deemed to be a faithful representation. She is placed beside William, emphasising the contrast in their stature.

p.285   'I go to Kensington as'. Bowen, p.222.

p.285   'The concern for his dear person'. Doebner, p.29.

p.285   'the cruel thought that my husband'. Ibid.

p.286   'Madam, your countrymen have'. Zee, p.317.

p.286   A Dutch soldier writing. Ibid., p.316.

p.287   'I know I need not beg'. Bowen, p.200.

p.287  'Ladies who had before'. Ibid., p.229.

p.288  'I am reflecting how hard'. Chapman, *Mary II*, p.221.

p.288  'When one listens to him'. Hopkirk, p.167.

p.288  'The more I see'. Orléans, 20 August 1690, p.57; Hopkirk, p.167.

p.289  'Will should have knotted'. Chapman, *Mary II*, p.236, taken from a contemporary broadsheet.

p.289  'My unlucky star'. Zee, p.362.

p.290  'that he who I dare no more name'. Doebner, p.54.

p.290  'I was ashamed to look'. Ibid.

p.290  'lessen my husband's kindness'. Ibid.

## Chapter 10 *The Quarrel*

Details of the quarrel, at least Sarah Marlborough's version of it, are recounted in *An Account of the Undeserv'd Ill Treatment of Her Royal Highness, Princess Anne of Denmark by King William and Queen Mary, Her Sister, wrote in a letter to Mrs Burnet*, in the Althorp Papers on loan to the British Library, D11.

p.293  In all this I see the hand of God. Doebner, p.45.

p.294  'Mary soon grew weary'. Marlborough, *Memoirs*, p.18.

p.295  'It was impossible for any body'. Ibid., p.19.

p.295  'Lord Devonshire's leavings'. Ibid., p.20.

p.295  palace of Richmond. Ibid., p.21.

p.295  'prove a tympane'. Evelyn, *Diary*, 19 July 1689, vol.ii, p.297.

p.296  'righteous judgement of God'. Doebner, p.15.

p.296  a new wet nurse. The details of Gloucester's childhood in this chapter are supplied by Jenkin Lewis, his Welsh servant. Lewis, pp.35–6.

p.296  'how my sister was'. Doebner, p.17.

p.297  'astonished to think how'. Marlborough, *Memoirs*, p.23.

p.297  'What was the meaning of'. Doebner, p.18.

p.297  'Pray, what friends have'. Marlborough, *Memoirs*, p.21.

p.298  James's Irish estates . . . 1699 to receive payment. Gregg, p.77.

p.298  'like a mad woman'. Doebner, p.18.

p.298  'Since that affair'. Marlborough, *Memoirs*, p.24.

p.298  peas. This incident is recalled in Sarah Marlborough's *An Account of the Undeserv'd Ill Treatment*, etc. Althorp Papers on loan to the British Library, D11, 73.

p.299  All over Christmas and into the New Year. Doebner, p.18.

p.299  'thought it an ungenerous thing'. Ibid.
p.299  'he did not only think'. Marlborough, *Memoirs*, p.25.
p.299  'I have reason to fear'. Doebner, pp.20–1.
p.299  'saw plainly that she'. Ibid., p.24.
p.300  According to Sarah. Marlborough, *Memoirs*, p.28.
p.300  to deter the hapless George from going to sea. Ibid., pp.27–9.
p.302  he was playing a double game. Gregg, p.83.
p.302  'I have been very desirous'. Brown, p.52.
p.303  The letter might have been backdated. Gregg, p.84.
p.303  James . . . was not inclined to believe. Ibid.
p.304  'for I doubt she is a jade'. Ibid., p.85.
p.304  Evelyn could only speculate. Evelyn, *Diary*, 24 January 1692, vol.ii, p.314.
p.305  'Having something to say to you'. Marlborough, *Memoirs*, pp.31–4.
p.307  'Your Majesty was in the right'. Brown, p.53.
p.309  'I am very sorry to find'. Ibid., p.54.
p.310  'as insensible as a statue'. Marlborough, *Memoirs*, p.42.
p.310  'I cannot believe it was their Dutch'. Gregg, p.88.
p.310  she 'responded that she knew the Princess'. Ibid.
p.310  'I am more yours'. Ibid.
p.310  'Mrs Freeman . . . must give me leave'. Brown, p.59.
p.311  'Can you think either of us'. Ibid., p.60.
p.312  'I have made the first step'. Marlborough, *Memoirs*, p.49.
p.312  'She trembled and looked'. Ibid., p.50.
p.313  'I hear Lord Marlborough'. Brown, pp.55–6.
p.313  'Jacobite Lady Ailesbury. Ailesbury, vol.i, pp.292–3.
p.314  'It is not a proper time'. Ibid., p.297.
p.314  'And though my duty'. Brown, p.54.
p.315  'I have received yours'. Marlborough, *Memoirs*, p.55.
p.315  'I am very sensibly touched'. Brown, pp.56–7.
p.316  Anne sent Lady Fitzharding. Marlborough, *Memoirs*, p.71.
p.316  'it is a comfort they'. Brown, p.58.
p.317  'I was yesterday at Berkeley House'. Ibid., pp.61–2.
p.317  'I have not yet seen Lady Charlotte'. Gregg, p.95.
p.318  'The Lady that has now'. Brown, pp.61–2.
p.318  no more notice of her than if she had been a rocker. Marlborough, *Memoirs*, p.73.
p.318  a favourite toyshop. Lewis, p.63.
p.318  a tallow-chandler. Marlborough, *Memoirs*, pp.68–9.
p.319  forbidden to place the text. Ibid., p.70.

p.319    to attend his wife's confinement. Evelyn, *Diary*, vol.6 April 1692, p.316.

p.319    Neither Mary nor Anne is ever recorded as referring to this undoubted sister. When Louise Marie died in 1712, Louis XIV sent Anne his condolences, but she replied only in the most general terms, never once mentioning Louise Marie by name.

p.319    'Although he was so active'. Lewis, p.41.

p.320    'his hat was big enough'. Ibid.


## *Chapter 11 An Untimely Death*

p.321    'Go, see now this cursed'. Strickland, vol.xi (1847), p.334.

p.321    As she wrote to. Bowen, p.263.

p.322    She had been feeling unwell. Burnet describes the onset and course of her illness in his *History*, pp.606–7.

p.322    The fact that Mary spent the night in her closet burning her papers is recounted in Burnet, *History*, p.606.

p.322    account book. Queen Mary's Account Book, 1678–89, in the Royal Library at Windsor Castle (RC IN 1142245).

p.322    'I find heer 817.14 to much'. Ibid.

p.322    'I hope the Prince will pardon'. Ibid.

p.323    There were bills for Richard Beauvoir. BM Add, Mss 5751 A VII.

p.323    'a poor woman at Hampton Court'. The Household Book of Queen Mary II, the Royal Archives, Windsor Castle (RA EB 13).

p.323    'for Mrs Miller a blind woman'. Ibid. Quotes by kind permission of Her Majesty Queen Elizabeth II.

p.323    'for cutting the boys . . . cosy winter coat'. BM Add. Mss 5751 A VII f.180.

p.324    The Little Sancy. This eventually came into the possession of Kaiser Wilhelm II. At the end of the Second World War, it fell into the hands of Russian soldiers and was never seen again.

p.324    'If I had had children'. Bowen, p.237.

p.325    'from being the most happy'. Burnet, *History*, p.606.

p.325    'He said, during the'. Ibid.

p.326    'Why are you crying?'. Chapman, *Mary II*, p.252.

p.326    'I believe I shall now'. Tenison, p.26.

p.326    Mary had read Charles Drelincourt's. Anon, *Royal Diary*, p.10.

p.326 'she seem'd neither to'. Ibid., p.11; Tenison, p.26.
p.327 'Others have need to'. Ibid., Ibid., p.27.
p.327 'I therefore challenge you'. Ken, pp.5–6.
p.328 'I have but a little time'. Anon, *Royal Diary*, p.11.
p.328 'Look again! Dr Radcliffe'. Strickland, vol.xi (1847) p.314.
p.329 'Pray, Madam, present'. Marlborough, *Memoirs*, p.75.
p.329 'to leave room for'. Ibid.
p.330 'no answer but a cold'. Ibid.
p.330 the letter she had written. Burnet, *History*, p.607.
p.331 'For perfumed sparadrape'. BM Add. Mss 5751 A f. 54; Strickland, vol.vii (1866), p.459.
p.332 'The news will have reached'. Haile, p.310.
p.332 'a child he loved'. Clarke, vol.ii, p.525.
p.332 'heard his poor daughter'. Ibid., pp.526–7.
p.334 'I beg Your Majesty's'. Brown, p.63.
p.335 'Who would have thought'. Chapman, *Mary II*, p.258.
p.335 so grossly swollen . . . sedan chair. Lewis, p.66.
p.335 'I hope Your Highness'. This was 'the half-witted Lord Caernarvon'. Marlborough, *Memoirs*, p.78.
p.335 'Oh, be doleful!'. Lewis, p.63.
p.336 The state funeral. *The Form of the Proceeding to the Funeral*, etc.
p.337 the ladies' trains dragged. Grew, p.236.
p.337 'A sparrow falls'. Tenison, p.20.
p.338 'she was canonised for a'. Clarke, vol.ii, p.526.

## Chapter 12 *The Succession*

p.340 'He bid me find means'. Haile, p.356.
p.341 Lord Ossory. This is not the same Lord Ossory who is listed as a member of Anne's Cockpit circle. Gallant and courageous, William's friend Lord Ossory died prematurely of a fever after Charles II had sent him on a fool's mission to the Tangier garrison in 1680. William was grief-stricken.
p.342 'This young man'. Zee, p.415.
p.342 'beautiful in his person'. Ibid., p.416.
p.343 'I don't know how'. Ibid., p.417.
p.343 'Sire, it is your honour'. Ibid., p.418.
p.344 'It has so much astonished'. Ibid., p.419.
p.345 'had no vice but'. Ibid., pp.423–4.
p.345 'It was of two sorts'. Ibid.

p.345 'The King is said'. Ibid., p.423; Dutton, p.168.
p.346 'I find that religion'. Zee, p.408.
p.347 'The princess is not ugly'. Ibid., p.411.
p.348 'Have the people'. Ibid., p.412.
p.349 'It's impossible to credit'. Ibid., p.450.
p.350 'I would rather see'. Haile, p.330.
p.350 'his own child should'. Clarke, vol.ii, p.575.
p.351 'the old bully'. Bevan, p.161.
p.351 'It is impossible to see him'. Ibid., p.162.
p.351 'I had done everything'. Zee, p.453.
p.353 'the head was opened'. Gregg, p.120.
p.353 'hung with black cloth'. Lewis, p.98.
p.353 'ye uneasiness that stiring'. Gregg, p.106.
p.354 'to know whether he'. Clarke, vol.ii, pp.559–60.
p.354 'he was not for permitting'. Ibid.
p.355 A suggestion has been made. Gregg, pp.121–2.
p.355 A continuation of the policy. Ibid.
p.355 he did not even know he had a grandfather. Lewis, p.55.
p.355 'the Prince of Wales'. Haile, p.344.
p.357 'I do not believe it'. William III to Princess Anne, 4 August 1700, Gregg, p.121.
p.358 'I lament King James'. Dalrymple, vol.ii, Appendices, Appendix Part 2, p.22.
p.359 'The Princess of Denmark'. Orléans, p.96.
p.362 Liselotte wickedly noted. Ibid., p.101.
p.362 On his deathbed. The scene is recalled in detail in Clarke, vol.ii, p.595.
p.364 'I am out of all patience'. Brown, pp.67–8.
p.364 'I think myself indispensably'. Haile, p.356.
p.364 'there is no doubt'. Clarke, vol.ii, p.602.
p.366 '*Je tire vers ma fin*'. Strickland, vol. xii (1848), p.32.
p.366 'As I know my heart'. Gregg, p.152; Strickland, vol.xii (1848), p.40.

## Chapter 13 *Broken Promises*

p.368 'Though I can never'. Letter from James Francis Edward to Anne, May 1711, Macpherson, vol.ii, pp.223–4.
p.368 felt well enough. Boyer, p.714.
p.369 She went to check the time. Ibid.
p.369 'the translation of the'. Sir David Hamilton, p.3.

p.369    Details of the Queen's illness were also given in a letter from Charles Ford to Jonathan Swift, 31 July 1714, Swift, *Correspondence*, vol.ii, pp.93–4.

p.370    'As for your poor unfortunate'. Brown, p.125.

p.370    'As long as I live'. Anne to Godolphin, 1 May 1705, Brown, p.232.

p.373    'it has not been my fault'. Gregg, p.273.

p.373    As young as fourteen. Butler, p.26.

p.374    'imbibed the most unconquerable'. Marlborough, *Memoirs*, p.87.

p.375    'I can not help being'. Brown, p.98.

p.375    'ye unfortunate ought'. Ibid., p.116.

p.376    'I desire you would order' Ibid., p.185.

p.376    'I beg my dear Mrs Freeman'. Gregg, p.173.

p.377    'I own I can not have'. Brown, pp.227–8.

p.377    'I can not help thanking'. Gregg, p.174.

p.377    'I must confess it is'. Ibid.

p.378    'I must own to you'. Brown, p.129.

p.379    'I must own I have' Ibid., p.153.

p.379    hardly cross the room except with two sticks. Ibid., p.127.

p.380    'Her Majesty was labouring'. Clerk, p.62.

p.380    'The poor lady'. Ibid., p.72.

p.381    'hunting the stag'. Swift, *Journal to Stella*, 7 August 1711, p.219.

p.381    'in a chaise with one'. Ibid.

p.381    'I agree that all'. Gregg, p.193.

p.382    a lingering feeling of guilt. Gregg makes a good case for this in his article, 'Was Queen Anne a Jacobite?'.

p.382    'received this with cheerfulness'. Sir David Hamilton, p.45.

p.383    Anne's personal policy was to keep. Gregg, 'Was Queen Anne a Jacobite?'.

p.383    'You know that I'. Gregg, p.222.

p.383    'Nothing will satisfie them'. Ibid.

p.383    'Your security and the nations'. Ibid., p.223.

p.384    'All I desire is'. Anne to Godolphin, 30 August 1706, Brown, pp.196–7.

p.384    'I desire you wd reflect'. Marlborough, *Private Correspondence*, vol.i, pp.71–5.

p.384    'It would be more pleasing'. Gregg, p.228.

p.385    'always making low'. Butler, p.191.

p.385    'I discovered that'. Ibid., p.193.

p.385 'I have a hundred'. Ibid., p.192.

p.385 'if this matter should'. Brown, pp.253–4.

p.385 'I do, and you must'. Butler, p.205.

p.387 'what is ye use'. Gregg, p.270.

p.387 'to have no more resentments'. Marlborough, *Memoirs*, p.155.

p.387 '*When as Queen Anne of great Renown*'. Gregg, p.275.

p.388 'And tho Your Majesty'. Ibid.

p.389 'Be quiet!'. Ibid., pp.276–7.

p.389 'I am so tired'. Ibid.

p.389 'Your Majesty chose'. Ibid.

p.389 'After the commands'. Brown, p.258.

p.390 'at the sight of that charming'. Marlborough, *Private Correspondence*, vol.ii, p.106.

p.390 'I scratched twice at'. Brown, p.263.

p.390 there would be enough space beside him for Anne. It was as well she checked. Anne's coffin was almost square, bigger than the Prince's, who was a big man.

p.390 'I thought she loved'. Gregg, p.283.

p.391 'I can not end'. Ibid.

p.391 'that after the service'. Ibid., pp.291–2.

p.391 'hoping that in time'. Ibid., p.293.

p.391 'You seem to be dissatisfied'. Anne to Marlborough, 25 October 1709, Brown, pp.285–6.

p.392 'I can't help but think'. Gregg, p.302.

p.392 'If this afternoon'. Ibid., p.307.

p.392 the last interview. We have only Sarah's record of it in Marlborough, *Memoirs*, pp.172–3.

p.393 'it was very hard'. Sir David Hamilton, p.25.

p.393 'in order to make it'. Gregg, p.313.

p.394 'It is true indeed'. Anne to Godolphin, 13 June 1710, Brown, p.303.

p.394 'when people are fond of'. Sir David Hamilton, p.12.

p.394 She said 'that she took'. Ibid.

p.394 'which I believe will'. Anne to Godolphin, 7 August 1710, Brown, p.305.

p.395 'The one is cunning'. Sir David Hamilton, p.23.

p.395 'persons may promise'. Ibid., p.16.

p.395 When Marlborough returned . . . he was angry. Ibid., p.25.

p.396 'that she would not build'. Gregg, p.329.

p.396 'is of the first quality'. Sir David Hamilton, p.38.

p.397 'You may be assured, Madam'. Macpherson, vol.ii, pp.223–4.

p.398   'things looked as though'. Sir David Hamilton, p.44.

p.398   she assured the bishops. Gregg, 'Was Queen Anne a Jacobite?'.

p.398   'the hearty concern'. Boyer, p.709.

p.399   The Queen fired off letters. Anne to the Dowager Electress Sophie, to the Elector of Hanover, and to the Electoral Prince of Hanover, 19 May 1714, Brown, pp.413–14.

p.399   'that the Princess Sophia'. Sir David Hamilton, p.61.

p.400   After her second stroke ... large and clear. Gregg, 'Was Queen Anne a Jacobite?'.

p.400   'I believe sleep was never'. Dr Arbuthnot to Jonathan Swift, 12 August 1714, Swift, *Correspondence*, vol.ii, p.122.

p.400   had not had time to sign her will. Ibid. The contents of the will are discussed in Gregg, *Queen Anne*, pp.397–8.

# Bibliography

## Manuscripts

Althorp Papers on loan to the British Library

Althorp Papers/Marlborough Papers, *An Account of the Undeserv'd Ill Treatment of Her Royal Highness, Princess Anne of Denmark by King William and Queen Mary, Her Sister, wrote in a letter to Mrs Burnet*

Bathurst Papers on loan to the British Library, 57/69 & 57/71

Blenheim Papers Add. Mss 61414; 61415

BM Add. Mss 5751 A; 4478B; 26657; 32095; 18740; 61415; 61101; 61232; 61420

Family Note Book of James, Duke of York in the Royal Library, Windsor

The Household Book of Mary II in the Royal Library, Windsor

Queen Mary's Account Book in the Royal Library, Windsor

## Pamphlets and printed documents

Burnet, Gilbert, Bishop of Salisbury, *A Sermon Preached at the Coronation of William III and Mary II King and Queen . . . at Westminster Abbey, 11 April 1689*

*A collection of the Newest and Most Ingenious Poems, Songs, Catches, etc., against Popery relating to the Times* (London, 1689)

*The Form of the Proceeding to the Funeral of her late Majesty Queen Mary II of Blessed Memory* (1695)

*Their Highness the Prince and Princess of Orange's Opinion about a general liberty of Conscience, etc, including Mijn Heer Fagel's First Letter to Mr Stewart* (1689)

Historical Manuscript Commission Reports (HMC): Dartmouth; Hamilton; Le Fleming; Portland; Ormonde; Rutland

Ken, Thomas, D.D. late Bishop of Bath and Wells, *A Letter to Dr Tenison, upon occasion of a Sermon, entitled, A Sermon Preach'd at the Funeral of Her Late Majesty Queen Mary, of Ever Blessed Memory, 29 March 1695*

*The Other Side of the Question: Or, An Attempt to Rescue the Characters of Two Royal Sisters, Queen Mary and Queen Anne, out of the Hands of Dowager Duchess of M ...* (London, 1744)

Tenison, Thomas, Archbishop of Canterbury, *A Sermon Preached at the Funeral of Her Late Majesty Queen Mary of Ever Blessed Memory in the Abbey-Church in Westminster, 5 March 1694–5*


## Books

Ailesbury, Thomas Bruce, 2nd Earl of, *Memoirs*, 2 vols. (Roxburghe Club, 1890)

*An Account of King William's and Queen Mary's Undeserv'd Ill Treatment of Her Sister, the Princess of Denmark* (1702)

Anon, *The Life of that Incomparable Princess, Mary, Our Late Sovereign Lady, of ever Blessed Memory* (London, 1695)

Anon, *The Royal Diary, Or King William's Interior Portraiture, To which is prefixt, The Character of his Royal Consort, Queen Mary II* (London, 1705)

Anon, *The Royal Progress; or, a Diary of the King's Journey* (London, 1695)

Anon, *The Secret History of Whitehall* (2nd edn, London, 1717)

Ashley, Maurice, *The Glorious Revolution of 1688* (London, 1966)

Aulnoy, Marie Catherine, Baronne d', *Memoirs of the Court of England in 1675*, translated by Mrs William Henry Arthur, edited by George David Gilbert (London, 1913)

Baily, F.E., *Sophia of Hanover and Her Times* (London, 1936)

# Bibliography

Bathurst, B., ed., *Letters of Two Queens* (London, 1924)

Baxter, Stephen, *William III and the Defence of European Liberty* (London, 1966)

Bentinck, Mechtild, Comtesse, ed., *Marie, Reine d'Angleterre, Lettres et Mémoires* (The Hague, 1880)

Bevan, Bryan, *King William III, Prince of Orange, the First European* (London, 1997)

Bowen, Marjorie, *The Third Mary Stuart* (London, 1929)

Boyer, Abel, *The History of the Reign of Queen Anne, Digested into Annals* (London, 1703)

Brown, Beatrice Curtis, *The Letters and Diplomatic Instructions of Queen Anne* (New York, 1968)

Bryant, Arthur, *King Charles II* (London, 1931)

Bucholz, R.O., *The Augustan Court: Queen Anne and the Decline of Court Culture* (Stanford, 1993)

Burnet, Gilbert, *An Essay on the Memory of the Late Queen* (London, 1695)

Burnet, Gilbert, *Bishop Burnet's History of His Own Time from the Restoration of Charles II to the Treaty of Peace at Utrecht, in the Reign of Queen Anne* (London, 1838)

Butler, Iris, *Rule of Three: Sarah, Duchess of Marlborough and her Companions in Power* (London, 1967)

Callow, John, *The Making of King James II: The Formative Years of a Fallen King* (London, 2000)

Carswell, John, *The Descent on England* (London, 1969)

Chapman, Hester, *Mary II, Queen of England* (London, 1953)

Chapman, Hester, *Privileged Persons: Four Seventeenth-Century Studies* (London, 1966)

Chesterfield, Philip Stanhope, 2nd Earl of, *Letters*, 2 vols. (London, 1937)

Childs, John, *The Army, James II and the Glorious Revolution* (Manchester, 1980)

Clarendon, Edward Hyde, 1st Earl of, *The Life of Edward, Earl of Clarendon, Lord High Chancellor of England, Written by Himself*, 3 vols. (Oxford, 1827)

Clarendon, Henry Hyde, 2nd Earl of, *The Correspondence*

of Henry Hyde, Earl of Clarendon and of his Brother, Laurence Hyde, Earl of Rochester; with the Diary of Lord Clarendon from 1687 to 1690, edited by S.W. Singer, 2 vols. (London, 1828)

Clarke, James Stanier, ed., *The Life of James II, Collected out of Memoirs Writ of His own Hand*, 2 vols. (London, 1816)

Clerk, Sir John, *Memoirs of the Life of Sir John Clerk of Penicuik, 1676–1755*, edited by John M. Gray (Edinburgh, 1892)

Coke, Roger, *A Detection of the Court and State of England during the Reigns of the Stuarts. As also the Inter-regnum*, vols. ii and iii (London, 1719)

Coke, Roger, *A Collection of Ordinances and Regulations for the Government of the Royal Household Made in Diverse Reigns from Edward III to King William and Queen Mary also Receipts for Ancient Cookery* (London, 1790)

Courtenay, Right Honourable Thomas Peregrine, *Memoirs of the Life, Works and Correspondence of Sir William Temple*, 2 vols. (London, 1836)

Dalrymple, Sir John, *Memoirs of Great Britain and Ireland*, 3 vols. (Edinburgh, 1771–88)

Defoe, Daniel, *A Tour through the Whole Island of Great Britain* (London, 1971)

Doebner, Dr, ed., *Memoirs of Mary, Queen of England, 1689–93, together with her letters and those of King James II and William III to the Electress Sophie of Hanover* (Leipzig, 1886)

Drelincourt, Charles, *A Christian's Defence Against the Fear of Death*, 4th edn (London, 1701)

Dutton, Ralph, *English Court Life* (London, 1963)

Elizabeth, Queen of Bohemia, *The Letters of Elizabeth, Queen of Bohemia*, compiled by L.M. Baker (London, 1953)

Ellis, Henry, *Original Letters Illustrative of English History*, 2nd series, 4 vols. (London, 1846)

*Ellis Correspondence, Letters Addressed to J. Ellis, Esq., 1686–8*, 2 vols. (London, 1829)

Evelyn, John, *The Life of Mrs Godolphin* (London, 1848)

Evelyn, John, *The Diary of John Evelyn*, edited from the original manuscript by William Bray, 2 vols. (London, 1901)

Fea, Allan, *James II and his Wives* (London, 1902)

Fiennes, Celia, *The Journeys of Celia Fiennes*, with an introduction by John Hillaby (London, 1983)

Foxcroft, Helen C., *The Life and Letters of Sir George Savile, 1st Marquis of Halifax*, 2 vols. (London, 1898)

Fuller, William, *A Plain Proof of the True Father and Mother of the Pretended Prince of Wales* (London, 1700)

Fuller, William, *The Whole Life of William Fuller Impartially Written by Himself* (London, 1703)

Green, David, *Queen Anne* (London, 1970)

Gregg, Edward, 'Was Queen Anne a Jacobite?' *History*, LVII (October 1972)

Gregg, Edward, *Queen Anne* (London, 1980)

Grew, Edwin and Marion, *The Court of William III* (London, 1910)

Haile, Martin, *Queen Mary of Modena: Her Life and Letters* (London, 1905)

Hamilton, Anthony, *Memoirs of Count Grammont*, edited by Sir Walter Scott (London, 1846)

Hamilton, Sir David, *The Diary of Sir David Hamilton, 1709–14*, edited by Philip Roberts (Oxford, 1975)

Hamilton, Elisabeth, *William's Mary* (London, 1972)

Hanover, Sophia, Electress of, *Memoirs*, translated by H. Forester (London, 1888)

Harris, Frances, *A Passion for Government: The Life of Sarah, Duchess of Marlborough* (Oxford, 1991)

Hay, Malcolm V., *The Enigma of James II* (London, 1938)

Hibbert, Christopher, *The Marlboroughs: John and Sarah Churchill, 1650–1744* (London, 2001)

Holmes, Geoffrey, *British Politics in the Age of Anne* (London, 1967)

Holmes, Geoffrey, *Britain after the Glorious Revolution 1689–1714* (London, 1969)

Hopkirk, Mary, *Queen Over the Water: Mary Beatrice of Modena, Queen of James II* (London, 1953)

Jesse, John Heneage, *Memoirs of the Court of England During the Reign of the Stuarts*, 4 vols. (London, 1855)

Jesse, John Heneage, *The Court of England from the Revolution in 1688 to the Death of George II*, 4 vols. (London, 1901)

Jones, David, *A Continuation of the Secret History of Whitehall* (London, 1697)

Jones, David, *The Tragical History of the Stuarts* (London, 1697)

Jones, J.R., *The Revolution of 1688 in England* (London, 1972)

Jones, J.R., *Court and Country: England 1658–1714* (London, 1978)

Kenyon, John P., *Robert Spencer, Earl of Sunderland, 1641–1702* (London, 1958)

Kenyon, John P., *The Stuarts* (London, 1969)

Kroll, Maria, *Sophie, Electress of Hanover* (London, 1973)

Lake, Dr Edward, *Diary of Dr Edward Lake in the Years 1677–78*, edited by George Percy Elliott (Camden Society, 1866)

Law, Ernest, *Kensington Palace* (London, 1899)

Lediard, Thomas, *The Life of John, Duke of Marlborough, with Original Letters and Papers*, 3 vols. (London, 1736)

Lewis, Jenkin, *Queen Anne's Son, Memoirs of the Duke of Gloucester*, edited by W.J. Loftie (London, 1881)

Luttrell, Narcissus, *A Brief Historical Relation of State Affairs*, 1678–1714, 6 vols. (Oxford, 1857)

Macpherson, James, *Original Papers Containing the Secret History of Great Britain from the Restoration to the Accession of the House of Hanover*, 2 vols. (London, 1775)

Marlborough, Sarah, Duchess of, *Private Correspondence of*

*Sarah, Duchess of Marlborough Illustrative of the Court and Times of Queen Anne*, 2 vols. (London, 1838)

Marlborough, Sarah, Duchess of, *Memoirs of Sarah, Duchess of Marlborough together with her Characters of her Contemporaries and her Opinions*, edited with an introduction by William King (London, 1930)

Miller, John, *Popery and Politics in England 1660–88* (London, 1973)

Miller, John, *James II: A Study in Kingship* (London, 1978)

Ogg, David, *England in the Reigns of James II and William III* (London, 1969)

Oldmixon, John, *The History of England during the Reigns of the Royal House of Stuart* (London, 1730)

Oman, Carola, *Mary of Modena* (London, 1962)

Orléans, Charlotte Elisabeth, Duchess of, *Letters from Liselotte*, translated and edited by M. Kroll (London, 1970)

Pepys, Samuel, *Diary and Correspondence of*, deciphered by Rev. J. Smith, Life and Notes by Richard, Lord Braybrooke, 4 vols. (New York, no date shown)

Pepys, Samuel, *Private Correspondence and Miscellaneous Papers*, edited by J.R. Tanner, 2 vols. (London, 1970)

Pinkham, Lucille, *William III and the Respectable Revolution* (Cambridge, Massachusetts, 1954)

Plumb, J.H., *The Growth of Political Stability in England, 1675–1725* (London, 1967)

Reresby, Sir John, *Memoirs*, edited by A. Browning (Glasgow, 1936)

Rowse, A.L., *The Early Churchills: An English Family* (London, 1956)

Russell, Lady Rachel, *Letters of Lady Rachel Russell in the Library at Woburn Abbey* (London, 1826)

Russell, Lady Rachel Wriothesley, *Some Account of the Life of Rachel Wriothesley, Lady Russell* (London, 1819)

Saint Evremond, Charles Marguetel de Saint Denis, Seigneur de, *The Letters of Saint Evremond*, edited by John Hayward (London, 1930)

Shrewsbury, Charles Talbot, Duke of, *Private and Original Correspondence of Shrewsbury with William III*, edited by W. Coxe (London, 1821)

Sidney, Henry, *Diary and Correspondence*, edited by R.S. Blencowe, 2 vols. (London, 1843)

Speck, W.A., *Reluctant Revolutionaries* (London, 1988)

Straka, Gerald M., *The Revolution of 1688: Whig Triumph or Palace Revolution?* (Lexington, Massachusetts, 1963)

Strickland, Agnes, *Lives of the Queens of England*, vols.viii–xii (London, 1848)

Strickland, Agnes, *Lives of the Queens of England*, (Mary II), vol.vii (London, 1866)

Swift, Jonathan, *The History of the Last Four Years of Queen Anne* (London, 1758)

Swift, Jonathan, *Swift's Journal to Stella 1710–13*, edited by Frederick Ryland (London, 1897)

Swift, Jonathan, *The Correspondence of Jonathan Swift, 1690–1713*, 2 vols. (Oxford, 1963)

Turner, F.C., *James II* (London, 1948)

Verney, Margaret M., *Memoirs of the Verney Family from the Restoration to the Revolution 1660 to 1696* (London, 1899)

Wood, Anthony à, *Life and Times* (London, 1932)

Zee, Henri and Barbara, van der, *William and Mary* (London, 1973)

# Index

The following abbreviations have been used:
JFE = James Francis Edward, Prince of Wales ('Old Pretender')
JII = King James II (*formerly* Duke of York and Albany)
MB = Mary Beatrice of Modena
SC = Sarah Churchill
WO = William III (*formerly* William, Prince, of Orange)

# Index